**THE SHIPS & AIRCRAFT
OF THE U.S. FLEET**

THE SHIPS & AIRCRAFT
OF THE U.S. FLEET

TENTH EDITION
COMPILED BY SAMUEL L. MORISON
AND JOHN S. ROWE

NAVAL INSTITUTE PRESS
ANNAPOLIS, MARYLAND

Cover: The carrier *Ranger* (CVA-61), taking in fueling lines. (Photo: Robert D. Moeser.)

Frontispiece: The carrier *Enterprise* (CVAN-65)

CONTENTS

PREFACE

It has now been some three years since the ninth edition of *The Ships and Aircraft of the U.S. Fleet* appeared. During that time, the Navy has changed just as much as it did in the six years between the eighth and ninth editions. Regrettably, in three years, the Navy has lost over 250 ships to the scrappers, with more scheduled. Others have been sold to foreign countries or sunk as targets.

The basic format of this edition has not essentially changed since the last one. However, one will note several improvements, especially in the appendices, primarily the result of comments received from readers of the ninth edition. The main text in this edition carries the Navy to early 1975, while the addenda update the main text to mid-1975. All data are from official unclassified Navy publications, the editors' own records, and other naval sources.

The editors are grateful to all the people who helped with this edition. It is almost impossible to list the names of everyone, but some individuals, we feel, should be cited. The first is Rear Admiral Samuel E. Morison, USNR (Retired), whose continued guidance and advice has proven to be invaluable. Then there is Vice Admiral Edwin B. Hooper, USN (Retired), Director of Naval History; Commander Richard T. Speer, USN, Head, Ships Histories Section, Naval Historical Center; Mr. Henry Vadnais, Assistant Head of the Curator Branch, Naval Historical Center; Rear Admiral Bobby Ray Inman, USN, Director, Naval Intelligence Command; Captain Joseph Dick, USN, Head, Ship Systems, Naval Intelligence Support Center; Lieutenant Commander Michael Tansey and Commander Robert Templeton, USN, Security Assistance Division, Office of Chief of Naval Operations; Commanders Roth, Morse, Test, Captain Magee, and Mr. W. Dailey, of the Ships Maintenance and Logistics Division, Office of Chief of Naval Operations; Mr. John Maffett and Mr. Stanley Krol, Navy Shipbuilding and Scheduling Office, Naval Sea Systems Command; Mr. Truman Strobridge and Captain B. L. Meaux, USCG, of the Coast Guard Public Affairs Office; Mr. William McEachern, Naval Air Systems Command; Mr. Robert L. Lawson, Mr. Christian Bielstein, Mr. William Davis, and Miss Darla Rowe; offices and organizations of the Department of the Navy and private businesses; and last, but certainly not least, Mr. Robert Carlisle, Head, Still Photo Branch, Office of Information, Department of the Navy. Many others who have been helpful prefer to remain anonymous.

All photographs, unless otherwise noted, are official Navy, Marine Corps, or Coast Guard photographs.

Finally, we wish to thank the readers who sent in their comments on the previous edition. Again, we encourage the readers to send in comments, corrections, and additional information to either one of the editors in care of the publisher.

Samuel L. Morison
John S. Rowe

THE SHIPS & AIRCRAFT
OF THE U.S. FLEET

ONE: WARSHIPS

A. AIRCRAFT CARRIERS

By the end of FY 1975, there were 21 aircraft carriers on the Naval Vessel Register. Of this total, 3 were rated as CVANs, 1 as a CVN, 6 as CVs, 7 as CVAs and 4 as CVSs. Active: 2 CVANs, 6 CVs and 6 CVAs. Reserve: 1 CVA and 4 CVSs. Under construction: 1 CVN, 1 CVAN. All carriers were originally rated as CV/CVB (41–43, 59, 60). All were reclassified as CVA on 1 Oc-

tober 1952. Current CVA/CVS mixed concept necessitates reverting to CV for all modern CVAs and CVN for CVANs. CVs will carry ten S-3 VIKINGS and 8 ASW helicopters at a loss of approximately half of a CVA's attack aircraft. See class footnotes and modernization tables for further reclassifications.

Class	Number	No. In Class	Full Load Displ.	Length Overall	Max. Draft	Extreme Beam	Number & Type of Reactors/Boilers & Engines	Screws/ SHP	Max. Speed (Kts.)	Accommodations[1] Officers	Enlisted	Armament[2]	Planes
Nimitz	CVAN-68	3	91,400	1092'	37'8"	252'	2R/A4W/A1G(G.E.)	4/280,000	30+	569	5,717	3 BPDMS	90+
John F. Kennedy	CV-67	1	87,000	1047'	35'11"	252'	8B(F.&W)/4GT(West.)	4/280,000	30+	505	5,222	3 BPDMS	70+
Enterprise	CVAN-65	1	89,600	1102'	35'9"	252'	8R/A2W(Westinghouse)	4/280,000	30+	425	4,475	2 BPDMS	84+
Kitty Hawk	CV-63	3	80,800	1046'	35'7"	249'	8B(F.&W)/4GT(West.)	4/280,000	30+	428	4,154	2 twin TERRIER launchers	70+
Forrestal	CVA-59	4	78,000	1040'	35'5"	252'	8B(B.&W)/4GT(West.)	4/260,000	30+	442	4,678	4 single 5"/54 cal. mts. (CVA-61), 2 BPDMS (CVA-59, CV-60, 62)	70+
Midway	CVA-41	3	64,000	972'	35'5"	238'	12B(B.&W)/4GT(West.)	4/212,000	30+	366	4,309	3 single 5"/54 cal. mts. (CVA-41, 43), 4 single 5"/54 cal. mts. (CVA-42)	70+
Hancock	CVA-19	3	44,700	899'	31'	192'	8B(B.&W)/4GT(West.)	4/150,000	30+	354	3,170	4 single 5"/38 cal. mts.	70+
Intrepid	CVS-11	2	42,000	899'	31'	192'	8B(B.&W)/4GT(West.)	4/150,000	25+	340	2,952	4 single 5"/38 cal. mts.	45+
"Essex"	CVS-9	2	40,600	890'	31'	196'	8B(B.&W)/4GT(West.)	4/150,000	30+	340	2,887	4 single 5"/38 cal. mts.	45+

[1] Includes air wings.   [2] CVA-59 and up carry (2/4) 40mm saluting guns.

2 NUCLEAR-POWERED ATTACK AIRCRAFT CARRIERS/1 NUCLEAR-POWERED AIRCRAFT CARRIER, *NIMITZ* CLASS

Name	Number	FY/SCB	Builder	Awarded	Keel	Launched	Commissioned	F/S
Carl Vinson	CVN-70	74/102	Newport News	4-5-74				Bldg.
Dwight D. Eisenhower	CVAN-69	70/102	Newport News	6-30-70[1]	8-14-70			Bldg.
Nimitz	CVAN-68	67/102	Newport News	6-30-70[1]	6-22-68	5-13-72		AA

[1] Definitized contract. Letter contract for construction awarded 5-16-68 (CVAN-68) and 6-29-70 (CVAN-69)

CVAN-69 originally named *Eisenhower*. Renamed as indicated 5-25-70. Will go to the Pacific Fleet after sea trials. CVN-70 is first USN ship named for a living person in over 175 years. Class has improved reactors. Initial cores will last 13 years before replacement is required.

Class has NTDS, automatic carrier landing system, and automated jet-fuel system. Replacement schedule in active fleet: CVAN-68 for CVA-31; CVAN-69 for CVA-42 and CVN-70 for CVA-43. Two additional sisters of this class (CVN-71/72) are planned.

1 CONVENTIONAL ATTACK AIRCRAFT CARRIER, *JOHN F. KENNEDY* CLASS

John F. Kennedy	CV-67	63/127C	Newport News	4-30-64	10-22-64	5-27-67	9-7-68	AA

She is the last conventionally powered carrier. Stack angles to starboard to prevent boile gases from drifting over stern and interfering with landings. She is equipped with NTDS

Reclassified CV on 12-1-74. This ship has three BPDMS launch systems.

1 NUCLEAR-POWERED ATTACK AIRCRAFT CARRIER, *ENTERPRISE* CLASS

Name	Number	FY/SCB	Builder	Awarded	Keel	Launched	Commissioned	F/S
Enterprise	CVAN-65	58/160	Newport News	11–15–57	2–4–58	9–24–60	11–25–61	PA

She is the largest warship in the world. Has unmistakable recognition features. Class was originally programmed as 6 units (CVAN-65/70), but to hold down costs only "Big E" was completed (without her planned TERRIER missile armament). Refueled at Newport News 64/65, 69/70. Present cores will last 10/13 years. Sides of "island" superstructure mount AN/SPS-32/33 three-dimensional radars. On 1–14–69, a ZUNI rocket, on an aircraft waiting to be launched, overheated and exploded, setting off numerous other fires and explosions. The explosions tore large holes in the after portion of the flight deck and wrecked the after portion of the hangar deck; 27 dead, 85 injured. Despite the damage, the "Big E" continued flight operations thus proving that big carriers can take considerable punishment.

3 CONVENTIONAL AIRCRAFT CARRIERS, *KITTY HAWK* CLASS

Name	Number	FY/SCB	Builder	Awarded	Keel	Launched	Commissioned	F/S
America	CV-66	61/127B	Newport News	11–25–60	1–9–61	2–1–64	1–23–65	AA
Constellation	CV-64	57/127A	NY Navy	7–23–56	9–14–57	10–8–60	10–27–61	PA
Kitty Hawk	CV-63	56/127	NY Ship	10–26–55	12–27–56	5–21–60	4–29–61	PA

CVA-63 to CV on 4–29–73. CVA-64 and 66 to CV in FY 1975. An improved *Forrestal* class.   CV-66 missile system also has capability to fire STANDARD after minor modifications.

2 CONVENTIONAL ATTACK AIRCRAFT CARRIERS/2 CONVENTIONAL AIRCRAFT CARRIERS, *FORRESTAL* CLASS

Name	Number	FY/SCB	Builder	Awarded	Keel	Launched	Commissioned	F/S
Independence	CV-62	55/80	NY Navy	7–31–54	7–1–55	6–6–58	1–10–59	AA
Ranger	CVA-61	54/80	Newport News	2–3–54	8–2–54	9–29–56	8–10–57	PA
Saratoga	CV-60	53/80	NY Navy	7–23–52	12–16–52	10–8–55	4–14–56	AA
Forrestal	CVA-59	52/80	Newport News	7–12–51	7–14–52	12–11–54	10–1–55	AA

CVA-60 to CV on 6–30–72; CVA-62 to CV on 2–28–73. First class of super carriers to be completed (*United States* (CVA-58) was first authorized super carrier; cancelled 4–23–49). CV-60 served as test ship for integrated CVA/CVS carrier concept. Carried ASW squadrons. Ships with ASW squadrons reclassified CV. They replace the costly and overage *Essex* class CVSs. Class lost forward 5" sponsons during late 1960s. They had proven to be a severe maintenance problem.

3 CONVENTIONAL ATTACK AIRCRAFT CARRIERS, *MIDWAY* CLASS

Name	Number	FY/SCB	Builder	Awarded	Keel	Launched	Commissioned	F/S
Coral Sea	CVA-43		Newport News	6–14–43	7–10–44	4–2–46	10–1–47	PA
Franklin D. Roosevelt	CVA-42		NY Navy	1–21–43	12–1–43	4–29–45	10–27–45	AA
Midway	CVA-41		Newport News	8–27–42	10–27–43	3–20–45	9–10–45	PA

Originally classed as CV. To CVB on 7–15–43. CVA-42, originally named *Coral Sea*; was renamed 5–8–45. Class incorporates the experiences and lessons learned from earlier classes during WW II (such as an armored flight deck). With modernizations, class recognition features differ considerable (see page 3). Three additional sisters (CVB-44, 56, 57) were cancelled.

MIDWAY CLASS MODERNIZATIONS

Number	Modernization Yard	FY/SCB	Decommissioned	Started	Recommissioned
CVA-41	PS Navy	55/110	10–14–55	9–1–55	9–30–57
CVA-41	SF Navy	66/101.66	2–15–66	2–15–66	1–31–70
CVA-42	PS Navy	54/110	4–23–54	5–1–54	4–6–56

Number	Modernization Yard	FY/SCB	Decommissioned	Started	Recommissioned
CVA-42		68/103.68	Modernization Cancelled		
CVA-43	PS Navy	57/110A	5–24–57	4–16–57	1–25–60

During the careers of the 3 *Midway* class CVAs, all have received extensive modernizations, primarily to prolong their useful lives, to update the ships' capabilities, and to enable the ships to exist in a modern warfare environment. After her second modernization, *Midway* resembled *Coral Sea*, but had a far larger and different flight deck layout. *FDR* was scheduled to receive the same modernization as *Midway* (second one), but this was cancelled due to time and cost of *Midway*'s modernization. *FDR* received austere overhaul instead. Centerline elevator of CVA-41, 42 was moved to port side deck edge. All now have three deck edge elevators.

3 CONVENTIONAL ATTACK AIRCRAFT CARRIERS, *HANCOCK* CLASS

Name	Number	Builder	Awarded	Commissioned	F/S	Decommissioned
Oriskany	CVA-34	NY Navy	8–8–47[1]	9–25–50	PA	
Bon Homme Richard	CVA-31	NY Navy	8–7–42	11–26–44	PR*	2 July 1971 at Bremerton
Hancock	CVA-19	Beth., Quincy	9–9–40	4–15–44	PA	

[1] Originally ordered 8–7–42. Suspended 1946/47. Redesigned and reordered as indicated. Completed to SCB-27A design.

CVA-19, originally named *Ticonderoga*, was renamed 5–1–43. CVA-34 has NTDS. CVA-19 and 34 will be decommissioned in FY 1976. *Antietam* (CVS-36) has been stricken.

2 CONVENTIONAL ANTISUBMARINE AIRCRAFT CARRIERS, *INTREPID* CLASS

Name	Number	Builder	Awarded	Commissioned	F/S	Decommissioned
Shangri-La	CVS-38	Norfolk Navy	8–7–42	9–15–44	AR*	30 July 1971 at Boston
Intrepid	CVS-11	Newport News	7–3–40	8–16–43	AR*	15 March 1974 at Quonset Point

During CVA-41 modernization, CVS-11 made 3 deployments to Vietnam as light CVA, retaining her CVS classification. CVS-38 replaced CVS-11 in light CVA role in mid-1969. Class is equipped with steam catapults. Sister *Ticonderoga* (CVS-14) has been stricken. Both ships are moored at Philadelphia Navy as part of the Philadelphia Inactive Ships Maintenance Facility (InactShipFac).

2 CONVENTIONAL ANTISUBMARINE AIRCRAFT CARRIERS, "ESSEX" CLASS

Name	Number	Builder	Awarded	Commissioned	F/S	Decommissioned
Bennington	CVS-20	NY Navy	12–15–41	8–6–44	PR*	15 January 1970 at Bremerton
Hornet	CVS-12	Newport News	9–9–40	11–29–43	PR*	26 June 1970 at Bremerton

Class is equipped with hydraulic catapults. Five sisters have been stricken. Ex-*Yorktown* (CVS-10) is a memorial at Patriots Point, South Carolina.

"ESSEX" CLASS MODERNIZATIONS[4]

Number	To CVS	Modernization Yard	FY/SCB	Awarded	Completed	Fram II FY
CVS-11	3–31–62	Newport News	52/27C	9–24–51	6–18–51	1965
CVS-11	—	NY Navy	57/125	1–24–56	5–2–57	—
CVS-12	6–27–58	NY Navy	52/27A	6–14–51	10–1–53	1965
CVS-12	—	PS Navy	56/125	8–24–55	8–15–56	—
CVT-16[1]	10–1–62	PS Navy	53/27C	7–21–52	9–1–55[2]	—
CVA-19	—	PS Navy	52/27C	7–17–51	3–1–54	—

Number	To CVS	Modernization Yard	FY/SCB	Awarded	Completed	Fram II FY
CVA-19	—	SF Navy	56/125	8–24–55	11–15–56	—
CVS-20	6–30–59	NY Navy	51/27A	10–26–50	11–30–52	1963
CVS-20	—	NY Navy	55/125	7–31–54	4–15–55	—
CVA-31	—	SF Navy	53/27C	7–21–52	11–1–55[2]	—
CVA-34[3]	—	SF Navy	57/125A	9–8–57	5–29–59	—
CVS-38	6–30–69	PS Navy	52/27C	7–17–51	2–1–55[2]	—

[1] See Section V for data on this ship.
[2] Authorization for SCB-27C also included 125 refit. Both done in 1 yard period.
[3] Completed to SCB-27A design.
[4] For modernization definitions, see 9th edition of this publication.

Nimitz (CVAN-68). During sea trials. 2–28–75. **Nimitz** class.

John F. Kennedy (CV-67). Note SPS-48 radar antenna aft of canted stack. 9–72. **John F. Kennedy** class.

Enterprise (CVAN-65). Note BPDMS launcher on port quarter. 6–71. **Enterprise** class.

Enterprise (CVAN-65). **Enterprise** class.

Constellation (CV-64). Note TERRIER launcher and fire control on starboard quarter. 6–71. **Kitty Hawk** class.

Independence (CV-62). Modified as multipurpose carrier. 10–74. **Forrestal** class.

Independence (CV-62). Note BPDMS on port quarter sponson. 10–74. **Forrestal** class.

Coral Sea (CVA-43). 5–70. **Midway** class.

Hornet (CVS-12) now laid up at Bremerton. 8–69. **"Essex"** class.

Hancock (CVA-19). Oldest active carrier. **Hancock** class.

Midway (CVA-41). Wider angled deck easily identifies this ship from her sisters. **Midway** class.

B. SURFACE COMBATANTS

Battleships   At the end of FY 1975, there were 4 battleships still on the NVR. All were in reserve, 2 on each coast. The *Iowa*s are the last of the bygone dreadnought era.

Class	Number	No. In Class	Full Load Displ.	Length Overall	Max. Draft	Extreme Beam	Number & Type of Boilers/Engines	Screws/ SHP	Max. Speed (Kts.)	Accommodations Officers	Enlisted	Armament
Iowa	BB-61	4	57,950	887'3"	38'	108'	8B(B&W)/4GT(G.E.)	4/212,000	33.5	95	2,270	3 triple 16"/50 cal. turrets, 10 twin 5"/38 cal. mts.

4 BATTLESHIPS, *IOWA* CLASS

Name	Number	Builder	Awarded	Commissioned	F/S	Decommissioned
Wisconsin	BB-64	Phil. Navy	6-12-40	4-16-44	AR*	8 March 1958 at New York
Missouri	BB-63	NY Navy	6-12-40	6-11-44	PR*	26 February 1955 at Bremerton
New Jersey	BB-62	Phil. Navy	7-1-39	5-23-43	PR*	17 December 1969 at Bremerton
Iowa	BB-61	NY Navy	7-1-39	2-22-43	AR*	24 February 1958 at Philadelphia

Illinois (BB-65) and *Kentucky* (BB-66) of this class were cancelled on 8–11–45 (BB-65) and 1–20–50 (BB-66). BB-62 was recommissioned 4–6–68 for Vietnam duty and made one deployment. She was preparing for second deployment when budget restrictions forced layup. Action to dispose of BB-61 and 64 was begun 6–6–73, then abruptly cancelled 11–9–73. BB-62/63 will survive as memorials after being stricken. From 3–10–55 to 12/59, *Missouri* served as accommodation and depot ship at Bremerton InactShipFac; she retains her original 40 mm mts. BB-61 and 64 carry 3″/50 cal. mts. BB-62 has no light guns. BB-61 and 64 were extensively cannibalized. Forward control tower of BB-62 was modified during 1967/68 reactivation to accommodate modern ECM/ECCM suite. The modifications centered around the upper portion of tower.

New Jersey (BB-62). World's last active battleship. 9–68. **Iowa** class.

Wisconsin (BB-64) in her original configuration. 1944. **Iowa** class.

Cruisers At the end of FY 1975, there were 40 cruisers on the NVR. Of that total, 10 were CGNs, 25 were CGs and 5 were CAs. Active: 5 CGNs, 23 CGs. Reserve: 2 CGs, 5 CAs. Building: 5 CGNs. A new class of cruisers, displacing approximately 12,000 tons, to carry four V/STOL or equivalent size helicopters, to be armed with 5″ guns, antiaircraft/cruise missiles is currently in the design stage. Funds for construction will be requested in the late 1970s.

Class	Number	No. In Class	Full Load Displ.	Length Overall	Max. Draft	Extreme Beam	Number & Type of Reactors/Boilers & Engines	Screws/ SHP	Max. Speed (Kts.)	Accommodations		Armament
										Officers	Enlisted	
MISSILE CRUISERS												
Virginia	CGN-38	5	10,000	585′	29′6″	63′	2R/D2G(G.E.)	2/	30+			2 twin MK 26 TARTAR D/ASROC launchers, 2 single 5″/54 MK 45 cal. mts., 2 MK 32 triple torpedo tube mts.
California	CGN-36	2	11,100	596′	31′6″	61′	2R/D2G(G.E.)	2/	30+	28	512	2 single MK 13 TARTAR "D" launchers, 2 single 5″/54 MK 45 cal. mts., 1 ASROC, 2 MK 32 triple torpedo tube mts.
Truxtun	CGN-35	1	9,000	564′	31′	58′	2R/D2G(G.E.)	2/60,000	29	36	492	1 twin MK 10 TERRIER/ASROC launcher, 1 single 5″/54 cal. mt., 2 single 3″/50 cal. mts., 2 MK 32 twin torpedo tube mts.
Belknap	CG-26	9	7,940	547′	29′	55′	4B(B&W)/2GT(G.E.)	2/85,000	32.5	31	387	1 twin MK 10 TERRIER/ASROC launcher, 1 single 5″/54 cal. mt., 2 single 3″/50 cal. mts., 2 MK 32 triple torpedo tube mts.
Bainbridge	CGN-25	1	8,590	565′	25′5″	58′	2R(D2G/(G.E.)	2/60,000	29	36	464	2 twin MK 10 TERRIER launchers, 2 twin 3″/50 cal. mts., 1 ASROC, 2 MK 32 triple torpedo tube mts.

continued

Class	Number	No. In Class	Full Load Displ.	Length Overall	Max. Draft	Extreme Beam	Number & Type of Reactors/Boilers & Engines	Screws/ Ship	Max. Speed (Kts.)	Accommodations Officers	Enlisted	Armament
Leahy	CG-16	9	7,800	533'	24'10"	55'	4B(B&W)/2GT(G.E.)	2/85,000	32.7	31	364	2 twin MK 10 TERRIER launchers, 2 twin 3"/50 cal. mts., 1 ASROC, 2 MK 32 triple torpedo tube mts.
Albany	CG-10	3	18,950	674'	33'6"	71'	4B(B&W)/4GT(G.E.)	4/120,000	30.4	86	1,186	2 twin TALOS launchers, 2 twin TARTAR launchers, 2 single 5"/38 cal. mts., 1 ASROC, 2 MK 32 triple torpedo tube mts.
Long Beach	CGN-9	1	16,247	721'3"	29'8"	73'3"	2R/C1W(West.)	2/80,000	30	79	1,081	2 twin TERRIER launchers, 1 twin TALOS launcher, 2 single 5"/38 cal. mts., 1 ASROC, 2 MK 32 triple torpedo tube mts.
Providence	CG-6	2	15,200	610'	25'5"	66'	4B(B&W)/4GT(G.E.)	4/100,000	32	75	1,045	1 triple 6"/47 cal. turret, 1 twin 5"/38 cal. mt., 1 twin TERRIER launcher
"Galveston"	CLG-3	2	15,142	610'	25'	66'	4B(B&W)/4GT(G.E.)	4/100,000	30.6	125	1,270	1 triple 6"/47 cal. turret, 1 twin TALOS launcher
HEAVY CRUISERS Des Moines	CA-134	3	20,950	716'5"	25'6"	76'4"	4B(B&W)/4GT(G.E.)	4/120,000	31.5	94	1,306	3 triple 8"/55 cal. turrets, 6 twin 5"/38 cal. mts., 10 twin 3"/50 cal. mts. (CA-134), 11 twin 3"/50 cal. mts. (CA-139)
"Boston"	CA-69	1	17,820	674'	29'	71'	4B(B&W)/4GT(G.E.)	4/120,000	33	113	1,512	2 triple 8"/55 cal. turrets, 5 twin 5"/38 cal. mts., 2 twin 3"/50 cal. mts., 2 twin TERRIER launchers
"Baltimore"	CA-68	1	17,350	674'9"	24'3"	70'8"	4B(B&W)/4GT(G.E.)	4/120,000	31	77	1,106	3 triple 8"/55 cal. turrets, 5 twin 5"/38 cal. mts., 6 twin 3"/50 cal. mts.

5 NUCLEAR-POWERED GUIDED MISSILE CRUISERS, *VIRGINIA* CLASS

Name	Number	FY/SCB	Builder	Awarded	Commissioned	F/S
	CGN-42	76/246	Newport News			Proj.
	CGN-41	75/246	Newport News	1-31-75		Bldg.
Mississippi	CGN-40	72/246	Newport News	1-21-72		Bldg.

Name	Number	FY/SCB	Builder	Awarded	Commissioned	F/S
Texas	CGN-39	71/246	Newport News	12-21-72		Bldg.
Virginia	CGN-38	70/246	Newport News	12-21-72		Bldg.

Class was originally authorized as guided missile frigates (nuclear powered) (DLGN). Reclassified and rerated as guided missile cruisers (nuclear powered) (CGN) on 6–30–75. Contract for construction was originally awarded under total package procurement concept. However, this process of designing/awarding was later abandoned and the various ships being built under this process were assigned SCB numbers (see also *Spruance* and *Tarawa* classes). Shorter than CGN-36 class because MK 26 combined HARPOON/STANDARD/ASROC missile launchers are used. The class was originally projected at 5 units. DLGN-41 and 42 were cancelled 5–6–71. However, Congress refused to let them die and has forced the Navy to build them. Class carries new lightweight 5" mount. Major new features of this class include new control and command systems. CGN-40 and later will have AEGIS radar weapon fire control system. All have helicopter hangar beneath fantail. Carry AN/SQS-26(CX) bow sonar.

2 NUCLEAR-POWERED GUIDED MISSILE CRUISERS, *CALIFORNIA* CLASS

Name	Number	FY/SCB	Builder	Awarded	Commissioned	F/S
South Carolina	CGN-37	68/241.66	Newport News	6-13-68	1-25-75	AA

Name	Number	FY/SCB	Builder	Awarded	Commissioned	F/S
California	CGN-36	67/241.66	Newport News	6-13-68	2-16-74	AA

Class was originally commissioned as guided missile frigates (nuclear-powered) (DLGN). Reclassified and rerated as indicated on 6–30–75. Three additional units of this class were deferred in favor of the *Virginia* class. Class is an improved *Truxtun* design. Like the *Virginias*, this class has dual-purpose launchers and mixed STANDARD/ASROC magazines. The new digital MK 86 gunfire control system is utilized for AAW/antisurface warfare/gunfire support. Two ships equipped with AN/SQS-26(CX) sonar. Have 3-dimensional warfare capability which is fully supported by three computer NTDS complex. CGN-37 in service on 9–30–74. CGN-36 scheduled to go to the Pacific in 1976.

1 NUCLEAR-POWERED GUIDED MISSILE CRUISER, *TRUXTUN* CLASS

Name	Number	FY/SCB	Builder	Awarded	Commissioned	F/S
Truxtun	CGN-35	62/222	NY Shipbuilding	6–23–62	5–27–67	PA

Was originally requested as DLG-35 of the *Belknap* class, but Congress authorized her as DLGN. Commissioned as guided missile frigate (nuclear powered) (DLGN) on indicated date. Reclassified and rerated as indicated on 6–30–75. Engineering plant for *Truxtun* and all succeeding CGNs duplicates *Bainbridge* class. Weapon and electronic installations duplicate *Belknap* class. Structural features differ. With closing down of ship's builder, Newport News remains the only yard with the capability to construct CGNs and larger combatants. Fitted with LAMPS under FY 1972.

9 CONVENTIONAL GUIDED MISSILE CRUISERS, *BELKNAP* CLASS

Name	Number	FY/SCB	Builder	Awarded	Commissioned	F/S
Biddle	CG-34	62/212	Bath Iron	1–16–62	1–21–67	AA
Fox	CG-33	62/212	Todd Shipyards	1–16–62	5–28–66	PA
William H. Standley	CG-32	62/212	Bath Iron	1–16–62	7–9–66	AA
Sterrett	CG-31	62/212	PS Navy	9–20–61	4–8–67	PA
Horne	CG-30	62/212	SF Navy	9–20–61	4–15–67	PA
Jouett	CG-29	62/212	PS Navy	9–20–61	12–3–66	PA
Wainwright	CG-28	61/212	Bath Iron	5–18–61	1–8–66	AA
Josephus Daniels	CG-27	61/212	Bath Iron	5–18–61	5–8–65	AA
Belknap	CG-26	61/212	Bath Iron	5–18–61	11–7–64	AA

Were originally commissioned as guided missile frigates (DLG); reclassified and rerated as indicated on 6–30–75. Very successful design. Subsequent CGN construction based on this class design. Class has NTDS, as do subsequent CGN classes. Class fitted with LAMPS under FY 1972. At least three additional units of this class were cancelled in favor of CGN construction. High rate of fire/reloading gives class deadly ASROC/TERRIER capabilities. Sonar is the SQ-26.

1 NUCLEAR-POWERED GUIDED MISSILE CRUISER, *BAINBRIDGE* CLASS

Name	Number	FY/SCB	Builder	Awarded	Commissioned	F/S
Bainbridge	CGN-25	56/189	Beth., Quincy	9–26–58	10–6–62	PA

Was originally commissioned as guided missile frigate (nuclear powered) (DLGN); reclassified and rerated as indicated on 6–30–75. Fitted with LAMPS system, except hangar, under FY 1974. AAW modernization (SCB-189.74) authorized under FY 1974. Assigned to Puget Sound Navy Yard on 11–5–73; arrived at yard and conversion begun on 6–30–74. NTDS will be fitted during AAW modernization.

9 CONVENTIONAL GUIDED MISSILE CRUISERS, *LEAHY* CLASS

Name	Number	FY/SCB	Builder	Awarded	Commissioned	F/S
Reeves	CG-24	59/172	PS Navy	12–8–58	5–15–64	PA
Halsey	CG-23	59/172	SF Navy	12–5–58	7–20–63	PA
England	CG-22	59/172	Todd Shipyards	11–7–58	12–7–63	PA
Gridley	CG-21	59/172	PS B. & DD	11–7–58	5–25–63	PA
Richmond K. Turner	CG-20	59/172	NY Shipbuilding	11–7–58	6–13–64	AA
Dale	CG-19	59/172	NY Shipbuilding	11–7–58	11–23–63	AA
Worden	CG-18	59/172	Bath Iron	11–7–58	8–3–63	PA
Harry E. Yarnell	CG-17	59/172	Bath Iron	11–7–58	2–2–63	AA
Leahy	CG-16	59/172	Bath Iron	11–7–58	8–4–62	AA

LEAHY CLASS ANTIAIR WARFARE MODERNIZATIONS (AAW)

Number	Modernized at	FY/SCB	Awarded	Started	Completed	Recommissioned
CG-24	Bath Iron	67/244	9–12–67	4–10–69	8–14–70	8–29–70
CG-23	Bath Iron	71/244	7–15–70	11–4–71	12–8–72	12–16–72
CG-22	Bath Iron	67/244	9–12–67	4–10–70	6–16–71	6–26–71
CG-21	Bath Iron	67/244	9–12–67	9–10–68	1–9–70	1–17–70
CG-20	Bath Iron	71/244	7–15–70	5–5–71	5–19–72	5–27–72

Number	Modernized at	FY/SCB	Awarded	Started	Completed	Recommissioned
CG-19[1]	Bath Iron	71/244	7–15–70	11–10–70	11–22–71	12–11–71
CG-18	Bath Iron	67/244	9–12–67	11–10–69	1–8–71	1–16–71
CG-17	Bath Iron	67/244	9–12–67	2–9–68	6–27–69	7–12–69
CG-16	Phil. Navy	66/244	12–29–65	2–15–67	8–17–68	5–4–68

[1] Contract for modernization originally awarded to Bath Iron Works on 9–12–67 under FY 1968; however, the modernization was deferred to FY 1971.

Modernization program included installation of NTDS, advanced communications, and ECM. Ships have AN/SQS-23 sonars. AN/SPS-48 air-search radar (integrates with NTDS) and MK 76, Mod. 5 fire control systems were installed.

3 CONVERTED HEAVY CRUISERS, ALBANY CLASS

Name	Number	Builder	Commissioned	Converted at	FY/SCB	Assigned	Started	Recommissioned	F/S
Columbus	CG-12	Beth., Fore R.	6–8–45	PS Navy	59/173	9–23–58	6–1–59	12–1–62	AR*
Chicago	CG-11	Phil. Navy	1–10–45	SF Navy	59/173	9–23–58	7–1–59	5–2–64	PA
Albany	CG-10	Beth., Fore R.	6–15–46	Boston Navy	58/173	11–26–57	1–2–59	11–3–62	AA

As originally projected, Oregon City (CA-122), Chicago (CA-136), and Fall River (CA-131) were to be converted to CG-10/12 under FY 1958. However, budget restrictions caused deferment of last two to FY 1959 program. Under original FY 1959 program, Columbus (CA-74) was to be converted to CG-13. However, to reduce costs further, the decommissioning Albany (CA-123) replaced CA-122 as CG-10. Further, with the deferment of CG-11/12 to FY1959, Columbus replaced CA-131 as CG-12, and the fourth CG conversion (CG-13) was dropped.

Albany is an ex-Oregon City class CA and the other two are ex-Baltimore class CAs. CA-123 and 136 were reclassified CG-10/11 on 11-1-58; CA-74 was reclassified CG-12 on 9-30-59. CG-10/11 have NTDS. Under FY 1968, CG-10 received AAW modernization SCB-002; was converted between 2-1-67 and 11-9-68 at Boston Naval Shipyard. CG-11/12 will not get AAW modernization due to age. CG-11 was fitted with LAMPS under FY 1973. CG-12 was decommissioned at Norfolk on 1-31-75. The hull numbers CG-13/15 were not used.

1 NUCLEAR-POWERED GUIDED MISSILE CRUISER, LONG BEACH CLASS

Name	Number	FY/SCB	Builder	Awarded	Keel Laid	Launched	Commissioned	F/S
Long Beach	CGN-9	57/169	Beth., Quincy	10–15–56	12–2–57	7–14–59	9–9–61	PA

Originally authorized as CLGN-160. To CGN-160 on 12-6-56; to CGN-9 on 7-1-57. Superstructure resembles that of CVAN-65, as both carry AN/SPS-32 and 33 radar arrays. Ship has NTDS and AN/SQS-23 bow-mounted sonar.

2 CONVERTED GUIDED MISSILE CRUISERS, PROVIDENCE CLASS

Name	Number	Builder	Commissioned	Converted at	FY/SCB	Awarded	Started	Recommissioned	F/S
Springfield	CG-7	Beth., Fore R.	9–9–44	Beth., Quincy	57/146A	1–10–57	8–1–57	7–2–60	AR*
Providence	CG-6	Beth., Fore R.	5–15–45	Boston Navy	57/146A	7–23–56	6–1–57	9–17–59	PR*

Ex-Cleveland class CLs. CL-82 (vice CL-65) to CLG-6 and CL-66 to CLG-7 on 5-23-57. Topeka (CLG-8), a sister, has been stricken, CG-6 decommissioned 8-31-73 at San Diego; CG-7 decommissioned 6-15-74 at Norfolk. Both are fitted as flagships. The hull number CG-8 was not used.

2 CONVERTED GUIDED MISSILE CRUISERS, "*GALVESTON*" CLASS

Name	Number	Builder	Commissioned	Converted at	FY/SCB	Awarded	Started	Recommissioned	F/S
Oklahoma City	CG-5	Cramp	12–22–44	Beth., SF	57/140A	1–10–57	5–21–57	9–7–60	PA
Little Rock	CG-4	Cramp	6–17–45	NY Shipbuilding	57/140A	12–21–56	1–30–57	6–30–70	AA

Originally commissioned as *Cleveland* class CLs. CL-92/91 reclassified CLG-4/5 on 5–23–57. CG-4 serves as flagship 6th Fleet. CG-5 also fitted as flagship. CG-4/7 are identical conversions, but are divided into two classes because of missile systems. CG-4/7 were reclassified and rerated from guided missile light cruisers (CLG) to guided missile cruisers (CG) on 6–30–75. The hull number CG-3 was not used. CAG-1/2 became CA-69/70.

3 HEAVY CRUISERS, *DES MOINES* CLASS

Name	Number	Builder	Awarded	Keel	Launched	Commissioned	F/S
Newport News	CA-148	Newport News	4–8–44	10–1–45	3–6–47	1–29–49	AR*
Salem	CA-139	Beth., Fore River	6–14–43	7–4–45	3–25–47	5–14–49	AR*

Name	Number	Builder	Awarded	Keel	Launched	Commissioned	F/S
Des Moines	CA-134	Beth., Fore River	9–25–43	5–28–45	9–27–46	11–16–48	AR*

Largest and most powerful CAs. Armed with fully automatic 8″ guns. CA-148 modified as 2nd Fleet flagship; made several deployments to Vietnam. No. 2 turret on CA-148 is inoperative because of internal explosion in turret on 10–1–72 while conducting a fire support mission off Vietnam. It was planned to repair it with No. 2 turret from CA-134, but due to costs and budget limitations, this was cancelled. Instead, the middle barrel was removed and the turret was realigned fore and aft in steaming position, where it is permanently frozen into position. The remaining 3″/50 mounts were removed from CA-148 in mid-1974. CA-134 was decommissioned 7–14–61 at Boston, CA-139 on 1–30–59 and CA-148 in 6/75 at Norfolk. CA-148 was the last active all-gun cruiser in USN. Nine additional sisters (CA-140/143, 149/153) were cancelled.

1 FORMER GUIDED MISSILE CRUISER, "*BOSTON*" CLASS

Name	Number	Builder	Commissioned	Converted at	FY/SCB	Awarded	Started	Recommissioned	F/S
Canberra	CA-70	Beth., Fore River	10–14–43	NY Shipbuilding	52/48	1–28–52	6–30–52	8–15–56	PR*

Ex-*Baltimore* class CA; was reclassified from CA-70 to CAG-2 on 1–4–52; reverted to CA-70 on 5–1–68. She carries the obsolete BW-1 TERRIER. Because it was obsolete and the 8″ guns were considered to be the main armament, the ship was reclassified back to its original CA number. As originally projected, *Oregon City* (CA-122) and *Chicago* (CA-136) were slated for conversion to CAG-1/2; were replaced by *Boston* (CA-69) as CAG-1 and *Canberra*. As CAGs, they were world's first guided missile armed warships. CAG-1/2 were to have received AAW modifications under FY 1968 (SCB-003), but this was cancelled. Sister-ship *Boston* (CA-69) and *Rochester* (CA-124) have been stricken.

1 HEAVY CRUISER, "*BALTIMORE*" CLASS

Name	Number	Builder	Awarded	Keel	Launched	Commissioned	F/S
Saint Paul	CA-73	Beth., Fore River	9–9–40	2–3–43	9–16–44	2–17–45	PR*

Last survivor of a class of 14 units and last active *Baltimore* class CA. Four of this class were converted to missile cruisers. CA-73 lacks forward 5″ gun (just below the bridge on the 01 level). As a result of over 26 years of continuous active service, *Saint Paul* is in rather poor material condition; decommissioned 4–30–71 at Bremerton. The Navy's last light cruiser (CL) was stricken on 1–15–71.

Mississippi (CGN-40). Artist's conception. 2–75. **Virginia** class.

South Carolina (CGN-37). One of a new class of cruisers. 10–74. **California** class.

South Carolina (CGN-37). 10–74. **California** class.

Truxtun (CGN-35). 7–70. **Truxtun** class.

Truxtun (CGN-35). Missile launcher doubles as ASROC launcher. 11–71. **Truxtun** class.

Bainbridge (CGN-25). Note ASROC and missile launchers forward and absence of lattice masts. 1970. **Bainbridge** class.

Sterett (CG-31) with SH-2D SEASPRITE on helicopter deck. 1972. **Belknap** class. (Photo: Kaman Aerospace.)

William H. Standley (CG-32). 1971. **Belknap** class.

Gridley (CG-21) in her post-AAW mod configuration. 1–70. **Leahy** class.

Chicago (CG-11). 6–73. **Albany** class.

Reeves (CG-24). Location of helicopter deck in this class differs from BELKNAP class. 7–72. **Leahy** class.

Long Beach (CGN-9). 1971. **Long Beach** class.

Springfield (CG-7). 8–73. **Providence** class.

Saint Paul (CA-73). Last active **"Baltimore"** class cruiser. 3–68. **"Baltimore"** class.

Newport News (CA-148). Note middle gun in #2 turret missing. 10–74. **Des Moines** class. (Photo: C. & S. Taylor.)

Oklahoma City (CG-5). Note difference in masts as compared to *Springfield* (CG-7). 1973. **"Galveston"** class.

Canberra (CA-70). **"Boston"** class.

Salem (CA-139). 6–52. **Des Moines** class.

Destroyers At the end of FY 1975, there were 134 destroyer types on the NVR. Of that total, 39 were DDGs and 95 were DDs. Active: 39 DDGs and 34 DDs. Reserve: 1 DD. Under construction: 28 DDs. In addition, 32 DDs were assigned to the Naval Reserve Training Force.

Class	Number	No. In Class	Full Load Displ.	Length Overall	Max. Draft	Extreme Beam	Number and Type of Boilers/Engines	SHP/ Screws	Max. Speed (Kts.)	Accommodations		Armament
										Officers	Enlisted	
Coontz	DDG-40	10	5,800	513'	23'5"	53'	4B(B&W)/2GT(DeLaval)	2/85,000	33	28	347	1 twin MK 10 TERRIER launcher, 1 single 5"/54 cal. mt., 1 ASROC, 2 MK 32 triple torpedo tube mts., 2 40mm saluting mts.
Mitscher	DDG-35	2	5,155	494'	21'	50'	4B(C.E.)/2GT(G.E.)	2/80,000	32	29	349	1 single MK 13 TARTAR launcher, 2 single 5"/54 cal. mts., 1 ASROC, 2 MK 32 torpedo tube mts.
Decatur	DDG-31	4	4,150	418'5"	22'	44'	4B(F.W.)/2GT(G.E.)	2/70,000	31	22	313	1 single MK 13 TARTAR launcher, 1 single 5"/54 cal. mt., 1 ASROC, 2 MK 32 triple torpedo tube mts.

continued

Class	Number	No. In Class	Full Load Displ.	Length Overall	Max. Draft	Extreme Beam	Number and Type of Boilers/Engines	SHP/ Screws	Max. Speed (Kts.)	Accommodations Officers	Accommodations Enlisted	Armament
Charles F. Adams	DDG-2	23	4,500	437′	27′3″	47′	4B(B&W)/2GT(G.E.)	2/70,000	30	24	330	1 twin MK 11 TARTAR launcher (DDG-2/14), 1 single MK 13 TARTAR launcher (DDG-15/23), 2 single 5″/54 cal. mts., 1 ASROC, 2 MK 32 triple torpedo tube mts.
Spruance	DD-963	30	7,800	563′4″	28′	54′	(4)LM-2500 Gas Turbines	2/80,000	30+			2 single 5″/54 MK 45 cal. mts., 1 BPDMS launcher, 1 ASROC, 2 MK 32 triple torpedo tube mts.
Hull	DD-945	5	4,050	418′5″	22′2″	45′1″	4B(B&W)/2GT(G.E.)	2/70,000	33	22	306	3 single 5″/54 cal. mts. (DD-945, 946 & 951), 2 single 5″/54 cal. mts. (remainder), 1 twin 3″/50 cal. mt. (DD-945, 946, 951), 1 ASROC (DD-948 & 950), 2 MK 32 triple torpedo tube mts.
Forrest Sherman	DD-931	9	4,050	418′	22′	45′	4B(B&W)/2GT(West.)	2/70,000	33	23	315	3 single 5″/54 cal. mts. (DD-931, 942, 944), 2 single 5″/54 cal. mts. (remainder), 1 twin 3″/50 cal. mt. (DD-931, 942, 944), 1 ASROC (DD-933, 937, 938, 940, 941 & 943), 2 MK 32 triple torpedo tube mts., 2 MK 11 Hedgehogs (DD-942, 944)
Carpenter	DD-825	2	3,459	391′	20′11″	41′	4B(B&W)/2GT(G.E.)	2/60,000	33	21	286	1 twin 5″/38 cal. mt., 1 ASROC, 2 MK 32 triple torpedo tube mts.
"Gearing"	DD-710	48	3,512	391′	20′	41′2″	4B(B&W)/2GT(West.)	2/60,000	32.2	24	298	2 twin 5″/38 cal. mts., 1 ASROC, 2 MK 32 triple torpedo tube mts.
"Allen M. Sumner"	DD-692	0	3,300	376′	21′	41′4″	4B(B&W)/2GT(G.E.)	2/60,000	32.5	19	276	3 twin 5″/38 cal. mts., 2 MK 32 triple torpedo tube mts.
"La Vallette"	DD-448	1	3,040	376′	20′	40′	4B(B&W)/2GT(G.E.)	2/60,000	35	24	299	4 single 5″/38 cal. mts. 3 twin 3″/50 cal. mts. 2 MK 32 triple torpedo tube mts, 2 MK 10 or 11 Hedgehogs

10 CONVENTIONAL GUIDED MISSILE DESTROYERS, *COONTZ* CLASS

Name	Number	FY/SCB	Builder	Awarded	Commissioned	F/S
Preble	DDG-46	57/142	Bath Iron	10–26–56	5–9–60	PA
Dewey	DDG-45	57/142	Bath Iron	10–26–56	12–7–69	AA
William V. Pratt	DDG-44	57/142	Phil. Navy	7–23–56	11–4–61	AA
Dahlgren	DDG-43	57/142	Phil. Navy	7–23–56	4–8–61	AA
Mahan	DDG-42	56/142	SF Navy	11–18–55	8–25–60	AA
King	DDG-41	56/142	PS Navy	11–18–55	11–17–60	PA
Coontz	DDG-40	56/142	PS Navy	11–18–55	7–15–60	AA
MacDonough	DDG-39	56/142	Beth., Quincy	1–27–56	11–4–61	AA
Luce (ex-Dewey)	DDG-38	56/142	Beth., Quincy	1–27–56	5–20–61	AA
Farragut	DDG-37	56/142	Beth., Quincy	1–27–56	12–10–60	AA

DLG-6/8 were originally authorized as DL-6/8, then reclassified DLG on 11–14–56 and completed to *Coontz* class design. DLG-9/11 were originally classified as DL-1/3, then reclassified DLG-9/11 on 11–14–56 "in order to continue the DL sequence of hull numbers." DLG-10/11 were two of the first three ships in USN to be equipped with NTDS. Class was originally designed to have 2 single 5″/54s fitted forward. Early units of this class were completed with #2 mt. absent. ASROC launcher was backfitted on these units when it became operational and the remainder of the class were completed with the launcher in place of the #2 5″ mt. DDG-38 was renamed 2–12–57. Reclassified and rerated from guided missile frigates (DLG) to guided missile destroyers (DDG) on 6–30–75. In 1974, DDG-40 served as test ship for the VULCAN CICWS system. System centers around a new 20mm gun employing the mount of the 3″/50 gun.

COONTZ CLASS ANTIAIR WARFARE MODERNIZATIONS

Number	Modernized at	FY/SCB	Awarded	Started	Completed	Recommissioned
DDG-46	Phil Navy	68/243	2–29–68	1–31–69	7–1–70	5–23–70
DDG-45	Phil Navy	69/243	8–22–68	11–24–69	4–23–71	3–13–71
DDG-44	Phil. Navy	72/243	1–12–72	10–10–72	10–18–73	10–6–73
DDG-43	Phil. Navy	72/243	9–30–71	2–28–72	3–29–73	3–17–73

Number	Modernized at	FY/SCB	Awarded	Started	Completed	Recommissioned
DDG-42[1]	Bath Iron	74/243	6-20-73	8-31-73		4-1-75
DDG-41	Boland	74/243	4-19-74	7-1-74		
DDG-40	Phil. Navy	71/243	7-24-70	2-28-71	4-27-72	3-18-72

[1] AAW modernization was originally authorized under FY 1973 and assigned to Philadelphia Naval Shipyard on 9-1-72. Cancelled 9/72 and reauthorized FY 1974. [2] Originally awarded to Norfolk Naval Shipyard on

Number	Modernized at	FY/SCB	Awarded	Started	Completed	Recommissioned
DDG-39	Phil. Navy	73/243	11-15-72	4-9-73	4-26-74	5-4-74
DDG-38	Phil. Navy	70/243	11-1-69	2-28-70	7-9-71	5-22-71
DDG-37[2]	Phil. Navy	66/243	10-13-66	5-1-68	3-10-69	9-13-69

12-29-65. Reawarded as indicated.

The class received same basic modernization as *Leahy* class with following exceptions: first 5 DDGs modernized received improved guidance capabilities for TERRIER missiles; DDG-37 received improved ASROC reload capabilities (deckhouse on 01 level just aft of ASROC launcher and under bridge). All of the class had the height of the mainmast increased and their 3"/50 cal. mts. removed. All have NTDS and AN/SQS-23 sonar. The two *Mitscher* class DLs and the *Norfolk* (DL-1) have been stricken.

2 CONVERTED GUIDED MISSILE DESTROYERS, *MITSCHER* CLASS (ex-Frigates)

Name	Number	FY/SCB	Builder	Commissioned	Converted at	FY/SCB	Awarded	Recommissioned	F/S
John S. McCain	DDG-36	48/5	Bath Iron	10-12-53	Phil. Navy	64/241	12-22-64	9-6-69	PA
Mitscher	DDG-35	48/5	Bath Iron	5-15-53	Phil. Navy	64/241	12-22-64	6-29-68	AA

DDG-35/36 were originally laid down as DD-927/928, then reclassified DL-2/3 on 2-9-51. They served as frigates from commissioning until conversion to DDG. DL-2/3 were reclassified DDG on 3-15-67. Both the *Decatur* and *Mitscher* class conversions have been somewhat less than successful. They are considered to be too top heavy. The construction of the DXG class DDGs has been deferred.

4 CONVERTED GUIDED MISSILE DESTROYERS, *DECATUR* CLASS (ex-Destroyers)

Name	Number	FY/SCB	Builder	Commissioned	Converted at	FY/SCB	Awarded	Recommissioned	F/S
Somers	DDG-34	56/85A	Bath Iron	4-3-59	SF Navy	64/240	12-22-64	2-10-68	PA
Parsons	DDG-33	56/85A	Ingalls	10-29-59	LB Navy	64/240	12-22-64	11-3-67	PA
John Paul Jones	DDG-32	53/85	Bath Iron	4-5-56	Phil. Navy	64/240	12-22-64	9-23-67	PA
Decatur	DDG-31	54/85	Beth., Quincy	12-7-56	Boston Navy	64/240	12-22-64	4-29-67	PA

DDG-31/32 originally commissioned as DD-936 and 932 of the *Forrest Sherman* class DDs; DDG-33/34 as DD-949 and 947 of the *Hull* class DDs. DD-936 reclassified DDG-31 on 9-15-66. The remainder were reclassified on 3-15-67. Class has massive appearance with two lattice radar masts and the block-like superstructure. During conversion ASROC was substituted for DASH. DD-936 was converted to DDG after suffering major collision damage as DD. It was cheaper to convert to DDG than to repair as DD.

23 GUIDED MISSILE DESTROYERS, *CHARLES F. ADAMS* CLASS

Name	Number	FY/SCB	Builder	Awarded	Commissioned	F/S
Waddell	DDG-24	61/155	Todd, Seattle	11-3-60	8-28-64	PA
Richard E. Byrd	DDG-23	61/155	Todd, Seattle	11-3-60	3-7-64	AA
Benjamin Stoddert	DDG-22	60/155	PS B & DD	3-25-60	9-12-64	PA
Cochrane	DDG-21	60/155	PS B & DD	3-25-60	3-21-64	PA
Goldsborough	DDG-20	60/155	PS B & DD	3-25-60	11-9-63	PA

Name	Number	FY/SCB	Builder	Awarded	Commissioned	F/S
Tattnall	DDG-19	59/155	Avondale	7-21-59	4-13-63	AA
Semmes	DDG-18	59/155	Avondale	7-21-59	12-10-62	AA
Conyngham	DDG-17	59/155	NY Shipbuilding	7-21-59	7-13-63	AA
Joseph Strauss	DDG-16	59/155	NY Shipbuilding	7-21-59	4-20-63	PA
Berkeley	DDG-15	59/155	NY Shipbuilding	7-21-59	12-15-62	PA

continued

Name	Number	FY/SCB	Builder	Awarded	Commissioned	F/S
Buchanan	DDG-14	58/155	Todd, Seattle	1-17-58	2-7-62	PA
Hoel	DDG-13	58/155	Defoe Shipbuilding	1-17-58	6-16-62	PA
Robison	DDG-12	58/155	Defoe Shipbuilding	1-17-58	12-9-61	PA
Sellers	DDG-11	58/155	Bath Iron	1-17-58	10-28-61	AA
Sampson	DDG-10	58/155	Bath Iron	1-17-58	6-24-61	AA
Towers	DDG-9	57/155	Todd, Seattle	3-28-57	6-6-61	PA
Lynde McCormick	DDG-8	57/155	Defoe Shipbuilding	3-28-57	6-3-61	PA

Name	Number	FY/SCB	Builder	Awarded	Commissioned	F/S
Henry B. Wilson	DDG-7	57/155	Defoe Shipbuilding	3-28-57	12-17-60	PA
Barney	DDG-6	57/155	NY Shipbuilding	3-28-57	8-11-62	AA
Claude V. Ricketts	DDG-5	57/155	NY Shipbuilding	3-28-57	5-5-62	AA
Lawrence	DDG-4	57/155	NY Shipbuilding	3-28-57	1-6-62	AA
John King	DDG-3	57/155	Bath Iron	3-28-57	2-4-61	AA
Charles F. Adams	DDG-2	57/155	Bath Iron	3-28-57	9-10-60	AA

DDG-2/9 were originally authorized as DD-952/959 of *Hull* class; reclassified DDG-952/959 on 8-16-56; but again reclassed DDG-2/9 on 6-26-57. DDG-5 was originally commissioned as *Biddle,* then renamed as indicated on 7-28-64. The ships are not identical. DDG-20/24 have SQS-23 bow-mounted sonar and an anchor located in the bull nose vice the port bow. The design of this class is rated as very successful. DDG-9 is first USN ship fitted with the Ship Anti-Missile Integrated Defense (SAMID) to help counter Soviet cruise missile threat (STYX,

SHADDOCK, etc.). During 1972-73, DDG-4 and 13 were fitted with the CHAPPAREL missile for operational evaluation. Six more of this class were constructed for two Allied nations. DDG-25/27 were built for Australia as *Perth* (D-38), *Hobart* (D-39) and *Brisbane* (D-41), respectively. DDG-28/30 were built for West Germany as *Lutjens* (D-185), *Molders* (D-186) and *Rommel* (D-187), respectively.

30 DESTROYERS, *SPRUANCE* CLASS

	Number	FY/SCB	Builder	Awarded		F/S
	DD-992	75/224.71	Ingalls	1-15-75		Bldg.
	DD-991	75/224.71	Ingalls	1-15-75		Bldg.
	DD-990	75/224.71	Ingalls	1-15-75		Bldg.
	DD-989	75/224.71	Ingalls	1-15-75		Bldg.
	DD-988	75/224.71	Ingalls	1-15-75		Bldg.
	DD-987	75/224.71	Ingalls	1-15-75		Bldg.
	DD-986	75/224.71	Ingalls	1-15-75		Bldg.
	DD-985	74/224.71	Ingalls	1-15-74		Bldg.
	DD-984	74/224.71	Ingalls	1-15-74		Bldg.
	DD-983	74/224.71	Ingalls	1-15-74		Bldg.
	DD-982	74/224.71	Ingalls	1-15-74		Bldg.
	DD-981	74/224.71	Ingalls	1-15-74		Bldg.
Moosbrugger	DD-980	74/224.71	Ingalls	1-15-74		Bldg.
Conolly	DD-979	74/224.71	Ingalls	1-15-74		Bldg.
Stump	DD-978	72/224.71	Ingalls	1-26-72		Bldg.

Name	Number	FY/SCB	Builder	Awarded		F/S
Briscoe	DD-977	72/224.71	Ingalls	1-26-72		Bldg.
Merrill	DD-976	72/224.71	Ingalls	1-26-72		Bldg.
O'Brien	DD-975	72/224.71	Ingalls	1-26-72		Bldg.
Comte de Grasse	DD-974	72/224.71	Ingalls	1-26-72		Bldg.
John Young	DD-973	72/224.71	Ingalls	1-26-72		Bldg.
Oldendorf	DD-972	72/224.71	Ingalls	1-26-72		Bldg.
David R. Ray	DD-971	71/224.71	Ingalls	1-15-71		Bldg.
Caron	DD-970	71/224.71	Ingalls	1-15-71		Bldg.
Peterson	DD-969	71/224.71	Ingalls	1-15-71		Bldg.
Arthur W. Radford	DD-968	71/224.71	Ingalls	1-15-71		Bldg.
Elliot	DD-967	71/224.71	Ingalls	1-15-71		Bldg.
Hewitt	DD-966	71/224.71	Ingalls	1-15-71		PA
Kinkaid	DD-965	70/224.71	Ingalls	6-23-70		PA
Paul F. Foster	DD-964	70/224.71	Ingalls	6-23-70		PA
Spruance	DD-963	70/224.71	Ingalls	6-23-70		AA

This class will replace WW II DDs still operating with the Fleet. The ships were originally awarded under total package procurement concept. However, this concept was abandoned in 1971 and an SCB number was assigned. They are the first major USN warships with gas turbine propulsion. Built primarily as ASW platforms, the ships can operate just as well in other fields; largest and lightest armed DDs in the world. Space and weight has been reserved for installation of two missile systems, a close-in defense missile system, AN/SQS-35,

ECM and two VULCAN CICWS systems. Ships also carry AN/SQS-53, MK 86 fire control system and AN/SPS-40A air-search. Because of technical difficulties in the operation of the new shipyard, especially built to build this class and the *Tarawa* class LHAs, costs of construction have increased and the class has fallen behind schedule. DD-993 through DD-998 of this class will be constructed for Iran by Ingalls. They will have more complete weapons and electronics suits than their U.S. counterparts.

5 DESTROYERS, *HULL* CLASS

Name	Number	FY/SCB	Builder	Awarded	Commissioned	F/S
Turner Joy (ex-Joy)	DD-951	56/85A	PS B & DD	1-27-56	8-3-59	PA
Richard S. Edwards	DD-950	56/85A	PS B & DD	1-27-56	2-5-59	PA
Morton	DD-948	56/85A	Ingalls	1-27-56	5-26-59	PA

Name	Number	FY/SCB	Builder	Awarded	Commissioned	F/S
Edson	DD-946	56/85A	Bath Iron	1-27-56	11-7-58	PA
Hull	DD-945	56/85A	Bath Iron	1-27-56	7-3-58	PA

9 DESTROYERS, *FORREST SHERMAN* CLASS

Name	Number	FY/SCB	Builder	Awarded	Commissioned	F/S
Mullinnix	DD-944	55/85	Beth., Quincy	10-23-54	3-7-58	AA
Blandy	DD-943	55/85	Beth., Quincy	10-23-54	11-26-57	AA
Bigelow	DD-942	55/85	Bath Iron	7-30-54	11-8-57	AA
Du Pont	DD-941	55/85	Bath Iron	7-30-54	7-1-57	AA
Manley	DD-940	55/85	Bath Iron	7-30-54	2-1-57	AA

Name	Number	FY/SCB	Builder	Awarded	Commissioned	F/S
Jonas Ingram	DD-938	54/85	Beth., Quincy	2-3-54	7-19-57	AA
Davis	DD-937	54/85	Beth., Quincy	2-3-54	2-28-57	AA
Barry	DD-933	53/85	Bath Iron	12-15-52	8-31-56	AA
Forrest Sherman	DD-931	53/85	Bath Iron	12-15-52	11-9-55	AA

These two classes, with minor differences, originally consisted of 11 *Forrest Sherman* class and 15 *Hull* class ships. DD-952/959 were converted to DDG-2/9 during construction and DD-936, 932, 949, and 947 were converted to DDG-31/34 after serving some dozen years as DDs. As originally scheduled all 18 ships were to convert to DDG-31/48. Costs and delays saw the cancellation of 14 of the conversions. Of the 14 non-converted, all were to receive major ASW modifications (see 9th edition, page 21 for modernization definition and modernization data table. Also photograph section of this edition for ASW configuration). In the end, only 9 of the 14 were modernized. DD-933 had an SCB-251 modernization which differed from the SCB-221 modernization that the remaining 8 received. Of the remaining 5 non-converted ships, all received minor ASW modifications. This included removal of the forward 3"/50 mount and the enlargement of the superstructure to provide extra space. The 5 received minor ASW modifications due to the costs and period of the major ASW modifications. DD-951 was renamed on 26 July 1957. On 11-9-73, DD-945 was picked to serve as the

operational test and evaluation platform for the new Mk 71 lightweight 8" gun. The 8" Mk 71 gun is an attempt to fill the gap to be left with the decommissioning of *Newport News* (CA-148). The gun weighs 172,000 pounds, has a rate of fire of 12 rounds per minute, and has a Mk 86 gunfire control system. Conversion of the *Hull* to test ship status was simple. The forward 5" mount was removed and replaced with the 8" mount. Magazine spaces and ammunition hoists were modified accordingly and the Mk 86 fire control installed. Conversion took place in the summer of 1975. If this system proves successful, it is likely that the *Forrest Sherman*, *Hull* and *Spruance* classes will be fitted with the gun mount. The hull numbers DD-934, 935, and 939 were assigned to Japanese/German war prizes. DD-960/961 were assigned to two DDs built in Japan for Japan under the Off-Shore Procurement Program of the International Logistics Program. DD-962 was assigned to the former HMS *Charity* which was acquired from England, by the USN, for transfer to Pakistan under ILP.

2 DESTROYERS, *CARPENTER* CLASS (FRAM I, ex-DDE)

Name	Number	Builder	Awarded	Commissioned	F/S
Robert A. Owens	DD-827	Bath Iron	11-10-44	11-5-49	NRT

Name	Number	Builder	Awarded	Commissioned	F/S
Carpenter	DD-825	Consol. Steel	11-29-44	12-15-49	NRT

These were originally laid down as *Gearing* class DDs. They were suspended after the war and laid up incomplete; resumed and completed as hunter-killer destroyers (DDK); reclassified DDK on 1-28-48 and reclassified DDE on 3-4-50 when the DDK and DDE classifications were merged. They were reclassified DD on 6-30-62 after completion of FRAM I. This class

was the only one to bear the DDK classification. It is a popular misconception that the *Lloyd Thomas* class DDs also wore the DDK classification. For NRT assignments, as indicated by the term "NRT" in the "F/S" column, see Section 7 of this publication.

48 DESTROYERS, *"GEARING"* CLASS (FRAM I)

Name	Number	Builder	Awarded	Commissioned	F/S
Meredith	DD-890	Consol. Steel	6-14-43	12-31-45	NRT
Orleck	DD-886	Consol. Steel	6-14-43	9-15-45	NRT
John R. Craig	DD-885	Consol. Steel	6-14-43	8-20-45	NRT
Newman K. Perry (ex-DDR)	DD-883	Consol. Steel	6-14-43	7-26-45	NRT
Bordelon (ex-DDR)	DD-881	Consol. Steel	6-14-43	6-5-45	AA
Dyess (ex-DDR)	DD-880	Consol. Steel	6-14-43	5-21-45	NRT
Vesole (ex-DDR)	DD-878	Consol. Steel	6-14-43	4-23-45	AA

Name	Number	Builder	Awarded	Commissioned	F/S
Rogers (ex-DDR)	DD-876	Consol. Steel	6-14-43	3-26-45	NRT
Hawkins (ex-DDR)	DD-873	Consol. Steel	6-14-43	2-10-45	AA
Damato (ex-DDE)	DD-871	Beth., Staten Is.	6-14-43	4-27-46	NRT
Brownson	DD-868	Beth., Staten Is.	6-14-43	11-17-45	AA
Stribling	DD-867	Beth., Staten Is.	6-14-43	9-28-45	AA
Cone	DD-866	Beth., Staten Is.	6-14-43	8-18-45	NRT
Harold J. Ellison (ex-DDR)	DD-864	Beth., Staten Is.	6-14-43	6-23-45	NRT

continued

Name	Number	Builder	Awarded	Commissioned	F/S
Steinaker	DD-863	Beth., Staten Is.	6-14-43	5-26-45	NRT
Vogelgesang	DD-862	Beth., Staten Is.	6-14-43	4-28-45	NRT
Leonard F. Mason	DD-852	Beth., Quincy	6-14-43	6-28-46	PA
Richard E. Kraus	DD-849	Bath Iron	6-14-43	5-23-46	AA
[Ozbourn]	DD-846	Bath Iron	6-14-43	3-5-46	Stricken
Bausell	DD-845	Bath Iron	6-14-43	2-7-46	PA
Fiske	DD-842	Bath Iron	6-14-43	11-28-45	NRT
Glennon	DD-840	Bath Iron	6-14-43	10-4-45	AA
Power	DD-839	Bath Iron	6-14-43	9-13-45	NRT
Sarsfield	DD-837	Bath Iron	6-14-43	7-31-45	AA
George K. MacKenzie	DD-836	Bath Iron	6-14-43	7-13-45	PA
Charles P. Cecil (ex-DDR)	DD-835	Bath Iron	6-14-43	6-29-45	NRT
Myles C. Fox (ex-DDR)	DD-829	Bath Iron	6-14-43	3-20-45	NRT
Agerholm	DD-826	Bath Iron	11-10-44	6-20-46	PA
Basilone (ex-DDE)	DD-824	Consol. Steel	11-29-44	7-26-49	AA
Robert H. McCard	DD-822	Consol. Steel	11-29-44	10-26-46	NRT
Johnston	DD-821	Consol. Steel	11-29-44	8-23-46	NRT
Rich (ex-DDE)	DD-820	Consol. Steel	11-29-44	7-4-46	NRT
Holder (ex-DDE)	DD-819	Consol. Steel	11-29-44	5-18-46	NRT

Name	Number	Builder	Awarded	Commissioned	F/S
New (ex-DDE)	DD-818	Consol. Steel	11-29-44	4-5-46	AA
Corry (ex-DDR)	DD-817	Consol. Steel	11-29-44	2-26-46	NRT
Higbee (ex-DDR)	DD-806	Bath Iron	8-7-42	1-27-45	NRT
Hollister	DD-788	Todd., Seattle	8-7-42	3-26-46	NRT
Richard B. Anderson	DD-786	Todd., Seattle	8-7-42	10-26-45	PA
Henderson	DD-785	Todd., Seattle	8-7-42	8-4-45	NRT
McKean (ex-DDR)	DD-784	Todd., Seattle	8-7-42	6-9-45	NRT
Gurke	DD-783	Todd., Seattle	8-7-42	5-12-45	PA
Rowan	DD-782	Todd., Seattle	8-7-42	3-31-45	PA
William C. Lawe	DD-763	Beth., SF	8-7-42	12-18-46	NRT
Southerland (ex-DDR)	DD-743	Bath Iron	8-7-42	12-22-44	NRT
Epperson (ex-DDE)	DD-719	Federal	8-7-42	3-19-49	NRT
Hamner	DD-718	Federal	8-7-42	7-11-46	NRT
[Theodore E. Chandler]	DD-717	Federal	8-7-42	3-22-46	Stricken
Wiltsie	DD-716	Federal	8-7-42	1-12-46	NRT
William M. Wood (ex-DDR)	DD-715	Federal	8-7-42	11-24-45	AA
William R. Rush (ex-DDR)	DD-714	Federal	8-7-42	9-21-45	NRT

Ninty-nine *Gearings* were commissioned from 12-22-44 (DD-743) to 7-26-49 (DD-824). The class is an enlarged version of *Sumner* class (engineering spaces of *Gearings* enlarged to increase range and endurance). Forty-nine sisters were cancelled and 5 were delivered incomplete (later scrapped). Post-completion conversions: 36 to DDR, 11 to DDE. All DDEs and DDRs except DD-713 class reverted to DD in early 1960s after completion of FRAMs. Current plans call for the last *Gearing* to leave the active fleet sometime beyond FY 1982. DD-837 and 849 serve as experimental ships. DD-849 served as AG-151 from 8-24-49 to 1-11-54. In 12/73, DD-821 served as a test ship for a new type of fuel oil derived from coal. All FRAM I's have one twin 5"/38 forward and aft, except DD-786, 826, 845, 867 and 890 which have two twin mounts forward. The stricken *Floyd B. Parks* (DD-884) was fitted with the CHAPARRAL missile for testing in 1972. The remaining ships of the *Chevalier, Lloyd Thomas* and *Kenneth D. Bailey* classes (all FRAM II) have been stricken.

DESTROYER, *"ALLEN M. SUMNER"* CLASS (FRAM II)

[Laffey]	DD-724	Bath Iron	8-7-42	2-8-44	Stricken

Fifty-eight ships of the *Allen M. Sumner* class were completed. As a result of the FRAM II modernization, this class was split into two distinct groups. The non-FRAMed units were referred to as the *English* class (15 units, all now stricken); the FRAM units were referred to as the *Allen M. Sumner* class (43 units). *Laffey* was assigned as NRT at Washington, D.C., and was moored across the river at Alexandria, Va. She will be replaced by a FRAM I DD, but because of the deeper draft of a FRAM I compared to a FRAM II, she will probably be based at Norfolk, Va.

1 DESTROYER, *"LA VALLETTE"* CLASS

Name	Number	Builder	Awarded	Commissioned	F/S
[Picking]	DD-685	Beth., Staten Is.	6-14-42	9-21-43	Stricken
[Porterfield]	DD-682	Beth., San Pedro	6-14-42	10-30-43	Stricken
Stoddard	DD-566	Seattle-Tacoma	9-9-40	4-15-44	DPR*

Originally the *Fletcher* class, these ships became *La Vallettes* when the *Fletcher* and 17 sisters received ASW modernizations (1949–51) and were reclassified DDE. All were recommissioned for the Korean War. During reactivation their pole mast was replaced with a tripod, the 40mm mts. with 3"/50s, electronics and communications were improved and all 20mm mts. and "K" guns were removed. Towards the latter years of her active life, DD-682 had all her secondary armament removed. DD-566 has a higher main gun director than the other two. The last unit of this class will be disposed of shortly. All were decommissioned at Long Beach on 9-6-69 (DD-685), 11-7-69 (DD-682) and 9-26-69 (DD-566) and are berthed at Mare Island.

John S. McCain (DDG-36). 11–71. **Mitscher** class.

Luce (DDG-38) as DLG-7. Class originally commissioned as frigates numbering DLG-6/15. Redesignated 30 June 1975. 6–71. **Coontz** class.

Decatur (DDG-31). Note SPS-48 three-dimensional search radar on after mast. 7–72. **Decatur** class.

Benjamin Stoddert (DDG-22). Note single-rail missile launcher as compared to that in *Buchanan* photo. 1972. **Charles F. Adams** class.

Buchanan (DDG-14). 1972. **Charles F. Adams** class.

Spruance (DD-963) during builder's trials 2–75. **Spruance** class.

Spruance (DD-963). 2–75. **Spruance** class.

Hull (DD-945). 10–71. **Hull** class.

Barry (DD-933). SCB-251 mod. Note stem anchor. 10–71. **Forrest Sherman** class.

Forrest Sherman (DD-931). 5–72. **Forrest Sherman** class.

Robert A. Owens (DD-827). 1966. **Carpenter** class.

Higbee (DD-806). 8–74. **"Gearing"** class.

Laffey (DD-724). Last of the **"Allen M. Sumner"** class. 9–70. **"Allen M. Sumner"** class.

Picking (DD-685). **"La Vallette"** class.

Richard B. Anderson (DD-786). One of few **"Gearing"** class FRAM I with both 5" mounts forward. 1971. **"Gearing"** class.

Frigates At the end of FY 1975, there were 68 frigates on the NVR. Active: 6 FFGs, 58 FFs. Under construction: 4 FFGs. Projected: 26 FFGs. The Navy's last WW II built ocean escort, *Gunason* (DE-795), was stricken on 9–1–73.

Class	Number	No. In Class	Full Load Displ.	Length Overall	Max. Draft	Extreme Beam	Number & Type of Boilers/Engines	Screws/ SHP	Max. Speed (Kts.)	Accommodations Officers	Enlisted	Armament
GUIDED MISSILE FRIGATES												
Oliver Hazard Perry	FFG-7	14	3,400	440'	24'5"	45'	(2)LM-2500 GST(G.E.)	1/41,000	30	17	168	1 single 76mm OTO/Melara COMPACT gun, 1 20mm VULCAN/PHALANX mt., 1 single MK 13 STANDARD/ HARPOON missile launcher, 2 MK 32 triple torpedo tube mts.
Brooke	FFG-1	6	3,426	414'	24'2"	44'	2B(F.W.)/1GT(West.)	1/35,000	27.2	17	281	1 single 5"/38 cal. mt., 1 single MK 22 TARTAR launcher, 1 ASROC, 2 MK 32 triple torpedo tube mts.
FRIGATES												
Knox	FF-1052	46	4,100	438'	25'	47'	2B(C.E.)/1GT(West.)	1/35,000	27	18	213	1 single 5"/54 cal. mt., 1 ASROC, 1 BPDMS (FF-1052, 1055, 1059, 1062/1067, 1071, 1072, 1074/1083), 2 MK 32 triple torpedo tube mts.
Garcia	FF-1040	10	3,403	414'	24'	44'	2B(F.W.)/1GT(West.)	1/35,000	27.5	17	211	2 single 5"/38 cal. mts., 1 ASROC, 2 MK 32 triple torpedo tube mts.
Bronstein	FF-1037	2	2,710	372'	23'	41'	2B(F.W.)/1GT(West.)	1/20,000	24	16	184	1 twin 3"/50 cal. mt., 1 single 3"/50 cal. mt., 1 ASROC, 2 MK 32 triple torpedo tube mts.

14 GUIDED MISSILE FRIGATES, *OLIVER HAZARD PERRY* CLASS

Name	Number	FY/SCB	Builder	Awarded	Commissioned	F/S
	FFG-20	76/261				Proj.
	FFG-19	76/261				Proj.
	FFG-18	76/261				Proj.
	FFG-17	76/261				Proj.
	FFG-16	76/261				Proj.
	FFG-15	76/261				Proj.
	FFG-14	76/261				Proj.

Name	Number	FY/SCB	Builder	Awarded	Commissioned	F/S
	FFG-13	76/261				Proj.
	FFG-12	76/261				Proj.
	FFG-11	76/261				Proj.
	FFG-10	75/261				Bldg.
	FFG-9	75/261				Bldg.
	FFG-8	75/261				Bldg.
Oliver Hazard Perry	FFG-7	75/261	Bath Iron Works	10-30-73		Bldg.

Originally classified and rated as patrol frigates (PF), they were reclassified and rerated as indicated on 6–30–75. Projected as a class of 50 units, they are part of an on-going construction program to replace WW II-built DDs and postwar-built FFs. As such, they are immediate successors to the *Knox* class. They are "designed for a particular portion of the surface escort mission rather than for operations throughout the escort mission spectrum." The reason for this is to keep costs low so that a greater number can be purchased. The FFGs will complement existing AAW and ASW ships rather than replace them. The primary raison d'etre is to protect amphibious forces, underway replenishment groups, and military and mercantile convoys. To facilitate construction and future modernization, the class will be built in a modular fashion. FFG-7 is tentatively scheduled to commission in July 1977. Two additional units of this class have been ordered by Australia.

6 GUIDED MISSILE FRIGATES, *BROOKE* CLASS

Name	Number	FY/SCB	Builder	Awarded	Commissioned	F/S
Julius A. Furer (ex-*Furer*)	FFG-6	63/199B	Bath Iron	5-24-63	11-11-67	AA
Richard L. Page	FFG-5	63/199B	Bath Iron	5-24-63	8-5-67	AA
Talbot	FFG-4	63/199B	Bath Iron	5-24-63	4-22-67	AA

continued

Name	Number	FY/SCB	Builder	Awarded	Commissioned	F/S
Schofield	FFG-3	62/199B	Lockheed	1-4-62	5-11-68	PA
Ramsey	FFG-2	62/199B	Lockheed	1-4-62	6-3-67	PA

Name	Number	FY/SCB	Builder	Awarded	Commissioned	F/S
Brooke	FFG-1	62/199B	Lockheed	1-4-62	3-12-66	PA

Missile versions of the *Garcia* class FFs. TARTAR launcher replaced #2 5″ mt. This class was originally projected at 19 units, but cost of $11 million more than a FF, per unit, plus other factors, limited construction to 6. Originally the class was to carry 5″/54s, but to cut costs, they were replaced with off-the-shelf 5″/38s. FFG-6 renamed 4–5–66. Despite DD size, the single screw of the FF/FFG and their limited speed rates them as FF/FFGs. DEG-7/11 were built in Spain, under the Off-Shore Procurement Program of ILP, for the Spanish Navy. In the summer of 1974, FFG-4 was fitted with a single 76mm OTO/Melara COMPACT gun, STIR radar and SQS-56 sonar to test and evaluate the equipment prior to its being fitted in the FFG-7 class. The LAMPS hangar and deck were converted to equip. test and stowage spaces. The 5″/38 was temporarily removed to compensate for the 76mm weight. FFG-4 is fitted with two single MK 25 ASW torpedo tubes. The ships of this class received LAMPS refits as indicated: FY 1972: FFG-3; FY 1973: FFG-4, 6; FY 1975: FFG-1, 2, 5. Class originally rated and classified as guided missile escort ships (DEG). Reclassified and rerated as indicated on 6–30–75. On the same date all escort ships (DE) were reclassified and rerated as frigates (FF). The construction of 8 sea control ships (CH) has been cancelled and the $29.4 million appropriated for design definition, under FY 1974, has been transferred to a new project to design a CVL-type carrier with catapults and arresting gear.

46 FRIGATES, *KNOX* CLASS

Name	Number	FY/SCB	Builder	Awarded	Commissioned	F/S
Moinester	FF-1097	67/200.66	Avondale	8-25-66	11-2-74	AA
Valdez	FF-1096	67/200.66	Avondale	8-25-66	7-27-74	AA
Truett	FF-1095	67/200.66	Avondale	8-25-66	6-1-74	AA
Pharris	FF-1094	67/200.66	Avondale	8-25-66	1-26-74	AA
Capodanno	FF-1093	67/200.66	Avondale	8-25-66	11-17-73	AA
Thomas C. Hart	FF-1092	67/200.66	Avondale	8-25-66	7-28-73	AA
Miller	FF-1091	67/200.66	Avondale	8-25-66	6-30-73	AA
Ainsworth	FF-1090	67/200.66	Avondale	8-25-66	3-31-73	AA
Jesse L. Brown	FF-1089	67/200.66	Avondale	8-25-66	2-17-73	AA
Barbey	FF-1088	67/200.66	Avondale	8-25-66	11-11-72	PA
Kirk	FF-1087	66/200.66	Avondale	8-25-66	9-9-72	PA
Brewton	FF-1086	66/200.66	Avondale	8-25-66	7-8-72	PA
Donald B. Beary	FF-1085	66/200.66	Avondale	8-25-66	7-22-72	AA
McCandless	FF-1084	66/200.66	Avondale	8-25-66	3-18-72	AA
Cook	FF-1083	66/200.66	Avondale	8-25-66	12-18-71	PA
Elmer Montgomery	FF-1082	66/200.66	Avondale	8-25-66	10-30-71	AA
Aylwin	FF-1081	66/200.66	Avondale	8-25-66	9-18-71	AA
Paul	FF-1080	66/200.66	Avondale	8-25-66	8-14-71	AA
Bowen	FF-1079	66/200.66	Avondale	8-25-66	5-22-71	AA
Joseph Hewes	FF-1078	66/200.66	Avondale	8-25-66	4-24-71	AA
Ouellet	FF-1077	65/200.65	Avondale	7-22-64	12-12-70	PA
Fanning	FF-1076	65/200.65	Todd, San Pedro	7-22-64	7-23-71	PA
Trippe	FF-1075	65/200.65	Avondale	7-22-64	9-19-70	AA
Harold E. Holt	FF-1074	65/200.65	Todd, San Pedro	7-22-64	3-26-71	PA
Robert E. Peary (ex-*Conolly*)	FF-1073	65/200.65	Lockheed	7-22-64	9-23-72	PA
Blakely	FF-1072	65/200.65	Avondale	7-22-64	7-18-70	AA
Badger	FF-1071	65/200.65	Todd, Seattle	7-22-64	12-1-70	PA
Downes	FF-1070	65/200.65	Todd, Seattle	7-22-64	8-28-71	AA
Bagley	FF-1069	65/200.65	Lockheed	7-22-64	5-6-72	PA
Vreeland	FF-1068	65/200.65	Avondale	7-22-64	6-13-70	AA
Francis Hammond	FF-1067	65/200.65	Todd, San Pedro	7-22-64	7-25-70	PA
Marvin Shields	FF-1066	65/200.65	Todd, Seattle	7-22-64	4-10-71	PA
Stein	FF-1065	65/200.65	Lockheed	7-22-64	1-8-72	PA
Lockwood	FF-1064	65/200.65	Todd, Seattle	7-22-64	12-5-70	PA
Reasoner	FF-1063	65/200.65	Lockheed	7-22-64	7-31-71	PA
Whipple	FF-1062	65/200.65	Todd, Seattle	7-22-64	8-22-70	PA
Patterson	FF-1061	64/199C	Avondale	7-22-64	3-14-70	AA
Lang	FF-1060	64/199C	Todd, San Pedro	7-22-64	3-28-70	PA
W. S. Sims	FF-1059	64/199C	Avondale	7-22-64	1-3-70	AA
Meyerkord	FF-1058	64/199C	Todd, San Pedro	7-22-64	11-28-69	PA
Rathburne	FF-1057	64/199C	Lockheed	7-22-64	5-16-70	PA
Connole	FF-1056	64/199C	Avondale	7-22-64	8-30-69	AA
Hepburn	FF-1055	64/199C	Todd, Seattle	7-22-64	7-3-69	PA
Gray	FF-1054	64/199C	Todd, Seattle	7-22-64	4-4-70	PA
Roark	FF-1053	64/199C	Todd, Seattle	7-22-64	11-22-69	PA
Knox	FF-1052	64/199C	Todd, Seattle	7-22-64	4-12-69	PA

These are enlarged and improved versions of *Garcia* class. Originally 56 units were authorized as DEs. DE-1102/1107 were cancelled in 1968, DE-1098/1100 were cancelled on 2–24–69. DE-1101, which was cancelled on 4–9–69, was to have had gas turbine propulsion. Originally FF-1078/1107 were rated as a separate class. They are the same design as *Knox* class, but have a different electronic suit. All were awarded to one builder to cut costs. This class has been criticized as being inferior to their foreign contemporaries, with the main objections being that they have a single screw and are under-armed. Ships fitted with BPDMS are indicated in armament column of the Frigate Characteristics table. Those ships not listed are scheduled to receive SEA CHAPARRAL (SAM) missile. To date the following ships have been refitted with LAMPS. FY 1972, FF-1063, 1066, 1074, 1078/1080; FY 1973, FF-1055, 1059,

1065, 1069, 1071/1073, 1075, 1081, 1083/1088; FY 1974, FF-1053, 1054, 1056/1058, 1060, 1076, 1089/1097; FY 1975, FF-1062, 1064, 1067, 1077, 1082. The following ships are scheduled to receive LAMPS in FY 1976: FF-1052, 1061, 1068 and 1070. LAMPS refit includes enlargement of existing DASH hangar and flight deck and improved electronics, communications, and control gear. Thirty-six ships of this class will receive AN/SQS-35 VDS as a supplement to their AN/SQS-26 (CX) bow-mounted sonar. FF-1070 serves as test and evaluation ship for NATO SEA SPARROW (BPDMS) missile system and associated fire control gear. In 1972,

FF-1064 was fitted with the 20mm VULCAN/PHALANX system (CIWS) for operational evaluation. FF-1071 has been fitted with the HARPOON AN/SWG-1(V) fire control system for evaluation. Some ships, such as FF-1068 and 1075, have had their ASROC launchers modified to fire the interim surface-to-surface STANDARD missile. FF-1078/1097 have been fitted with the Test Evaluation and Monitoring System (TEAMS) which speeds repairs to shipboard radar and sonar systems. FF-1073 was renamed 5–12–71.

10 FRIGATES, *GARCIA* CLASS

Name	Number	FY/SCB	Builder	Awarded	Commissioned	F/S
O'Callahan	FF-1051	63/199A	Defoe	3–21–63	7–13–68	PA
Albert David	FF-1050	63/199A	Lockheed	3–20–63	10–19–68	PA
Koelsch	FF-1049	63/199A	Defoe	3–21–63	6–10–67	AA
Sample	FF-1048	63/199A	Lockheed	3–20–63	3–23–68	PA
Voge	FF-1047	63/199A	Defoe	3–21–63	11–25–66	AA
Davidson	FF-1045	62/199A	Avondale	1–3–62	12–7–65	PA
Brumby	FF-1044	62/199A	Avondale	1–3–62	8–5–65	AA
Edward McDonnell	FF-1043	62/199A	Avondale	1–3–62	2–15–65	AA
Bradley	FF-1041	61/199A	Beth., S.F.	6–22–61	5–15–65	PA
Garcia	FF-1040	61/199A	Beth., S.F.	6–22–61	12–21–64	AA

Modified and enlarged version of the *Bronstein* class. The *Brooke* class FFGs were built to same design. Class refitted with LAMPS as indicated: FF-1040, 1041, 1044 and 1051 in FY 1972; FF-1043, 1045 in FY 1973; FF-1049 in FY 1974; and FF-1047 in FY 1975. FF-1048 and 1050 are not scheduled to receive LAMPS. MK 25 ASW torpedoes in transom have been removed from all ships of this class except FF-1044. From 1967/68 FF-1041 was fitted with BPDMS for testing and evaluation. FF-1047 and 1049 are fitted with NTDS. DE-1042 and 1046 were built under the Off-Shore Procurement Program of ILP for Portugal.

2 FRIGATES, *BRONSTEIN* CLASS

McCloy	FF-1038	60/199	Avondale	6–13–60	10–21–63	AA
Bronstein	FF-1037	60/199	Avondale	6–13–60	6–16–63	PA

Lead class of a new generation of escorts. Design influenced succeeding classes. Class first to have "macks." DE-1039 was built under Off-Shore Procurement plan of ILP for Portugal. All of the *Dealey, Courtney* and *Claud Jones* DEs were stricken between 7–1–72 and 12–16–74. All were scrapped except *Dealey* (DE-1006) which was sold to Uruguay, *Hartley* (DE-1029) sold to Colombia, and all of the *Claud Jones* class (DE-1033/36) which were sold to Indonesia. The two *Wagner* class DERs, the *Kirkpatrick* (DER-318), the last of the *Harveson* class DERs and the last five units of the *Savage* class DERs have all been stricken. On 6–30–75, *Camp* (DER-251) and *Forster* (DER-334), both on loan to South Vietnam, were reclassified and rerated as frigates, radar picket (FFR).

Downes (FF-1070). Note NATO SEA SPARROW launcher on stern. 5–73. **Knox** class.

FFG-7 class: *Oliver Hazard Perry* (FFG-7). Class was formerly **PF-109** class. Artist's concept. 1974.

Julius A. Furer (FFG-6). Missile version of **Garcia** class. **Brooke** class.

Barbey (FF-1088). Overhead view showing sphere which houses classified electronics. 9–74. **Knox** class.

Talbot (FFG-4). Note 76mm OTO/Melara gun mount forward (USN MARK 75) and MK 92 fire control system aft of missile launcher. Installed for evaluation. 12–74. **Brooke** class.

Whipple (FF-1062). Note fantail-mounted BPDMS. 10–74. **Knox** class.

Harold E. Holt (FF-1074). LAMPS SH-2D SEASPRITE approaches for landing. Note also wider helicopter deck. 4–72. **Knox** class.

Garcia (FF-1040). 8–72. **Garcia** class.

Bagley (FF-1069). 3–72. **Knox** class.

Brumby (FF-1044). Note telescopic helicopter hangar extended slightly outward. 5–72. **Garcia** class.

McCloy (FF-1038). 10–71. **Bronstein** class.

C. PATROL COMBATANTS

At the end of FY 1975, there were 19 patrol ships on the NVR; 12 were PGs and 7 were PHMs. Active: 4 PGs and 1 PHM. Building: 6 PHMs. In addition, 8 PGs were assigned to the Naval Reserve Force. Twenty-three more PHMs are projected for construction.

Class	Number	No. In Class	Full Load Displ.	Length Overall	Max. Draft	Extreme Beam	Number & Type of Gas Turbines/ Engines	Screws/ SHP	Max. Speed (Kts.)	Accommodations Officers	Enlisted	Armament
PATROL COMBATANT MISSILE (Hydrofoil)[1]												
Pegasus	PHM-1	10+	239	147'6"	9'5"	29'	2D(Mercedes-Benz)/ 1 LM-2500 GST(G.E.)	0/1,600 or 18,000	40+	4	17	2 quad HARPOON missile launchers, 1 single 76mm MK 75 OTO/Melara COMPACT mt.
PATROL COMBATANTS												
Asheville	PG-84	12	245	165'	9'6"	23'6"	2D(Cummings)/ 1 LM-1500 GST(G.E.)	2/13,000	37.5	4	27	2 single MK 32 STANDARD missile launchers (PG-86, 87, 98, 100), 1 single 3"/50 cal. mt., 1 single 40mm mt. (PG-84/90, 92/94)

[1] *Characteristics are approximate with foils retracted. See class notes for foil-extended characteristics.*

10 PATROL COMBATANT MISSILE (Hydrofoil), PEGASUS CLASS

Name	Number	FY/SCB	Builder	Awarded	Commissioned	F/S
	PHM-10	/602.73				Proj.
	PHM-9	76/602.73				Proj.
	PHM-8	76/602.73				Proj.
	PHM-7	75/602.73				Bldg.
	PHM-6	75/602.73				Bldg.
	PHM-5	75/602.73				Bldg.
	PHM-4	75/602.73				Bldg.
	PHM-3	74/602.73				Bldg.
Hercules	PHM-2	73/602.73	Boeing, Seattle	2-1-73		Bldg.
Pegasus (ex-Delphinus)	PHM-1	73/602.73	Boeing, Seattle	2-1-73		Bldg.

This is a new type of patrol ship developed in conjunction with the Federal Republic of Germany and Italy for NATO. Class will be 30 ships with the designed mission "to operate offensively against major surface combatants and other surface craft; to conduct surveillance, screening, and special operations." Approximate characteristics with foils extended are as follows: length overall, 138'; max. draft, 23'5"; max. speed, 48 knots. Each missile launcher is a 4-tubed cannister affair with a reload for each tube. Maximum missile capacity per ship is 16 HARPOON missiles. The missile system will be independent of the secondary armament. Class is based on modified *Tucumcari* design. PHM-1 was renamed 4-26-74. Construction of PHM-2 was suspended in 8/74 because of a lack of funds. The first two ships were being built with research and development funds. Due to inflation and cost overruns the money ran out before construction of the two was completed. More funds to complete PHM-2 were requested from Congress and construction was resumed in July 1975. Class originally rated as patrol hydrofoil guided missile ships (PHM). Rerated as indicated on 6-30-75.

12 PATROL COMBATANTS, *ASHEVILLE* CLASS

[Green Bay]	PG-101	66/600.65	Peterson	7-26-66	12-5-69	Stricken
Douglas	PG-100	66/600.65	Tacoma	7-26-66	2-6-71	AA
[Beacon]	PG-99	66/600.65	Peterson	7-26-66	11-21-69	Stricken
Grand Rapids	PG-98	66/600.65	Tacoma	7-26-66	9-5-70	AA
Chehalis	PG-94	66/600.65	Tacoma	7-26-66	11-8-69	NRT
Welch	PG-93	66/600.65	Peterson	7-26-66	9-8-69	NRT
Tacoma	PG-92	66/600.65	Tacoma	7-26-66	7-14-69	NRT
Canon	PG-90	65/600.65	Tacoma	1-18-65	7-26-68	NRT
Marathon	PG-89	65/600.65	Tacoma	1-18-65	5-11-68	NRT
Crockett	PG-88	65/600.65	Tacoma	1-18-65	6-24-67	NRT
Ready	PG-87	64/600.65	Tacoma	6-20-64	1-6-68	AA
Antelope	PG-86	64/600.65	Tacoma	6-20-64	11-4-67	AA
Gallup	PG-85	63/600.65	Tacoma	6-28-63	10-22-66	NRT
Asheville	PG-84	63/600.65	Tacoma	6-28-63	8-6-66	NRT

These are the first large patrol ships built for USN since WW II and the first mass-produced class with gas turbine propulsion in USN. They can shift from diesels to turbine power, underway, without losing speed. Class was originally classified as PGMs; reclassified PG on 4-1-67 to differentiate from the PGMs built under ILP. Hull numbers duplicate British "Flower" class corvettes obtained under reverse lend-lease during WW II. PG-86 and 87 have MK 87 fire control system which can be aimed automatically by high-speed digital computer. Remaining units have MK 63 fire control systems. The transferred *Benicia* (PG-96) served as test and evaluation ship for the STANDARD missile. Missile gear and missiles were removed before transfer. Four of the *Ashevilles* are currently armed with missiles. Each unit carries one missile per launcher in the ready position and one reload per launcher. The after 40mm mount was removed to compensate for the weight of the missile launchers, missiles, and associated gear. PG-84, 88, and 89 were transferred from the Pacific Fleet to the Great Lakes in October 1974 for duty as NRT ships. Officially joined NRT force in July 1975. All three are homeported at Chicago, Ill. The only two units left in the Pacific Fleet, PG-85 and 90, are homeported at San Diego and are assigned to COSRIVRON 1. Five units of this class have been transferred to foreign navies. Two non-gas turbine *Asheville* class units are being constructed for transfer to South Vietnam. The *Asheville* class were originally rated as patrol gunboats (PG). Rerated as patrol combatants (PG) on 6-30-75.

Ready (PG-87) firing STANDARD missile. **Asheville** class. (Photo: General Dynamics.)

Pegasus (PHM-1) prior to launching. Built to modified *Tucumcari* design. 11–8–74. **Pegasus** class.

Pegasus (PHM-1). Note stern foils and missile tubes. 11–8–74. **Pegasus** class.

Marathon (PG-89). Abaft the large funnel (for turbine exhaust) are two small diesel exhaust stacks, one each side. 1968. **Asheville** class.

Grand Rapids (PG-98). Late 1972, *Grand Rapids* received the STANDARD (ARM) missile system and two new diesel engines. 8–73. **Asheville** class.

D. COMMAND SHIPS

At the end of FY 1975, there were 2 command ships on the NVR. *Northampton* is laid up at the Philadelphia Inactive Ships Maintenance Facility (InactShipFac) and *Wright* is laid up at Norfolk InactShipFac. These ships are unique.

Class	Number	No. In Class	Full Load Displ.	Length Overall	Max. Draft	Extreme Beam	Number & Type of Boilers/Engines	Screws/ SHP	Max. Speed (Kts.)	Accommodations Officers	Enlisted	Armament
Wright	CC-2	1	19,570	684'	28'	110'	4B(B&W)/4GT(G.E.)	4/120,000	30.8	222	1,498	4 twin 40mm mts., 2 40mm saluting guns
Northampton	CC-1	1	17,204	676'	26'6"	71'	4B(B&W)/2GT(G.E.)	4/120,000	32	227	1,448	2 40mm saluting mts.

1 CONVERTED LIGHT CARRIER, *WRIGHT* CLASS

Name	Number	FY/SCB	Converted at	Awarded	Started	Completed	Recommissioned	F/S
Wright	CC-2	62/228	PS Navy	2-19-62	6-11-62	5-11-63	5-11-63	AR*

Originally commissioned on 2–9–47 as *Wright* (CVL-49), second of the *Saipan* class light carriers. She was decommissioned on 3–15–56, reclassified AVT-7 on 5–15–59, and reclassified CC-2 on 9–1–62. Conversion to command ship was rated as highly successful. The forward two-thirds of hangar deck is fitted as command and communications spaces; after third is used to store and repair helicopters that are carried by the ship. As an active ship, she carried the most powerful radio antenna installed on a ship. Sister *Saipan* (CVL-48) was to become CC-3, but conversion was stopped and she was reauthorized for conversion to *Arlington* (AGMR-2). *Wright* is almost indistinguishable from *Arlington*. The major differences are that *Wright* lacks gun mounts at forward corners of former flight deck and has pylon radar masts between #1 and #2 stacks. *Wright* was decommissioned on 5–27–70.

1 CONVERTED HEAVY CRUISER, *NORTHAMPTON* CLASS

Name	Number	Builder	Awarded	Keel	Cancelled	Reordered	Launched	Commissioned	F/S
Northampton	CC-1	Beth., Quincy	8-7-42	8-31-44	8-11-45	7-1-48	1-27-51	3-7-53	AR*

She was originally ordered as CA-125 of the *Oregon City* class CAs. Construction was cancelled when 56.1 percent completed and she remained on stocks until reordered as tactical command ship. She was reclassified CLC-1 on 11–1–47; to CC-1 on 9–15–61. When active, *Northampton* served primarily as flagship of 6th and 2nd fleets. Her hull was one deck higher than other modern CAs to accommodate staff of 165 officers and 275 enlisted as well as extra communications gear. Until 1963 she carried largest radar antenna afloat. Until decommissioned on 4–8–70, she carried tallest unsupported antenna afloat (125'). She can operate, but not stow or support, helicopters. As completed there were 4 single 5"/54s and 4 twin 3"/50s mounted. All gradually removed over the years. Since World War II, the USN has programmed 4 ships for conversion to command ships. No command ship has been programmed to be built from the keel up. Besides the three already mentioned, there was the uncompleted *Hawaii* (CB-3). She wore the classification CBC-1 (large tactical command ship) from 1952 to 1954.

Wright (CC-2). 1963. **Wright** class.

Northampton (CC-1) prior decommissioning. Note absence of armament. **Northampton** class.

E. SUBMARINES

At the end of FY 1975, there were 146 submarines on the NVR. Total breakdown: 44 SSBN, 92 SSN, 10 SS/SSG. Active: 41 SSBN, 65 SSN and 9 SS. Reserve: 2 SSN and 1 SSG. Under Construction: 3 SSBN and 26 SSN. Projected: 7 SSBN and 9 SSN. Of the 65 active SSNs, 8 were rated as second line and are of limited value. In addition to the submarines mentioned in this section, three additional ones serve as AGSSs and can be found in the Auxiliary Section. All SSTs/X craft/IXSSs have been stricken. See Section 13 for strike data.

Class	Number	No. in Class	Standard Displacement		Length Overall	Max. Draft	Extreme Beam	Number and Type of Reactors/Engines	Screws/ SHP	Max. Speed (Knots.)		Accommodations		Armament
			Surface	Submerged						Surface	Submerged	Officers	Enlisted	
FLEET BALLISTIC MISSILE SUBMARINES														
	SSBN-726	10	16,600	18,700	560'	35'5"	42'		1/35,000	23.5+		16	117	24 TRIDENT I Missiles
Benjamin Franklin	SSBN-640	12	7,320	8,250	425'	31'4"	33'	1R/S5W(West.)	1/15,000	20+	30+	20	148	16 POSEIDON missiles, 4 21" torpedo tubes fwd.
Lafayette	SSBN-616	19	7,250	8,250	425'	31'4"	33'	1R/S5W(West.)	1/15,000	20+	30+	14	126	16 POSEIDON missiles, 4 21" torpedo tubes fwd.

Class	Number	No. in Class	Standard Displacement Surface	Submerged	Length Overall	Max. Draft	Extreme Beam	Number and Type of Reactors/Engines	Screws/ SHP	Max. Speed (Knots.) Surface	Submerged	Accommodations Officers	Enlisted	Armament
Ethan Allen	SSBN-608	5	6,955	7,880	410'	30'9"	33'	1R/S5W(West.)	1/15,000	20+	30+	15	127	16 A-2 POLARIS missiles, 4 21" torpedo tubes fwd.
George Washington	SSBN-598	5	6,019	6,888	382'	30'	33'	1R/S5W(West.)	1/15,000	20+	31+	12	127	16 A-3 POLARIS missiles, 4 21" torpedo tubes fwd.

NUCLEAR-POWERED ATTACK SUBMARINES

Class	Number	No. in Class	Standard Displacement Surface	Submerged	Length Overall	Max. Draft	Extreme Beam	Number and Type of Reactors/Engines	Screws/ SHP	Max. Speed (Knots.) Surface	Submerged	Accommodations Officers	Enlisted	Armament
Los Angeles	SSN-688	28	6,000	6,900	360'	32'	33'	1R/S5W(West.)	1/	20+	32+			4 21" torpedo tubes midships, SUBROC
Glenard P. Lipscomb	SSN-685	1	5,813	6,480	365'		31'8"	1R/S5Wa(West.)	1/12,000	20+	25+	12	108	4 21" torpedo tubes midships, SUBROC
Narwhal	SSN-671	1	4,450	5,350	303'	29'	38'	1R/S5G(G.E.)	1/17,000	20+	30+	12	95	4 21" torpedo tubes midships, SUBROC
Sturgeon	SSN-637	37	3,640	4,640	292'3"	28'9"	31'8"	1R/S5W(West.)	1/15,000	20+	30+	12	95	4 21" torpedo tubes midships, SUBROC
Tullibee	SSN-597	1	2,317	2,640	273'	21'	23'7"	1R/S2C(G.E.)	1/2,500	15+	20+	6	50	4 21" torpedo tubes midships
"Thresher"	SSN-593	13	3,700	4,300	278'	28'5"	31'7"	1R/S5W(West.)	1/15,000	20+	30+	12	91	4 21" torpedo tubes midships, SUBROC
Halibut	SSN-587	1	3,850	5,000	350'	21'5"	29'7"	1R/S3W(West.)	2/6,600	15+	20+	10	88	4 21" torpedo tubes fwd., 2 21" torpedo tubes aft.
Triton	SSN-586	1	5,939	6,670	447'	24'	37'	2R/S4G(G.E.)	2/34,000	27+	20+	14	156	4 21" torpedo tubes fwd., 2 21" torpedo tubes aft.
Skipjack	SSN-585	5	3,075	3,513	252'	29'5"	31'7"	1R/S5W(West.)	1/15,000	16+	30+	8	85	6 21" torpedo tubes fwd.
Skate	SSN-578	4	2,570	2,861	267'7"	22'5"	25'	1R/S3W or 1R/S4W (Both West.)	2/6,600	20+	25+	8	87	6 21" torpedo tubes fwd., 2 21" torpedo tubes aft.
Seawolf	SSN-575	1	3,765	4,200	338'	23'1"	28'	1R/S2Wa(West.)	2/15,000	20+	20+	10	95	6 21" torpedo tubes fwd.
Nautilus	SSN-571	1	3,764	4,040	319'5"	25'5"	28'	1R/S2W(West.)	2/15,000	20+	20+	10	95	6 21" torpedo tubes fwd.

CONVENTIONALLY POWERED SUBMARINES

Class	Number	No. in Class	Standard Displacement Surface	Submerged	Length Overall	Max. Draft	Extreme Beam	Number and Type of Reactors/Engines	Screws/ SHP	Max. Speed (Knots.) Surface	Submerged	Accommodations Officers	Enlisted	Armament
Barbel	SS-580	3	2,145	2,894	219'1"	28'	29'	3D(F.M.)/2EM(G.E.)	1/3,150	14.5	20.7	9	69	6 21" torpedo tubes fwd.
"Grayback"	SSG-574	1	2,540	3,515	318'	19'	27'	3D(F.M.)/2EM(Ell.)	2/5,500	20	17	10	78	4 21" torpedo tubes fwd., 2 21" torpedo tubes aft.
Darter	SS-576	1	1,720	2,388	284'6"	19'	27'2"	3D(F.M.)/2EM(Ell.)	2/6,000	19.5	14.3	8	75	6 21" torpedo tubes fwd., 2 21" torpedo tubes aft.
Sailfish	SS-572	2	2,455	3,160	350'5"	18'5"	28'5"	4D(F.M.)/2EM(West.)	2/6,000	19.5	14.3	12	79	6 21" torpedo tubes fwd.
"Tang"	SS-563	3	2,122	2,700	277'	19'	27'1"	3D(F.M.)/2EM(Ell.)	2/3,200	15.5	16	8	75	6 21" torpedo tubes fwd., 2 21" torpedo tubes aft.

10 FLEET BALLISTIC MISSILE SUBMARINES, *UNNAMED* CLASS

Name	Number	FY/SCB	Builder	Awarded	Commissioned	F/S	Name	Number	FY/SCB	Builder	Awarded	Commissioned	F/S
	SSBN-735	/304.75				Proj.		SSBN-730	/304.75				Proj.
	SSBN-734	/304.75				Proj.		SSBN-729	76/304.75				Proj.
	SSBN-733	/304.75				Proj.		SSBN-728	75/304.75	Gen. Dyn., Groton	2–28–75		Bldg.
	SSBN-732	/304.75				Proj.		SSBN-727	75/304.75	Gen. Dyn., Groton	2–28–75		Bldg.
	SSBN-731	/304.75				Proj.		SSBN-726	74/304.74	Gen. Dyn., Groton	7–25–74		Bldg.

continued

This class of 10 units is truly awesome in size and armament. Surpassing some of our heavy cruisers in displacement, the submarines will be armed with 24 TRIDENT I (C-4) missiles, with MIRV warheads, that have a range of 4,000 miles. They will replace the SSBN-598 and 608 classes. Originally the class was scheduled to be built at a rate of 3 a year, starting in FY 1975; however, this has now been changed to 2 per year. In the early 1980s, the TRIDENT I missiles will be replaced by TRIDENT II (D-5) missiles that will have a range of approximately 6,000 miles and MIRV warheads that will be able to change course in mid-flight. Compared to its predecessors, the SSBN-640 class, the TRIDENTs will have a quieter propulsion system, a higher at-sea/in-port ratio, and greater systems reliability. The class will be built with the modular technique like the *Tarawa's* and *Spruance's*. This will greatly facilitate modernization, overhaul, and general maintenance. Current schedule calls for first *Tridents* to put to sea in late 1979, but due to high national priority of this project, this may be advanced as much as 18 months. Pacific homeport will be Bangor, Washington. The Atlantic homeport has not been selected, but presumed to be Charleston, South Carolina. SSBN-726 was originally assigned the hull number SSBN-711. However, it was reclassified SSBN-1 on 2-21-74 and again reclassified SSBN-726 on 4-10-74.

12 FLEET BALLISTIC MISSILE SUBMARINES, *BENJAMIN FRANKLIN* CLASS

Name	Number	FY/SCB	Builder	Awarded	Commissioned	F/S
Will Rogers	SSBN-659	64/216	Gen. Dyn., Groton	7-29-63	4-1-67	AA
Mariano G. Vallejo	SSBN-658	64/216	Mare Island	8-8-63	12-16-66	AA
Francis Scott Key	SSBN-657	64/216	Gen. Dyn., Groton	7-29-63	12-3-66	AA
George Washington Carver	SSBN-656	64/216	Newport News	7-29-63	6-15-66	AA
Henry L. Stimson	SSBN-655	64/216	Gen. Dyn., Groton	7-29-63	8-20-66	AA
George C. Marshall	SSBN-654	64/216	Newport News	7-29-63	4-29-66	AA

Name	Number	FY/SCB	Builder	Awarded	Commissioned	F/S
James K. Polk	SSBN-645	63/216	Gen. Dyn., Groton	11-1-62	4-16-66	AA
Lewis and Clark	SSBN-644	63/216	Newport News	11-1-62	12-22-65	AA
George Bancroft	SSBN-643	63/216	Gen. Dyn., Groton	11-1-62	1-22-66	AA
Kamehameha	SSBN-642	63/216	Mare Island	8-31-62	12-10-65	AA
Simon Bolivar	SSBN-641	63/216	Newport News	11-1-62	10-29-65	AA
Benjamin Franklin	SSBN-640	63/216	Gen. Dyn., Groton	11-1-62	10-22-65	AA

19 FLEET BALLISTIC MISSILE SUBMARINES, *LAFAYETTE* CLASS

Name	Number	FY/SCB	Builder	Awarded	Commissioned	F/S
Nathanael Greene	SSBN-636	62/216	Portsmouth Navy	7-21-61	12-19-64	AA
Sam Rayburn	SSBN-635	62/216	Newport News	7-20-61	12-2-64	AA
Stonewall Jackson	SSBN-634	62/216	Mare Island	7-21-61	8-26-64	AA
Casimir Pulaski	SSBN-633	62/216	Gen. Dyn., Groton	7-20-61	8-14-64	AA
Von Steuben	SSBN-632	62/216	Newport News	7-20-61	9-30-64	AA
Ulysses S. Grant	SSBN-631	62/216	Gen. Dyn., Groton	7-20-61	7-17-64	AA
John C. Calhoun	SSBN-630	62/216	Newport News	7-20-61	9-15-64	AA
Daniel Boone	SSBN-629	62/216	Mare Island	7-21-61	4-23-64	AA
Tecumseh	SSBN-628	62/216	Gen. Dyn., Groton	7-20-61	5-29-64	AA
James Madison	SSBN-627	62/216	Newport News	7-20-61	7-28-64	AA

Name	Number	FY/SCB	Builder	Awarded	Commissioned	F/S
Daniel Webster	SSBN-626	61/216	Gen. Dyn., Groton	1-31-61	4-9-64	AA
Henry Clay	SSBN-625	61/216	Newport News	1-31-61	2-20-64	AA
Woodrow Wilson	SSBN-624	61/216	Mare Island	2-9-61	12-27-63	AA
Nathan Hale	SSBN-623	61/216	Gen. Dyn., Groton	1-31-61	11-23-63	AA
James Monroe	SSBN-622	61/216	Newport News	1-31-61	12-7-63	AA
John Adams	SSBN-620	61/216	Portsmouth Navy	7-23-60	5-12-64	AA
Andrew Jackson	SSBN-619	61/216	Mare Island	7-23-60	7-3-63	AA
Alexander Hamilton	SSBN-617	61/216	Gen. Dyn., Groton	7-22-60	6-27-63	AA
Lafayette	SSBN-616	61/216	Gen. Dyn., Groton	7-22-60	4-23-63	AA

Both classes are based on the same design, but SSBN-640 has quieter machinery and larger crew. All SSBN-616 and 640 class have received POSEIDON refits (see following table and text). Eventually it is planned to refit 10 of the POSEIDON-carrying SSBNs with the TRIDENT I (C-4) missile. All SSBNs have emergency diesels, batteries, and snorkles. SSBN-626 has diving planes mounted on bow vice sail. It is one of a kind in class. SSBNs operate with hull numbers painted out. SSBN bases located as follows: Pacific: Guam, Pearl Harbor. Atlantic: Charleston, South Carolina, Holy Loch, Scotland, and Rota, Spain.

POSEIDON (C-3) CONVERSIONS

Number	FY/SCB	Converted at	Awarded	Started	Completed
SSBN-659	73/355.73	Portsmouth Navy	9-18-72	10-10-72	2-8-74
SSBN-658	73/355.73	Newport News	8-18-72	8-21-72	12-19-73

Number	FY/SCB	Converted at	Awarded	Started	Completed
SSBN-657	72/353.71	PS Navy	12-27-71	2-20-72	5-17-73
SSBN-656	72/353.71	Gen. Dyn., Groton	11-11-71	11-12-71	4-7-73

Number	FY/SCB	Converted at	Awarded	Started	Completed
SSBN-655	72/353.71	Newport News	11-12-71	11-15-71	3-22-73
SSBN-654	72/353.71	PS Navy	8-15-71	9-14-71	2-8-73
SSBN-645	72/353.71	Newport News	7-16-71	7-15-71	11-17-72
SSBN-644	71/353.71	PS Navy	1-28-71	4-30-71	7-21-72
SSBN-643	71/353.71	Portsmouth Navy	1-21-71	4-28-71	7-31-72
SSBN-642	72/353.71	Gen. Dyn., Groton	7-12-71	7-15-71	10-27-72
SSBN-641	71/353.71	Newport News	2-12-71	2-15-71	5-12-72
SSBN-640	71/353.71	Gen. Dyn., Groton	2-24-71	2-25-71	5-15-72
SSBN-636	71/353.68	Newport News	7-21-70	7-22-70	9-21-71
SSBN-635	70/353.68	Portsmouth Navy	2-18-70	1-19-70	9-2-71
SSBN-634	71/353.68	Gen. Dyn., Groton	7-14-70	7-15-70	10-29-71
SSBN-633	70/353.68	Gen. Dyn., Groton	1-2-70	1-10-70	4-30-71
SSBN-632	69/353.68	Gen. Dyn., Groton	7-8-69	7-11-69	11-19-70
SSBN-631	70/353.68	PS Navy	10-6-69	10-3-69	12-16-70

Number	FY/SCB	Converted at	Awarded	Started	Completed
SSBN-630	69/353.68	Mare Island	6-23-69	8-4-69	2-22-71
SSBN-629	68/353.68	Newport News	4-19-68	5-11-69	8-11-70
SSBN-628	70/353.68	Newport News	1-6-69	11-10-69	2-18-71
SSBN-627	68/353.68	Gen. Dyn., Groton	11-17-67	2-3-69	6-28-70
SSBN-626	75/355.73	Gen. Dyn., Groton			
SSBN-625	75/355.73	Gen. Dyn., Groton			
SSBN-624	74/355.73	Newport News	9-28-73	10-1-73	
SSBN-623	73/355.73	PS Navy	6-15-73	6-15-73	
SSBN-622	75/355.73	Newport News	12-24-74		
SSBN-620	74/355.73	Portsmouth Navy	2-1-74	2-1-74	
SSBN-619	73/355.73	Gen. Dyn., Groton	3-15-73	3-19-73	
SSBN-617	73/355.73	Newport News	1-15-73	1-15-73	
SSBN-616	73/355.73	Gen. Dyn., Groton	10-15-72	10-15-72	11-7-74

Conversion to handle the POSEIDON missile includes removal of a liner in the missile tubes to accommodate the larger circumference of the POSEIDON, replacement of the MK 84 fire control system with the MK 88 fire control system, overhauling the ships, and refueling their reactors. *James Madison*, the first SSBN to receive the refit, made the first deployment with POSEIDON on 3-31-71.

5 FLEET BALLISTIC MISSILE SUBMARINES, *ETHAN ALLEN* CLASS

Name	Number	FY/SCB	Builder	Awarded	Commissioned	F/S
Thomas Jefferson	SSBN-618	61/180	Newport News	7-22-60	1-4-63	PA
John Marshall	SSBN-611	59/180	Newport News	7-1-59	5-21-62	PA
Thomas A. Edison	SSBN-610	59/180	Gen. Dyn., Groton	7-1-59	3-10-62	PA
Sam Houston	SSBN-609	59/180	Newport News	7-1-59	3-6-62	AA
Ethan Allen	SSBN-608	59/180	Gen. Dyn., Groton	7-17-58	8-8-61	PA

This modified *Thresher* class design is the first class of true SSBNs. They have greater depth and quieter machinery than SSBN-598 class. They are scheduled for POLARIS A-3 refit. Class to be replaced by *Trident* SSBNs.

5 FLEET BALLISTIC MISSILE SUBMARINES, *GEORGE WASHINGTON* CLASS

Name	Number	FY/SCB	Builder	Awarded	Commissioned	F/S
Abraham Lincoln	SSBN-602	59/180A	Portsmouth Navy	7-30-58	3-11-61	PA
Robert E. Lee	SSBN-601	59/180A	Newport News	7-30-58	9-16-60	PA
Theodore Roosevelt	SSBN-600	58/180A	Mare Island	3-13-58	2-13-61	PA
Patrick Henry	SSBN-599	58/180A	Gen. Dyn., Groton	12-31-57	4-9-60	PA
George Washington	SSBN-598	58/180A	Gen. Dyn., Groton	12-31-57	12-30-59	PA

These are first generation SSBNs. SSBN-598/600 were originally authorized as SSNs of *Skipjack* class. When it was decided to construct this class, *Scorpion* (SSN-598) had already been laid down and materials for the unnamed SSN-590 had already been assembled. A supplement to the FY 1958 program authorized the construction of the first three SSBNs. This was done by modifying the *Skipjack* class design. The hull was cut in half, just aft of the sail, and a 130' missile section inserted. This was also done for SSBN-601 and 602. *Scorpion* (SSN-598) and the unnamed SSN-590 were reclassified SSGN-598 and 599 on 4-8-58, and a third SSN was classified SSGN-600 on the same date. The name *Scorpion* was cancelled at the same time. SSGN-598/600 were reclassified SSBNs on 6-26-58. Class was originally fitted with the POLARIS (A-1) missiles. These missiles were replaced with POLARIS (A-3) missiles at General Dynamics, Groton (SSBN-601 at Mare Island Naval Shipyard) between 6-20-64 and 6-3-67. The refit included overhaul, refueling and replacement of the compressed-air missile ejection system with a gas-steam ejection system. Class is "depth limited."

28 NUCLEAR-POWERED ATTACK SUBMARINES, *LOS ANGELES* CLASS

Name	Number	FY/SCB	Builder	Awarded	Commissioned	F/S
	SSN-715	76/303.70				Proj.
	SSN-714	76/303.70				Proj.
	SSN-713	75/303.70				Bldg.
	SSN-712	75/303.70				Bldg.
	SSN-711	75/303.70				Bldg.
	SSN-710	74/303.70	Gen. Dyn., Groton	10–31–73		Bldg.
	SSN-709	74/303.70	Gen. Dyn., Groton	12–10–73		Bldg.
	SSN-708	74/303.70	Gen. Dyn., Groton	10–31–73		Bldg.
	SSN-707	74/303.70	Gen. Dyn., Groton	12–10–73		Bldg.
	SSN-706	74/303.70	Gen. Dyn., Groton	10–31–73		Bldg.
	SSN-705	73/303.70	Gen. Dyn., Groton	10–31–73		Bldg.
	SSN-704	73/303.70	Gen. Dyn., Groton	10–31–73		Bldg.
	SSN-703	73/303.70	Gen. Dyn., Groton	12–10–73		Bldg.
	SSN-702	73/303.70	Gen. Dyn., Groton	10–31–73		Bldg.
	SSN-701	73/303.70	Gen. Dyn., Groton	12–10–73		Bldg.
	SSN-700	73/303.70	Gen. Dyn., Groton	10–31–73		Bldg.
Jacksonville	SSN-699	72/303.70	Gen. Dyn., Groton	1–24–72		Bldg.
Bremerton	SSN-698	72/303.70	Gen. Dyn., Groton	1–24–72		Bldg.
Indianapolis	SSN-697	72/303.70	Gen. Dyn., Groton	1–24–72		Bldg.
New York City	SSN-696	72/303.70	Gen. Dyn., Groton	1–24–72		Bldg.
Birmingham	SSN-695	72/303.70	Newport News	1–24–72		Bldg.
Groton	SSN-694	71/303.70	Gen. Dyn., Groton	1–31–71		Bldg.
Cincinnati	SSN-693	71/303.70	Newport News	2–4–71		Bldg.
Omaha	SSN-692	71/303.70	Gen. Dyn., Groton	1–31–71		Bldg.
Memphis	SSN-691	71/303.70	Newport News	2–4–71		Bldg.
Philadelphia	SSN-690	70/303.70	Gen. Dyn., Groton	1–8–71		Bldg.
Baton Rouge	SSN-689	70/303.70	Newport News	1–8–71		Bldg.
Los Angeles	SSN-688	70/303.70	Newport News	1–8–71		AA

This is a new class of SSN designed to dive deeper and operate faster than previous USN "nukes." U.S. Navy SSN designs are a technical compromise. To obtain high speeds, the submarines can become too big and noisy, but at very high speeds, detection does not become a real problem. Currently in the research and development stage is a class of SSN that will be armed with tactical cruise missiles. The class will be larger than the 688s and the cruise missiles will have a range of approximately 1,500 miles.

1 NUCLEAR-POWERED ATTACK SUBMARINE, *GLENARD P. LIPSCOMB* CLASS

Name	Number	FY/SCB	Builder	Awarded	Commissioned	F/S
Glenard P. Lipscomb	SSN-685	68/302	Gen. Dyn., Groton	10–14–70	12–21–74	AA

This is a prototype design with turbine electric drive, rather than geared drive, to test advanced silencing techniques for superquiet operations. The propulsion system is more advanced than that of the 688 class. The submarine is larger and slower than the *Sturgeon* class and has full combat capability.

1 NUCLEAR-POWERED ATTACK SUBMARINE, *NARWHAL* CLASS

Name	Number	FY/SCB	Builder	Awarded	Commissioned	F/S
Narwhal	SSN-671	64/245	Gen. Dyn., Groton	7-28-64	7-12-69	AA

This is the largest built-for-purpose SSN in Navy; similar to SSN-637 class, but has improved propulsion system equipped with a natural circulation reactor. Next to steam turbines, primary coolant pumps are the noisiest component of a pressurized water propulsion system. The bow was designed for optimum performance of the long-range sonar it houses.

37 NUCLEAR-POWERED ATTACK SUBMARINES, *STURGEON* CLASS

Name	Number	FY/SCB	Builder	Awarded	Commissioned	F/S
Richard B. Russell	SSN-687	69/300	Newport News	7–25–69		AA
L. Mendel Rivers	SSN-686	69/300	Newport News	7–25–69	2–1–75	AA
Cavalla	SSN-684	68/300	Gen. Dyn., Groton	7–24–69	2–9–73	AA
Parche	SSN-683	68/300	Ingalls	6–25–68	8–17–74	PA
Tunny	SSN-682	67/300	Ingalls	6–25–68	1–26–74	AA
Batfish	SSN-681	67/300	Gen. Dyn., Groton	6–25–68	9–1–72	AA
William H. Bates	SSN-680	67/300	Ingalls	6–25–68	5–5–73	AA
Silversides	SSN-679	67/300	Gen. Dyn., Groton	6–25–68	5–5–72	AA
Archerfish	SSN-678	67/300	Gen. Dyn., Groton	6–25–68	12–17–71	AA
Drum	SSN-677	66/300.66	Mare Island	3–15–67	4–15–72	PA
Billfish	SSN-676	66/300.66	Gen. Dyn., Groton	7–15–66	3–12–71	AA
Bluefish	SSN-675	66/300.66	Gen. Dyn., Groton	7–15–66	1–8–71	AA
Trepang	SSN-674	66/300.66	Gen. Dyn., Groton	7–15–66	8–14–70	AA
Flying Fish	SSN-673	66/300.66	Gen. Dyn., Groton	7–15–66	4–29–70	AA
Pintado	SSN-672	66/300.66	Mare Island	12–29–65	9–11–71	PA
Finback	SSN-670	65/300.65	Newport News	3–9–65	2–4–70	AA
Seahorse	SSN-669	65/300.65	Gen. Dyn., Groton	3–9–65	9–19–69	AA
Spadefish	SSN-668	65/300.65	Newport News	3–9–65	8–14–69	AA
Bergall	SSN-667	65/300.65	Gen. Dyn., Groton	3–9–65	6–13–69	AA
Hawkbill	SSN-666	65/300.65	Mare Island	12–18–64	2–4–71	PA
Guitarro	SSN-665	65/300.65	Mare Island	12–18–64	9–9–72	PA
Sea Devil	SSN-664	64/188A	Newport News	5–28–64	1–30–69	AA
Hammerhead	SSN-663	64/188A	Newport News	5–28–64	6–28–68	AA
Gurnard	SSN-662	64/188A	Mare Island	10–24–63	12–6–68	PA
Lapon	SSN-661	64/188A	Newport News	5–28–64	12–14–67	AA
Sand Lance	SSN-660	64/188A	Portsmouth Navy	10–24–63	9–25–71	AA
Ray	SSN-653	63/188A	Newport News	3–26–63	4–12–67	AA
Puffer	SSN-652	63/188A	Ingalls	3–26–63	8–9–69	PA
Queenfish	SSN-651	63/188A	Newport News	3–26–63	12–6–66	PA
Pargo	SSN-650	63/188A	Gen. Dyn., Groton	3–26–63	1–5–68	AA
Sunfish	SSN-649	63/188A	Gen. Dyn., Groton	3–26–63	3–15–69	AA
Aspro	SSN-648	63/188A	Ingalls	3–26–63	2–20–69	PA
Pogy	SSN-647	63/188A	Ingalls	12–7–67	5–15–71	PA

Name	Number	FY/SCB	Builder	Awarded	Commissioned	F/S
Grayling	SSN-646	63/188A	Portsmouth Navy	9–5–62	10–11–69	AA
Tautog	SSN-639	62/188A	Ingalls	11–30–61	8–17–68	PA
Whale	SSN-638	62/188A	Gen. Dyn., Groton	11–30–61	10–12–68	AA
Sturgeon	SSN-637	62/188A	Gen. Dyn., Groton	11–30–61	3–3–67	AA

SSN-647 was originally ordered from NY Shipbuilding on 3–23–63. The contract was cancelled on 6–5–67 for convenience of the government and she was towed to Philadelphia in 6/67 and laid up incomplete. Towed to Ingalls in 1/68 for completion (parted tow off Florida during a storm). *Guitarro* (SSN-665) sank 5–15–69, in 35' of water, while being outfitted at Mare Island. She was raised 5–19–69. Her electrical/electronic gear was heavily damaged, and the completion was delayed 28 months. A Court of Inquiry ruled the sinking resulted from negligence. SSN-680 was originally named *Redfish*; renamed 6–25–71 in honor of a deceased congressman. Class was built to modified *Thresher* design (SUBSAFE features included) and is easily recognizable from previous SSNs by taller sails and lower position of diving planes on sails. SSN-678/684, 686, and 687 are 10' longer than rest of class to accommodate extra electronic and sonar gear. SSN-666 and 670 are fitted as DSRV motherships. SSN-687 placed "in service" 5–5–75.

1 NUCLEAR-POWERED ATTACK SUBMARINE, *TULLIBEE* CLASS

Tullibee	SSN-597	58/178	Gen. Dyn., Groton	11–15–57	11–9–60	AA

Tullibee was originally laid down as SSKN; to SSN on 8–15–59. She is the smallest SSN with combat capability and the first SSN to be designed for ASW. The first USN submarine to use the bow entirely for sonar. She has turbo-electric drive, an early attempt to produce a quiet propulsion plant. Torpedo tubes amidships angled out from center line; no SUBROC; rated second line.

13 NUCLEAR-POWERED ATTACK SUBMARINES, "*THRESHER*" CLASS

Haddock	SSN-621	61/188	Ingalls	8–24–60	12–22–67	PA
Gato	SSN-615	60/188	Gen. Dyn., Groton	6–9–60	1–25–68	AA
Greenling	SSN-614	60/188	Gen. Dyn., Groton	6–9–60	11–3–67	AA
Flasher	SSN-613	60/188	Gen. Dyn., Groton	6–9–60	7–22–66	PA
Guardfish	SSN-612	60/188	NY Shipbuilding	6–9–60	12–20–66	PA
Dace	SSN-607	59/188	Ingalls	3–3–59	4–4–66	AA
Tinosa	SSN-606	59/188	Portsmouth Navy	12–17–58	10–17–64	AA
Jack	SSN-605	59/188	Portsmouth Navy	3–13–59	3–31–67	AA

Name	Number	FY/SCB	Builder	Awarded	Commissioned	F/S
Haddo	SSN-604	59/188	NY Shipbuilding	3–3–59	12–16–64	AA
Pollack (ex-*Barb*)	SSN-603	59/188	NY Shipbuilding	3–3–59	5–26–64	AA
Barb (ex-*Pollack*, *Plunger*)	SSN-596	58/188	Ingalls	3–3–59	8–24–63	PA
Plunger (ex-*Pollack*)	SSN-595	58/188	Mare Island	3–23–59	11–21–62	PA
Permit	SSN-594	58/188	Mare Island	1–27–58	5–29–62	PA

SSN-595 was originally named *Pollack*; renamed 7–23–59. SSN-596 was originally named *Plunger*; renamed *Pollack* on 4–28–59; renamed *Barb* on 7–23–59. SSN-603 originally named *Barb*; renamed 7–23–59. SSN-595, 596 and 607 were originally authorized as SSGNs of *Halibut* class; reclassified SSN on 10–15–59. Lead ship of this class, *Thresher* (SSN-593), was lost on 4–10–63 off New England coast, with 129 men aboard, while conducting deep diving tests. Court of Inquiry fixed loss on improperly welded patch on outer hull done by Portsmouth Navy Yard. Loss delayed construction of class while SUBSAFE features were installed. As a result SSN-605 is 297'5" long, SSN-613/615 are 292'2" long, and all 4 are approximately 500 tons heavier. This class represents the first of a series of a new type of attack submarine.

1 NUCLEAR-POWERED ATTACK SUBMARINE, *HALIBUT* CLASS

Halibut	SSN-587	56/137A	Mare Island	3–9–56	1–4–60	PR*

Halibut was originally commissioned as SSGN; 4 others reordered as SSNs of *Thresher* class. She was originally designed as conventional SSG, but was converted to nuclear power during design stage. As SSGN she was designed to carry 5 REGULUS I or 2 REGULUS II missiles. When SSBN program superseded the REGULUS program, she became SSN on 8–15–65, and the missile gear was removed. She was employed in experimental duties until decommissioned at Mare Island in FY 1976. Rated second line. As SSGN she carried a crew of 11 officers and 108 men. The submarine lacks speed and maneuverability.

1 NUCLEAR-POWERED ATTACK SUBMARINE, *TRITON* CLASS

Triton	SSN-586	56/132	Gen. Dyn., Groton	10–5–55	11–10–59	AR*

The world's longest submarine, she was originally commissioned as SSRN. When the Navy abandoned the SSR concept, *Triton* was reclassified as SSN on 3–1–61. The projected conversion of this ship to an underwater version of *Northampton* and *Wright* was dropped. Rated as second line, the ship became a "white elephant" when there was no logical method or operation in which she could be used. As a result, she was decommissioned on 5–3–69 at New London, becoming the first nuclear-powered warship to be laid up.

5 NUCLEAR-POWERED ATTACK SUBMARINES, *SKIPJACK* CLASS

Name	Number	FY/SCB	Builder	Awarded	Commissioned	F/S
Snook	SSN-592	57/154	Ingalls	1–18–57	10–24–61	PA
Shark	SSN-591	57/154	Newport News	1–31–57	2–9–61	AA
Sculpin	SSN-590	57/154	Ingalls	1–18–57	6–1–61	PA
Scamp	SSN-588	57/154	Mare Island	7–23–56	6–5–61	PA
Skipjack	SSN-585	56/154	Gen. Dyn., Groton	10–5–55	4–15–59	AA

These were the first tear-drop designed nuclear submarines and first SSN class to have single screw. *Scorpion* (SSN-589) was declared overdue and presumed lost on 5–7–68; officially declared lost 6–6–68 west of the Azores, cause of sinking unknown. The class is rated as second line. Original hull of *Scorpion* and materials for SSN-590 were used to construct SSBN-598 and 599.

4 NUCLEAR-POWERED ATTACK SUBMARINES, *SKATE* CLASS

Seadragon	SSN-584	56/121	Portsmouth Navy	9–29–55	12–5–59	PA
Sargo	SSN-583	56/121	Mare Island	9–29–55	10–1–58	PA
Swordfish	SSN-579	55/121	Portsmouth Navy	7–18–55	9–15–58	PA
Skate	SSN-578	55/121	Gen. Dyn., Groton	7–18–55	12–23–57	AA

This class represents the first production model of SSNs. The design is similar to, but smaller than, *Nautilus* with *Guppy* hull and twin propellers. Rated second line.

1 NUCLEAR-POWERED ATTACK SUBMARINE, *SEAWOLF* CLASS

Seawolf	SSN-575	52/64A	Gen. Dyn., Groton	7–21–52	3–30–57	PA

Completed with S2G sodium-cooled reactor, which was replaced in 1959 with pressurized water plant after the sodium reactor developed leaks and other problems. Originally intended as an attack submarine, *Seawolf* is now used mainly for experiments.

1 NUCLEAR-POWERED ATTACK SUBMARINE, *NAUTILUS* CLASS

Nautilus	SSN-571	52/64	Gen. Dyn., Groton	8–20–51	9–30–54	AA

Nautilus is the world's first nuclear-powered warship, and like *Seawolf*, has *Guppy* hull. She is rated second line. Now twenty years old, she is used strictly in experiments. Completely overhauled in 1974 for further service.

3 CONVENTIONALLY POWERED ATTACK SUBMARINES, *BARBEL* CLASS

Name	Number	FY/SCB	Builder	Awarded	Commissioned	F/S
Bonefish	SS-582	56/150	NY Shipbuilding	6–29–56	7–9–59	PA
Blueback	SS-581	56/150	Ingalls	6–29–56	10–15–59	PA
Barbel	SS-580	56/150	Portsmouth Navy	8–24–55	1–17–59	PA

These are the last conventional SSs built for USN, with the hull based on experiments conducted with *Albacore*. As completed the diving planes were located on the bow; later moved to the sail. They were the first submarines to have controls centralized in an "attack center" to increase efficiency, and this practice was adopted for all succeeding submarine classes.

1 CONVENTIONALLY POWERED GUIDED MISSILE SUBMARINE, "*GRAYBACK*" CLASS

Growler	SSG-577	55/161	Portsmouth Navy	7–31–54	8–30–58	PR*

Along with *Grayback*, *Growler* was originally ordered as SS of the *Darter* class; to SSG on 7–26–56 and converted to carry REGULUS during construction by inserting a 50′ section amidships and adding two cylindrical hangars to handle/store the missiles. Each hangar is 11″ high and extends 70′ aft from the bow. Decommissioned 5–25–64 at Mare Island along with *Grayback*. *Grayback* was later taken out of reserve and converted to an LPSS (see Amphibious Section). It was planned to convert this ship to an LPSS too, but the excessive cost and time to convert *Grayback* forced cancellation of *Growler*'s conversion. With less than six years' service, *Growler* represents a valuable asset in that she is virtually brand new.

1 CONVENTIONALLY POWERED ATTACK SUBMARINE, *DARTER* CLASS

Darter	SS-576	54/116	Gen. Dyn., Groton	6–30–54	10–20–56	PA

An improved *Tang* class with console controls. She is exceptionally quiet. Two sisters were completed as SSGs.

2 CONVENTIONALLY POWERED ATTACK SUBMARINES, *SAILFISH* CLASS

Name	Number	FY/SCB	Builder	Awarded	Commissioned	F/S
Salmon	SS-573	52/84	Portsmouth Navy	2-27-52	8-25-56	PA
Sailfish	SS-572	52/84	Portsmouth Navy	2-27-52	4-14-56	PA

Originally commissioned as SSRs; to SS on 3-1-61 when SSR concept was abandoned. Both have been FRAMed. SS-573 to AGSS on 6-29-68 for duty as test and evaluation submarine for the DSRV. When the project was delayed, she was reclassified back to SS on 6-30-69. They are the largest non-nuclear SSs built for USN since the 1930s.

3 CONVENTIONALLY POWERED ATTACK SUBMARINES, "*TANG*" CLASS

Name	Number	FY/SCB	Builder	Awarded	Commissioned	F/S
Gudgeon	SS-567	49/2A	Portsmouth Navy	10-12-48	11-21-52	PA
Trout	SS-566	49/2A	Electric Boat	5-14-48	6-27-52	PA
Wahoo	SS-565	48/2A	Portsmouth Navy	2-1-48	5-30-52	PA

These were the first postwar SSs to be completed. *Gudgeon* was the first SS to circumnavigate the world. Original length of the class was 269'2". Over the years, SS-565 and 566 have been lengthened to 277' and SS-567 to 283'. Class has been FRAMed. Two sisters are now in Italian Navy. *Tang* (SS-563) was converted to an AGSS (see Auxiliary section).

SSBN-726 class. Model of Navy's TRIDENT submarine. 9-73.

Summary *Guppy* disposals since last edition. *Guppy III* (9 in class): All 9 have been transferred to foreign countries for further service. *Guppy IIA* (10): 7 sold to foreign navies for further service, 2 scrapped, and 1 sunk as target. *Guppy II* (10): 9 sold to foreign navies for further service and 1 scrapped. *Guppy 1A* (10): 5 sold foreign (4 for service and 1 for cannibalization and scrapping), 1 is a salvage training hulk, 1 is to be sunk as a target, and the disposition of 3 is pending.

It should be noted that from 1 August 1972 until 1 October 1973, when she was stricken, the target and training submarine *Barracuda* (SST-3) was classified as SS-T3 and rated as an attack submarine. This was merely a force level adjustment and no actual conversion to an attack role was undertaken.

Tecumseh (SSBN-626). **Lafayette** class.

George Washington Carver (SSBN-656). **Lafayette** class.

Ethan Allen (SSBN-608). **Ethan Allen** class.

Ethan Allen (SSBN-608). 8–71. **Ethan Allen** class.

Abraham Lincoln (SSBN-602). Hull configuration of SSBNs differentiates them from SSNs. **George Washington** class.

Los Angeles (SSN-688). Launch photo. 4–6–74. **Los Angeles** class.

Glenard P. Lipscomb (SSN-685). 8–4–73. **Glenard P. Lipscomb** class.

Narwhal (SSN-671). Similar to but longer than **Sturgeon** class units. 1969. **Narwhal** class.

Finback (SSN-670). 1970. **Sturgeon** class.

Cavalla (SSN-684). 10–72. **Sturgeon** class.

Hawkbill (SSN-666) with Deep Submergence Rescue Vehicle (DSRV-1) aboard. 1971. **Sturgeon** class.

Tullibee (SSN-597). **Tullibee** class.

Plunger (SSN-595). 1972. **"Thresher"** class.

Halibut (SSN-587). Note hangar deck for former missile armament faired into hull. Reclassified SSN from SSGN when REGULUS program was abandoned. Can also carry DSRV. **Halibut** class.

Triton (SSN-586). 1966. **Triton** class.

Snook (SSN-592). First class to be built to tear drop design. **Skipjack** class.

Sargo (SSN-583). **Skate** class.

Seawolf (SSN-575). **Seawolf** class.

Nautilus (SSN-571). The world's first nuclear-powered submarine is now 21 years old. **Nautilus** class.

Barbel (SS-580). **Barbel** class.

Growler (SSG-577). Note missile hangar forward. **"Grayback"** class.

Darter (SS-576). Fins are PUFF sonar domes. **Darter** class.

Salmon (SS-573). **Sailfish** class.

Gudgeon (SS-567). **"Tang"** class. 1968.

TWO: AMPHIBIOUS WARFARE SHIPS

At the end of FY 1975, there were a total of 106 amphibious warfare ships on the NVR. Active: 2 LCC, 5 LKA, 14 LPD, 7 LPH, 1 SS (ex-LPSS), 13 LSD and 20 LST. Reserve (USN): 2 LPR, 1 LPSS, 1 LSD and 4 LST. Reserve (MarAd): 1 LCC, 6 LKA, 1 LPA, 3 LSD and 3 LST. Naval Reserve Training: 1 LKA and 2 LPA. Building; 5 LHA. In addition to the aforementioned breakdown, 14 LSTs are assigned to the Military Sealift Command for employment as cargo carriers. Although officially rated as amphibious ships, they are in actual fact auxiliaries. All 14 units are in reserve at Sasebo, Japan. For the purpose of this publication, all ships transferred to the permanent custody of MarAd, but still on the NVR, are considered to be stricken (see Section 14 for names and hull numbers).

Class	Number	No. In Class	Full Load Displ.	Length Overall	Max. Draft	Extreme Beam	Number & Type of Boilers/Engines	Screws/ SHP	Max. Speed (Kts.)	Accommodations Officers	Accommodations Enlisted	Troops Officers	Troops Enlisted	Armament
Blue Ridge	LCC-19	2	19,000	620'	27'	108'	2B(F.W.)/1GT(G.E.)	1/22,000	20	269	1,169	—	—	2 twin 3"/50 cal. mts., 2 BPDMS (LCC-20), 2 40mm saluting mts. (LCC-20)
"Adirondack"	AGC-15	1	12,560	459'	24'7"	63'	2B(C.E.)/1GT(G.E.)	1/6,000	16	60	553	—	—	1 single 5"/38 cal. mt., 2 twin 40mm mts.
Tarawa	LHA-1	5	39,300	820'	26'	106'	2B(C.E.)/4GT(West.)	2/140,000	24	90	812	172	1,731	2 BPDMS, 3 MK 45 single 5"/54 cal. mts., 6 MK 67 machineguns, 2 40mm saluting mts.
Charleston	LKA-113	5	20,700	550'	28'	82'	2B(C.E.)/1GT(West.)	1/22,000	20	31	362	15	211	4 twin 3"/50 cal. mts.
Tulare	LKA-112	1	16,818	564'	28'	76'	2B(C.E.)/1GT(DeLaval)	1/22,000	23.4	31	362	18	301	6 twin 3"/50 cal. mts.
Rankin	LKA-103	3	10,664	459'	26'3"	61'1"	2B(C.E.)/2GT(G.E.)	1/6,000	16.3	25	335	9	129	1 single 5"/38 cal. mt., 4 twin 40mm mts.
Winston	LKA-94	2	13,700	459'	28'	63'2"	2B(F.W.)/2GT(G.E.)	1/6,000	16.5	28	335	11	88	4 twin 40mm mts.
"Uvalde"	AKA-88	1	13,000	459'	28'	63'	2B(C.E.)/2GT(G.E.)	1/6,000	16	37	335	12	85	4 twin 40mm mts.
Francis Marion	LPA-249	1	16,838	564'	27'8"	76'	2B(F.W.)/2GT(G.E.)	1/22,000	22.4	64	505	96	1,561	4 twin 3"/50 cal. mts.
Paul Revere	LPA-248	1	16,838	564'	27'	76'	2B(F.W.)/2GT(G.E.)	1/19,200	22.5	77	484	96	1,561	4 twin 3"/50 cal. mts.
"Haskell"	APA-117	1	10,679	455'	24'	62'	2B(F.W.)/2GT(West.)	1/8,500	18.4	50	459	51	916	2 single 5"/38 cal. mts., 4 twin 40mm mts.
Austin	LPD-4	12	16,900	569'	21'6"	105'2"	2B(B&W)/2ST(DeLaval)	2/24000	21	27	446	103	801	4 twin 3"/50 cal. mts.
Raleigh	LPD-1	2	14,651	521'9"	22'	104'	2B(B&W)/2ST(DeLaval)	2/24,000	20	27	435	73	996	4 twin 3"/50 cal. mts.
Iwo Jima	LPH-2	7	18,000	602'	29'	84'	2B(C.E.)/1GT(West.)	1/22,000	23	47	605	143	1,581	2 BPDMS(LPH-2, 3, 11, 12), 3 twin 3"/50 cal. mts. (LPH-3), 4 twin 3"/50 cal. mts. (remainder), 2 40mm saluting guns
"Knudson"	LPR-101	1	2,130	306'	15'2"	37'	2B(F.W.)/2GT(G.E.)	2/12,000	24	29	225	8	113	1 single 5"/38 cal. mt., 1 quad 40mm mt., 3 twin 40mm mts., 1 DCT
"Laning"	LPR-55	1	2,130	306'	13'	37'	2B(F.W.)/2GT(G.E.)	2/12,000	23.6	27	335	8	113	1 single 5"/38 cal. mt., 1 quad 40mm mt., 3 twin 40mm mts. 2 DCT
Grayback	SS-574	1	2,240	334'	17'	27'	3D(F.M.)/2EM(Ell.)	2/5,500	16.7	9	78	7	60	6 21" torpedo tubes fwd., 2 21" torpedo tubes aft.
"Perch"	LPSS-313	1	1,659	312'	18'	27'	2D(G.M.)/4EM(G.E.)	2/2,305	13.8	6	68	4	68	2 single 40mm mts.
Anchorage	LSD-36	5	13,700	555'	18'	84'	2B(C.E.)/2GT(DeLaval)	2/24,000	20	21	376	25	312	4 twin 3"/50 cal. mts.
Thomaston	LSD-28	8	11,525	510'	20'	90'	2B(B&W)/2GT(G.E.)	2/24,000	22.5	21	384	29	312	6 twin 3"/50 cal. mts.
Cabildo	LSD-16	3	9,078	458'	17'6"	72'	2B(B&W)/2GT(NN SB)	2/7,000	16	21	295	18	150	2 quad 40mm mts., 2 twin 40mm mts.
"Casa Grande"	LSD-13	1	9,078	458'	17'6"	72'	2B(B&W)/2GT(NN SB)	2/7,000	16	18	305	18	182	2 quad 40mm mts.
Newport	LST-1179	20	8,400	567'	15'	68'	6D(G.M.)(1179/81) (Alco)(rest)	2/16,000	20	12	174	20	411	2 twin 3"/50 cal. mts.

Class	Number	No. In Class	Full Load Displ.	Length Overall	Max. Draft	Extreme Beam	Number & Type of Boilers/Engines	Screws/ SHP	Max. Speed (Kts.)	Accommodations Officers	Accommodations Enlisted	Troops Officers	Troops Enlisted	Armament
"De Soto County"	LST-1171	3	7,804	442'	17'6"	62'	6D(F.M.)	2/13,700	16.5	15	173	30	604	3 twin 3"/50 cal. mts.
"Terrebonne Parish"	LST-1156	2	5,777	384'	16'1"	56'	4D(G.M.)	2/6,000	15.5	16	189	15	376	3 twin 3"/50 cal. mts.
	LST-511	12	4,080	328'	12'	50'	2D(G.M.)	2/1,700	11.6	9	109	18	116	2 twin 40mm mts., 4 single 40 mm mts.
	LST-1	4	3,640	328'	14'1"	50'	2D(G.M.)	2/1,700	11.5	9	107	14	119	None

2 AMPHIBIOUS COMMAND SHIPS, *BLUE RIDGE* CLASS

Name	Number	Commissioned	F/S
Mount Whitney	LCC-20	1–16–71	AA
Blue Ridge	LCC-19	11–14–70	PA

Originally all LCCs were classed as AGC; AGC-19 and 20 to LCC on 10–1–68; AGC-16 to LCC on 1–1–69. First amphibious command ships built from keel up. At a distance the class resembles AGMR-1. They are built with a flight deck arrangement which provides more antenna space. The class design and machinery arrangement are similar to LPH-2 class. Both fitted with NTDS. A third sister AGC-21 was cancelled in 1969. Flag accommodations: 217 officers and 471 enlisted.

1 AMPHIBIOUS COMMAND SHIP, "ADIRONDACK" CLASS

Pocono	LCC-16	12–29–45	MAR*

Built on a C2-S-AJ1 hull design. LCC-16 acquired 2–15–45. Originally 3 in class, AGC-15 was stricken 6–1–61; LCC-17 was transferred to permanent custody of MarAd on 9–1–71, but is not stricken; LCC-16 was decommissioned 9–16–71 at Norfolk and transferred to temporary custody of MarAd on 2–1–72 for layup. The remaining 3 units of the *Mount McKinley* class LCCs have been disposed of. *Eldorado* (LCC-11) was stricken and *Mount McKinley* (LCC-7) and *Estes* (LCC-12) were transferred to the permanent custody of MarAd on 9–1–71 for layup.

INSHORE FIRE SUPPORT SHIPS (LFR)—The 9 LFRs listed in the 9th edition have been stricken. With the cancellation of the Amphibious Fire Support Ship (LFS), before it reached the construction stage, the striking of the 9 LFRs leaves the USN without an effective, reliable fire support ship.

5 AMPHIBIOUS ASSAULT SHIPS (GENERAL PURPOSE), *TARAWA* CLASS

Name	Number	FY/SCB	Builder	Awarded	Commissioned	F/S
Da Nang	LHA-5	71/410.68	Ingalls	11–6–70		Bldg.
Nassau	LHA-4	71/410.68	Ingalls	11–6–70		Bldg.
Belleau Wood	LHA-3	70/410.68	Ingalls	11–15–69		Bldg.
Saipan	LHA-2	70/410.68	Ingalls	11–15–69		Bldg.
Tarawa	LHA-1	69/410.68	Ingalls	5–1–69		PA

This is a new type of amphibious assault ship, combining features of LPDs, LSDs, and LPHs. Originally ordered under the concept definition/contract formulation process; it was assigned an SCB number when the CD/CF process was abandoned. Four additional sisters were cancelled in 1973. It is highly automated which reduces size of crew. Stern is fitted with a well deck as in LSD/LPDs for landing craft to enter. This is underneath a hangar deck that runs from amidships aft and measures 78' × 268'; can handle small amphibious landing craft up to and including the LCU. Class has a large hangar deck, vehicle storage and maintenance facilities for tanks, trucks, and jeeps and has sophisticated internal and external communications systems and extensive medical facilities. Cargo can be moved automatically by conveyors. Each ship has 9 elevators for moving helos, personnel, cargo, and equipment. Technical and labor difficulties have delayed construction of this class. LHA-1 is 2 years behind schedule. LHA-5 is 32 months behind schedule. When these ships are completed, they, plus the LPHs, should provide a formidable troop lift "punch" to our amphibious forces. Current schedule calls for LHA-1 to commission in 1975 and LHA-5 in 12/76. The ships can carry sixteen CH-46, six CH-53, and four UH-1E helicopters. In January 1975, *Saipan* was damaged during a storm at Pascagoula when she broke her mooring lines at the fitting-out dock and grounded on the opposite bank from the yard. She was pulled off the same day. Moderate damage.

5 AMPHIBIOUS CARGO SHIPS, *CHARLESTON* CLASS

Name	Number	Commissioned	F/S
El Paso	LKA-117	1–17–70	AA
St. Louis	LKA-116	11–22–69	PA
Mobile	LKA-115	9–20–69	PA
Durham	LKA-114	5–24–69	PA
Charleston	LKA-113	12–14–68	AA

Class was the first USN LKAs built from the keel up. All LKAs were originally classes as AKAs; AKA-113 to LKA on 12–14–68; remainder of class on 10–1–68. *Charleston* was the first USN ship with a fully automated propulsion plant. Class has helo deck aft and same machinery layout as LPH-2 class.

1 AMPHIBIOUS CARGO SHIP, *TULARE* CLASS

Name	Number	Commissioned	F/S
Tulare	LKA-112	1–12–56	NRT

Built on MarAd C4-S-1A hull design as SS *Evergreen Mariner, Tulare* is near sister to LPA-248/249; to LKA on 1–1–69. See Section 7 for NRT assignment.

3 AMPHIBIOUS CARGO SHIPS, *RANKIN* CLASS

Name	Number	Commissioned	F/S
Vermilion	LKA-107	6–23–45	MAR*
Seminole	LKA-104	3–8–45	MPR*
Rankin	LKA-103	2–25–45	MAR*

Built on a C2-S-AJ3 hull design. All 3 were reclassified from AKA on 1–1–69. There were originally 6 ships in class. One has been stricken and 2 were transferred to the permanent custody of MarAd and are laid up, but not stricken. LKA-103 decommissioned 5–11–71 and LKA-107 on 4–14–71 at Little Creek. LKA-104 decommissioned 12–23–70 at San Diego. Transfers to temporary custody of MarAd as follows: LKA-103 on 8–12–71, LKA-104 on 5–20–71, and LKA-107 on 7–27–71.

2 AMPHIBIOUS CARGO SHIPS, *WINSTON* CLASS

Name	Number	Commissioned	F/S
Merrick	LKA-97	3–31–45	MPR*
Winston	LKA-94	1–19–45	MPR*

These ships were built on a C2-SB-1 hull design and were originally commissioned as AKAs. They were decommissioned at San Diego as follows: LKA-94 in 1969 and LKA-97 on 9–17–69. LKA-94 was transferred to temporary custody of MarAd on 12–15–69. LKA-97 followed on 2–17–70. Both are laid up.

1 AMPHIBIOUS CARGO SHIP, *"UVALDE"* CLASS

Name	Number	Commissioned	F/S
Yancey	LKA-93	10–11–44	MAR*

Yancey was built on C2-S-B1 hull design and commissioned as AKA. On 1–1–69, all AKAs from AKA-112 down, still on NVR, were reclassified as LKA. Since the 9th edition, *Arneb* (LKA-56) has been stricken. *Thuban* (LKA-19), *Algol* (LKA-54), *Capricornus* (LKA-57), and *Muliphen* (LKA-61) have been transferred to the permanent custody of MarAd for layup (not stricken).

1 AMPHIBIOUS TRANSPORT, *FRANCIS MARION* CLASS

Name	Number	Commissioned	F/S
Francis Marion	LPA-249	7–6–61	NRT

This transport was completed 5–25–54 as SS *Prairie Mariner* on a MarAd C4-S-1A hull design. Acquired from MarAd and converted to APA under FY 1959. A near sister to LKA-112/LPA-248. Reclassified LPA on 1–1–69.

1 AMPHIBIOUS TRANSPORT, *PAUL REVERE* CLASS

Name	Number	Commissioned	F/S
Paul Revere	LPA-248	9–3–58	NRT

The *Paul Revere* was completed 12–22–53 as SS *Diamond Mariner* on a MarAd C4-S-1A hull design. Acquired from MarAd and converted to APA under FY 1957. Reclassified LPA on 1–1–69.

1 AMPHIBIOUS TRANSPORT, *"HASKELL"* CLASS

Name	Number	Commissioned	F/S
Bexar	LPA-237	10–9–45	MPR*

Built on a VC2-S-AP5 MarComm hull design. Sole survivor of a class of 122 ships. Originally commissioned as APA, she was decommissioned 12/69 at San Diego, and transferred to the temporary custody of MarAd on 8–7–70 for layup. Of the 7 sisterships mentioned in the 9th edition, 1 was stricken and 6 were transferred to the permanent custody of MarAd. The 3 survivors of the *Bayfield* class LPAs have been stricken.

12 AMPHIBIOUS TRANSPORT DOCKS, *AUSTIN* CLASS

Name	Number	Commissioned	F/S
Ponce	LPD-15	7–10–71	AA
Trenton	LPD-14	3–6–71	AA
Nashville	LPD-13	2–14–70	AA
Shreveport	LPD-12	12–12–70	AA
Coronado	LPD-11	5–23–70	AA
Juneau	LPD-10	7–12–69	PA
Denver	LPD-9	10–26–68	PA
Dubuque	LPD-8	9–1–67	PA
Cleveland	LPD-7	4–21–67	PA
Duluth	LPD-6	12–18–65	PA
Ogden	LPD-5	6–19–65	PA
Austin	LPD-4	2–6–65	AA

LPD-6 originally awarded to the New York Navy Yard, but reassigned to Philadelphia Naval Shipyard on 11–24–65 for completion after the New York Naval Shipyard closed down. LPD-7/13 are fitted as flagships and have an extra superstructure deck. Class is enlarged version of the *Raleigh* class. Fitted with telescopic hangars for helo maintenance. Well deck measures 168′ × 50′; landing craft load cargo by using overhead monorails.

2 AMPHIBIOUS TRANSPORT DOCKS, *RALEIGH* CLASS

Vancouver	LPD-2	5–11–63	PA
Raleigh	LPD-1	9–8–62	AA

There are the first of a new type of amphibious warfare ships which evolved from the LSD. A third unit of this class, *La Salle* (LPD-3), serves as an AGF (see Auxiliary section).

7 AMPHIBIOUS ASSAULT SHIPS, *IWO JIMA* CLASS

Inchon	LPH-12	6–20–70	AA
New Orleans	LPH-11	11–16–68	PA
Tripoli	LPH-10	8–6–66	PA
Guam	LPH-9	1–16–65	AA
Guadalcanal	LPH-7	7–20–63	AA
Okinawa	LPH-3	4–14–62	PA
Iwo Jima	LPH-2	8–26–61	AA

The world's first ships specifically designed to operate helicopters, this class approximates the size of the WW II CVEs. They carry a full Marine Battalion with assorted gear and up to twenty CH-46 helicopters. LPH-12 has davits aft for 2 LCVPs. LPH-10/12 have enclosed 3″/50 mounts forward of the bridge. All are being retrofitted with 2 BPDMS systems. *Guam* (LPH-9) was modified in late 1971 to serve as test and evaluation ship for the Sea Control Ship con-

cept. Her LPH capabilities were removed, but she retains classification. With the death of the Sea Control Ship, it is reported that this ship will be converted to serve as a mothership for minesweeping helicopters. Conversion of LPH-1, a former *Commencement Bay* class CVE, was cancelled. LPH-4, 5, and 8 were former *Essex* class CVA/CVS, and LPH-6 was the former *Casablanca* class CVE, *Thetis Bay*. All are now stricken.

1 AMPHIBIOUS TRANSPORT (SMALL), *"KNUDSON"* CLASS

Name	Number	Commissioned	F/S
Balduck	LPR-132	5–7–45	PR*

Formerly DE-716 of the *Rudderow* class DEs. Was converted during construction. A non-FRAM, she was decommissioned 11/57 at Mare Island. All APDs still on the NVR were reclassified LPR on 1–1–69.

1 AMPHIBIOUS TRANSPORT (SMALL), *"LANING"* CLASS

Begor (ex DE-711)	LPR-127	3–14–45	PR*

Ex-*Rudderow* class DE that was converted to APD during construction. She is the sole survivor of the class. Decommissioned 7/62 at San Diego. Many of these ships serve in foreign navies in various capacities.

1 SUBMARINE, *GRAYBACK* CLASS

Grayback (ex-LPSS, SSG, SS)	SS-574	3–7–58	PA

Originally laid down as an SS of *Darter* class. Reclassified to SSG on 7–26–56. Converted to carry REGULUS missiles by inserting a 50′ section into the hull. When the POLARIS superseded the REGULUS program, she was decommissioned on 6–1–64 at Mare Island. Authorized for conversion to LPSS under FY 1965; converted at Mare Island and reclassified to LPSS from SSG on 8–30–68. Recommissioned as LPSS on 5–9–69. During conversion, the hull was lengthened 6′, the hangar doors were altered to serve her new role, she was re-engined, and improved electronics/sonar were added. She is the only USN submarine homeported outside the U.S. Reclassified back to SS on 6–30–75. Although *Grayback* has been reclassified as an SS, she still performs the duties and functions of an LPSS.

1 AMPHIBIOUS TRANSPORT SUBMARINE, *"PERCH"* CLASS

Name	Number	Commissioned	F/S
Sealion	LPSS-315	3-8-44	AR*

Originally commissioned as Fleet submarine of the *Balao* class, *Sealion* was converted to troop transport at Mare Island; recommissioned 3-13-48. To SSP on 3-31-48; to ASSP on 1-31-50; to APSS on 10-24-56; to LPSS on 1-1-69. Decommissioned 2/70 at Philadelphia. Sistership *Perch* was stricken as an IXSS. *Sealion* is the only USN submarine to sink a battleship.

5 DOCK LANDING SHIPS, *ANCHORAGE* CLASS

Name	Number	FY/SCB	Builder	Awarded	Commissioned	F/S
Fort Fisher	LSD-40	67/404.66	Gen. Dyn., Quincy	5-2-67	12-9-72	PA
Mount Vernon	LSD-39	66/404.66	Gen. Dyn., Quincy	2-25-66	5-13-72	PA
Pensacola	LSD-38	66/404.66	Gen. Dyn., Quincy	2-25-66	3-27-71	AA
Portland	LSD-37	66/404.66	Gen. Dyn., Quincy	2-25-66	10-3-70	AA
Anchorage	LSD-36	65/404.65	Ingalls	6-29-65	3-15-69	PA

This class strongly resembles previous LSD classes with two exceptions: has tripod mast and enclosed 3″ mounts forward on either side of the bridge. Well deck measures 430′ × 50′. The ships can accommodate landing craft up to and including LCUs. The cranes have 50-ton capacity.

8 DOCK LANDING SHIPS, *THOMASTON* CLASS

Name	Number	Commissioned	F/S
Monticello	LSD-35	3-29-57	PA
Hermitage	LSD-34	12-14-56	AA
Alamo	LSD-33	8-24-56	PA
Spiegel Grove	LSD-32	6-8-56	AA
Point Defiance	LSD-31	3-31-55	PA
Fort Snelling	LSD-30	1-24-55	AA
Plymouth Rock	LSD-29	11-29-54	AA
Thomaston	LSD-28	9-17-54	PA

All were built at Ingalls Shipbuilding. They have accommodations for over 300 troops. The well deck measures 391′ × 48′.

3 DOCK LANDING SHIPS, *CABILDO* CLASS

Name	Number	Commissioned	F/S
Donner	LSD-20	7-31-45	MAR*
Comstock	LSD-19	7-2-45	PR*
Cabildo	LSD-16	3-15-45	MPR*

There were originally 11 ships in this class. Two were cancelled at the end of WW II (one, after being completed for merchant service, was reacquired in the mid-1950s as *Taurus* (AK-273), later AKR-8, and served until stricken in the late 1960s). Of the 9 commissioned, 1 was loaned to Greece, 1 has been stricken, 1 to Spain, and 3 are in the permanent custody of MarAd. LSD-20 has been FRAMed. All have helicopter platforms. Decommissioning was as follows: at Bremerton, LSD-19 in 1/70; at Norfolk, LSD-20 on 12-23-70; at San Diego, LSD-16 in 1970. LSD-16 was transferred to the temporary custody of MarAd on 7-9-70 and LSD-20 followed on 4-27-71. *Fort Marion* (LSD-22), only ship of the *Fort Marion* class, and *Catamount* (LSD-17) have both been stricken.

1 DOCK LANDING SHIP, *"CASA GRANDE"* CLASS

Rushmore	LSD-14	7-3-44	MAR*

Originally a 7-ship class, all of the ships were for lend-lease to Britain. Four ships (LSD-9/12) were actually transferred to Britain and 3 were retained by USN for service. Two of the 3 retained are now decommissioned and in the permanent custody of MarAd. LSD-14 was decommissioned 9-30-70 at Norfolk and transferred to the temporary custody of MarAd on 2-10-71 for layup. Of the 8 *Ashland* class LSDs, 6 were stricken as LSDs, 1 was converted to an MCS and later stricken, and 1 is still on loan to Taiwan.

20 TANK LANDING SHIPS, *NEWPORT* CLASS

Name	Number	FY/SCB	Builder	Awarded	Commissioned	F/S
Bristol County	LST-1198	67/405.67	National Steel	7-15-66	8-5-72	PA
Barnstable County	LST-1197	67/405.67	National Steel	7-15-66	5-27-72	AA
Harlan County	LST-1196	67/405.67	National Steel	7-15-66	4-8-72	AA
Barbour County	LST-1195	67/405.67	National Steel	7-15-66	2-12-72	PA
La Moure County	LST-1194	67/405.67	National Steel	7-15-66	12-18-71	AA
Fairfax County	LST-1193	67/405.67	National Steel	7-15-66	10-16-71	AA
Spartanburg County	LST-1192	67/405.67	National Steel	7-15-66	9-1-71	AA
Racine	LST-1191	67/405.67	National Steel	7-15-66	7-9-71	PA
Boulder	LST-1190	67/405.67	National Steel	7-15-66	6-4-71	AA
San Bernadino	LST-1189	67/405.67	National Steel	7-15-66	3-27-71	PA
Saginaw	LST-1188	66/405.66	National Steel	7-15-66	1-23-71	AA
Tuscaloosa	LST-1187	66/405.66	National Steel	7-15-66	10-24-70	PA
Cayuga	LST-1186	66/405.66	National Steel	7-15-66	8-8-70	PA

Name	Number	FY/SCB	Builder	Awarded	Commissioned	F/S
Schenectady	LST-1185	66/405.66	National Steel	7-15-66	6-13-70	PA
Frederick	LST-1184	66/405.66	National Steel	7-15-66	4-11-70	PA
Peoria	LST-1183	66/405.66	National Steel	7-15-66	2-21-70	PA
Fresno	LST-1182	66/405.66	National Steel	7-15-66	11-22-69	PA
Sumter	LST-1181	66/405.66	Phil. Navy	12-29-65	6-20-70	AA
Manitowoc	LST-1180	66/405.66	Phil. Navy	12-29-65	1-24-70	AA
Newport	LST-1179	65/405.65	Phil. Navy	12-29-64	6-7-69	AA

These are the fastest and largest LSTs ever built. The new design is a radical departure from the old LST concept—features include a clipper bow, over-the-bow ramp vice bow doors, and a rounded bottom. The bow configuration is similar to that of ANL. Two derrick arms at the bow support a 40-ton, 112' aluminum bow ramp. When ramp is run out and lowered to beach, the uppermost portion of the bow splits and folds back. "Horns," boxlike superstructure, and staggered arrangement of stacks provides salient recognition features. The tank deck is connected to main deck by a hinged ramp, just forward of the bridge and aft of the bow ramp. Class has stern doors for discharging cargo into landing craft; "tunnel" in superstructure to facilitate passage of vehicles and cargo from stern to bow. Has helicopter deck but no hangar. A 30' turntable at each end of tank deck permits vehicles to turn around without having to shift into reverse. LST-1180 and 1181 were transferred from the Pacific to Atlantic on 1-15-73.

3 TANK LANDING SHIPS, "*DE SOTO COUNTY*" CLASS

Name	Number	Commissioned	F/S
Wood County	LST-1178	8-5-59	MAR*
Lorain County	LST-1177	10-3-58	MAR*
Suffolk County	LST-1173	8-15-57	AR*

This was the last LST class with traditional bow doors. Of the 8 in class, LST-1171 and 1175 were transferred to Italy, LST-1172 was cancelled, LST-1174 was transferred to Brazil, and LST-1176 now serves as an AGP (see Auxiliary Section). Decommissioning was as follows: at Norfolk: LST-1178 on 5-1-72; LST-1173 on 8-25-72; and LST-1177 on 9-1-72. LST-1178 was transferred to the temporary custody of Marad on 8-15-72. LST-1177 followed on 1-31-73.

2 TANK LANDING SHIPS, "*TERREBONNE PARISH*" class

Whitfield County	LST-1169	9-14-54	PR*
Terrell County	LST-1157	3-14-53	PR*

The ships are highly maneuverable; have controllable pitch-propellers. Originally there were 15 in class. Two were transferred to Turkey, 3 to Spain, and 1 to Venezuela. One was converted to MSS-2 (see Combatant Ships) and 6 were stricken and transferred to MarAd for layup

after short hitches as MSC cargo carriers. The transfer of remaining two ships to MSC was cancelled. LST-1157 is in poor material condition. LST-1157 decommissioned 3-25-71 at Bremerton and LST-1169 decommissioned 3-15-73 at Yokosuka, Japan (since towed to Bremerton for berthing). The last steam-powered LST, *Talbot County* (LST-1153), has been stricken.

12 TANK LANDING SHIPS, "*LST-511*" CLASS

Name	Number	Commissioned	F/S
Sedgewick County	LST-1123	2-19-45	PR*
[St. Clair County]	LST-1096	2-2-45	Stricken
unnamed	LST-1072	4-12-45	MSC
Orleans Parish	LST-1069	3-31-45	MSC
[Meeker County]	LST-980	2-26-44	Stricken
[Litchfield County]	LST-901	1-11-45	Stricken
[Kemper County]	LST-854	12-14-44	Stricken
[Henry County]	LST-824	11-30-44	Stricken
Harris County	LST-822	11-23-44	MSC
[Hampshire County]	LST-819	11-14-44	Stricken
[Floyd County]	LST-762	9-5-44	Stricken
Duval County	LST-758	8-19-44	MAR*
Daviess County	LST-692	5-10-44	MSC
unnamed	LST-649	10-26-44	MSC
unnamed	LST-629	7-28-44	MSC
unnamed	LST-623	6-21-44	MSC
unnamed	LST-613	5-19-44	MSC
unnamed	LST-607	4-24-44	MSC
unnamed	LST-579	7-21-44	MSC

All LSTs were originally unnamed. Those on NVR and not assigned to MSC (formerly MSTS) were named on 7-1-55. LSTs serving with MSC are unarmed, noncommissioned, and civilian manned. LSTs have served in a variety of roles such as ARL/ARB/ARVE/ARVA and APB. LST-1069 served a hitch as MCS-6 before reverting to her original hull number. Six of the LSTs reactivated for the Vietnam War were converted to AGPs although only 3 were actually classified as such (all 6 have been disposed of). Cargo boom and repair shops were added. LST-758 was transferred to the temporary custody of MarAd on 4-5-73 for layup. See Section 12 for LSTs transferred overseas since the 9th edition.

4 TANK LANDING SHIPS, "*LST-1*" CLASS

unnamed	LST-491	12-3-43	MSC
unnamed	LST-287	12-15-43	MSC
unnamed	LST-230	11-3-43	MSC
unnamed	LST-47	11-8-43	MSC

LST-1/488 were designated ATL in design stages. Differ from LST-511 class primarily in having an elevator from the tank deck to the upper deck vice a ramp in the LST-511 class.

Mount Whitney (LCC-20). Note that deck structures limit arc of gunfire. 11–70. **Blue Ridge** class.

Mount Whitney (LCC-20). 11–70. **Blue Ridge** class.

Pocono (LCC-16). Last WW II LCC still on the Navy List. **"Adirondack"** class.

Saipan (LHA-2) being outfitted at the builder's yard. 9–74. **Tarawa** class.

AMPHIBIOUS WARFARE SHIPS

Tarawa (LHA-1) launching ceremony. 12–73. **Tarawa** class.

Mobile (LKA-115). 8–71. **Charleston** class.

St. Louis (LKA-116). Note armament and landing craft. 1969. **Charleston** class.

AMPHIBIOUS WARFARE SHIPS

Tulare (LKA-112). **Tulare** class.

Vermilion (LKA-107). 8–70. **Rankin** class.

Merrick (LKA-97). **Winston** class.

Yancey (LKA-93). **"Uvalde"** class.

Francis Marion (LPA-249). 5–68. One of the last two LPAs in service. **Francis Marion** class.

Paul Revere (LPA-248). 1971. **Paul Revere** class.

Bexar (LPA-237). Only WW II LPA still on the Navy List. **"Haskell"** class.

Cleveland (LPD-7) with minesweeping helicopters aboard. 2–73. **Austin** class.

Shreveport (LPD-12). Note staggered funnels amidships and telescopic hangar. 11–70. **Austin** class.

Raleigh (LPD-1) with AV-8 HARRIER taking off. 4–71. **Raleigh** class.

Vancouver (LPD-2). 4–67. **Raleigh** class.

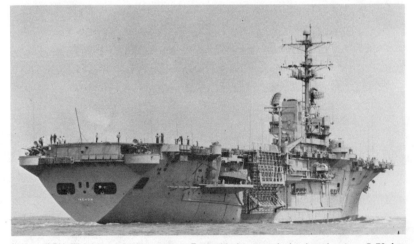

Inchon (LPH-12) with original armament. Each ship has two deck-edge elevators. 5–70. **Iwo Jima** class.

Iwo Jima (LPH-2). Note BPDMS launchers, one on port quarter and another forward of island. 1974. **Iwo Jima** class.

Balduck (LPR-132). **"Knudson"** class.

Begor (LPR-127). **"Laning"** class.

Grayback (SS-574). The two former REGULUS hangars were divided by the addition of a pressure bulkhead into wet and dry compartments, the former operating as a pressure lock. 12–69. **Grayback** class.

AMPHIBIOUS WARFARE SHIPS

Sealion (LPSS-315). Retained as LPSS due to cancellation of conversion of *Growler* (SSG-577). **"Perch"** class.

Portland (LSD-37). **Anchorage** class. 1970. (Photo: General Dynamics.)

Pensacola (LSD-38). Note tripod mast of this class. **Anchorage** class. 2–71. (Photo: General Dynamics.)

Hermitage (LSD-34). 1966. **Thomaston** class.

AMPHIBIOUS WARFARE SHIPS

Comstock (LSD-19). One of the few remaining WW II LSDs. **Cabildo** class.

Rushmore (LSD-14). Oldest LSD on the Navy List. **"Casa Grande"** class.

Spartanburg County (LST-1192). New design meets 20-knot amphibious lift requirement. 8–71. **Newport** class.

AMPHIBIOUS WARFARE SHIPS

Barbour County (LST-1195). Funnels are different sizes and staggered. 1972. **Newport** class.

Whitfield County (LST-1169). 5–70. **"Terrebonne Parish"** class.

Unnamed LST-1072 in MSC configuration.

Wood County (LST-1178) refueling the ill-fated Tucumcari (PGH-2). **"De Soto County"** class.

Blanco County (LST-344). Since disposed of. She was the last of this class in regular USN service. Four surviving sisters remain in MSC.

THREE: MINE WARFARE SHIPS

At the end of FY 1975, there were 46 mine warfare vessels on the NVR. Total breakdown: 9 MSCs and 37 MSOs. Active: 3 MSOs. Reserve: 12 MSOs. In addition 9 MSCs and 22 MSOs were assigned to Naval Reserve training duties. There are no plans to construct additional mine warfare ships. There are no surface minelayers or mine countermeasures support ships on the NVR. The currently favored procedure is to sweep with helicopter-towed sleds. This is a comparatively new development, but it is limited to fairly deep water.

Class	Number	No. in Class	Full Load Displ.	Length Overall	Max. Draft	Extreme Beam	Number & Type of Boilers/Engines	Screws/ SHP	Max. Speed (Kts.)	Accommodations		Armament
										Officers	Enlisted	
"Redwing"	MSC-200	7	412	145'	12'	28'	2D(G.M.)	2/880	12.8	5	35	1 twin 20mm mt.(MSC-201,203,204,207)
"Falcon"	MSC-190	2	363	144'3"	10'	28'	2D(Packard)	2/1,200	13.6	4	35	1 twin 20mm mt.(MSC-199)
Acme	MSO-508	4	750	173'	14'	36'	2D(Packard)	2/2,280	14.9	8	70	1 twin 20mm mt.
Dash	MSO-428	4	775	172'	14'	36'	2D(G.M.)	2/1,520	14	8	70	1 single 40mm mt.
Aggressive	MSO-422	28	775	172'	13'	35'	4D(Packard)	2/2,280	14	5	69	1 single 40mm mt.(MSO-437, 459, 461, 462, 464, 471, 494/496) 1 twin 20mm mt. (MSO-427, 439, 458, 464, 489, 492), 1 .50 cal. machine gun (remainder)
Agile	MSO-421	1	755	172'	13'	35'	4D(Packard)	2/3,040	14	8	70	1 single 40mm mt.

Mine Countermeasures Support Ships (MCS) The last of the mine countermeasures support ships, *Ozark* (MSC-2), was transferred to the permanent custody of MarAd on 9-1-71 for layup.

Minelayers (MMF and MMD) With the disposal of the fleet minelayer *Terror* and the 10 surviving ships of the *Robert H. Smith* class fast minelayers, the USN has no surface ship with the capability to lay mines.

7 COASTAL MINESWEEPERS, "REDWING" CLASS

Name	Number	Commissioned	F/S
Woodpecker	MSC-209	2-3-56	NRT
Whippoorwill	MSC-207	10-20-55	NRT
Warbler	MSC-206	7-23-55	NRT
Vireo	MSC-205	6-7-55	NRT
Thrush	MSC-204	11-8-55	NRT
Thrasher	MSC-203	8-16-55	NRT
Shrike	MSC-201	3-21-55	NRT

Originally there were 10 ships in this class. Class leader and MSC-202 were transferred to Spain and another was disposed of. See NRT section for individual NRT assignments. Six MSCs of the MSC-294 class. MSC-320/325, are under construction. MSC-320/321 are being built for South Korea, and MSC-322/325 are being built for Saudi Arabia. Remainder of *Redwing* and *Falcon* class MSCs will be disposed of in FY 1976.

2 COASTAL MINESWEEPERS, "FALCON" CLASS

Name	Number	Commissioned	F/S
Phoebe	MSC-199	4-29-55	NRT
Peacock	MSC-198	3-16-55	NRT

Basically, *Redwing* and this class are the same; see statistics table. Originally there were 10 in class. Six were loaned to Indonesia and 2 were stricken (MSC-194 as result of collision).

Fleet Minesweepers (MSF) All 29 MSFs listed in the 9th edition have been stricken and disposed of as follows: *Auk* class (25), 20 were sold to Mexico, 1 became a salvage training hulk, and 4 were scrapped; *Admirable* class (4), 1 transferred to Mexico and 3 scrapped.

4 OCEAN MINESWEEPERS, *ACME* CLASS

Name	Number	Commissioned	F/S
Affray	MSO-511	12–8–58	NRT
Advance	MSO-510	6–16–58	PR*
Adroit	MSO-509	3–4–57	NRT
Acme	MSO-508	9–27–56	PR*

Fitted as flagships. These ships have wooden hulls and stainless steel engines. MSO numbers not listed have been stricken, transferred under ILP, or cancelled. MSO-510 decommissioned 12–23–70 and MSO-508 11–6–70, both at San Diego. Of the 3 *Ability* class MSOs, the class leader was stricken and the 2 survivors serve as AGs (see Auxiliary Section).

4 OCEAN MINESWEEPERS, *DASH* CLASS

Dominant	MSO-431	11–8–54	NRT
Direct	MSO-430	7–9–54	NRT
Detector	MSO-429	1–26–54	NRT
Dash	MSO-428	8–14–53	NRT

Originally all MSOs were classified as AMs. All were reclassified on 2–7–55.

28 OCEAN MINESWEEPERS, "*AGGRESSIVE*" CLASS

Venture	MSO-496	2–3–58	AR*
Swerve	MSO-495	7–27–57	AR*
Sturdy	MSO-494	10–23–57	AR*
Pledge	MSO-492	4–20–56	NRT
Leader	MSO-490	11–16–55	AA
Gallant	MSO-489	9–14–55	NRT
Conquest	MSO-488	7–20–55	NRT
Vital	MSO-474	6–9–55	AR*
Skill	MSO-471	11–7–55	AR*
Pluck	MSO-464	8–11–54	NRT
Pinnacle	MSO-462	10–21–55	AR*
Observer	MSO-461	8–31–55	AR*
Nimble	MSO-459	5–11–55	AR*
Lucid	MSO-458	5–4–55	PR*
Inflict	MSO-456	5–11–54	NRT
Implicit	MSO-455	3–10–54	NRT
Impervious	MSO-449	7–15–54	NRT

Name	Number	Commissioned	F/S
Illusive	MSO-448	11–14–53	PA
Fortify	MSO-446	7–16–54	NRT
Fidelity	MSO-443	1–19–55	AA
Fearless	MSO-442	9–22–54	NRT
Exultant	MSO-441	6–22–54	NRT
Exploit	MSO-440	3–31–54	NRT
Excel	MSO-439	2–24–55	NRT
Esteem	MSO-438	9–10–55	NRT
Enhance	MSO-437	4–16–55	NRT
Engage	MSO-433	6–29–54	NRT
Constant	MSO-427	9–8–54	NRT

This is the largest class of MSOs. Built to replace the MSFs which were useless in sweeping magnetic mines. All were built in private yards. MSO-433 was originally named *Elusive*, renamed 3–6–53 to avoid confusion with MSO-448. At least a half dozen of the ships have caught fire. All were lost except MSO-437, 439, and 441. MSO-437 caught fire on 1–6–75 20 miles southwest of San Diego when diesel fuel was ignited by the ship's overheated engines. MSO-439 caught fire 11–13–73 while moored at San Francisco. The wardroom area was destroyed. Sabotage suspected. MSO-441 caught fire after an internal explosion 8–12–60 while sailing off the coast of Georgia. Originally there were 53 ships in the class. Twelve were transferred overseas, 1 was scrapped after grounding, 3 were disposed of due to irreparable damage from fires, and the remainder were scrapped (5 during modernization). Because of the new helicopter minesweeping methods, all MSOs are being laid up or assigned to NRT. Decommissioned at Charleston: MSO-459 on 11–24–70; MSO-461 on 7–28–72; MSO-462 on 11–24–70; MSO-471 on 12–15–70; MSO-474 on 9–22–72; MSO-494, 495 on 7–1–71; MSO-496 on 8–2–71. At San Diego: MSO-458 on 12-23-70. At Long Beach: MSO-434 on 9–22–72. MSO-434 and 467 were assigned to NRT before layup. MSO-438 was originally assigned to NRT on 11–1–72 and MSO-488 on 9–1–72. Both were activated on 1–27–73 for the sweeping of North Vietnam waters and deployed overseas. They reverted to NRT 8–31–73 upon completion of Operation "End Sweep." As a result of the mining of North Vietnamese waters in early 5/72, dispositions, layups, and NRT assignments of several MSOs were cancelled. All status changes for MSOs were reapproved 5–31–72. MSO-443 serves as evaluation and test ship for the Naval Coastal Systems Laboratory.

1 OCEAN MINESWEEPER, *AGILE* CLASS

Agile	MSO-421	6–21–56	AR*

Agile is the only ship of this class. 36 MSOs were transferred overseas without serving in USN. MSO-421 was decommissioned 7–28–72 at Charleston.

OCEAN MINESWEEPER MODERNIZATIONS

Number	FY/SCB	Converted at	Awarded	Started	Completed
MSO-490	69/502	Harbor Boat Building	6–30–70	11–30–70	1–31–72
MSO-488	69/502	Harbor Boat Building	6–30–70	10–30–70	9–30–71
MSO-456	68/502	Dillingham	5–15–68	11–30–68	2–10–70
MSO-449	68/502	Dillingham	5–15–68	11–30–68	12–4–70
MSO-448	69/502	Harbor Boat Building	6–30–70	11–30–70	2–14–72
MSO-446	68/502	Dillingham	5–15–68	10–31–68	9–28–70
MSO-445	68/502	Dillingham	5–15–68	12–31–68	4–7–71

Number	FY/SCB	Converted At	Awarded	Started	Completed
MSO-443	68/502	Beth., Baltimore	5–7–68	9–30–68	12–9–70
MSO-442	68/502	Beth., Baltimore	5–7–68	9–30–68	10–19–70
MSO-441	68/502	Beth., Baltimore	5–7–68	8–31–68	6–8–70
MSO-438	69/502	Harbor Boat Building	6–30–70	9–30–70	8–13–71
MSO-437	69/502	Harbor Boat Building	6–30–70	10–30–70	11–22–71
MSO-433	68/502	Dillingham	5–15–68	10–31–68	8–14–70

Originally all MSOs in commission in the mid-1960s were to be modernized. However, only 19 MSOs actually started modernization. The modernization of MSO-460, 468, 470, 472, and 519 was cancelled on 10–16–70 and the hulks were disposed of. *Avenge* (MSO-423) caught fire on 10–6–69 while undergoing modernization at Bethlehem Steel. She was so badly damaged that she was stricken on 2–1–70 and disposed of. Another ship, MSO-445, caught fire at sea on 4–24–73 enroute to Guam from Subic Bay and sank. Fire was blamed on negligence. Only 12 modernized units survive. The entire modernization of the MSOs was

cancelled when the emphasis switched to minesweeping helos. MSO-433, 441/443, 445/446, 449, and 456 remained In Commission, Special, during modernization. Other ships decommissioned/recommissioned as follows: MSO-437 on 10–29–70/12–10–71, MSO-438 on 9–29–70/ 8–27–71, MSO-448 on 11–29–70/3–2–72, MSO-488 on 10–29–70/10–21–71, and MSO-490 on 11–29–70/2–11–72. *Force* (MSO-445) replaced *Loyalty* (MSO-457) in program. Modernization included replacement or refurbishment of all machinery, piping, degaussing gear, electrical systems, and improvement of habitability.

Woodpecker (MSC-209). All remaining MSCs serve as Reserve Training vessels. **"Redwing"** class.

Peacock (MSC-198). **"Falcon"** class.

MINE WARFARE SHIPS

Affray (MSO-511). **Acme** class.

Fidelity (MSO-443) following modernization. 12–70. **"Aggressive"** class.

Direct (MSO-430). Except for engines, same as unmodernized **"Aggressive"** class. **Dash** class.

Lucid (MSO-458). 1968. **"Aggressive"** class.

MINE WARFARE SHIPS

FOUR: COMBATANT CRAFT

At the end of FY 1975, there were 19 combatant craft of all types in service. Combatant craft are not on the NVR. Of the 19 craft, there were 17 PTFs, 1 PCH, and 1 PGH. Active: 1 PCH and 1 PGH. All of the 17 PTFs were assigned to Naval Reserve training duties. In addition to the aforementioned craft, the term "combatant craft" also includes landing craft, mine countermeasures craft, and riverine warfare craft. Since the previously mentioned three types of craft are small, the characteristics table that follows only gives statistical data on the major combatant craft. Brief summaries of the other craft are given in parts B through D.

Class	Number	No. in Class	Full Load Displ.	Length Overall	Max. Draft	Extreme Beam	Number Type of Engines	Foils or Screws/ SHP	Max. Speed (Kts.)	Accommodations Officers	Accommodations Enlisted	Armament
High Point	PCH-1	1	110	116'	6'	32'	(2)Gas Turbines(Proteus)/ (2)Diesels(Packard)	4/6,200	45	1	12	2 .50 cal. mg., 2 twin Mk 32 ASW torpedo tubes
Flagstaff	PGH-1	1	57	74'4"	14'	22'	(1)Gas Turbine(Rolls-Royce)	1/3,620	40	1	10	Removed
"*Osprey*"	PTF-23	4	89	96'	7'	23'2"	2D(N.D.)	2/6,200	38	4	12	1 single 40mm mt., 2 single 20mm mt., 1 .50 cal. mg./81mm mortar
"*Trumpy*"	PTF-17	6	84	80'5"	8'	24'7"	2D(N.D.)	2/6,200	40	3	16	1 single 40mm mt., 2 single 20mm mt., 1 .50 cal. mg./81mm mortar
"*Nasty*"	PTF-3	7	80	80'4"	6'7"	24'7"	2D(N.D.)	2/6,200	38	4	16	1 single 40mm mt., 2 single 20mm mt., 1 .50 cal. mg./81mm mortar

A. PATROL CRAFT
1 PATROL CRAFT (Hydrofoil), "*HIGH POINT*" CLASS

Name	Number	FY/SCB	Builder	Awarded	In Service	F/S
High Point	PCH-1	60/202	Boeing, Seattle	6–14–60	8–15–63	PSA

Rated as experimental, she is built entirely of aluminum except for high-yield steel foils and struts. Hull-borne, she is powered by a 600 BHP diesel that produces a speed of 12 knots. From 8–9–71 to 7/73, *High Point* underwent a conversion at Puget Sound Naval Shipyard to serve as operational test and evaluation platform for the HARPOON missile system. She received a new control system, struts, modified foils, and a steerable strut forward. The craft is fitted with a HARPOON quadruple cannister launcher on the centerline aft of the superstructure. Two of these launchers, with associated gear, and the missile system will be fitted on each of the *Pegasus* class PHMs. Temporarily loaned to Coast Guard 3/75 for operational testing.

1 PATROL GUNBOAT (Hydrofoil), *FLAGSTAFF* CLASS

Name	Number	FY/SCB	Builder	Awarded	In Service	F/S
Flagstaff	PGH-1	66/252	Grumman	4–28–66	9–14–68	PSA

Flagstaff, of aluminum construction, is powered by a controllable pitch propeller driven by a geared transmission system. The main lifting surface is forward. She saw service in Vietnam. During 1971 she was armed with a 152mm cannon of the type used in the Army's *Sheridan* armored reconnaissance vehicle. Removed after firing trials. Hull-borne, the craft is powered by two diesels that propel a water jet system. Temporarily loaned to the Coast Guard 11-1-74 to 12–20–74 for operational testing as USCG *Flagstaff* (WPBH-1). Her near sister *Tucumcari* (PGH-2) ran aground on 11–16–72 and was damaged beyond economical repair. She was taken out of service on 11–7–73 and her hulk transferred to Naval Research and Development Laboratory, Annapolis, for tests.

4 FAST PATROL CRAFT, "OSPREY" CLASS

Number	In Service	F/S
PTF-26	4-8-68	NRT
PTF-25	4-8-68	NRT
PTF-24	3-13-68	NRT
PTF-23	3-13-68	NRT

Built by Sewart Seacraft, these craft were a commercial design that didn't quite work out. Aluminum hulls. PTFs were originally on the NVR. They were reclassified "boats" on 9-23-70 and dropped from the NVR as a result of the reclassification. After service in Vietnam, all PTFs were assigned to NRT. An attempt is being made to keep the lessons learned in riverine warfare alive by keeping a nucleus riverine force as part of the Naval Reserve Force (see Section 7). As part of the nucleus force, all PTFs and several dozen riverine craft were assigned to NRT.

6 FAST PATROL CRAFT, "TRUMPY" CLASS

PTF-22	9-23-70	NRT
PTF-21	9-23-70	NRT
PTF-20	10-5-68	NRT
PTF-19	10-5-68	NRT
PTF-18	7-1-68	NRT
PTF-17	7-1-68	NRT

Built by John Trumpy and Sons, Annapolis, Maryland, this class duplicates PTF-3 class. The craft have double planked mahogany hulls. PTF-21/22 were in commission from 5-14-69 to 9-23-70.

7 FAST PATROL CRAFT, "NASTY" CLASS

PTF-12	7-7-65	NRT
PTF-11	7-7-65	NRT
PTF-10	4-22-65	NRT
PTF-7	3-1-64	NRT
PTF-6	3-1-64	NRT
PTF-5	3-1-64	NRT
PTF-3	1-1-63	NRT

These were built in Norway by Boatservice (PTF-3, 5/7) and Westermoen (remainder). Originally 14 in class, 1 was disposed of and 6 were sunk while on lease to the South Vietnamese Navy. PTF-3, 5/7 were leased to Vietnam 1-26-65 and returned to USN in 1970 where they were returned to service. Hulls of the 14 units in class were completed in Norway and shipped to U.S. for outfitting. PTF-1/2 (Ex PT-810 and 811) were stricken in 1965 and sunk as targets.

High Point (PCH-1) launching HARPOON missile. **High Point** class. 1973. (Photo: McDonnell Douglas.)

Flagstaff (PGH-1). **Flagstaff** class.

COMBATANT CRAFT

Flagstaff (PGH-1) in Coast Guard markings. On loan from 11–1–74 to 12–20–74 to USCG. Mission included evaluation of hydrofoils for search and rescue, enforcement of laws and treaties, and port safety and security. While on loan, sustained considerable damage to rear struts in collision with whale. **Flagstaff** class.

Flagstaff (PGH-1) as USCGC WPBH-1. Note absence of armament. 1975. **Flagstaff** class.

PTF-23. **"Osprey"** class.

PTF-6. **"Nasty"** class.

B. LANDING CRAFT

Smaller landing craft types now have their own classification category in the Navy's ship-type nomenclature list under the general category of "Combatant Craft." With the exception of the LCUs, these craft have no hull numbers. However, with the exception of the LCUs, all other landing craft are assigned identification numbers for record keeping. Besides the types listed below, the Marines use a variety of landing vehicles, tracked (LVT), descendants of the "Alligators" of World War II.

AALC—Amphibious Assault Landing Craft. Four prototypes were completed in 1974/75 as competing designs. Two, known as AALC-JEFF(A) were built by Aerojet General Corporation and Tacoma Boatbuilding Company to one design, and the other two, completed to a different design and known as AALC-JEFF(B), were built by Bell Aerosystems Company. Essentially air cushion vehicles, both designs are fitted with ramps fore and aft for carrying vehicles. It is planned that these craft will replace such landing craft as the LCUs and smaller craft presently in the inventory. Both designs are powered by gas turbines and can carry up to 75 tons of cargo or equipment.

LCA—Fully tracked landing vehicle with 30-ton capacity. It is used to transfer supplies and equipment from ships to inland points without offloading at a beach.

LCM—56' LCM(6) developed in World War II and still manufactured. A versatile, useful craft, many were converted to riverine warfare craft. The 73'8" LCM(8) is a further development. Hundreds are used by the Army and Navy. The craft is transportable by LKA, LPD, and LSD.

LCPL—Original designation of the "Higgins Boat" of Guadalcanal fame. Current LCPLs are 36' launches used as landing guide and control craft. Many served as armed river/coastal patrol craft and gunboats in Vietnam.

LCPR—World War II ramped version of the original LCPL. This is one of the earliest landing types still in service and is used by reconnaissance swimmer teams.

LCU—Originally 2 marks of World War II tank landing craft, LCT (5) and LCT (6); these went through several postwar reclassifications before becoming LCU. They were classified as service craft until 8–14–68 when they became "boats." Some World War II built units survive. To date, 1,670 of these craft have been authorized (some were cancelled before being built). Modern versions of the extremely handy craft serve with USN and in many foreign navies. Sizes and armaments vary; some have experimental propulsion rigs. They are used to land tanks and heavy gear on beaches; were widely used in Vietnam. Unlike other small landing craft, LCUs have hull numbers. Approximately 80 LCUs were converted to YFUs and salvage craft. LCU-1667/1680 are under construction.

LCVP—Davit-launched; lands troops, small vehicles. One of the most successful, versatile landing craft. The craft is still built to the same World War II design, but with minor modifications. Early craft had plated plywood hulls, now they are reinforced plastic. Some craft were armed for Vietnam river operations.

LWT—Designed to salvage stranded landing craft and to beach and tend pontoon causeways and anchors. Early LWTs are pontoon craft fitted with powerful winch and A-frame and 2 outboard diesels. They first proved themselves on World War II invasion beaches. New type has greater speed and pulling capacity and can be transported by LST, LSD, or LPD.

AALC. Model of Aerojet-General JEFF(A). 1971.

AALC. Artist's concept of JEFF(B). (Photo: Textron's Bell Aerospace Division.)

COMBATANT CRAFT

AALC. JEFF(B) under construction. Scheduled for rollout early 1976. (Photo: Textron's Bell Aerospace Division.)

LCM(8). 1970.

LCPL. 1968.

LCU-1656. 1971.

C. MINE COUNTERMEASURES CRAFT

Like landing craft, small mine warfare types are now carried under "combatant craft" heading. The mine warfare force is always the first to suffer during peacetime, as it is now. Three of the mine warfare craft developed for the Vietnam War have been discarded. These are the drone minesweeper, small (MSD), the river minesweeper (MSM) and the patrol minesweepers (MSR). Except for the MSS-1, none of the mine countermeasures craft are on the NVR.

MHA—Classification established for civilian craft that might be acquired on mobilization. They would be fitted with sonar capability for emergency use.

MSA—Like MHAs, this symbol would apply to mobilized ex-civilian craft equipped with minimum minesweeping capability.

MSB—Originally designed as assault sweepers to be carried on parent ships. As built, they were too heavy for boom handling; used since in harbors and channels. Many were used in Vietnam (4 were either sunk or disposed of as a result of war damage). They are transportable by large ships, but must be loaded and off-loaded by heavy cranes. The craft require shore base or MCS support. Of the 16 craft still in use by the Navy, all are 57'2" long except MSB-29 which is 82' long. All MSBs were rated as service craft until 8–14–68 when they were rerated as combatant craft. All are active and based at Charleston, South Carolina.

MSI—111' nonmagnetic mine craft. Originally designed as smaller replacement for MSCs, the MSI is slowly being phased out of service. The first two craft, *Cove* (MSI-1) and *Cape* (MSI-2), were built during 1958/59. Originally the hull numbers MSI-1/54 were allotted to the USN, and MSI-55/101 to ILP. However, after construction of the first two, it was decided not to build any more MSIs for the USN. Subsequently, MSI-3/18 were built and transferred under ILP. The hull numbers MSI-19/54 are unused at this time. MSI-1/2 have 1 screw, the remainder 2. MSI-3/18, 55/101 have 50 percent more power. MSI-1/2 served with NRT from November 1969 to 1 July 1970 when both were replaced by *Embattle* (MSO-434). MSI-1 was transferred on loan to Johns Hopkins University, Silver Springs, Maryland, on 7–31–70 for service as a research ship. MSI-2 was transferred to the Naval Undersea Center, San Diego, California, on 9–25–70 as the R/V *Cape* for service as a research ship. She is civilian manned but under USN operational control. She is neither "In service" nor in commission.

MSL—36' assault sweeping craft, with moored/magnetic/acoustic capability. *Catskill* (MCS-1) and *Ozark* (MCS-2) carried 20 of these craft when they were active. Newest Mark MSL has diesel engine and plastic hull. Sixteen of these craft are still in operation, all based at Charleston, South Carolina.

MSS—Rated as Minesweeper, Special (Device). To date there have been 2 MSSs. MSS-1 is the ex-Liberty ship SS *Harry L. Glucksman* (ex-MCE-2445). Completed in 1943, She was built as an EC2-S-C1 Maritime hull design. Conversion included removal of all internal machinery, piping, shafting, etc. The hull was strengthened, and a shock-mounted pilot house was installed forward. The ship can withstand mine explosions without sinking. She was acquired from MarAd in summer of 1966. Conversion authorized under FY 1966 (SCB-500), and awarded to American Shipbuilding Company, Lorain, Ohio, on 8–30–66. The conversion was completed on 6–16–69 and she was placed in service on the same date. Her crew consisted of 1 officer and 8 enlisted men. She was placed "in reserve, out of service" on 3–15–73 at Charleston and is currently berthed at Philadelphia. MSS-2 was originally *Washtenaw County* (LST-1166) of the *Terrebonne Parish* class LSTs. She was reclassified MSS-2 on 2–9–73 and her name was cancelled on the same date. Conversion was austere, primarily consisting of filling the tank deck with styrofoam to prevent her sinking and the mounting of

shock absorbers. She was specifically converted for participating in the sweeping of mines from North Vietnamese waters. Called "Operation End Sweep." After a channel or area was swept, MSS-2's mission was to sail through the area to see if any mines were left and either detonate them with her hull or mark them for sweeping. She was decommissioned as LST and placed in service as MSS-2 on 2–9–73. Upon completion of the operation, she was placed out of service on 8–30–73 and stricken on the same date.

MSB-17. 1966.

MSL-18. 1968.

MSS-1. Side pods contain propulsion units. 4–69.

D. RIVERINE WARFARE CRAFT

As a result of the riverine craft's successes in Vietnam, it was decided to keep a nucleus riverine warfare force active. The force consists of less than 100 riverine craft, most, if not all, being assigned to two coastal river squadrons and three coastal river divisions based at San Francisco, San Diego, New Orleans, Little Creek, and Great Lakes, Illinois. (See Section 7 for further data on NRT assignments). Existing riverine warfare craft are listed below.

ASPB—Construction of these craft resulted from Vietnamese war requirements. They were built in two MKs with welded steel hulls; they were used to escort other USN riverine craft and to interdict enemy shipping. They have provisions to handle shallow draft minesweeping gear. The ASPBs are faster than Monitors (MON), but similarly armed.

ATC—Two versions. The regular ATCs were converted from LCM (6) landing craft to carry troops and other equipment for logistic support. They can carry a maximum of 40 troops or a 105mm howitzer and its prime mover. They are heavily armored. There is also the "mini" ATC which is used for riverine and swimmer delivery operations. It has an aluminum hull, is unarmed, and is 36′ long as compared to 65′5″ length of the regular ATCs. One "mini" ATC is powered by gas turbines, the remainder by diesels.

CCB—Converted from LCM (6) landing craft. They are miniature versions of *Northampton* (CC-1) and *Wright* (CC-2) and are heavily armored. The CCB carries between 11 and 15 command staff and is used mainly by boat group commanders.

MON—Converted from LCM (6) landing craft, they are designed to provide direct and indirect fire support to forces ashore and to serve as security guard for afloat or ashore boat bases. They are heavily armored. Of the 2 MONs still in the USN, one is armed with 105mm howitzer and the other with two Army M-10-8 flame throwers (main armament of the 2 craft).

PBR—Built to 2 MKs. The first 160 boats are MK I and the remainder MK II. They were adopted from commercial design and are excellent craft for shallow water operations. All MK I PBRs were built by United Boat Builders, Bellingham, Washington. Statistics and characteristics of both MKs vary. A couple of hundred were transferred to Vietnam.

PCF—These are the famous "Swift" Boats. They were adopted from commercial, all-metal boats that support off-shore drilling rigs. The first 104 boats are MK I, remainder MK II. All have basically the same characteristics, but configuration varies. Less than twelve of the MK I and II series remain in USN. Majority of those built were transferred to Vietnam. Others were transferred to countries in Southeast Asia, Latin America, etc.

Note: There are several new types of riverine craft under development, one of which is the CPIC, a 99′, 45-kt. gunboat that is armed with a twin 30mm gun mount and a very reliable new fire control system. Only one has been completed and will be transferred to South Korea after testing by the U.S. Navy. There is also a MK I PB and a MK III PB; both are 65′ long. Both Iran and the Philippines have ordered approximately 40 craft of the MK III PB for their navies. Two MK I PBs were delivered to the U.S. Navy in 1973 for test and evaluation. U.S. Navy procurement of the CPIC (to succeed the PTF), the MK III PB and additional units of the MK I PB are under consideration.

ASPB MARK II.

ASPB MARK I.

ATC. Note blunt bow. 1967.

CCB. Note modification to traditional LCM bow; note minesweeping gear aft. 1967.

COMBATANT CRAFT

Monitor. Similar to CCB except for antenna array and small shelter abaft forward gun.

PBR MARK II. 1969.

PBR MARK II unit of COASTAL RIVER SQUADRON TWO, Little Creek, Virginia. 12–73.

PCF MARK I. 2–69.

PCF MARK II. 12–73.

COMBATANT CRAFT

FIVE: AUXILIARY SHIPS

By the end of FY 1975, there were 255 auxiliaries on the NVR. Of the total 122 were active, 20 were in reserve, 19 were in the temporary custody of MarAd, 65 were assigned to MSC and 14 were on loan/charter to government/non-government agencies. In addition, 15 auxiliaries were under construction.

Class	Number	No. in Class	Full Load Displ.	Length Overall	Max. Draft	Extreme Beam	Number and Type of Boilers/Engines	Screws/ SHP	Max. Speed (Kts.)	Accommodations Officers	Accommodations Enlisted	Armament
Samuel Gompers	AD-37	5	20,700	645'	23'	85'	2B(C.E.)/1GT(DeLaval)	1/20,000	18	135	1,668	1 single 5"/38 cal. mt., 2 40mm saluting guns
Shenandoah	AD-26	2	14,700	492'	28'	70'	2B(F.W.)/2GT(West.)	1/8,500	18	45	780	1 single 5"/38 cal. mt.(AD-36), 2 40mm saluting guns (AD-26), 4 single 20mm mts.
"Klondike"	AD-22	1	15,337	492'	27'	70'	2B(B&W)/2GT(G.E.)	1/8,500	18	80	819	2 single 3"/50 cal. mts., 2 40mm saluting guns
Dixie	AD-14	5	18,000	530'6"	26'	73'3"	4B(B&W)/2GT(Parsons)	2/11,000	18.2	60	1,011	1 single 5"/38 cal. mt., (except AD-14; None), 2 40mm saluting mts., 4 single 20mm mts.
Kilauea	AE-26	8	19,937	564'	28'	81'	3B(F.W.)/2GT(G.E.)	1/22,000	20	38	373	4 twin 3"/50 cal. mts.
Nitro	AE-23	3	17,500	512'	29'	72'	2B(C.E.)/2GT(Beth.)	1/16,000	20.6	20	330	2 twin 3"/50 cal. mts.
Suribachi	AE-21	2	17,400	512'	29'	72'	2B(C.E.)/2GT(Beth.)	1/16,000	18	16	370	2 twin 3"/50 cal. mts.
"Mount Hood"	AE-11	2	15,277	459'	28'	63'	2B(C.E.)/1GT(G.E.)	1/6,000	15	20	270	4 single 3"/50 cal. mts.(AE-12), 2 single 3"/50 cal. mts. (AE-14)
Rigel	AF-58	2	15,500	502'	29'	72'	2B(C.E.)/1GT(G.E.)	1/16,000	20	22	330	2 twin 3"/50 cal. mts.
Denebola	AF-56	1	11,948	455'	23'9"	62'	2B(C.E.)/1GT(West.)	1/8,500	18.3	18	286	None
Aludra	AF-55	1	12,891	459'	26'4"	65'	2B(B&W)/1GT(G.E.)	1/6,000	15.6	20	277	4 twin 3"/50 cal. mts.
"Bald Eagle"	AF-50	1	13,860	459'	26'	63'	2B(F.W.)/1GT(G.E.)	1/6,000	16	18	46	3 twin 40mm mts.
"Alstede"	AF-48	2	13,860	459'	28'5"	63'	2B(B&W)/1GT(G.E.)	1/6,000	16.5	21	243	2 twin 40mm mts.
Mars	AFS-1	7	16,263	581'	24'	79'	3B(B&W)/1GT(DeLaval)	1/22,000	20	34	441	4 twin 3"/50 cal. mts.
Alacrity	AG-520	2	934	191'	12'	36'1"	2D(G.M.)	2/2,700	15	8	75	none
S. P. Lee	AG-192	1	1,297	208'	14'	39'	2D	1/1,200	15	9	17	none
Flyer	AG-178	1	11,000	459'	26'	63'	2B/1GT	1/6,000	17	14	41	none
Kingsport	AG-164	1	11,100	455'	22'	62'	2B(B&W)/1GT(West.)	1/8,500	17	19	108	none
Compass Island	AG-153	2	16,076	563'7"	31'	76'	2B(F.W.)/1GT(G.E.)	1/19,250	20	35	384	4 single 20mm mts. (AG-153)
Sequoia	AG-23	1	120	105'	5'	21'	2D(Winton)	1/400	12	7 total		none
Point Loma	AGDS-2	1	14,000	492'	22'	78'	2B(F.W.)/2GT(West.)	2/6,000	15	10	164	none
Plainview	AGEH-1	1	320	212'	25'	40'	2D(Detroit)/2 Gas Turbines (General Electric)	2/28,000	50	4	20	2 MK 32 triple torpedo tube mts.
"Banner"	AGER-1	1	700	180'	8'5"	33'	2D(G.M.)	1/1,000	12	7	75	3 single .50 cal. mg.
La Salle	AGF-3	1	13,900	521'9"	23'	104'	2B(B&W)/2ST(DeLaval)	2/24,000	20	135	1,475	4 twin 3"/50 cal. mts.
Glover	AGFF-1	1	3,575	415'	24'5"	44'	2B(F.W.)/1GT(West.)	1/35,000	27	17	231	1 single 5"/38 cal. mt., 1 ASROC, 2 MK 32 triple torpedo tube mts.
Range Sentinel	AGM-22	1	11,800	456'	23'	63'	2B(C.E.)/1GT(West.)	1/8,500	18	27	94	none
Vanguard	AGM-19	2	24,710	595'	25'	75'	2B(B&W)/1GT(G.E.)	1/8,700	15	21	68	none
General H. H. Arnold	AGM-9	2	14,300	522'11"	25'	72'	2B(B&W)/1GT(West.)	1/9,000	14	88	105	none
"Range Tracker"	AGM-1	1	15,200	455'	28'6"	62'	2B(C.E.)/1GT(West.)	1/8,500	17	14	76	none
Arlington	AGMR-2	1	19,800	684'	28'	109'	4B(B&W)/4GT(G.E.)	4/120,000	32.5	50	989	4 twin 3"/50 cal. mts.

Class	Number	No. in Class	Full Load Displ.	Length Overall	Max. Draft	Extreme Beam	Number and Type of Boilers/Engines	Screws/ SHP	Max. Speed (Kts.)	Accommodations Officers	Accommodations Enlisted	Armament
Annapolis	AGMR-1	1	23,850	557'	30'7"	104'	4B(C.E.)/2GT(A.C.)	2/16,000	19	48	700	4 twin 3"/50 cal. mts.
Gyre	AGOR-21	2	950	176'	14'6"	36'	2D(Caterpillar)	2/1,700	12	21 total		none
Chain	AGOR-17	1	1,970	213'6"	15'	41'	2D(C.B.)	2/2,440	14	10	84	none
Hayes	AGOR-16	1	3,080	246'5"	18'8"	75'	2D(G.M.)	2/5,400	15	11	33	none
"Eltanin"	AGOR-8	1	3,886	266'	19'	52'	2D(Alco)	2/2,700	12	14	34	none
Robert D. Conrad	AGOR-3	9	1,370	209'	15'3"	37'6"	2D(CTC)	1/10,000	13	9	17	none
Graham County	AGP-1176	1	7,100	445'	18'	62'	2D(Nordberg)	2/13,700	16.5	35	601	3 twin 3"/50 cal. mts.
Wilkes	AGS-33	2	2,540	283'	15'	48'	2D(G.E.)	1/3,000	15	12	29	none
Chauvenet	AGS-29	2	3,800	393'	15'	54'	2D(Alco)	1/3,400	15	24	131	none
Silas Bent	AGS-26	2	2,580	285'	15'	48'	2D(West.)	1/3,000	15	12	32	none
Bowditch	AGS-21	2	13,050	455'	27'6"	62'	2B(C.E.)/1GT(West.)	1/9,350	17	14	47	none
Albacore	AGSS-569	1	1,500[1]	200'	22'	27'	2D(G.M.)/1EM(West.)	1/15,000	12[2]	5	47	none
Tang	AGSS-563	1	2,122	277'	19'	27'1"	3D(F.M.)/2EM(Ell.)	2/3,200	15.5	8	75	6 21" TT fwd., 2 21" TT aft.
Dolphin	AGSS-555	1	846	152'	18'	19'5"	2D(Detroit)/1EM(Ell.)	1/1,650	15	5	15	none
"Haven"	AH-12	1	14,892	520'	26'	72'	2B(B&W)/1GT(G.E.)	1/9,000	18.3	147	1,256	none
Wyandot	AK-283	1	14,000	459'2"	26'3"	63'	2B(C.E.)/1GT(G.E.)	1/6,000	16.5	38	385	none
Norwalk	AK-279	4	11,300	455'	22'	62'	2B(B&W)/1GT(G.E.)	1/8,500	16.5	18	71	none
Schuyler Otis Bland	AK-277	1	15,910	454'	27'	66'	2B(F.W.)/1GT(G.E.)	1/13,750	18.5			none
Lt. James E. Robinson	AK-274	1	15,199	455'	29'	62'	2B(C.E.)/1GT(West.)	1/8,500	18	15	40	none
"Eltanin"	AK-270	1	4,942	262'2"	18'7"	51'5"	2D(Alco)	2/3,200	13	14	34	none
Marine Fiddler	AK-267	1	22,094	520'	33'	72'	2B(B&W)/1GT(West.)	1/9,000	15.8	14	43	none
Pvt. Leonard C. Brostrom	AK-255	1	22,056	520'	32'	72'	2B(B&W)/1GT(G.E.)	1/9,000	17	14	50	none
"Lt. George W. G. Boyce"	AK-251	2	15,199	455'	29'	62'	2B(F.W.)/1GT(West.)	1/6,000	17	18	38	none
Greenville Victory	AK-237	2	15,200	455'	29'	62'	2B(B&W)/1GT(West.)	1/8,500	18	15	40	none
Sea Lift	AKR-9	1	21,700	540'	27'	83'	2B/2GT	2/19,400	20	5	49	none
Comet	AKR-7	1	18,286	499'	27'	78'	2B(B&W)/1GT(G.E.)	2/13,200	18	73 total		none
	AO-177	2	27,500	588'6"	35'	88'	2B/1GT	1/24,000	20	135 total		.2 CIWS (see class notes)
Sealift Pacific	AO-168	9	32,000	587'	32'	84'	2D(Colt-Pielstick/ Enterprise)	1/15,000	26	26 total		none
American Explorer	AO-165	1	31,300	615'	32'	80'	2B(B&W)/1GT(DeLaval)	1/22,000	20	16	37	none
Maumee	AO-149	3	32,953	620'	32'	84'	2B(C.E.)/1GT(West.)	1/20,460	18	17	35	none
Neosho	AO-143	6	38,000	655'	35'	86'	2B(B&W)/2GT(G.E.)	2/28,000	19	20	303	6 twin 3"/50 cal. mts. (AO-145, 146, 148), 4 twin 3"/50 cal. mts. (remainder).
"Mission"	AO-111	0	21,880	524'	31'	68'	2B(B&W)/1GT(G.E.)	1/10,000	16	14	38	none
Mispillion	AO-105	5	35,091	644'	36'	75'	4B(B&W)/2GT(West.)	2/13,500	16	18	288	4 single 3"/50 cal. mts. (AO-106, 108), none (remainder)
Suamico	AO-49	4	21,880	524'	31'	68'	2B(B&W)/1GT(G.E.)	1/6,000	15	14	38	none
"Cimarron"	AO-22	7	25,500	553'	33'	75'	4B(F.W.)/2GT(Beth.)	2/13,500	18	20	270	4 single 3"/50 cal. mts. (AO-51, 64, 98, 99), 2 single 3"/50 cal. mts. (AO-54, 56), none (remainder)
Sacramento	AOE-1	4	52,483	793'	38'5"	107'	4B(C.E.)/2GT(G.E.)	2/100,000	26	33	565	4 twin 3"/50 cal. mts.
Alatna	AOG-81	2	7,300	302'	60'11"	19'	2D(Alco)	2/3,400	12	11	40	none
"Tonti"	AOG-76	3	6,050	325'	19'	48'	1D(Nordberg)	1/1,400	10	11	30	none
"Patapsco"	AOG-1	3	4,570	311'	17'	49'	4D(G.M.)	2/3,750	14	9	114	2 twin 3"/50 cal. mts., 2 twin 20mm mts. (AOG-55, 56)
Wichita	AOR-1	7	38,100	659'	34'	96'	3B(F.W.)/2GT(G.E.)	2/38,000	20	27	362	2 twin 3"/50 cal. mts.
"Barrett"	AP-196	1	19,600	533'	27'	73'	2B(B&W)/1GT(G.E.)	1/13,750	19	426	1,723	none
"Blackford"	APB-45	1	3,910	328'	14'	50'	2D(G.M.)	2/1,800	10	38	395	2 quad 40mm mts., 6 twin 20mm mts.

continued

Class	Number	No. in Class	Full Load Displ.	Length Overall	Max. Draft	Extreme Beam	Number and Type of Boilers/Engines	Screws/ SHP	Max. Speed (Kts.)	Accommodations Officers	Accommodations Enlisted	Armament
"Benewah"	APB-35	3	4,080	328'	14'	50'	2D(G.M.)	2/1,800	12	38	1,283	2 single 3"/50 cal. mts., 2 quad 40mm mts., 8 .50 cal. mg.
Grand Canyon	AR-28	1	14,700	492'	28'	70'	2B(B&W)/2GT(A.C.)	1/8,500	18	80	1,191	4 single 20mm mts.
Markab	AR-23	1	14,383	491'8"	26'6"	72'3"	2B(F.W.)/1GT(G.E.)	1/8,500	18	57	804	4 single 3"/50 cal. mts.
Delta	AR-9	2	13,009	490'	26'	70'	2B(B&W)/1GT(N.N.)	1/8,500	16	46	957	1 single 5"/38 cal. mt. (AR-12), 4 single 3"/50 cal. mts., 2 twin 40mm mts. (AR-12), 8 twin 20mm mts. (AR-12)
Vulcan	AR-5	4	16,330	530'	24'5"	73'	4B(B&W)/2GT(N.Y.S.)	2/12,000	18.7	63	1,272	4 single 5"/38 cal. mts. 4 single 20mm mts. (AR-5), 2 6-pdr. mts. (AR-5), 2 40mm saluting mts. (AR-6, 8)
"Aristaeus"	ARB-1	2	3,640	328'	14'	50'	2D(G.M.)	2/1,800	12	24	248	1 single 3"/50 cal. mt. (ARB-5), 2 quad 40mm mts.
Aeolus	ARC-3	2	7,040	438'	19'3"	58'2"	2B(Wickes)/2GT(West.)	2/6,600	17	23	198	none
Neptune	ARC-2	2	7,444	370'	18'	47'	2B(C.E.)/2RS(Skinner)	2/4,800	14	28	168	none
"Achelous"	ARL-1	4	3,853	328'	14'	50'	2D(G.M.)	2/1,800	12	18	248	2 quad 40mm mts., 8 single 20mm mts. (ARL-8, 31)
Bolster	ARS-38	6	2,040	214'	15'	44'	4D(C.B.)	2/2,440	14	10	89	1 single 40mm mt. (ARS-38/42), 2 MK 68 mg.
Escape	ARS-6	9	1,970	214'	15'	44'	4D(C.B.)	2/2,440	14.3	10	91	1 single 40mm mt. (ARS-7, 23/25), 2 twin 20mm mts. (ARS-6, 8), 2 MK 68 mg.
L. Y. Spear	AS-36	4	22,640	644'	24'5"	85'	2B(F.W.)/1GT(G.E.)	1/20,000	20	94	1,254	2 single 5"/38 cal. mts.
Simon Lake	AS-33	2	21,000	644'	22'5"	85'	2B(C.E.)/1GT(DeLaval)	1/20,000	18	95	1,326	2 twin 3"/50 cal. mts.
Hunley	AS-31	2	18,300	619'	23'4"	83'	6D(F.M.)	1/15,000	18	91	1,312	2 twin 3"/50 cal. mts.
Proteus	AS-19	1	18,500	574'	25'5"	73'	8D(A.C.)	2/11,000	16	85	1,212	1 single 5"/38 cal. mt. 2 single 20mm mts.
Fulton	AS-11	6	16,050	530'	26'	73'4"	8D(G.M.)	2/11,200	16	80	1,032	2 single 5"/38 cal. mts. (except AS-11 and 18), 4 single 20mm mts. (AS-11 & 18), 2 single 20mm mts. (AS-12 & 17), (1) single 20mm mt. (AS-16)
Pigeon	ASR-21	2	4,555	251'	21'5"	86'	4D(Alco)	2/6,000	15	16	147	2 single .50 cal. mg.
"Chanticleer"	ASR-7	6	2,290	251'	16'	44'	4D(Alco/G.M.)	1/3,000	15	11	109	2 single 20 mm mts.
"Sotoyomo"	ATA-121	2	860	143'	14'	34'	1D(G.M.)	1/1,500	12.5	7	42	2 single 20mm mts.
	ATF-166	3	2,400	240'	17'	48'	2D	2/4,500	15	47 total		none
"Cherokee"	ATF-66	22	1,640	205'	17'	39'	1D(G.M.)	1/3,000	15	5	87	1 single 3"/50 cal. mt. (except ATF-76, 85, 149 & 158)
Edenton	ATS-1	3	3,125	282'8"	18'3"	50'	4D(Paxman)	2/6,800	16	9	91	2 twin 20mm mts. (ATS-1 & 3), (2) single 20mm mts. (ATS-2)
Norton Sound	AVM-1	1	13,590	540'7"	20'11"	71'7"	4B(B&W)/2GT(A.C.)	2/12,000	19.5	91	623	2 twin MK 26 STANDARD missile launchers.
Lexington	CVT-16	1	42,000	899'	31'	192'	8B(B&W)/4GT(West.)	4/150,000	28	115	1,500	none (no aircraft permanently assigned)

[1] Displacement is surface displacement for all AGSSs.   [2] Speed is surface speed for all AGSSs

5 DESTROYER TENDERS, SAMUEL GOMPERS CLASS

Name	Number	FY/SCB	Builder	Awarded	Commissioned	F/S
	AD-42	76/700				Proj.
	AD-41	76/700				Proj.
	AD-40	73/700				Bldg.

Name	Number	FY/SCB	Builder	Awarded	Commissioned	F/S
Puget Sound	AD-38	65/700.65	PS Navy	12-29-64	4-27-68	AA
Samuel Gompers	AD-37	64/244	PS Navy	10-31-63	7-1-67	PA

The first postwar-constructed ADs. Hull and machinery duplicates AS-33 and 36 classes. They can serve all types of ships up to and including Virginia class CGNs. Class has a helicopter hangar. Construction of AD-39 was cancelled 12-11-65 to pay for cost overruns in other construction programs. AD-41 was originally authorized in FY 1975. Appropriated funds for the ship were switched to AS-39 and 40 to pay for cost and inflation escalations in that program. Two more units of this class are projected. The entire class is badly needed to replace World War II construction ADs.

2 DESTROYER TENDERS, *SHENANDOAH* CLASS

Name	Number	Commissioned	F/S
Bryce Canyon	AD-36	9–15–50	PA
Shenandoah	AD-26	8–13–45	AA

Built on modified C3 hulls. From 3–7–46 until 8–14–47 construction of AD-36 was suspended. Both units have been FRAMed. Originally 9 in class, 3 were cancelled at end of WW II (were begun as ASs), 1 now serves as AR-28, 1 was leased to Indonesia, 1 has been disposed of, and 1 is in permanent custody of MarAd.

1 DESTROYER TENDER, "*KLONDIKE*" CLASS

Name	Number	Commissioned	F/S
Everglades	AD-24	5–25–51	AR*

Modified C3 hulls. There were originally 4 ships in this class. Two were stricken (since scrapped) and 1 was converted to AR-22 (since stricken). AD-24 was completed 5–23–46, but laid up until commissioned; decommissioned 8–15–70 at Charleston. Towed to Philadelphia 11/70 to replace *Chandeleur* (AV-10) as accommodation and depot ship for the Philadelphia Inactive Ships Maintenance Facility. Placed in service, in reserve 2–3–71. *Cascade* (AD-16) has been stricken and disposed of.

5 DESTROYER TENDERS, *DIXIE* CLASS

Name	Number	Commissioned	F/S
Yosemite	AD-19	3–25–44	AA
Sierra	AD-18	3–20–44	AA
Piedmont	AD-17	1–5–44	AA
Prairie	AD-15	8–5–40	PA
Dixie	AD-14	4–25–40	PA

Similar in appearance to *Vulcan* class ARs and *Fulton* class ASs. There were originally 6 in class. *New England* (AD-32), was cancelled in 1945. All have been FRAMed. AD-14 is oldest active ship in Fleet. All have helo decks aft. They were originally intended as DASH maintenance facilities. Regular helos can not operate from them.

8 AMMUNITION SHIPS, *KILAUEA* CLASS

Name	Number	FY/SCB	Builder	Awarded	Commissioned	F/S
Kiska	AE-35	68/703	Ingalls	3–8–68	12–16–72	PA
Mount Baker	AE-34	68/703	Ingalls	3–8–68	7–22–72	AA
Shasta	AE-33	67/703	Ingalls	3–8–68	2–26–72	PA
Flint	AE-32	67/703	Ingalls	3–8–68	11–20–71	PA

Name	Number	FY/SCB	Builder	Awarded	Commissioned	F/S
Mount Hood	AE-29	66/703	Beth., Sparrows Pt.	1–26–66	5–1–71	PA
Santa Barbara	AE-28	66/703	Beth., Sparrows Pt.	1–26–66	7–11–70	AA
Butte	AE-27	65/703	Gen. Dyn., Quincy	3–30–65	12–14–68	AA
Kilauea	AE-26	65/703	Gen. Dyn., Quincy	3–30–65	8–10–68	PA

A new class of AEs, easily recognizable because of helo deck/hangar aft and superstructure just forward of it. The ships are fitted with fin stabilizers and equipped with FAST. Two more ships of this class are projected between FY 1975/79. *Virgo* (AE-30), ex AKA-20, and *Chara* (AE-31), ex AKA-58, converted units of the *Andromeda* class AKAs, have been stricken and disposed of.

3 AMMUNITION SHIPS, *NITRO* CLASS

Name	Number	Commissioned	F/S
Haleakala	AE-25	11–3–59	PA
Pyro	AE-24	7–24–59	PA
Nitro	AE-23	5–1–59	AA

These are an improved *Suribachi* class; FAST/helicopter deck retrofitted. They can handle missiles up to size of TALOS.

2 AMMUNITION SHIPS, *SURIBACHI* CLASS

Name	Number	Commissioned	F/S
Mauna Kea	AE-22	3–30–57	PA
Suribachi	AE-21	11–17–56	AA

Class is the first built-for-purpose AEs. FAST and helo deck retrofitted.

2 AMMUNITION SHIPS, "*MOUNT HOOD*" CLASS

Name	Number	Commissioned	F/S
Firedrake	AE-14	6–21–44	MPR*
Wrangell (ex-SS Midnight)	AE-12	5–28–44	MAR*

Both were built by North Carolina Shipbuilding Company on C2-S-AJ1 hulls. AE-14 was originally named SS *Winged Racer*. This class originally consisted of 8 ships. The class leader sank in World War II, and 5 others have been stricken and disposed of. AE-12 was decommissioned on 12–21–70 at Norfolk; AE-14 followed on 3–19–71 at Mare Island. AE-12 was transferred to the temporary custody of MarAd on 4–29–71 for layup; AE-14 followed on 7–21–71.

2 STORE SHIPS, *RIGEL* CLASS

Name	Number	Commissioned	F/S
Vega	AF-59	11–10–55	PA
Rigel	AF-58	9–2–55	AA

The only built-for-purpose AFs in USN, they were built to USN specifications using a MarAd R3-S-4A design. The two store ships of the *Asterion* class have been stricken and disposed of.

1 STORE SHIP, *DENEBOLA* CLASS

Denebola (ex-SS *Hibbing Victory*)	AF-56	1–20–54	MSC

Completed in 1944 to VC2-S-AP3 hull design and acquired by USN 5–3–52. Sister ship *Regulus* (AF-57) was stricken after she received irreparable damage when she grounded in Hong Kong harbor during a typhoon. *Denebola* was decommissioned on 7–1–75 and transferred to MSC for further service, in fleet support operations, on the same date as USNS *Denebola* (T-AF-56). *Denebola* continues a trend, that was begun by *Taluga* (AO-62), of transferring auxiliaries to MSC for operation by civilian crews. This is patterned after the Royal Navy and its Royal Fleet auxiliary. One of the prime reasons for this transfer is that it frees USN personnel for assignment to other stations and it has proven to be more efficient.

1 STORE SHIP, *ALUDRA* CLASS

Aludra (ex-SS *Matchless*)	AF-55	7–7–52	MPR*

Acquired from MarAd on 12–18–50. Built on R2-S-BV1 hull design. *Aludra* was decommissioned in 9/69 at Mare Island; transferred to temporary custody of MarAd on 10–1–69 for berthing. With the loss of *Regulus* (AF-57), plans to reactivate this ship as a replacement for *Regulus,* in late 1971, were actively considered. However, the reactivation did not take place because of a change in force level requirements for AFs.

1 STORE SHIP, "*BALD EAGLE*" CLASS

Arcturus	AF-52	11–18–61	MAR*

Built on a C2-S-B1 hull design, there were originally 4 ships in class. Two were stricken and disposed of and 1, USNS *Grommet Reefer* (T-AF-53), was wrecked in a storm off Italy on 12–15–52 and was declared a total loss. AF-52 was originally acquired from MarAd on 3–1–50 for service with MSTS as USNS *Golden Eagle* (T-AF-52). With the enlargement of the Fleet in 1961 as a result of the Berlin Crises, additional Fleet AFs were needed and AF-52 was transferred to Fleet service. She was renamed *Arcturus* 10–13–61; commissioned into Fleet as indicated. Decommissioned 3–16–73 at Norfolk; transferred to temporary custody of MarAd on 10–18–73 for berthing.

2 STORE SHIPS, "*ALSTEDE*" CLASS

Name	Number	Commissioned	F/S
Procyon (ex-SS *Flying Scud*)	AF-61	11–24–61	MPR*
Pictor (ex-SS *Great Republic*)	AF-54	9–13–50	MPR*

These were built on an R2-S-BV-1 hull design and completed 1943 as merchant ships. There were originally 6 ships in class. AF-48, 60 and 62 were struck and disposed of. AF-49 was transferred to the permanent custody of MarAd. AF-54 was acquired from MarAd 9–13–50 and AF-61 was acquired on 8–8–61. AF-54 was decommissioned 12/69; AF-61 followed on 12–8–70 at Mare Island. Both were transferred to temporary custody of MarAd for layup— AF-54 on 8–11–70 and AF-61 on 2–4–71. The MSC-operated *Bondia* (AF-42) and the USN-operated *Hyades* (AF-28) have been disposed of.

7 COMBAT STORE SHIPS, *MARS* CLASS

San Jose	AFS-7	10–23–70	PA
San Diego	AFS-6	5–24–69	AA
Concord	AFS-5	11–27–68	AA
White Plains	AFS-4	11–23–68	PA
Niagara Falls	AFS-3	4–29–67	PA
Sylvania	AFS-2	7–11–64	AA
Mars	AFS-1	12–21–63	PA

The *Mars* class was designed to replace AF/AKS/AVS types. They have built-in helicopter deck aft with capability to maintain and store H-46 helicopters, "M" frames vice the usual kingposts and booms, and 5 cargo holds (1 refrigerated). Three more of this class are projected for authorization between FY 1975/79.

2 MISCELLANEOUS, *ALACRITY* CLASS (ex-MSO)

Assurance	AG-521	11–21–58	AA
Alacrity	AG-520	10–1–58	AA

These ships were originally commissioned as MSO-520 and 521 of the *Ability* class. Lead ship, *Ability* (MSO-519), was stricken and scrapped. MSO-520 was reclassified AG on 6–1–73 and MSO-521 on 3–1–73. Minesweeping gear was removed, AN/SQR-15 TASS sonar system was installed, fuel tanks were modified, and habitability was improved. The ships perform tests in the Caribbean. TASS was operationally tested with the 6th Fleet from mid-1970 to late 1973 by the now stricken *Hammerberg* (DE-1051), *Courtney* (DE-1021), and *Lester* (DE-1022).

1 MISCELLANEOUS, *S.P. LEE* CLASS

Name	Number	Commissioned	F/S
S.P. Lee (ex AGS-31)	AG-192	12-2-68	Loan

Completed on indicated date as AGS-31. Resembles AGOR-3 class. Upon completion, she was transferred to MSC for service as USNS *S.P. Lee* (T-AGS-31). Placed in reserve in late 1969 because of lack of operating funds. Reactivated 9-10-70; reclassified AG-192 on 9-25-70 and transferred to operational control of Naval Electronics Laboratory, San Diego, as replacement for the stricken *Rexburg* (PCER-855) and *Marysville* (PCER-857). Fitted as hydrographic research ship. She was taken out of service on 2-27-74 and transferred as loan to the Geological Survey, Department of the Interior, for further service. The former antiaircraft light cruiser, *Spokane* (AG-191), ex CLAA-120, has been stricken and scrapped.

1 MISCELLANEOUS, *FLYER* CLASS

Name	Number	Commissioned	F/S
Flyer (ex-SS American Flyer, SS Water Witch)	AG-178	3-1-65	MSC

Completed in 1945 to a C2-S-B1 hull design as *Water Witch,* she was acquired from MarAd on 2-9-65 and instated on the NVR on the indicated date, under the operational control of Naval Electronics Systems Command. The 3 *Phoenix* class AGs (AG-172/174) have been stricken and disposed of.

1 MISCELLANEOUS, *KINGSPORT* CLASS

Name	Number	Commissioned	F/S
Kingsport	AG-164	3-1-50	MSC

Completed in 1944 as SS *Kingsport Victory* on a VC2-S-AP3 hull design. She was acquired from MarAd on the indicated date and transferred to MSC for service as USNS *Kingsport Victory* (T-AK-239). She was renamed and reclassified *Kingsport* (AG-164) on 11-1-64; converted at Philadelphia Naval Shipyard to world's first satellite communications ship for participation in "Project Advent." Antenna sphere installed aft of superstructure. Upon completion of the project in 1966, the antenna sphere was removed and the ship was reconverted to a hydrographic vessel for further service as such. Operated by the Naval Electronics Systems Command.

2 MISCELLANEOUS, *COMPASS ISLAND* CLASS

Name	Number	Commissioned	F/S
Observation Island (ex YAG-57)	AG-154	12-5-58	MPR*
Compass Island (ex YAG-56)	AG-153	12-3-56	AA

Built on a C4-S-1A hull design by New York Shipbuilding Corporation, AG-153 was originally named SS *Garden Mariner* and AG-154 was SS *Empire State Mariner.* They were acquired from MarAd 3-29-56 (153) and 9-10-56 (154) as YAGs; to EAG on 6-19-56 and commissioned as such. To AG on 4-1-68. AG-153 served as test ship for FBM guidance and navigation systems. AG-154 served as test ship for POLARIS/POSEIDON. AG-154 played a prominent part in the development of SINS. Decommissioned 9-29-72 at Pearl Harbor and transferred to temporary custody of MarAd on 1-26-73 for layup. Conversion of EAG-155, a third unit of this class, was cancelled.

1 MISCELLANEOUS, *SEQUOIA* CLASS

Name	Number	Commissioned	F/S
Sequoia	AG-23	3-25-33	ASA

Originally commissioned on above date, but is no longer a commissioned ship. She is officially under control of the Secretary of the Navy and is used by high government officials as a yacht. Based at Washington, D.C.

1 AUXILIARY DEEP SUBMERGENCE SUPPORT SHIP, *POINT LOMA* CLASS

Name	Number	Commissioned	F/S
Point Loma	AGDS-2	2-28-58	PA

Built on a S2-ST-23a hull design, she was commissioned as USS *Point Barrow* (AKD-1). Decommissioned 5-29-58 and transferred to MSC for further service on the same date as USNS *Point Barrow* (T-AKD-1). Built for Arctic service, she closely resembles an LSD. She was placed in MSC ready reserve on 9-28-72. Returned to USN 2-28-74 and placed in commission on same date. Reclassified and renamed *Point Loma* (AGDS-2) on 2-28-74. She replaced *Apache* (ATF-67) and *White Sands* (AGDS-1) as support ship for *Trieste III.* Modifications to *Point Loma* will include removal of canopy over well deck and installation of large gasoline tanks for storing *Trieste III* ballast. Formerly used to transport SATURN booster rockets to Cape Kennedy Space Center.

1 HYDROFOIL RESEARCH SHIP, *PLAINVIEW* CLASS

Name	Number	Commissioned	F/S
Plainview	AGEH-1	3-1-69	PSA

Authorized in FY 1962, she was placed in service on the indicated date. *Plainview* has a maximum speed of 50 knots, but potential of 80 knots. Used to test hydrofoil concepts, she has aluminum hull, steel alloy struts and foils, and automatic pilot controls.

1 ENVIRONMENTAL RESEARCH SHIP, "BANNER" CLASS

Name	Number	Commissioned	F/S
Pueblo	AGER-2	3–13–67	PA

Completed in late World War II as the Army Supply Ship FS-344. She was acquired by USN on 4–12–66 and commissioned as Pueblo (AKL-44). Reclassified AGER on 6–1–67. The ship was actually outfitted as an electronic surveillance ship. She was boarded and captured on 1–23–68 by the North Korean Navy and towed to Wonson, North Korea; crew was released 12/68. She is reportedly being used by the North Korean Navy. Remains on the NVR as an active ship. Sisters Banner (AGER-1) and Palm Beach (AGER-3) have been stricken and disposed of.

1 MISCELLANEOUS COMMAND SHIP, LA SALLE CLASS

La Salle	AGF-3	2–22–64	AA

Originally commissioned as LPD-3 of the Raleigh class amphibious transport docks. She was reclassified AGF-3 on 7–1–72. Modified for AGF duties as Philadelphia Navy Yard. During modification, elaborate command and communications facilities were installed, accommodations for admiral and staff provided, extra air conditioning added, and she was painted white to reflect heat. She is homeported at Bahrain, Persian Gulf, as flagship Middle East Force, replacing the stricken Valcour (AGF-1), ex AVP-55. The hull number AGF-2 was not used.

1 FRIGATE RESEARCH SHIP, GLOVER CLASS

Glover	AGFF-1	11–13–65	AA

Originally authorized as AG-163, she was commissioned as an escort research ship (AGDE) on the indicated date. Rerated and reclassified as a frigate research ship (AGFF) on 6–30–75. Ship has full combat capabilities and is used to test sonar theories and systems. Last used to test SQS-35 VDS for Knox class FFs.

1 MISSILE RANGE INSTRUMENTATION SHIP, RANGE SENTINEL CLASS

Range Sentinel	AGM-22	9–20–44	MSC

Built on a VC2-S-AP5 hull design, she was originally commissioned as Sherburne (APA-205) of the Haskell class APAs. Decommissioned in 1946 and laid up. She was stricken from NVR on 10–1–58 and transferred to MarAd for layup. Reclassified AGM-22 on 4–16–69; reacquired and reinstated on the NVR on 10–22–69. Authorized for conversion to AGM under FY 1969 (SCB-731). Converted at Northwest Marine Iron Works, Portland, Oregon. Started conversion 10–20–69; delivered to MSC for service on 10–21–71. Renamed Range Sentinel on 4–26–71.

2 MISSILE RANGE INSTRUMENTATION SHIPS, VANGUARD CLASS

Name	Number	Commissioned	F/S
Redstone	AGM-20	10–22–47	MSC
Vanguard	AGM-19	10–21–47	MSC

Both built on a T2-SE-A2 hull design, these ships were acquired on the above dates as Mission DePala (AO-114) (AGM-20) and Mission San Fernando (AO-122) (AGM-19). They served with the Naval Overseas Transportation Service until 10–1–49 when both were taken over by the newly created Military Sea Transportation Service. Both were stricken for the third and last time, as AOs on 9–4–57 (122) and 3–13–58 (114). They were reacquired on 9–28–64 (AGM-19) and 9–19–64 (AGM-20) and reinstated on the NVR on 7–1–64 for conversion to AGMs. Mission DePala renamed Johnstown and Mission San Fernando renamed Muscle Shoals on 4–8–65. Johnstown was renamed Redstone and Muscle Shoals renamed Vanguard on 9–1–65. Converted at Bethlehem Steel Company, Quincy, Massachusetts, they were delivered to MSC and placed in service on 2–28–66 (19) and 6–30–66 (20). Conversion included addition of a 72' midbody. A third ship of this class, Mercury (AGM-21), was stricken and sold to Matson Navigation Company for service as a merchantship. Of the 6 Sword Knot class (AGM-13/18), 5 were disposed of and 1 was converted to an AGS.

2 MISSILE RANGE INSTRUMENTATION SHIPS, GENERAL H. H. ARNOLD CLASS

General Hoyt S. Vandenberg	AGM-10	4–1–44	MSC
General H. H. Arnold	AGM-9	8–17–44	MSC

These ships were built on a C4-S-A3 hull design as USS General R. E. Callan (AP-139) (AGM-9) and USS General Harry Taylor (AP-145) (AGM-10) and commissioned on indicated date. After brief service in MSC in early 1950s, both were laid up in MarAd. Acquired by the Air Force on 7–15–61, converted to AGMs, and renamed. They were operated by USAF until 7–1–64 when both were acquired by the Navy and instated on the NVR on the same date. Transferred to MSC for service as USNS General H. H. Arnold (T-AGM-9) and USNS General Hoyt S. Vandenberg (T-AGM-10), they serve as satellite and missile tracking ships. They carry a 40' UHF radar dish, a 30' radar dish, and a "star tracker" radar. The AKL type AGM, Range Recoverer (AGM-2), was reclassified YFRT-524 on 5–16–72 and her name cancelled. She operated out of Newport, Rhode Island, until stricken.

1 MISSILE RANGE INSTRUMENTATION SHIP, "RANGE TRACKER" CLASS

Wheeling (ex-SS Seton Hall Victory)	AGM-8	6–21–62	MSC

Completed on a VC2-S-AP3 hull design; acquired from MarAd on indicated date. Wheeling has a Navy contingent of 18 to operate the ship's helicopters. There were originally 6 in class. All except AGM-8 have been stricken and disposed of.

1 MAJOR COMMUNICATIONS RELAY SHIP, *ARLINGTON* CLASS

Name	Number	Commissioned	F/S
Arlington (ex-Saipan)	AGMR-2	7–14–46	PR*

Originally commissioned as *Saipan* (CVL-48). Decommissioned 10–3–57 and laid up. Reclassified AVT-6 on 5–15–59. Authorized for conversion to CC under FY 1962. Reclassified CC-3 on 1–1–64. Contract for conversion awarded to Alabama DD & SB Company. When a need for a third CC was cancelled, conversion of *Saipan* was halted in 2/64 when she was 64 percent completed. Reauthorized for conversion to AGMR under FY 1964 vice *Vella Gulf* (CVE-111). Conversion costs $26,886,424.00. She was reclassified AGMR-2 on 9–1–64; renamed *Arlington* on 4–8–65; recommissioned as *Arlington* (AGMR-2) on 8–27–66. Decommissioned 1–14–70 at San Diego.

1 MAJOR COMMUNICATIONS RELAY SHIP, *ANNAPOLIS* CLASS

Name	Number	Commissioned	F/S
Annapolis	AGMR-1	2–5–45	AR*

Originally commissioned as *Gilbert Islands* (CVE-107) of the *Commencement Bay* class CVEs. As such, she is the last CVE type still on the NVR. She was decommissioned in 1946, and recommissioned 9–7–51 for the Korean War, but operated in the Atlantic. She was decommissioned 1–15–55 at Boston, struck from the NVR on 6–1–61, but reinstated on the NVR on 11–1–61, along with *Vella Gulf*, for eventual conversion to AGMRs. She was converted to AGMR at New York Naval Shipyard 1962/64. Reclassified from AKV-39 to AGMR-1 on 6–1–63, and renamed *Annapolis* on 6–22–63. She was recommissioned 3–7–64 as AGMR. Decommissioned 12–20–69 at Philadelphia.

2 OCEANOGRAPHIC RESEARCH SHIPS, *GYRE* CLASS

Name	Number	Commissioned	F/S
Moana Wave	AGOR-22	1–16–74	Loan
Gyre	AGOR-21	11–14–73	Loan

Both ships were authorized FY 1971. They were built at Halter Marine Service, Inc., New Orleans, under a contract awarded 6–23–72, and completed on indicated dates. Rated as AGOR (Utility). AGOR-21 is assigned to Texas A&M University and AGOR-22 to the University of Hawaii. The ships have a 150 HP retractable propeller pod which can only be used when the main engines are not in use. The Navy plans to build several of these workboat-type AGORs to replace obsolete AGORs presently being operated by civilian institutions in support of Navy programs.

1 OCEANOGRAPHIC RESEARCH SHIP, *CHAIN* CLASS

Name	Number	Commissioned	F/S
Chain	AGOR-17	3–31–44	Loan

Originally commissioned as ARS-20 of the *Escape* class. Decommissioned 11–9–46 at Orange, Texas, converted to an AGOR in the mid-1950s and reactivated. She was reclassified AGOR on 4–1–67, and is operated by Woods Hole Institute. Sister ship, *Snatch* (AGOR-18), has been stricken.

1 OCEANOGRAPHIC RESEARCH SHIP, *HAYES* CLASS

Hayes	AGOR-16	7–21–71	MSC

This ship was authorized FY 1967 (SCB-726), and was built at Todd, Seattle, under contract awarded 12–10–68, and completed on indicated date. *Hayes* has a catamaran hull, and has excellent maneuverability, negating the need for bow thrusters, but has severe pitching problems. She has a center well between the two hulls, allowing research apparatus to be lowered and raised from within the ship.

1 OCEANOGRAPHIC RESEARCH SHIP, "*ELTANIN*" CLASS

Mizar	AGOR-11	3–7–58	MSC

This ship was built on a C1-ME2-13A hull design by Avondale and was placed in service with MSC on the indicated date as USNS *Mizar* (T-AK-272). She is ice-strengthened for Arctic operations. She was reclassified AGOR on 4–15–64 and converted to such. She is operated by MSC for the Naval Research Laboratory. This ship was instrumental in locating the hulks of the sunken *Thresher* (SSN-593) and *Scorpion* (SSN-589). Her sister ship *Eltanin* (AGOR-8) has been leased to Argentina.

9 OCEANOGRAPHIC RESEARCH SHIPS, *ROBERT D. CONRAD* CLASS

Name	Number	Commissioned	F/S
Knorr	AGOR-15	1–14–70	Loan
Melville	AGOR-14	8–27–69	Loan
Bartlett	AGOR-13	3–31–69	MSC
De Steiguer	AGOR-12	2–28–69	MSC
Thomas Washington	AGOR-10	9–7–65	Loan
Thomas G. Thompson	AGOR-9	8–24–65	Loan

continued

Name	Number	Commissioned	F/S
Lynch	AGOR-7	3-27-65	MSC
James M. Gilliss	AGOR-4	11-5-62	Loan
Robert D. Conrad	AGOR-3	11-29-62	Loan

First class of built-for-purpose AGORs. AGOR-9 originally named *Silas Bent*; renamed 3-12-64. All completed on dates indicated in above table. Originally 11 in class, 1 is leased to Brazil and 1 is leased to New Zealand. AGOR-3 is operated by Lamont-Doherty, Geological Observatory, Columbia University; AGOR-4 is operated by the University of Miami; AGOR-9, University of Washington; AGOR-10 and 14, Scripps Institution of Oceanography; AGOR-15, Woods Hole Institute. Two additional units of this class, AGOR-19 and 20, were cancelled on 2-24-69. The *Josiah Willard Gibbs* (AGOR-1), formerly *San Carlos* (AVP-51), was leased to Greece.

1 PATROL CRAFT TENDER, *GRAHAM COUNTY* CLASS

Graham County	AGP-1176	4-17-58	AA

Originally commissioned on indicated date as LST-1176 of the *De Soto County* class. She was scheduled to be decommissioned on 5-22-72; however, this was cancelled and she was converted to an AGP. Reclassified AGP on 8-1-72. She received an austere conversion at Philadelphia Navy Yard February/May 1972, which included welding bow doors shut, converting tank deck to machine shops/store rooms. Boat booms were added to sides, along with numerous bitts; generator and steam risers were added to provide steam to PGs moored alongside. Serves as tender to *Asheville* class PGs based in the Mediterranean.

2 SURVEY SHIPS, *WILKES* CLASS

Wyman	AGS-34	11-3-71	MSC
Wilkes	AGS-33	6-28-71	MSC

Improved *Silas Bent* class. Completed on indicated dates. These ships resemble AGOR-3 class, but are larger. Carry 38 scientists in addition to crew. Fitted with anti-roll devices and small bow propulsion unit to maintain heading when dead in water. Both built by Defoe, Bay City. Authorized FY 1967.

2 SURVEY SHIPS, *CHAUVENET* CLASS

Harkness	AGS-32	1-29-71	MSC
Chauvenet	AGS-29	11-13-70	MSC

Completed on indicated dates. These are large surveying ships with helicopter deck and hangar and ice-strengthened steel hulls. Main wartime mission is to survey spots that meet fleet and landing force requirements.

2 SURVEY SHIPS, *SILAS BENT* CLASS

Name	Number	Commissioned	F/S
Kane	AGS-27	5-19-67	MSC
Silas Bent	AGS-26	7-24-65	MSC

Completed on indicated dates. AGS-26, 27, 33 and 34 are operated by MSC for Oceanographer of the Navy. *Kellar* (AGS-25) has been leased to Portugal.

2 SURVEY SHIPS, *BOWDITCH* CLASS

[Michelson (ex-SS Joliet Victory)]	AGS-23	12-15-68	Stricken
Dutton (ex-SS Tuskegee Victory)	AGS-22	9-12-58	MSC
Bowditch (ex-SS South Bend Victory)	AGS-21	9-12-58	MSC

Built on a VC2-S-AP3 hull and placed in service with MSC on the indicated dates. Support SSBN operations. Converted between 10-1-57 and 12-31-58 at Charleston Navy (AGS-21) and Phil. Navy (AGS-22). The two converted AKAs of the *Tanner* class (AGS-15/16), the 5 converted MSFs of the *Auk* class (AGS-17/20, 28) and the converted ATF of the *Cherokee* class (AGS-24) have all been stricken.

1 AUXILIARY SUBMARINE, *ALBACORE* CLASS

Albacore	AGSS-569	12-5-53	AR*

High-speed experimental submarine with no combat capability. First teardrop hull design. SSN-580 and 585 classes were evolved from the design of this submarine. She has virtually been rebuilt four times at Portsmouth Naval Shipyard to test new submarine equipment and theories. Decommissioned 9-1-72 at Portsmouth; berthed at Philadelphia.

1 AUXILIARY SUBMARINE, *TANG* CLASS

Tang	AGSS-563	10-25-51	PA

Originally commissioned as leadship of *Tang* class. As such, she was the first postwar-built SS to be completed. Overhauled and converted to AGSS at Mare Island Naval Shipyard between July 1975 and May 1976 as replacement for *Tigrone* (AGSS-419). Unlike *Tigrone*, *Tang* retains her torpedo tubes forward and aft. As built, *Tang* was 269'2" long. She and the remainder of the class (see Submarine section) have undergone reconstruction several times. *Tang* has received a FRAM II modernization.

1 AUXILIARY SUBMARINE, *DOLPHIN* CLASS

Name	Number	Commissioned	F/S
Dolphin	AGSS-555	8–17–68	PA

The original hull number SS-555 was cancelled on 3–26–45. Reassigned in 1961 to this experimental submarine. Built at Portsmouth Naval Shipyard of aluminum, HY-80 steel, and fiberglass. Designed for deep-diving of limited endurance and for oceanographic research. The sub is highly automated; has no conventional diving planes. In addition to oceanographic research, *Dolphin* also tests new equipment and performs weapon tests and evaluations. On 11–24–68 this sub submerged to a greater depth than any other operating submarine.

MISCELLANEOUS AUXILIARY SUBMARINES (AGSS) The 9th edition listed an additional 21 AGSSs; all 21 have been stricken. However, before this, the following things occurred: 5 of the GUPPY IA Class AGSSs were reclassified back to SS on 6–30–71 and were stricken as such a little over two years later. The 6th *Guppy* IA, *Chopper* (AGSS-342), plus all the *Torsk, Sand Lance, Charr, Balao, Pompon, Angler* and *Gato* classes were reclassified IXSS on 6–30–71 and were stricken as such in 12/71. *Chopper* replaced *Hake* (AGSS-256) as salvage training hulk for Service Squadron 8. Eight units became memorials and the remainder were scrapped or are awaiting disposition. *Baya* (AGSS-318) was stricken in 10/72.

1 HOSPITAL SHIP, "*HAVEN*" CLASS

Sanctuary	AH-17	6–20–45	MAR*

Built on a C4-S-B2 hull design. There were originally 6 in class; 5 have been stricken. *Haven* (AH-12) was sold and converted to a chemical carrier. *Benevolence* (AH-13) was sunk in a collision in 1950 in San Francisco Bay, *Tranquility* (AH-14) was transferred to MarAd for layup (since disposed of), *Consolation* (AH-15) was chartered on 3–16–60 to the People to People Health Foundation for operation as a private hospital ship under the name SS *Hope*. Returned to USN 9–16–74 and stricken for disposal. *Repose* (AH-16) was disposed of after serving on active duty in the Vietnamese War and later as a non-operative annex to the Long Beach Naval Hospital. *Sanctuary* was recommissioned for Vietnam service on 11–15–66. Scheduled decommissioning in late 1971 for layup cancelled. Decommissioned 12–15–71 at Hunters Point for conversion to Dependent Support Ship, Medical facilities upgraded, facilities to handle maternity, gynecology, obstetrics added; exchange facilities added. "Designed to aid military dependents in overseas ports where other U.S. facilities are not available". Red crosses on sides of ship removed. Officially rated as Hospital Ship (AH), but because of her dependent support role she no longer qualifies as such under Geneva Convention rules. Recommissioned 11–18–72. First USN ship with a mixed crew of men and women. As a result of budgetary problems, *Sanctuary* was decommissioned at Philadelphia on 3–26–75.

1 CARGO SHIP, *WYANDOT* CLASS

Name	Number	Commissioned	F/S
Wyandot (ex-AKA-92)	AK-283	9–30–44	MSC

Built on a C2-S-B1 hull design. Commissioned as indicated as AKA-92 of the *Andromeda* class. Decommissioned in late 1950s and laid up; later stricken. Reacquired and reinstated in 1961 for the Berlin crisis. Recommissioned in 1962. Transferred to MSTS in 3/63 for service as USNS *Wyandot* (T-AKA-92). Reclassified AK on 1–1–69. Disposal in May 1973 cancelled and ship retained. Employed in Arctic resupply operations.

4 CARGO SHIPS, *NORWALK* CLASS

Marshfield (ex-SS Marshfield Victory)	AK-282	5–28–70	MSC
Victoria (ex-SS Ethiopia Victory)	AK-281	10–15–65	MSC
Furman (ex-SS Furman Victory)	AK-280	10–7–64	MSC
Norwalk (ex-SS Norwalk Victory)	AK-279	12–30–63	MSC

Built on a VC2-S-AP3 hull design during WW II. Conversion to AK completed on indicated dates for AK-280/282. AK-279 was delivered on the indicated date. All acquired from MarAd in 1960s for service as FBM resupply ships for AS(FBM) tenders deployed overseas. Hold #3 rigged with silos for 16 FBM missiles. All carry POLARIS missiles; AK-282 also carries POSEIDON. Also carry general cargo of stores, provisions as well as spare parts, torpedoes and petroleum products. AK-279/281 were modified to carry POSEIDON. Three out of 4 units of this class retained first half of "Victory" names. Ex-SS *Ethiopia Victory* was completely renamed.

1 CARGO SHIP, *SCHUYLER OTIS BLAND* CLASS

Schuyler Otis Bland	AK-277	7–20–61	MSC

Only ship of its type. Built on MarAd C3-S-DX1 hull design. It was originally completed on 7–26–51 as SS *Schuyler Otis Bland*. Acquired from MarAd and instated on the NVR on the above date as a replacement for *Kingsport Victory* (AK-239).

1 CARGO SHIP, *LT. JAMES E. ROBINSON* CLASS

Lt. James E. Robinson	AK-274	3–1–50	MSC

Originally completed on a VC2-S-AP3 hull design as the SS *Czechoslovakia Victory* on 3–11–44. This ship was acquired from MarAd on the above date and instated on the NVR for service with MSTS as USNS *Lt. James E. Robinson* (T-AKV-3). Reclassified AK-274 on 5–7–59; then reclassified AG-170 on 12–1–62 for special project work. She was reclassified back to AK-274 on 7–1–64. For all ships with the abbreviation "MSC" indicated in the F/S column, see Section 8 for further data on the ships.

1 CARGO SHIP, "ELTANIN" CLASS

Name	Number	Commissioned	F/S
Mirfak	AK-271	12–30–57	MSC

Built on a C1-ME2-13a hull design; completed on the above date. Ice-strengthened. Two sisters converted to AGOR-8 and AGOR-11.

1 CARGO SHIP, MARINE FIDDLER CLASS

Name	Number	Commissioned	F/S
Marine Fiddler	AK-267	12–10–52	MAR*

Built on a C4-S-B5 hull design in World War II; served with the Army 1946/52. Acquired on the above date and instated on the Naval Vessel Register on the same date for service with MSTS as USNS Marine Fiddler (T-AK-267). This ship has massive booms with 150-ton lift capability. Transferred to the temporary custody of MarAd on 9–14–73 for layup.

1 CARGO SHIP, PVT. LEONARD C. BROSTROM CLASS

Name	Number	Commissioned	F/S
Pvt. Leonard C. Brostrom	AK-255	8–9–50	MSC

Built on a C4-S-B1 hull design in WW II, this ship was completed as SS Marine Eagle. She served with the Army until 1950, when she was taken over by the Navy on 7–31–50 and instated on the Naval Vessel Register on the above date. Received present name during Army service. Has massive booms with 150-ton lift capability. Near sister-ship of AK-267. Both AK-267 and 255 are capable of carrying locomotives and other heavy equipment as deck cargo. The 3 Antares class AKs listed in the 9th edition have been stricken; two, the Sgt. Jack J. Pendleton (AK-276) and Pvt. Joseph F. Merrell (AK-275), as a result of irreparable damage from grounding (AK-276) and collision (AK-275) damage. The third, Betelgeuse (AK-260), served as test ship for a new method of mothballing ships before being stricken.

2 CARGO SHIPS, "LT. GEORGE W. G. BOYCE" CLASS

Name	Number	Commissioned	F/S
Sgt. Truman Kimbro (ex-SS Hastings Victory)	AK-254	8–9–50	MSC
[Sgt. Morris E. Crain] (ex-SS Mills Victory)	AK-244	3–1–50	Stricken
Sgt. Andrew Miller (ex-SS Radcliffe Victory)	AK-242	3–1–50	MSC

Built to a VC2-S-AP2 hull design. Instated on the NVR on the indicated dates. AK-254 was acquired on 7–31–50; AK-242, on 3–1–50. Served with the Army prior to MSC service.

2 CARGO SHIPS, GREENVILLE VICTORY CLASS

Name	Number	Commission	F/S
Pvt. John R. Towle	AK-240	3-1-50	MSC
Greenville Victory	AK-237	3-1-50	MSC

Built on a VC2-S-AP3 hull design. Difference between AP3 and AP2 design is higher SHP in AP3 type; appearance of both is the same. Saw service with Army Transportation Service before being acquired by USN and instated on the NVR on the above date. The 6 AKs of the Alamosa class have been stricken and disposed of. As of 11–1–71 there are no more AKLs in USN.

1 VEHICLE CARGO SHIP, SEA LIFT CLASS

Sea Lift	AKR-9	4-25-67	MSC

Built on a MarAd C4-ST-67a hull design. Originally authorized as AK-278; reclassified LSV-9 on 6–1–63, then to AKR-9 on 1–1–69. Delivered to USN on above date. Transferred to MSC for service on 5–19–67. An improved AKR-7 design. Has roll-on/roll-off capability. She has two 70-ton, two 10-ton and fourteen 15-ton booms. Proposed sisters to Sea Lift were dropped.

1 VEHICLE CARGO SHIP, COMET CLASS

Comet	AKR-7	1-27-58	MSC

Built on a MarAd C4-ST-14a hull design as AK-269. To LSV-7 on 6–1–63; to AKR-7 on 1–1–69. Completed on the indicated date. Roll on/roll off with 5 ramps, including one in stern. AKR-8 was the stricken Taurus (ex-LSD-23). Altair (AKS-32), the remaining 2 AKVs of the Bogue class, and Rabaul (AKV-21) have all been stricken. AKV-21 was actively considered for reactivation as an interm Sea Control Ship. However, Guam (LPH-9) got the honors. The last net layer (ANL), Cohoes (ANL-78), has been stricken.

2 OILERS, UNNAMED CLASS

Name	Number	FY/SCB	Builder	Awarded	Commissioned	F/S
	AO-178	76/739				Proj.
	AO-177	76/739				Proj.

First of new class of Fleet Oilers. To number 10 units. The class will replace existing WW II vintage AOs presently operating with the fleet. Capacity of 120,000 barrels of Navy distillate and JP-5 fuels. Each unit will carry 2 VULCAN/PHALANX 20mm mts. for armament. AO-177 originally requested under FY 1975, but cut by Congress. Rerequested under FY 1976 along with AO-178. Remainder to be requested under FY 1977/1979.

AUXILIARY SHIPS

9 TANKERS, *SEALIFT PACIFIC* CLASS

Name	Number	Builder	Awarded	Delivered	F/S
Sealift Antarctic	AO-176	Bath Iron Works	6–20–72		MSC
Sealift Arctic	AO-175	Bath Iron Works	6–20–72		MSC
Sealift Caribbean	AO-174	Bath Iron Works	6–20–72	2–10–75	MSC
Sealift Mediterranean	AO-173	Bath Iron Works	6–20–72	11–6–74	MSC
Sealift Atlantic	AO-172	Bath Iron Works	6–20–72	8–26–74	MSC
Sealift Indian Ocean	AO-171	Todd, Los Angeles	6–20–72		MSC
Sealift China Sea	AO-170	Todd, Los Angeles	6–20–72		MSC
Sealift Arabian Sea	AO-169	Todd, Los Angeles	6–20–72	2–6–75	MSC
Sealift Pacific	AO-168	Todd, Los Angeles	6–20–72	8–14–74	MSC

Being built for operation by MSC as replacements for "Suamico" class tankers. Each has a capacity of approximately 220,000 barrels with the additional capability of handling 4 separate liquid cargoes. All 9 tankers were built for private steamship companies after MSC agreed with the companies to charter the ships upon completion of a "bareboat" basis (i.e., without crew) for a period of 5 years, with option to extend the charter. The agreement to build and charter was done without congressional approval, thus obviating the need for an SCB number and FY authorization. However, from now on MSC has agreed to submit all build and charter agreements to Congress for approval prior to any final agreements.

1 TANKER, *AMERICAN EXPLORER* CLASS

Name	Number	Commissioned	F/S
American Explorer	AO-165	10–27–59	MSC

Built by Ingalls to a T5-S-RM2a hull design and completed on the indicated date. AO-166/167, the first of a new class of Fleet Oiler, were both cancelled on 5–25–65.

3 TANKERS, *MAUMEE* CLASS

Yukon	AO-152	5–17–57	MSC
Shoshone	AO-151	4–15–57	MSC
Maumee	AO-149	12–17–56	MSC

Built to a MarAd T5-S-12a hull design and delivered to USN on above dates for service with MSTS. A fourth sister, Potomac(AO-150), exploded and sank in 9/61. The stern was salvaged and built around a new commercial tanker; rest of the ship was scrapped. AO-149 was ice-strengthened 1969/70. The 12 Cumberland class (AO-153/164) were stricken in the late 1950s and transferred to MarAd for layup (since disposed of).

6 OILERS, *NEOSHO* CLASS

Name	Number	Commissioned	F/S
Ponchatoula	AO-148	1–12–56	PA
Truckee	AO-147	11–23–55	AA
Kawishiwi	AO-146	7–6–55	PA
Hassayampa	AO-145	4–19–55	PA
Mississinewa	AO-144	1–18–55	AA
Neosho	AO-143	9–24–54	AA

Largest AOs built for USN and first AOs built to a non-MarAd hull design. AO-143/144, 147 are fitted with helicopter decks above the fantail. All are fitted as flagships. The entire class is scheduled to be transferred to MSC for further service as fleet oilers starting with Mississinewa in FY 1976.

TANKER, *"MISSION"* CLASS

[Mission Santa Ynez]	AO-134	10–22–47	MarAd

Built on T2-SE-A2 hull design. She is the survivor of a 27-ship class (AO-111/137). This ship was acquired by USN on above date and served with Naval Overseas Transportation Service until 10–1–49 when she was transferred to the newly formed MSTS for service as USNS Mission Santa Ynez (T-AO-134). One unit of this class, USNS Mission Capistrano (T-AO-112), was converted to AG-162 (since stricken). Three other units became AGM-19/21.

5 JUMBOIZED OILERS, *MISPILLION* CLASS

Waccamaw	AO-109	6–25–46	MSC
Pawcatuck	AO-108	5–10–46	AA
Passumpsic	AO-107	4–1–46	MSC
Navasota	AO-106	2–27–46	PA
Mispillion	AO-105	12–29–45	MSC

Built on a T3-S2-A3 hull design. AO-109 became AOR-109 on 12–11–50. She was to be converted to the first replenishment oiler (AOR), but conversion was cancelled and she reverted to AO on 5–7–51. The entire class has been jumboized under the following programs: FY 1963: AO-106, AO-109; FY 1964: AO-105, 107/108. AO-107 was decommissioned on 7–24–73 and transferred to MSC for further service as USNS Passumpsic (T-AO-107) and AO-105 followed on 7–26–74. Transfer of AO-109 to MSC occurred on 2–24–75. AO-106 and 108 will transfer to MSC in FY 1976. MSC units are disarmed and are operated by a civilian crew. A Navy detachment remains on board to handle communications. Ships continue role of support to the operating fleet.

4 TANKERS, *SUAMICO* CLASS

Name	Number	Commissioned	F/S
Schuylkill (ex-SS Louisburg)	AO-76	4-9-43	MSC
Saugatuck (ex-SS Newton)	AO-75	2-19-43	MAR*
Millicoma (ex-SS Conestoga)	AO-73	3-5-43	MSC
Tallulah (ex-SS Valley Forge)	AO-50	9-5-42	MSC

Built on a T2-SE-A1 hull design. Originally laid down as merchant tankers, these ships were acquired during construction by USN for service with fleet and commissioned as Fleet Oilers. All were struck 1946/47 and transferred to Maritime Commission for layup. All were reacquired in January/February 1948 for service with the Naval Overseas Transportation Service as tankers. All were transferred to MSTS on 10-1-49 for service as USNS (T-AO). Eight of this class have been disposed of since the last edition: one was scrapped as a result of irreparable grounding damage and 7 were scrapped because of material condition and age. AO-75 was transferred to the temporary custody of MarAd on 11-5-74 for layup.

7 OILERS, "CIMARRON" CLASS

Name	Number	Commissioned	F/S
Canisteo	AO-99	12-3-45	AA
Caloosahatchee	AO-98	10-10-45	AA
[Tolovana]	AO-64	2-24-45	Stricken
Taluga	AO-62	8-25-44	MSC
Marias	AO-57	2-12-44	MSC
Aucilla(ex-SS Escanaba)	AO-56	12-22-43	MAR*
Chikaskia	AO-54	11-10-43	MAR*
Ashtabula	AO-51	8-7-43	PA

Built on a T3-S2-A1 hull design. All were acquired from the Maritime Commission. Four of this class were converted to Escort Carriers (CVE) (since stricken). AO-51, 98, 99 have been jumboized, but more extensively than AO-105 class. They have an extra "M" frame and 2 gun mounts vice a forward helo deck, superstructure was extensively rebuilt and stack heightened. AO-62 decommissioned 5-4-72 at Long Beach and transferred to MSC for further service. AO-57 decommissioned and transferred to MSC on 10-2-73 for further service. Like the AO-105 class transferred to MSC, they continue their fleet operations. 115 civilian seamen and officers replace the regular navy crew on each ship. AO-54 decommissioned 12/69 at Philadelphia, and transferred to temporary custody of MarAd on 9-4-70 for layup. AO-56 decommissioned 12-18-70 at Philadelphia and transferred to temporary custody of MarAd on 10-7-71 for layup.

4 FAST COMBAT SUPPORT SHIPS, *SACRAMENTO* CLASS

Name	Number	Commissioned	F/S
Detroit	AOE-4	3-28-70	AA
Seattle	AOE-3	4-5-69	AA
Camden	AOE-2	4-1-67	PA
Sacramento	AOE-1	3-14-64	PA

A new type of ship combining functions of AF/AO/AE/AK. Carries 2 to 3 H-46 helicopters for VERTREP operations. A fifth unit of this class was authorized FY 1968, but cancelled on 11-4-69.

2 GASOLINE TANKERS, *ALATNA* CLASS

Name	Number	Commissioned	F/S
Chattahoochee	AOG-82	10-22-57	MPR*
Alatna	AOG-81	7-17-57	MPR*

Built on a T1-MET-24a hull. Built for polar service, they have an ice-resistant belt. Except for lack of midship mast, they resemble *Eltanin* class AGORs/AKs. Delivered on above dates.

3 GASOLINE TANKERS, "TONTI" CLASS

Name	Number	Commissioned	F/S
Petaluma (ex-SS Raccoon Bend)	AOG-79	9-7-50	MSC
Nodaway (ex-SS Belridge)	AOG-78	9-7-50	MSC
Rincon (ex-SS Tarland)	AOG-77	7-1-50	MSC

Built on a T1-M-BT2 hull design in 1945 for commercial service. Acquired from MarAd and placed in service with MSTS on the above date. They have been in continuous service with MSC ever since. The class leader served the Colombian Navy. A fifth unit of the class has been scrapped.

3 GASOLINE TANKERS, "PATAPSCO" CLASS

Name	Number	Commissioned	F/S
Pinnebog	AOG-58	10-20-45	Loan
Noxubee	AOG-56	10-19-45	DAA
Chewaucan	AOG-50	2-19-45	DAA

Built to USN design by Maritime Commission. AOG-56 stricken 7-1-60, but reinstated on NVR 8-23-65 for Vietnam service. Recommissioned 9-10-66. AOG-58 was operated by MSTS from 2-27-52 until 9/57 when she was loaned to the Air Force.

7 REPLENISHMENT FLEET OILERS, *WICHITA* CLASS

Name	Number	FY/SCB	Builder	Awarded	Commissioned	F/S
Roanoke	AOR-7	72/707.72	National Steel	12-15-72		Bldg.
Kalamazoo	AOR-6	67/707	Gen. Dyn., Quincy	7-19-67	8-11-73	AA
Wabash	AOR-5	67/707	Gen. Dyn., Quincy	7-19-67	11-20-71	PA
Savannah	AOR-4	66/707	Gen. Dyn., Quincy	7-6-66	12-5-70	AA
Kansas City	AOR-3	66/707	Gen. Dyn., Quincy	7-6-66	6-6-70	PA
Milwaukee	AOR-2	65/707	Gen. Dyn., Quincy	6-2-65	11-1-69	AA
Wichita	AOR-1	65/707	Gen. Dyn., Quincy	6-2-65	6-7-69	PA

A new type of ship. They carry ammunition and petroleum, as well as a limited amount of provisions and freight. Have a built-in helicopter platform aft, but no hangar. They resemble AOEs at a distance, but have smaller superstructure and stack. AOR-7 was launched on 12-7-74.

1 TRANSPORT, *"BARRETT"* CLASS

Name	Number	Commissioned	F/S
Geiger	AP-197	9-11-52	MPR*

Built by New York Shipbuilding on a P2-S1-DN3 hull design. Completed on indicated date. Acquired by USN, from MarAd, on 9-13-52 and assigned to MSTS for service. Last of "troopers." There were originally three in the class: *Barrett* (AP-196) was stricken and transferred to the New York State Maritime Academy on 9-5-73 as its training ship SS *Empire State V*; *Upshur* (AP-198) was stricken and transferred to the Maine Maritime Academy on 4-2-73 as its training ship SS *State of Maine* (replaced ex-USS *Ancon* (AGC-4); AP-197 taken out of service on 4-27-71 and transferred to temporary custody of MarAd on the same date for layup.

1 SELF-PROPELLED BARRACKS SHIP, *"BLACKFORD"* CLASS

Kingman	APB-47	6-27-45	PR

Laid down as LST-1113 of the LST-511 class. Named and reclassified *Kingman* (AKS-18) on 12-8-44. Reclassified APB-47 on 3-6-45. Decommissioned 1-15-47 at San Diego.

3 SELF-PROPELLED BARRACKS SHIPS, *"BENEWAH"* CLASS

Name	Number	Commissioned	F/S
Nueces	APB-40	11-30-45	PR*
Mercer	APB-39	9-10-45	PR*
Echols	APB-37	None	PR*

All originally classified as APLs. Reclassified APB on 8-11-44 (37) and 8-7-44 (39 & 40). APB-37 was never commissioned. Three additional sisters have been disposed of (APB-35 as IX-311). APB-37, laid up in an "in reserve, in service" status since 1/47 at Norfolk. *Echols* was to have been reactivated and modernized for service as command ship for Riverine Force in Vietnam. Scheduled for recommissioning 1969, but Vietnamization of war led to cancellation of reactivation. APB-40 was recommissioned on 5-3-68 for Vietnam service. APB-39 followed on 5-9-68. APB-40 was decommissioned 3-13-70 at San Diego. APB-39 was laid up in an "in service, in reserve" status on 1-7-70 at Mare Island. She was towed to Todd Shipyards, Seattle, in 4/74 for reactivation as a non-self-propelled barracks ship, and her status was changed to "in reserve, out of commission" on 4-29-74. Only berthing spaces and other associated spaces were activated. Remaining spaces remain inactive. Reactivation completed 5-24-74. Employed at Puget Sound Naval Shipyard as a berthing craft for the crew of *Sperry* (AS-12) while the ship undergoes a long overhaul at yard. Status of craft remains as indicated despite her current employment.

1 REPAIR SHIP, *GRAND CANYON* CLASS (ex-AD)

Grand Canyon	AR-28	4-5-46	AA

Originally commissioned as AD-28 of *Shenandoah* class. This ship was built to a C3 hull design. Reclassified to AR-28 on 3-12-71 as replacement for *Cadmus* (AR-14).

1 REPAIR SHIP, *MARKAB* CLASS (ex-AD)

Markab (ex-SS Mormacpenn)	AR-23	6-15-41	PSR*

Built on a C3 hull design, this ship was originally commissioned as AK-31. She was reclassified AD-21 on 3-14-42. Decommissioned 1/47 at Orange, Texas. Recommissioned 2-26-52; decommissioned 7-31-55 at Charleston. She was reclassified AR-23 on 4-15-60 and recommissioned 7-1-60. Decommissioned on 12-19-69 at Mare Island and placed "in service, in reserve" on the same date for service as accommodation and depot ship at Mare Island InactShipFac, replacing *Pelias* (AS-14). The hull numbers AR-24/27 were not used. *Klondike* (AR-22), formerly accommodation and depot ship at San Diego InactShipFac, was stricken without replacement and is awaiting disposal.

2 REPAIR SHIPS, *DELTA* CLASS

Name	Number	Commissioned	F/S
Briareus (ex-SS *Hawaiian Planter*)	AR-12	11–15–43	MAR
Delta (ex-SS *Hawaiian Packer*)	AR-9	6–16–41	PSR*

Built on a C3 hull design. AR-12 was decommissioned 9–9–55 for duty as accommodation and depot ship at Norfolk. She was replaced by *Bushnell* (AS-15) on 6–30–70, then transferred to temporary custody of MarAd on 6–7–72 for layup. AR-9 was originally commissioned as AK-29; reclassified AR-9 on 7–1–42. Recommissioned 10/59. Decommissioned 6–20–70 at Bremerton and placed "in service, in reserve" as accommodation and depot ship at Bremerton on the same date, replacing *Euryale* (AS-22). The two ships of the *Amphion* class (AR-13/14) were transferred overseas; *Amphion* (AR-13) to Iran and *Cadmus* (AR-14) to Taiwan. Two additional sisters of this class, AR-15 and 16, were cancelled at the end of WW II. The 4 Liberty ship AR conversions, AR-17/21, were struck and transferred to MarAd for layup (3 have since been disposed of).

4 REPAIR SHIPS, *VULCAN* CLASS

Jason	AR-8	6–19–44	PA
Hector	AR-7	2–7–44	PA
Ajax	AR-6	10–30–43	PA
Vulcan	AR-5	6–16–41	AA

Built to a similar design as the *Fulton* class ASs and the *Dixie* class ADs. AR-8 was originally commissioned as ARH-1; to AR-8 on 9–9–57.

2 BATTLE DAMAGE REPAIR SHIPS, "*ARISTAEUS*" CLASS

Sarpedon	ARB-7	3–20–45	PR
Midas	ARB-5	5–23–44	PR

ARB-5 was originally laid down as LST-514 and ARB-7 as LST-956. They were reclassified ARB on 11–3–43 (5) and 8–14–44 (7). Both were decommissioned in 1/47 at San Diego.

2 CABLE REPAIRING SHIPS, *AEOLUS* CLASS

Thor (ex-*Vanadis*)	ARC-4	7–9–45	MSC
Aeolus (ex-*Turandot*)	ARC-3	6–18–45	MSC

Built on an S4-SE2-BE1 hull design as *Turandot* (AKA-47) and *Vanadis* (AKA-49). Commissioned as indicated. Both were decommissioned and stricken in 1946. Transferred to Maritime Commission for layup. AKA-47 was reacquired 11–4–54 and AKA-49 on 4–14–55 for conversion to ARCs. AKA-47 was renamed and reclassified on 3–17–55; AKA-49 followed on 11–14–

55. ARC-3 was recommissioned 5–14–55, followed by ARC-4 on 1–3–56. ARC-3 was decommissioned 10–1–73 and transferred to MSC for further service as USNS *Aeolus* (T-ARC-3). ARC-4 was decommissioned on 7–2–73 at Portsmouth, N.H., and transferred to MSC as USNS *Thor* (T-ARC-4). However, *Thor* was reduced to MSC ready-reserve in July 1974 as there are no funds to operate her. ARC-5 was the former USCGC *Yamacraw* (WARC-333).

2 CABLE REPAIR SHIPS, *NEPTUNE* CLASS

Name	Number	Commissioned	F/S
Albert J. Meyer	ARC-6	5–13–63	MSC
Neptune	ARC-2	6–1–53	MSC

Built on an S3-S2-BP1 hull design. ARC-2 was originally completed in WW II as SS *William H. G. Bullard*. Acquired by USN; commissioned on indicated date. This ship was decommissioned 11–8–73 at Norfolk and transferred to MSC on the same date for further service as USNS *Neptune* (T-ARC-2). ARC-6 was completed in 1945 with her present name. She was acquired from the Army as a loan on the indicated date. Acquired from the Army permanently in 9/66. She is employed as a hydrographic research ship. This class is quickly distinguished from the *Aeolus* class with one stack vice the two on ARC-3/4. ARC-1 was *Portunus* (ex-LSM-275).

4 LANDING CRAFT REPAIR SHIPS, "*ACHELOUS*" CLASS

Indra (ex LST-1147)	ARL-37	5–28–45	ASR*
Bellerophon (ex LST-1132)	ARL-31	3–19–45	PR
Sphinx (ex LST-963)	ARL-24	12–12–44	PR*
Egeria (ex LST-136)	ARL-8	12–18–43	PR

Originally laid down as LST-1 class (8) and LST-511 class (remainder) LSTs. These are the survivors of a class of 37 units. About a half-dozen serve foreign navies; some serve privately in merchant service. All were reclassified from LST to ARL on 11–3–43 (8) and 8–14–44 (remainder). All named on dates they were reclassified. ARL-8 was decommissioned 1/47 at San Diego; ARL-24 recommissioned 10/67 for Vietnam service; decommissioned 9–30–71 at Bremerton. ARL-37 was recommissioned 1/68 and made one tour of Vietnam before decommissioning 4/70 at Orange, Texas. Reactivated and placed "in service, in reserve" in 7/75 for duty as accommodation and depot ship at Norfolk InactShipFac, replacing *Bushnell* (AS-15). ARL-24 and 37 were fully modernized upon reactivation. Employed as floating maintenance bases for riverine craft in Vietnam.

6 SALVAGE SHIPS, *BOLSTER* CLASS

Name	Number	Commissioned	F/S
Recovery	ARS-43	5-15-46	AA
Reclaimer	ARS-42	12-20-45	PA
Opportune	ARS-41	10-5-45	AA
Hoist	ARS-40	7-21-45	AA
Conserver	ARS-39	6-9-45	PA
Bolster	ARS-38	5-1-45	PA

9 SALVAGE SHIPS, *ESCAPE* CLASS

Name	Number	Commissioned	F/S
Gear (ex-HMS *Pacific Salvor*)	ARS-34	9-24-43	Loan
Safeguard	ARS-25	10-31-44	PA
Grasp	ARS-24	8-22-44	PA
Deliver	ARS-23	7-18-44	PA
Curb	ARS-21	5-12-44	Loan
Cable	ARS-19	3-6-44	Loan
Preserver	ARS-8	1-11-44	AA
Grapple	ARS-7	12-16-43	PA
Escape	ARS-6	11-20-43	AA

Both classes are equipped to salvage ships of all types. Shallow drafts permit close-in salvage and emergency repair work. In addition to above, one unit of *Escape* class serves as AGOR-17 and two other units serve the Coast Guard. *Gear* originally classed as BARS-4 and intended for transfer to England under indicated name; retained by USN. Reclassified ARS-34 on 9-23-42 and renamed *Gear*. She was decommissioned 12-23-46 at San Diego; reactivated and placed "in service" 2-24-53 for charter to Murphy Marine Salvage Company. Placed under operational control of USN Supervisor of Salvage. As of 7/73, *Gear* is rated as "special, in service." Sister-ship *Clamp* (ARS-33) is scheduled for reinstatement on the NVR and reactivation for service in the same capacity as *Gear*. Her reactivation schedule is not known at this writing. ARS-19 and 21 are on loan to private salvage firms. ARS-19 was decommissioned 9-15-47 and loaned on same date. ARS-21 was decommissioned 12-20-46 and loaned on 5-10-47. Both are under the operational control of Supervisor of Salvage. It is currently proposed to replace *Curb* and/or *Cable* with *Clamp*. The 2 *Gypsy* class ARSDs, 2 *Laysan Island* class ARSTs, 2 *Fabius* class ARVAs, and the remaining *Aventinus* class ARVE unit have all been stricken and disposed of.

4 SUBMARINE TENDERS, *L. Y. SPEAR* CLASS

Name	Number	FY/SCB	Builder	Awarded	Commissioned	F/S
	AS-40	73/737.72	Lockheed	11-20-74		Bldg.
	AS-39	72/737.72	Lockheed	11-20-74		Bldg.
Dixon	AS-37	66/702	Gen. Dyn., Quincy	4-20-66	8-7-71	PA
L. Y. Spear	AS-36	65/702	Gen. Dyn., Quincy	5-12-65	2-28-70	AA

These tenders are designed to handle the latest SSNs. Each can take 4 SSN alongside and provide logistical support to another 12 SSN. Has the capability to repair nuclear power plants. AS-36 replaced *Bushnell* (AS-15) and *Dixon* replaced *Nereus* (AS-17) in the active Fleet. A fifth unit of this class, AS-38, was authorized in FY 1969, but she was cancelled on 3-27-69 and the funds diverted to pay for cost overruns on other shipbuilding projects. A fifth and sixth unit of this class is planned.

2 SUBMARINE TENDERS, *SIMON LAKE* CLASS

Name	Number	Commissioned	F/S
Canopus	AS-34	11-4-65	AA
Simon Lake	AS-33	11-7-64	AA

Designed as tenders for SSBNs, they can repair SSBN nuclear power plants and support and/or replace an SSBNs missiles. Each can take 3 SSBNs alongside at one time and render logistical support to another 9 SSBN. A third unit of this class, AS-35, was authorized FY 1965, but cancelled 12-3-64 when a requirement for a fifth FBM tender was dropped.

SIMON LAKE CLASS/*HUNLEY* CLASS POSEIDON (C-3) CONVERSIONS

Number	FY/SCB	Conversion Yard	Awarded	Started	Completed
AS-34	68/733.68	PS Naval Shipyard	8-29-67	6-3-69	2-3-70
AS-33	69/733.68	PS Naval Shipyard	7-1-68	7-7-70	3-9-71
AS-32	75/736.73	PS Naval Shipyard	8-13-73	9-3-74	
AS-31	73/736	PS Naval Shipyard	7-6-72	4-1-73	1-22-74

2 SUBMARINE TENDERS, *HUNLEY* CLASS

Name	Number	Commissioned	F/S
Holland	AS-32	9-7-63	PA
Hunley	AS-31	6-16-62	AA

First class of AS were specifically designed as AS (FBM). They can be distinguished from AS-33 and 36 classes by the stack amidships vice aft. The class was originally completed with a 32-ton hammerhead crane aft of stack. The crane proved cumbersome and a maintenance problem and was replaced by two 47-ton cranes similar to those on the *Fulton* class, located one to starboard and one to port aft. *Aegir* (AS-23) and *Euryale* (AS-22) have been stricken and disposed of.

1 SUBMARINE TENDER, *PROTEUS* CLASS

Name	Number	Commissioned	F/S
Proteus	AS-19	1-31-44	PA

Originally commissioned on indicated date as *Fulton* class AS; decommissioned 9-26-47 at New London. She was authorized for conversion to FBM tender under FY 1959. Alterations included the addition of a 44-foot midbody amidships, with a travelling crane running athwartships on the top of the new midbody. Recommissioned 7-8-60. Established SSBN bases at Holy Loch, Rota and Guam. The 2 *Griffin* class (AS-13/14) have been disposed of.

6 SUBMARINE TENDERS, *FULTON* CLASS

Name	Number	Commissioned	F/S
Orion	AS-18	9-30-43	AA*
Nereus	AS-17	10-24-45	PR*
Howard W. Gilmore	AS-16	5-24-44	AA
Bushnell	AS-15	4-10-43	MAR*
Sperry	AS-12	5-1-42	PA
Fulton	AS-11	9-12-41	AA

Built to the same design as *Vulcan* class ARs and *Dixie* class ADs. There were originally 7 in the class; *Proteus* was modified for use as AS(FBM) (see preceding class). All have been FRAMmed. AS-16 was originally named *Neptune*, then renamed as indicated on 6-8-43. This class can handle SSNs. AS-16 has kingposts and booms amidships; others have large cranes. AS-15 was decommissioned at Norfolk on 6-30-70 and was placed "in service, in reserve" on the same date as accommodation and depot ship at Norfolk InactShipFac. Replaced *Briareus* (AR-12) and was in turn replaced by *Indra* (ARL-37) in July 1975. Status was changed from "in service, in reserve" to "in reserve, out of commission" on the same date. Transferred to temporary custody of MarAd in 8/75 for layup. AS-17 was decommissioned 10-27-71 at Mare Island and laid up. AS-11 is one of the oldest active ships in the fleet.

2 SUBMARINE RESCUE SHIPS, *PIGEON* CLASS

Ortolan	ASR-22	7-14-73	AA
Pigeon	ASR-21	4-28-73	PA

First built-for-purpose ASR class. These ships have a catamaran hull (each hull 251' × 26') with a 34-foot well between hulls. They are equipped with a 200-ton crane aft, personnel transfer capsules, and a decompression chamber. They have built-in helicopter decks, but no hangar; they can carry DSRVs for rescue of crew members of sunken submarines. *Pigeon* replaced *Chanticleer* (ASR-7) on the active list. The converted ATFs of the *Penguin* class (ASR-12, 19/20) have been disposed of.

6 SUBMARINE RESCUE SHIPS, "*CHANTICLEER*" CLASS

Name	Number	Commissioned	F/S
Tringa	ASR-16	1-28-47	AA
Sunbird	ASR-15	1-28-47	AA
Petrel	ASR-14	9-24-46	AA
Kittiwake	ASR-13	7-18-46	AA
Florikan	ASR-9	4-5-43	PA
Coucal	ASR-8	1-23-43	PA

Based on tug design. All armament was removed 1957/58. These ships carry the latest rescue equipment, but are not equipped for deep rescue like the *Pigeon* class. Class leader has been disposed of. Sister ship *Greenlet* (ASR-10) was sold to Turkey; *Macaw* (ASR-11) was lost in WW II.

2 AUXILIARY OCEAN TUGS, "*SOTOYOMO*" CLASS

Tatnuck (ex-ATR-122)	ATA-195	2-26-45	PR*
[Penobscot (ex-ATR-115)]	ATA-188	12-14-44	Stricken
Accokeek (ex-ATR-108)	ATA-181	10-7-44	MAR*

Originally classed as Rescue Tugboats (ATR); all reclassified 5-15-44. Many of this class serve in foreign navies, the merchant marine and Coast Guard. ATA-181 was decommissioned 6-30-72 at Norfolk and transferred to temporary custody of MarAd on 9-19-72 for layup. ATA-188 was decommissioned 7-2-71 at Boston. ATA-195 was decommissioned 7-1-71 at Bremerton. Both laid up in InactShipFacs. *Wandank* (ATA-204) and *Koka* (ATA-185), previously on loan to the Department of the Interior and the Department of Health, Education and Welfare, respectively, were returned to USN on 5-22-73 and 12-1-73, respectively, and were transferred permanently to their respective civilian departments on the same dates. The unnamed ATA-240 has been disposed of.

3 FLEET OCEAN TUGS, *UNNAMED* CLASS

Name	Number	FY/SCB	Builder	Awarded	Commissioned	F/S
	ATF-168	76/740.75				Proj.
	ATF-167	76/740.75				Proj.
	ATF-166	75/740.75				Bldg.

A new class of fleet tug. With the exception of the ATSs, this is the first oceangoing tug constructed since WW II. She has accommodations for a salvage and diving detachment of 20 men and is to be manned by MSC upon completion. Habitability standards will be up to civilian standards. She will be able to tow any ship up to 60,000 tons and will carry a 10-ton crane. Besides salvage and towing, she will have the capability to fight fires on ships at sea. First tug is scheduled for delivery in 8/77. A total of 10 units of this class is planned.

AUXILIARY SHIPS

22 FLEET OCEAN TUGS, "CHEROKEE" CLASS

Name	Number	Commissioned	F/S
Shakori	ATF-162	12–20–45	AA
Salinan	ATF-161	11–9–45	AA
Papago	ATF-160	10–3–45	AA
Paiute	ATF-159	8–27–45	AA
Mosopelea	ATF-158	7–28–45	MSC
Nipmuc	ATF-157	7–8–45	AA
Luiseno	ATF-156	6–16–45	DAA
Atakapa	ATF-149	12–8–44	MSC
Tawakoni	ATF-114	9–15–44	PA
Takelma	ATF-113	8–3–44	PA
Quapaw	ATF-110	5–6–44	PA
Molala	ATF-106	9–29–43	PA

Name	Number	Commissioned	F/S
Moctobi	ATF-105	7–25–44	PA
Hitchiti	ATF-103	5–27–44	PA
Cocopa	ATF-101	3–25–44	PA
Chowanoc	ATF-100	2–21–44	PA
Abnaki	ATF-96	11–15–43	PA
[Tawasa]	ATF-92	7–17–43	Stricken
Seneca	ATF-91	4–30–43	MAR*
Mataco	ATF-86	5–29–43	PA
Lipan	ATF-85	4–29–43	MSC
Cree	ATF-84	3–28–43	PA
Ute	ATF-76	12–31–42	MSC

Originally classified as ATs, all were reclassified ATF on 5–15–44. There are two subdivisions within the class. From ATF-96 on, the tugs have no stack; the preceding units have one stack. This is one of the more successful designs in the USN and the basis for design of the ASR-7 class. Many of these tugs serve other Navies in a variety of missions; 2 units serve in the Coast Guard. ATF-158 was decommissioned 7–2–73 at Norfolk and transferred to MSC for further service. ATF-85 was decommissioned 7–31–73 at Sasebo, Japan, and transferred to MSC for further service. ATF-149 was decommissioned on 7–1–74 and ATF-76 on 8–30–74. Both were transferred to MSC for further service. All serve as USNS (T-ATF), are unarmed and civilian manned. ATF-91 was decommissioned 7–1–71 at Norfolk and transferred to the temporary custody of MarAd on 11–18–71 for layup.

3 SALVAGE AND RESCUE SHIPS, *EDENTON* CLASS

Name	Number	Commissioned	F/S
Brunswick	ATS-3	12–9–72	PA
Beaufort	ATS-2	1–22–72	PA
Edenton	ATS-1	1–23–71	AA

Originally designed to replace ATA/ATFs, but because of the size and expense of each ship this will not be done. These ships were originally rated as salvage tugs, but rerated as indicated on 2–16–71. Each ship has controllable pitch propellers, twin rudders, bow thruster, 70-ton self-tensioning towing winch, one 10-ton crane forward and one 20-ton crane aft and can also fight fires on other ships and support dives up to depths of 950 feet. ATS-4 was authorized FY 1972 and ATS-5/6 in FY 1973. However, construction was deferred. All of this class were built in England.

1 GUIDED MISSILE SHIP, *NORTON SOUND* CLASS

Name	Number	Commissioned	F/S
Norton Sound	AVM-1	1–8–45	PA

First commissioned as AV-11 of *Currituck* class AVs, *Norton Sound* was converted in 1949 for service as a weapons and systems test ship; reclassified AVM on 8–8–51. She served as a test ship for such weapons as ASROC, TARTAR, TERRIER, and BPDMS. The latest weapon systems tested were the MK 45 lightweight 5″/54 gun and MK 26 guided missile launcher. This ship has been modified for her testing missions many times and is currently employed as a test ship for the AEGIS weapon system and associated gear. Originally, it was planned to convert two *Alaska* class large cruisers (CB) to serve as experimental guided missile ships (one on each coast). Because of the initial cost of $50 million per ship and the restricted budgets of the era, the project (SCB-26) was abandoned and *Norton Sound* was given an austere conversion instead.

1 TRAINING AIRCRAFT CARRIER, *LEXINGTON* CLASS

Name	Number	Commissioned	F/S
Lexington	CVT-16	2–17–43	AT

Originally laid down as *Cabot;* renamed 6–16–42. She was originally commissioned as an *Essex* class carrier and rated as a warship. Decommissioned 4–23–47. She was modernized in the early 1950s (see *Essex* class modernization table in Section 1) and reclassified CVA-16 on 10–1–52. Recommissioned 8–15–55; to CVS on 10–1–62. She replaced *Antietam* (CVS-36) as a training carrier at Pensacola on 12–29–62. Reclassified CVT on 1–1–69. She was rerated from warship to auxiliary on 9–23–70. All guns and fire control gear were removed during her 7/69 to 1/70 overhaul. The ship is subordinated to the Naval Air Training Command and has a reduced crew.

Samuel Gompers (AD-37). Note two large centerline cranes and two small traveling cranes on each side. 1971. **Samuel Gompers** class.

Shenandoah (AD-26). Familiar 5″ mount forward has been removed. 7–73. **Shenandoah** class.

Everglades (AD-24). **"Klondike"** class.

Piedmont (AD-17). Ships in this class are among the oldest still in commission. **Dixie** class.

Butte (AE-27). 2–70. **Kilauea** class.

Kiska (AE-35). Note enclosed 3" mounts atop superstructure abaft stack compared to open 3" mounts on BUTTE (AE-27). 10–72. **Kilauea** class.

Pyro (AE-24). 1972. **Nitro** class.

Suribachi (AE-21). Note forward 3" armament as compared to that of PYRO (AE-24). 1969. **Suribachi** class.

AUXILIARY SHIPS

Firedrake (AE-14). 1970. **"Mount Hood"** class.

Rigel (AF-58). After 3″ mounts removed when helicopter platform was installed. 1968. **Rigel** class.

Denebola (AF-56) prior to transfer to MSC for further service. 1971. **Denebola** class.

Aludra (AF-55). **Aludra** class.

Arcturus (AF-52). **"Bald Eagle"** class.

Procyon (AF-61). 1963. **"Alstede"** class.

Sylvania (AFS-2). Note "M" frames, which replaced king posts and conventional booms. **Mars** class.

San Jose (AFS-7). Some units of this class have closed 3″ mounts forward, some are open. 7–71. **Mars** class.

AUXILIARY SHIPS

S.P. Lee (AG-192) as AGS-31. Now on loan to Department of Interior. **S.P. Lee** class.

Alacrity (AG-520) as MSO-520. Minesweeping gear was removed for her new role. 4–69. **Alacrity** class.

Observation Island (AG-154). Served as POLARIS/POSEIDON test ship. 3–71. **Compass Island** class.

Compass Island (AG-153). **Compass Island** class.

Sequoia (AG-23). **Sequoia** class.

Point Loma (AGDS-2) as POINT BARROW (AKD-1). **Point Loma** class.

Plainview (AGEH-1). **Plainview** class.

Pueblo (AGER-1). 1967. **"Banner"** class. (Photo: PHCS(AC) J. M. Lahr.)

AUXILIARY SHIPS

Glover (AGFF-1). Except for no armament aft and her raised fantail, *Glover* can easily be confused with **Brooke/Garcia** classes. 10–69. **Glover** class.

Redstone (AGM-20). 5–70. **Vanguard** class.

La Salle (AGF-3). 6–72. **La Salle** class.

Longview (AGM-3). 5–70. **"Range Tracker"** class.

Arlington (AGMR-2). Frequently and easily confused in appearance with *Wright* (CC-2). **Arlington** class.

Annapolis (AGMR-1). Hurricane bow installed during conversion. **Annapolis** class.

Gyre (AGOR-21). Small, utility type AGOR of simple design. Open deck aft provides quick change of mission capabilities. Note two thin, tall stacks. 1973. **Gyre** class.

Snatch (AGOR-18). Since stricken; she is sister to *Chain* (AGOR-17). **Chain** class.

AUXILIARY SHIPS

General H.H. Arnold (AGM-9). **General H.H. Arnold** class. (Photo: Todd Shipyards.)

Hayes (AGOR-16). One of the three catamaran hull ships in the Navy. 1971. **Hayes** class. (Photo: Camera Craft.)

Hayes (AGOR-16). 1971. **Hayes** class. (Photo: Camera Craft.)

Mizar (AGOR-11). 1969. **"Eltanin"** class.

Knorr (AGOR-15). 11–69. **Robert D. Conrad** class.

Graham County (AGP-1176) arriving Philadelphia Naval Shipyard for conversion to AGP. 2–8–72. **Graham County** class.

Lynch (AGOR-7). 1973. Note differences in appearance between this ship and *Knorr* (AGOR-15). **Robert D. Conrad** class.

109

Wyman (AGS-34). Class is larger version of *Robert D. Conrad* AGORs. 9–71. **Wilkes** class.

Chauvenet (AGS-29). 1973. **Chauvenet** class.

Silas Bent (AGS-26). 1965. **Silas Bent** class.

Dutton (AGS-22). Navy's largest surveying ships. Designed to chart the ocean floor and to record magnetic fields and gravity. **Bowditch** class.

AUXILIARY SHIPS

Albacore (AGSS-569) in PHASE III configuration. **Albacore** class.

Tang (AGSS-563) as SS-563. **Tang** class.

Dolphin (AGSS-555). Diving planes replaced by new type of rudder. 1968. **Dolphin** class.

Sanctuary (AH-17). 1966. **"Haven"** class.

Norwalk (AK-279). **Norwalk** class.

Sgt. Truman Kimbro (AK-254). **"Lt. George W. G. Boyce"** class.

Sea Lift (AKR-9). **Sea Lift** class.

Pvt. John R. Towle (AK-240). **Greenville Victory** class.

Comet (AKR-7). **Comet** class.

Sealift Pacific (AO-168). Bulk oil tankers built as replacements for the aging **"Suamico"** class tankers. 6–7–74. **Sealift Pacific** class. (Photo: Joseph J. Ernest.)

Ponchatoula (AO-148). 3–70. **Neosho** class.

Maumee (AO-149). **Maumee** class.

Mission Buenaventura (AO-111). Since stricken. Class leader of 27 **"Mission"** class AOs. **"Mission"** class.

Mispillion (AO-105). 1972. **Mispillion** class.

Schuylkill (AO-76). 10–71. **"Suamico"** class.

Ashtabula (AO-51). One of the jumboized **"Cimarron"** class oilers. 10–70 **"Cimarron"** class.

Detroit (AOE-4). Fast carrier task force replenishment ships. 4–72. **Sacramento** class.

Passumpsic (AO-107) in her MSC configuration. **Mispillion** class.

Seattle (AOE-3). 1–70. **Sacramento** class.

Chewaucan (AOG-50). Normally refuel other vessels at anchor, but have secondary underway refueling capability. 1973. **"Patapsco"** class.

Kalamazoo (AOR-6). Note similarity to AOE. This class has shorter hull, higher helicopter platform, and stubby stack. 6–73. **Wichita** class.

Wichita (AOR-1). 1971. **Wichita** class.

Geiger (AP-197). USN's last AP. "**Barrett**" class.

Mercer (APB-39). "**Benewah**" class. 1968.

Grand Canyon (AR-28). 1967. **Grand Canyon** class.

Markab (AR-23). **Markab** class.

Delta (AR-9). **Delta** class.

Hector (AR-7). Note similarity to **Dixie** and **Fulton** class tenders. 1971. **Vulcan** class.

AUXILIARY SHIPS

Zeus (ARB-4). Since stricken. She represents the class. 1944. "**Aristaeus**" class.

Aeolus (ARC-3). 3–70. **Aeolus** class.

Indra (ARL-37). "**Achelous**" class.

Neptune (ARC-2). **Neptune** class.

Bolster (ARS-38). 2–73. **Bolster** class.

Safeguard (ARS-25). 3–72. **Escape** class.

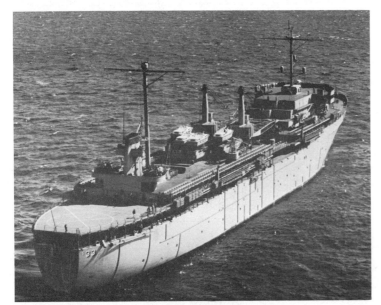

Simon Lake (AS-33). SSBN tender. 1965. **Simon Lake** class.

L.Y. Spear (AS-36). 10–69. **L.Y. Spear** class.

AUXILIARY SHIPS

L.Y. Spear (AS-36). 1–70. **L.Y. Spear** class.

Holland (AS-32). 1974. **Hunley** class.

Proteus (AS-19). Converted **Fulton** class AS. First FBM tender. **Proteus** class.

AUXILIARY SHIPS

Hunley (AS-31) with *Sunfish* (SSN-649) alongside. 7–69. **Hunley** class.

Fulton (AS-11). One of oldest active ships in the Navy. 12–71. **Fulton** class.

Ortolan (ASR-22). Note stubby profile. 8–73. **Pigeon** class.

Ortolan (ASR-22). Note large work areas of catamaran ships. 7–73. **Pigeon** class.

AUXILIARY SHIPS

Florikan (ASR-9). Note tug design of this class. 8–71. **"Chanticleer"** class.

Mosopelea (ATF-158). 10–68. **"Cherokee"** class.

Accokeek (ATA-181). 1970. **"Sotoyomo"** class.

Beaufort (ATS-2). 8–74. **Edenton** class.

Brunswick (ATS-3) conducting an exercise tow of *Constellation* (CV-64). 10–74. **Edenton** class. (Photo: Robert L. Lawson.)

Norton Sound (AVM-1). Note BPDMS and missile launchers aft. **North Sound** class.

Lexington (CVT-16). 2–72. **Lexington** class.

SIX: SERVICE CRAFT

Because of the diverse nature of the U.S. Navy's service craft, this section will be handled in a different manner from the preceding sections. Each classification will be listed with its long title. Then the general characteristics of the type, from the smallest to the largest, will be listed. Units in the classification still on the NVR will be followed by a summation of the craft status in the specific classification. Each classification will conclude with appropriate comments. Unless noted in the Comments Section of each classification, all active service craft are rated as "Active, in service" or "In reserve, out of service." Further, unless noted all service craft are unnamed. A glossary of terms used in this chapter appears at the end of the section. **Service Craft Summary:** Active: 921½; Reserve: 174½; Loan: 46½; ILP: 71; Building: 32; Lend-lease: 4; **Grand Total:** 1245½.

AFDB—Large Auxiliary Floating Dry Dock (non-self-propelled)
Displacement: 30,800/38,500 tons (light)
Lifting capacity: 32,250/90,000 tons (nominal)
Length overall: 825'/927'
Length on pontoons: 398'9"/827'
Maximum draft: 67'4"/78'
Light draft: 8'8"/9'
Over blocks draft: 39'10"/46'
Inside width: 119'6"/133'7" (clear)
Units: AFDB-1/5, Los Alamos (AFDB-7) (Sections A, B, E & G), AFDB-7 (Sections C & D).
Summary: Active: 1 unit and 1 partial unit; Reserve 4 and 1 partial unit; Loan 1 partial unit
Comments: AFDBs are normally used to dock CVA/BB types (Los Alamos docks SSBNs). The docks consist of 7 to 10 steel sections that are detachable for towing and maintenance. The 6 AFDBs are divided into 3 classes: AFDB-1 class (1/2), AFDB-3 class (3), and AFDB-4 class (4, 5, 7). AFDB-1 and Los Alamos (AFDB-7) are the only active units. AFDB-1 is based at Subic Bay and Los Alamos at Holy Loch. Sections C & D of AFDB-7 were replaced by the reactivated Sections E & G of AFDB-7 in early 1974 and sections C & D were inactivated at that time. This was done in lieu of overhauling Sections C & D. Completed between 7/43 and 3/45.

AFDL—Small Auxiliary Floating Dry Dock (non-self-propelled)
Displacement: 800/13,000 tons (light)
Lifting capacity: 1,000/6,500 tons (nominal)
Length overall: 200'/489'
Length on pontoons: 200'/448'
Maximum draft: 28'6"/46'10"
Light draft: 3'3"/13'5"
Over blocks draft: 15'11"/26'
Inside width: 45'/70' (clear)
Units: AFDL-1, 2, 6/12, 15, 16, 19/23, 25, 26, 28/30, 33, 37/41, 43/45, 47, 48. **Summary:** Active: 7; Reserve: 2; Loan: 14; ILP: 10.
Comments: AFDLs are normally used to dock DD/SS/LST/DE/ATA/AN/MSO types. They con-

sist of one steel or concrete section. Unlike the AFDBs, they are not detachable into sections. The AFDLs are divided into 5 classes: AFDL-1 class (1, 2, 6, 8/12, 15, 16, 19/21, 25, 26, 28/30), AFDL-7 class (7, 22, 23, 33), AFDL-35 class (37/41, 43/45), AFDL-47 class (47) and AFDL-48 class (48). All completed between 9/43 and 6/56.

AFDM—Medium Auxiliary Floating Dry Dock (non-self-propelled)
Displacement: 6,400/8,000 tons
Lifting capacity: 15,000 and 18,000 tons (nominal)
Length overall: 615'8" and 622'
Length on pontoons: 544' and 552'
Maximum draft: 31'9"/52'9"
Light draft: 5'8"/6'2"
Over blocks draft: 28'/31'1"
Inside width: 87'6"/93'2" (clear)
Units: AFDM-1/3, 5/7, Richland (AFDM-8), 9, 10. **Summary:** Active: 4; Reserve: 0; Loan: 5
Comments: AFDMs consist of 3-piece steel sections attached together to form one dock. They are normally used to dock CG/CLG/DD types. All AFDMs are ex-YFDs. The AFDMs are divided into two classes: AFDM-1 class (1/2) and AFDM-3 class (3, 5/10). Completed between 7/42 and 3/45.

AGDS—Auxiliary Deep Submergence Support Vehicle
Displacement: 5,200 (light)
Lifting capacity: 3,500 tons (nominal)
Length overall: 491'8"
Length on pontoons: 414'1"
Maximum draft: 32'10"
Light draft: 5'8"
Over blocks draft: 21'2"
Inside width: 59' (clear)
Units: None. **Summary:** None

Comments: Originally, this ship was a one-piece steel auxiliary repair dry dock with the hull number ARD-20. In the mid-1960s, she was taken out of reserve and modified for service as a tender and support ship for the *Trieste* II. Named *White Sands* on 3–9–68. Non-self-propelled, the fleet tug *Apache* (ATF-67) was assigned to act as her consort and provide the towing. Reclassified AGDS-1 on 8–1–73. On 2–28–74, both *White Sands* and *Apache* were replaced by *Point Loma* (AGDS-2). *White Sands* (AGDS-1) has since been stricken, but she is listed here for accounting purposes. The classification, as applied to AGDS-2, does not mean the same thing as applied to AGDS-1 (see Glossary Section, Part a, for definition of AGDS as applied to each ship). AGDS-1 was completed in 3/44.

APL—Barracks Craft (non-self-propelled)
Displacement: 2,580 tons (full load)
Length overall: 260′
Extreme beam: 49′
Maximum draft: 11′
Accommodations: Officers: 96 (53 & 54), 6 (remainder); Enlisted: 338 (53 & 54), 680 (remainder)
Units: APL-2, 4, 5, 15, 18, 19, 29, 31, 32, 34, 42, 43, 45, 47, 50, 53, 54, 57, 58. **Summary:** Active: 14; Reserve: 2; Loan: 1; ILP: 2.
Comments: Non-self-propelled craft used to berth troops and ships' crews (when their ships are in overhaul). They have also been used to berth sailors and marines in transit to other stations. 19 units on NVR fall into 4 classes: APL-2 class (2, 4, 5, 15), APL-17 class (18, 19, 29, 31, 32, 34), APL-41 class (42, 43, 45, 47, 50) and APL-53 class (53, 54, 57, 58). APL-45 was stricken 11–1–72, but reinstated in 1974 for further service. Completed between 7/44 and 9/45.

ARD—Auxiliary Repair Dry Dock (non-self-propelled)
Displacement: 4,200/5,200 tons (light)
Lifting capacity: 3,500 tons (nominal)
Length overall: 485′8″/491′8″
Length on pontoons: 414′1″
Maximum draft: 32′7″/32′10″
Light draft: 5′1″/5′8″
Over blocks draft: 21′2″/21′9″
Inside width: 49′/59′ (clear)
Units: ARD-5/9, 12/15, 17, *Windsor* (ARD-22), 23, 24, 28, *Arco* (ARD-29), 30, 32. **Summary:** Active:4; Reserve: 0; Loan: 0; ILP: 12
Comments: One-piece steel docks used to dock DD/SS/LST types. The 16 ARDs still on the NVR are divided into 2 classes which are as follows: ARD-1 class (5/9) and ARD-12 class (12/15, 17, 22/24, 28/30, 32). *Windsor* (ARD-22) and *Arco* (ARD-29) held commissioned status before they were transferred to foreign countries. In addition to the above, 3 ARDs were converted to ARDMs (see next subsection) and a fourth ARD became AGDS-1. Completed between 6/42 and 8/44.

ARDM—Medium Auxiliary Floating Dry Dock (non-self-propelled)
Displacement: 5,200 tons (light) (1/3), 5,300 tons (light) (4)
Lifting capacity: 3,500 tons (1/2), 5,500 tons (3), 17,800 tons (4) (all nominal)
Length overall: 491′8″ (1/2), 512′7″ (3), 492′ (4)
Length on pontoons: 414′1″ (1/2)
Maximum draft: 32′10″ (1/2), 41′9″ (3), 33′ (4)
Light draft: 5′8″ (1/2), 7′2″ (3)
Over blocks draft: 21′2″ (1/2), 30′ (3)
Inside width: 59′ (1/2), 39′3″ (3) (all clear)
Units: *Oak Ridge* (ARDM-1), *Alamagordo* (ARDM-2), ARDM-3, 4. **Summary:** Active: 3; Reserve: 0; Building: 1.
Comments: ARDM-1/3 originally completed between 2/44 and 6/44 as ARD-19 (1), ARD-26 (2) and ARD-18 (3). ARD-19, 26 were converted to ARDM-1/2 in 1961–65. ARDM-3 received a less austere conversion than ARDM-1/2 in 1968–69. ARDM-1 commissioned 12/63 as *Oak Ridge* (ARDM-1). ARDM-2 followed on 8–3–65 as *Alamagordo* (ARDM-2). She sank 11–10–65 at Charleston while docking an SSBN. She was decommissioned, raised, repaired and recommissioned 6/66. ARDM-3 was placed "in service" 10/71. Serves at Charleston with ARDM-2. ARDM-1 serves at Rota, Spain. The construction of ARDM-4 was authorized under FY 1975. ARDM-5/7 are projected. They will replace existing ARDs and will be able to handle all SSBNs except *Trident* class.

DSRV—Deep Submergence Research Vehicle (self-propelled)
Full load displacement: 32 tons (in air)
Length overall: 49′2″
Extreme beam: 8′ (diameter measurement)
Propulsion: Battery-powered electric motors
Screws/max. speed: 1/5 kts.
Accommodations: off.: 3; Survivors: 24
Operating depth: 5,000 ft.
Units: DSRV-1/2. **Summary:** Active: 2; Reserve: 0
Comments: Designed to rescue survivors from sunken submarines, the 2 units can operate deeper than the survival depth of any existing submarine in the U.S. Navy. Built in response to the *Thresher* (SSN-593) disaster. DSRV-1 placed "in service" on 8–7–71 and commissioned in 10/71. DSRV-2 placed "in service" on 8–7–72. Originally 6 units were planned, but costs and construction delays limited the class to 2 units. Both units are assigned to the Pacific Fleet.

DSV—Deep Submergence Vehicle (self-propelled)
Weight: 84 tons (1), 21 tons (3/4)
Length overall: 78′6″ (1), 25′ (3/4)
Extreme beam: 15′3″ (1), 8′ (3/4)
Propulsion: Battery-powered electric motors
Screws/max. speed: 1/2 knots
Crew: 3 (1), 2 (3/4)

Units: *Trieste* II (DSV-1), *Alvin* (DSV-2), *Turtle* (DSV-3), *Sea Cliff* (DSV-4), *Nemo* (DSV-5).
Summary: Active 4; Loan: 1.
Comments: Characteristics for DSV-2 and 5 are not available. DSV-1 and 5 were originally completed in 1950s for private service. DSV-1 was purchased in 1958 as *Trieste I;* rebuilt in early 1960s, and renamed *Trieste II.* Classed as "equipment" until 9-1-69 when she was instated on the NVR as X-2 and placed "in service" on the same date. She was reclassified DSV-1 on 6-1-71 and assigned to the Pacific Fleet. DSV-2 was built for the U.S. Navy in mid-1960s; classed as "equipment." She accidentally sank on 10-16-68, approximately 120 miles south of Cape Cod, when a cable being used to hoist the mini-sub aboard the mother ship broke and the sub fell back into the sea. With the entry hatch open, she flooded and sank. She was raised 8-28-69 by *Mizar* (AGOR-11) and the commercial research sub *Aluminaut*, rebuilt 1970-71 and instated on the NVR on 6-1-71 as DSV-2 (retains her original name). Placed "In service" on the same date. Active, Atlantic Fleet. DSV-3/4 completed 1968-69 for the Navy with the unofficial classification *Autec I* and *II*, respectively. Originally rated as "equipment" and both instated on the NVR on 6-1-71 as DSV-3/4, respectively (retaining original names). Both were placed "in service" on the same date and assigned to the Pacific Fleet. DSV-5 was acquired in mid-1960s as "equipment," and was instated on the NVR on 6-1-71 as DSV-5 (retaining her original name). Placed "In service" on the same date. She is currently on loan to Southwest Research Institute, San Antonio, Texas. DSV-1, 3 and 4 were placed in commission (miscellaneous) 1/73.

IX—Unclassified Miscellaneous
Full load displacement: 1,785 (501)/2,200 (21)
Length overall: 175' (between perp.) (21)/229'8" (501)
Extreme beam: 45' (21)/50' (501)
Propulsion: Diesels (all except IX-21 and 310 which are non-self-propelled)
Screws/max. speed: 2/11 kts. (501) to 13 kts. (308)
Accommodations: 13 (307)/62 (308)
Units: *Constitution* (IX-21), IX-306, *Brier* (IX-307), *New Bedford* (IX-308), IX-310, *Elk River* (IX-501): **Summary:** Active: 6; Reserve: 0
Comments: This type represents a diverse group of ships. Characteristics of IX-310 are not available. IX-21 is the frigate *Constitution,* the oldest active ship in USN. She has been in full commission since 10/71 having been in special commission prior to that date; serves as flagship of Commandant First Naval District. She was overhauled and rebuilt 1927-30 and is currently undergoing overhaul in the former Boston Naval Shipyard. The ship is scheduled to be opened for visitors in time for the United States Bicentennial; she will remain in Boston. IX-306 is the former Army FS-221. Acquired from the Army on 1/69, instated on the NVR, and placed in service on the same date. She serves as a test ship for the MK 48 torpedo. Her bow is painted blue, which makes the ship easily recognizable; she operates in the Caribbean. *Brier* (IX-307) is the former USCG *Brier* (WLI-299). Acquired by USN from the Coast Guard on 3-10-69, and placed in service in 9/69 as "equipment." She was classed as IX-307 and instated on the NVR on 8-29-70; retained Coast Guard name. Assigned to Naval Ordnance Lab., Solomons, Md. *New Bedford* (IX-308) was originally the Army Supply ship FS-289. She was acquired from the Army on 3-1-50 as AKL-17, assigned to MSTS for service, and named *New Bedford* on 11-20-61. Rerated as "equipment" on

8-26-63 and her name dropped. She was transferred from the Atlantic to Naval Torpedo Station, Keyport, Washington, for further service. Her name was restored in 2/69, she was classed as IX-308 and rerated as "service craft" (thus putting the ship back on NVR) all in 2/69. Continued service until 10/71 when her status was changed to "in service." She continues her assignment at Keyport. IX-309 was reclassified YAG-61. IX-310 was instated on the NVR and placed in service on 4-1-71. She consists of two barges held together with a deck housing running athwartships across the two barges at the midship section, and appears H-shaped from the air. This vessel is under the administrative and operational control of Naval Underwater Systems Center, Newport, R.I. and is in Lake Seneca, N.Y., where she serves as sonar test ship. *Elk River* (IX-501) was originally commissioned on 5-27-45 as LSMR-501. She was converted for service as the SEALAB III mothership 1968-69 at Avondale Shipyards and placed "in service, special" in 1/69. Placed "in service, active" in 1/73. With discontinuance of the SEALAB III program, the ship now supports deep submergence activities off San Clemente Island, California. She also has capability to operate as mothership for deep-diving salvage operations. The ship has an open well deck amidships and carries a 65-ton capacity crane. During modification, the ship was lengthened from 203'6" to 225' and bulges were added amidships to improved stability and for additional workspace.

NR—Submersible Research Vehicle (self-propelled)
Submerged displacement: 400 tons
Length overall: 136'4"
Extreme beam: 12'4"
Propulsion: 2 nuclear reactors
Screws/max. speed: 2/12 kts.
Accommodations: 7 total
Units: NR-1. **Summary:** Active: 1; Reserve: 0
Comments: A highly successful research submarine. She was placed in service on 10-27-69. Equipped with lights, TV viewers, viewing ports, movie cameras and retractable arm for picking up objects off ocean floor. In addition, she is equipped with retractable "wheels" on the bottom of the hull so she can drive along the ocean floor. Active Atlantic Fleet. A second unit is projected. NR-1 is the first nuclear-powered service craft.

SWOB—Ship Waste Off-Loading Barge (non-self-propelled)
Capacity: 7,500 gallons.
Units: SWOB-1/26. **Summary:** Active: 0; Reserve: 0; Building: 26.
Comments: New type of service craft. Characteristics are not available. Authorized under FY 1974 program. Contract for construction was awarded to the Marine Power and Equipment Company, Inc., Seattle, Wash., on 6-28-74.

YAG—Miscellaneous Auxiliary (self-propelled)
Displacement: 11,400 (full load) (39), 440 tons (light) (61)
Length overall: 442' (39), 174" (61)
Extreme beam: 67' (39), 33' (61)
Propulsion: Reciprocating steam (39), diesel (61)
Screws/max. speed: 1/11 (39), 7 (61)
Accommodations: 49 (39), 23 (61)
Units: *George Eastman* (YAG-39), YAG-61. **Summary:** Active: 1; Reserve: 1.
Comments: *George Eastman* was originally completed in WW II as SS *George Eastman*. She was acquired on 10–20–53 and instated on the NVR as YAG-39 (no name) and placed in service on the same date. Placed out of service on 11–1–57 at San Diego; placed in commission 10–20–62 and assigned former merchant ship name on 7–3–63. Decommissioned 9/67 at Mare Island. YAG-61 was originally completed in WW II as YW-87. Converted to a MObile NOise Barge in 5/69 and reclassified as IX-309. Unofficially known as MONOB 1. Reclassified YAG-61 on 7–1–70 and based at Port Everglades, Florida, where she conducts research for the Naval Ship Research and Development Center. The former YAG-60 (ex-*Butternut*, ANL-9), still exists as a fire-fighting training hulk. YAG-61 has been in service since 6/70.

YC—Open Lighter (non-self-propelled)
Displacement: 175 tons/1,400 tons
Length overall: 80'/175'
Extreme beam: 27'/53'
Propulsion: None
Screws/max. speed: None
Accommodations: None
Units: YC-306, 316, 360, 688, 695, 699, 705, 706, 709, 712, 713, 721, 724, 725, 728, 735, 746, 752, 754, 756, 757, 760, 763, 764, 769, 772, 775, 781, 783, 787, 789, 794, 799, 800, 802/805, 813, 821, 823/826, 828/833, 972, 978/981, 983, 984, 1027, 1029, 1056, 1058/1060, 1062, 1065, 1068/1071, 1073/1077, 1080, 1081, 1084/1092, 1107, 1109, 1112, 1116/1121, 1273, 1275, 1321/1324, 1326/1329, 1333, 1134, 1351, 1352, 1360, 1366/1368, 1371/1373, 1375/1383, 1385, 1386, 1389/1392, 1394, 1395, 1398/1402, 1406/1411, 1413, 1417, 1419, 1430/1451, 1456, 1458/1462, 1464/1497, 1499/1504, 1509/1516. **Summary:** Active: 195; Reserve: 25; Loan: 2.
Comments: Essentially, these are barges with houses on them. Used to store materials, to house shops, etc. All completed between 1915 and 1969.

YCF—Car Floats (non-self-propelled)
Full load displacement: 420 tons
Length overall: 150'
Extreme beam: 34'
Propulsion: None
Screws/max. speed: None
Accommodations: None
Units: YCF-14/16. **Summary:** Active: 1; Reserve: 2.
Comments: Barges used to transport railroad cars, by being towed from one place to the other. The active unit, YCF-16, is in service in the Third Naval District. Completed 1941–42.

YCV—Aircraft Transportation Lighter (non-self-propelled)
Full load displacement: 2,480 tons
Length overall: 200'
Extreme beam: 65'
Propulsion: None
Screws/max. speed: None
Accommodations: None
Units: YCV-8/11, 15, 16, 18. **Summary:** Active: 6; Reserve: 0; Loan: 1.
Comments: Used to transport dismantled and/or complete aircraft in inland waters. These are barge-type craft which were completed between 3/44 and 10/45.

YD—Floating Crane (non-self-propelled)
Full load displacement: 393 tons/4,917 tons
Length overall: 87'/205'
Extreme beam: 30'/110'
Propulsion: None
Screws/max. speed: None
Accommodations: None
Units: YD-26, 71, 73, 75, 77, 82, 86/91, 113/117, 120, 121, 127, 145, 149, 150, 152, 153, 154, 156, 157, 159, 162, 163, 166, 169/172, 174, 180, 181, 183, 188, 189, 191/193, 196/200, 203/211, 213, 214, 216/220, 222/226, 228/234. **Summary:** Active: 63; Reserve: 6; Loan: 1; ILP: 10.
Comments: These are floating cranes with lifting capacity ranging from 10 to 350 tons. Of the active units, only YD-233 is in commission. The remaining active units are "in service." YD-217/219 are on loan from the Army since 1966 (217) and 1967 (remainder). YD-171 is a German war prize which has the heaviest lift of all and is the largest YD. All were completed 1913–70. YDs provide mobility that enables heavy lift cranes to get to places not accessible to land cranes.

YDT—Diving Tenders (self-propelled and non-self-propelled)
Full load displacement: 650 tons/2,000 tons
Length overall: 81'/261'
Extreme beam: 27'/48'
Propulsion: Two diesels (YDT-14 & 15 only)
Screws/max. speed: 2/10 kts. (YDT-14 & 15 only)
Accommodations: 10/17
Units: YDT-10, *Phoebus* (YDT-14), *Suitland* (YDT-15), YDT-16. **Summary:** Active: 4; Reserve: 0.
Comments: Diving tenders used in support of salvage and diving operations. YDT-10 (ex YFNG-1) and YDT-16 (ex YFNB-43) are non-self-propelled. YDT-14 (ex-YF-294) and YDT-15 (ex YF-336) are self-propelled. Completed between 11/42 and 6/45.

YF—Covered Lighters (self-propelled)
Full load displacement: 650 tons
Length overall: 133′
Extreme beam: 31′
Propulsion: Two diesels
Screws/max. speed: 2/10 kts.
Accommodations: 11
Units: *Lynnhaven* (YF-328), YF-862, *Kodiak* (YF-866), *Keyport* (YF-885). **Summary:** Active 2; Reserve: 2.
Comments: Primarily used for coastal and inland water resupply operations. Before inactivation, *Kodiak* made shuttle runs from the West Coast of U.S. to Kodiak, Alaska, carrying freight and supplies. *Lynnhaven* is a YF-269 class; the remainder are YF-852 class. Two sisters serve as YDTs. Completed between 11/42 and 11/45.

YFB—Ferryboat or Launch (self-propelled)
Full load displacement: approx. 325 tons/773 tons
Length overall: 116′/180′ (approx.)
Extreme beam: 33′/59′ (approx.)
Propulsion: Two diesels (82 has 3)
Screws/max. speed: 2/8 to 10 kts.
Accommodations: 17
Units: *Aquidneck* (YFB-14), YFB-82, 83, 86/91. **Summary:** Active: 6; Reserve: 1; ILP: 2.
Comments: Used to carry personnel and/or cars and equipment from point to point. Usually assigned to Navy yards where facilities are spread out, such as Pearl Harbor, or as interisland cargo ships in the Philippines, Guam, Wake Island, etc. YFB-88/91 are ex LCU-1636, 1638/1640. YFB-82 is the former LCU-1040 and YFB-86 is ex-YFU-1, LCU-524. All units are one-ship classes, except YFB-88/91 which are YFB-88 class. Completed between 5/37 and 1971.

YFD—Yard Floating Drydock (non-self-propelled)
Displacement: 800 tons/13,000 tons (light)
Lifting capacity: 1,000 tons/20,000 tons (nominal)
Length overall: 200′/658′11″
Length on pontoons: 200′/587′3″
Maximum draft: 28′6″/49′8″
Light draft: 3′5″/8′3″
Over blocks draft: 15′11″/28′
Inside width: 45′/98′
Units: YFD-7/9, 23, 54, 68/71, 83. **Summary:** Active: 1; Reserve: 0; Loan: 9.
Comments: This classification represents a miscellaneous group of dry docks that can be used to dock CG/CLG/DD/AO/AK/ANL/MSO/SS. They range in size from one sectional steel to six sectional timber docks. The docks with two sections or more can be separated into sections for ease of maintenance or towing. In addition to the above, all the existing AFDMs were formerly YFDs. All units are single-unit classes. YFD-83 is ex-AFDL-31 and is on loan to the Coast Guard since January 1947. YFD-71 is the single active unit. She was returned from commercial lease in 1/73 and placed in service for Navy use. The remaining units are still on commercial lease. Completed between 11/42 and 7/45.

YFN—Covered Lighter (non-self-propelled)
Full load displacement: 350 tons/722 tons
Length overall: 110′/127′
Extreme beam: 30′/35′
Propulsion: None
Screws/max. speed: None
Accommodations: None
Units: YFN-260, 262, 263, 266, 272, 274, 276, 278, 279, 283, 284, 299, 305/308, 311, 313, 362, 364, 367/372, 375, 413, 414, 540, 640/642, 644/652, 654, 656/659, 691, 692, 694, 697, 704, 705, 707, 717, 792/798, 800/803, 806, 814/816, 818, 820, 821, 901/903, 905/907, 910/912, 917, 920, 922, 927, 934, 941, 945, 946, 948, 951/956, 958/959, 962/966, 968, 970, 972, 973, 977/981, 983, 984, 988, 989, 991, 992, 1102, 1126, 1128/1130, 1154/1156, 1158, 1159, 1163, 1172/1178, 1180, 1181, 1183, 1187/1192, 1194/1200, 1202/1206, 1208, 1209, 1211/1214, 1217/1223, 1237/1243, 1250/1253. **Summary:** Active: 144; Reserve: 34; Loan: 2; ILP: 1.
Comments: Non-self-propelled lighters used to haul freight and cargo from point to point by tow. A house covers the craft in order to protect equipment/freight from the sea, rain, etc. YFN-540 is ex YC-650, YFN-1126, 1128/1130 is ex YCF-73, 86/88. All were completed between 4/40 and 1/71.

YFNB—Large Covered Lighter (non-self-propelled)
Full load displacement: 2,000 tons and 2,700 tons
Length overall: 261′
Extreme beam: 48′
Propulsion: None
Screws/max. speed: None
Accommodations: 10/29
Units: YFNB-2, 4/6, 8, 13, 19, 22, 23, 25, 30/32, 34/37 39, 41, 42. **Summary:** Active: 13; Reserve: 5; Loan: 2.
Comments: These craft are larger versions of the YFNs. All YFNBs are ex-YFNs, except YFNB-19 which is the ex-YRBM-19. YFNB-6 and 13 are operated by MSC. All completed between 10/44 and 8/45.

YFND—Dry Dock Companion Craft (non-self-propelled)
Full load displacement: 350 tons/590 tons
Length overall: 110′
Extreme beam: 31′ and 35′
Propulsion: None
Screws/max. speed: None
Accommodations: None
Units: YFND-5, 6, 19, 27, 29. **Summary:** Active: 3; Reserve: 0; ILP: 2.
Comments: Non-self-propelled tenders to dry docks. Equipment needed to operate a dry dock, but not part of the dry dock or not kept on the dock is kept on this craft, which is usually tied up alongside the dock. Also, spare parts, lathes, and other tools are sometimes kept on board and operated on board. Basically, YFNDs are annexes to docks. All are former YFNs which were completed between 12/41 and 8/45.

YFNX—Lighter (Special Purpose) (non-self-propelled)
Full load displacement: 310 tons/720 tons
Length overall: 112′ (32) and 110′ (remainder)
Extreme beam: 31′/36′
Propulsion: None
Screws/max. speed: None
Accommodations: None
Units: YFNX-6, 7, 15, 19/26, 30/32. **Summary:** Active: 13; Reserve: 1.
Comments: These are barge-type craft used for special purposes. YFNX-21, 23/26, 30, 31 are ex-YFNs, YFNX-15 is an ex-YNG, YFNX-19 is an ex-YC and YFNX-32 is an ex-YRBM. Completed between 4/42 and 8/70.

YFP—Floating Power Barge (non-self-propelled)
Full load displacement: 590/6,920 tons
Length overall: 110′ and 338′
Extreme beam: 32′/50′
Propulsion: None
Screws/max. speed: None
Accommodations: None
Units: YFP-3, 11, 12. **Summary:** Active: 3; Reserve: 0.
Comments: These craft provide power to remote stations or places where it is impossible or would cost too much to run power lines. They are equipped with large generators. YFP-3 is an ex-YC, YFP-11, 12 are ex-YFNs. Completed between 4/45 and 4/65.

YFR—Refrigerated Covered Lighter (self-propelled)
Full load displacement: 600 tons (443 & 890) and 610 tons (888)
Length overall: 133′ (888 & 890) and 134′ (443)
Extreme beam: 31′ (443) and 30′ (remainder)
Propulsion: Two diesels
Screws/max. speed: 2/10 kts.
Accommodations: 11
Units: YFR-443, 888, 890. **Summary:** Active: 0; Reserve: 1; Loan: 1; ILP: 1.
Comments: These built-for-purpose lighters are used to store bulk frozen foodstuffs. All are YFR-443 class and were completed between 11/45 and 10/45. Similar to YFs in appearance.

YFRN—Refrigerated Covered Lighter (non-self-propelled)
Full load displacement: 690 tons/860 tons
Length overall: 150′/153′
Extreme beam: 34′ (385) and 35′ (412 & 997)
Propulsion: None
Screws/max. speed: None
Accommodations: None
Units: YFRN-385, 412, 997, 1235. **Summary:** Active 1; Reserve: 3.
Comments: Non-self-propelled versions of the YFR. Characteristics for YFRN-1235 are not available. YFRN-385, 412 and 997 are ex-YFs. Completed between 9/43 and 10/45 (1235 excluded).

YFRT—Covered Lighter (Range Tender) (self-propelled)
Full load displacement: 935 tons (524) and 650 tons (remainder)
Length overall: 177′ (524) and 133′ (remainder)
Extreme beam: 30′/32′
Propulsion: Two diesels
Screws/max. speed: 2/10
Accommodations: 11/24
Units: YFRT-287, 411, 418, 451, 520, 522, 523. **Summary:** Active: 5; Reserve: 1; Loan: 1.
Comments: YFRT-287, 418, and 523 are former YFs. YFRT-524 was ex-USNS *Range Recoverer* (T-AGM-2). She was reclassified on 5–16–72 and her name dropped. She operated out of Newport, R.I. until stricken. Completed between 8/40 and 9/45.

YFU—Harbor Utility Craft (self-propelled)
Full load displacement: 320 tons/380 tons
Length overall: 116′/135′
Extreme beam: 29′/33′
Propulsion: Two diesels
Screws/max. speed: 2/10 and 11 kts.
Accommodations: 14/20
Units: YFU-44, 50, 53, 55, 56, 67, 68, 71, 72, 74/77, 79/83, 89, 91, 93, 94, 97/102. **Summary:** Active: 13; Reserve: 12; Loan: 1; ILP: 2.
Comments: Used as supply/heavy equipment carriers in large bases in the Continental U.S. or its territories, such as Guam. All are converted LCUs, except YFU-71, 72, 74/77, 79/83 which are built-for-purpose to a modified LCU design. Completed between 11/43 and 1972.

YGN—Garbage Lighter (non-self-propelled)
Full load displacement: 500 tons (40/78) and 855 tons (remainder)
Length overall: 120′ (40/78) and 124′ (remainder)
Extreme beam: 35′
Propulsion: None
Screws/max. speed: None
Accommodations: None
Units: YGN-69, 70, 73, 80/83. **Summary:** Active: 7; Reserve: 0.
Comments: These non-self-propelled versions of the YG were completed between 7/43 and 1/71. Ships' wastes are loaded into these craft and they are towed to and from dumping grounds. The last of the garbage lighters (self-propelled) (YG) have been stricken.

YHLC—Salvage Lift Craft, Heavy (non-self-propelled)
Units: *Crilly* (YHLC-1), *Crandall* (YHLC-2). **Summary:** Active: 0; Reserve: 2.
Comments: Characteristics of these two craft are not available. Both were originally completed for the German Navy in 1943 as *Energie* (1) and *Ausdauer* (2). Acquired by the USN

from Germany in 1966. They were employed in Vietnam (1966–71). In order to salvage craft, the two YHLCs team up and a web of three-inch steel cables is woven under the sunken hulk. Then by a method of ballasting and using the tides, the craft is lifted between the two YHLCs and taken to shallow ground, where it is left or broken up. Both were placed out of service in 10/71 at Subic Bay. On 5–22–74, a contract for the clearing of the Suez Canal was awarded by the Egyptian government to Murphy Marine Salvage. In turn Murphy Marine leased these two craft to assist in the operation. They were reactivated in 6/74 and placed "in service." Both craft placed "out of service" in early 1975. Both are berthed at the MarAd James River reserve fleet.

YM—Dredge (non-self-propelled)
Full load displacement: approx. 47 tons/164 tons
Length overall: approx. 43'/162'
Extreme beam: approx. 15'/38'
Propulsion: None
Screws/max. speed: None
Accommodations: 34/75
Units: YM-17, 22, 32, 33, 35/38, 52. **Summary:** Active: 8; Reserve: 1.
Comments: Used to keep channels, pier spaces, and ship basins clear of silt buildup which can prevent ships from navigating to or through them. The dredges were completed between 1924 and 1971.

YMLC—Salvage Lift Craft, Medium (non-self-propelled)
Units: None. **Summary:** Active: 0; Reserve: 0.
Comments: These smaller versions of YHLC-1/2 were acquired from the Royal Navy in 1967 and placed in service in 9/67. YMLC-5, 6 were active in the Pacific and Atlantic Fleets.

YNG—Gate Craft (non-self-propelled)
Full load displacement: 225 tons
Length overall: 110'
Extreme beam: 34'
Propulsion: None
Screws/max. speed: None
Accommodations: 18/20
Units: YNG-11, 17. **Summary:** Active: 2.
Comments: Gate craft are used to tend submarine nets protecting local harbor entrances or as harbor control vessels (usually stationed at or near harbor entrances in this duty). All are of the YNG-1 class. They were completed in 7/41 and 6/41, respectively.

YO—Fuel Oil Barge (self-propelled)
Full load displacement: 1,095 tons/2,700 tons
Length overall: 156'/174'
Extreme beam: 29'/38'
Propulsion: One/two diesels
Screws/max. speed: 1 or 2/9 to 11 kts.
Accommodations: 16/34
Units: *Casinghead* (YO-47), *Crownblock* (YO-48), YO-106, 129, 153, 154, 171, 174, 194, 199, 200, 202, 203, 205, 213, 215, 219, 220, 223/225, 227, 228, 230, 241, 248, 257, 264. **Summary:** Active: 16; Reserve: 9; Loan: 0; ILP: 3.
Comments: Used to refuel ships that are moored to piers or anchored in harbors or roadsteads. As completed, all YOs were armed. Now unarmed. YO-241, 248, 257 and 264 are former YOGs. Completed 1/41 and 12/45.

YOG—Gasoline Barge (self-propelled)
Full load displacement: 1,490 tons (107), 1,390 tons (remainder)
Length overall: 183' (107), 174' (remainder)
Extreme beam: 30' (107), 33' (remainder)
Propulsion: One/two diesels
Screws/max. speed: 2/11 kts.
Accommodations: 23
Units: YOG-58, 65, 67, 68, 73, 78, 79, 87/89, 93. *Lt. Thomas W. Fowler* (YOG-107), YOG-196. **Summary:** Active: 3; Reserve: 8; Loan: 0; ILP: 2.
Comments: These craft duplicate the 174' YO class, but carry gasoline/aviation fuels from fuel depot to ships moored to piers, or anchored in harbors or roadsteads. YOG-107 is ex-YO-244 and YOG-196 is ex-YO-196. Completed between 11/43 and 1/46.

YOGN—Gasoline Barge (non-self-propelled)
Full load displacement: 350 tons/1,360 tons
Length overall: 165'
Extreme beam: 35'/42'
Propulsion: None
Screws/max. speed: None
Accommodations: None
Units: YOGN-8/10, 16, 26, 110, 111, 113/115, 120, 122/124. **Summary:** Active: 14; Reserve: 0.
Comments: Non-self-propelled versions of the YOGs. Barge-type craft with tanks inside the hull. YOGN-123 is ex-YON-252. Completed between 7/42 and 9/52.

YON—Fuel Oil Barge (non-self-propelled)
Full load displacement: 395 tons/1,460 tons
Length overall: 87'/174'
Extreme beam: 28'/40'
Propulsion: None
Screws/max. speed: None
Accommodations: None
Units: YON-1, 2, 80, 81, 84/88, 90, 91, 96/98, 100/102, 235, 239, 240, 255, 256/262, 265, 267/269, 271/275, 279/300. **Summary:** Active: 54; Reserve: 0; Building: 5.
Comments: Non-self-propelled versions of the YO, these are barge-like craft with tanks in the hull. YON-1 was completed 5/42. This type of craft is still under construction. YON-235 is a former YW, YON-255, 256 are on loan from the Army, YON-265, 267, 279 are ex-YOGNs. Four additional YON were approved for construction under FY 1975.

YOS—Oil Storage Barge (non-self-propelled)
Full load displacement: 290 tons/690 tons
Length overall: 80' and 110'
Extreme beam: 34'
Propulsion: None
Screws/max. speed: None
Accommodations: None
Units: YOS-8/12, 15/17, 20/24, 28. **Summary:** Active: 13; Reserve: 0; Loan: 1.
Comments: Barge craft used for oil storage. They were completed between 12/40 and 4/46. YOS-28 is an ex-YC.

YP—Patrol Craft (self-propelled)
Full load displacement: 60 tons/67 tons
Length overall: 75'/81'
Extreme beam: 17' and 18'
Propulsion: Two diesels
Screws/max. speed: 1 or 2/10 to 12 kts.
Accommodations: 10
Units: YP-587, 589/591, 654/672. **Summary:** Active: 23; Reserve: 0.
Comments: Small patrol craft used as training ships at the Naval Academy and Officer Candidate School. All are unarmed. YPs below 654 are YP-78 class; remainder are YP-254 class. YP-589, 590 were reinstated on the Naval Vessel Register on 5–10–65. Completed between 9/43 and 4/73.

YPD—Floating Pile Driver (non-self-propelled)
Full load displacement: 590 tons/680 tons
Length overall: 104'/111'
Extreme beam: 31'/46'
Propulsion: None
Screws/max. speed: None
Accommodations: None
Units: YPD-32, 37, 41/43, 45. **Summary:** Active: 4; Reserve: 1; ILP: 1.
Comments: Craft are used to drive pilings and beams for piers and other structures that need deep supports. YPD-32 and 45 are ex-YCs. Completed between 1942 and 4/69.

YR—Floating Workshops (non-self-propelled)
Full load displacement: 60 tons/67 tons
Length overall: 110'/261'
Extreme beam: 30'/48'
Propulsion: None
Screws/max. speed: None
Accommodations: 17/65
Units: YR-9, 23/27, 29, 34/38, 44, 46, 48, 50, 59, 60, 63/65, 67, 68, 70, 72, 73, 75/78, 83. **Summary:** Active: 16; Reserve: 5; Loan: 1; ILP: 5; Lend-lease: 4.
Comments: Supplements existing workshops in naval bases or used as workshops in areas where there are none. The 4 units listed as lend-lease were lent to Russia in 1945 and were neither returned nor accounted for. YR-60, 67, 78 were reinstated on the NVR on 10–1–71. Completed between 11/41 and 10/46. YR-9 is an ex-YFNB and YR-23 is an ex-YC.

YRB—Repair and Berthing Barges (non-self-propelled)
Full load displacement: 100 tons/590 tons
Length overall: 111' (1) and 110' (remainder)
Extreme beam: 30'/35'
Propulsion: None
Screws/max. speed: None
Accommodations: 8/21
Units: YRB-1, 22, 25, 28. **Summary:** Active: 3; Reserve: 1.
Comments: Used as craft for berthing enlisted men and/or making minor repairs. Otherwise similar to YRs. YRB-22 is an ex-YC and remainder are ex-YFNs. Completed between 8/40 and 4/45.

YRBM—Repair, Messing and Berthing Barges (non-self-propelled)
Full load displacement: 245 tons/2,700 tons
Length overall: 110'/261'
Extreme beam: 34'/49'
Propulsion: None
Screws/max. speed: None
Accommodations: 17/434
Units: YRBM-1/6, 8, 9, 11/15, 20, 23/30. **Summary:** Active: 21; Reserve: 1.
Comments: Enlarged versions of YR/YRB craft. YRBM-20 is an ex-YFNB. She has been "in commission" since 1/73. Completed between 11/44 and 6/71.

YRDH—Floating Dry Dock Workshop (Hull) (non-self-propelled)
Full load displacement: 750 tons
Length overall: 151'
Extreme beam: 35'
Propulsion: None
Screws/max. speed: None
Accommodations: 47
Units: YRDH-1, 2, 6, 7. **Summary:** Active: 1; Reserve: 3.
Comments: Companion craft for dry docks. Machinery on aboard used for hull repairs of ships in dry dock. YRDH-6, the only active craft, has been in service since 1/73. YRDH-1, 2 are former YRs. Completed between 12/43 and 7/44.

YRDM—Floating Dry Dock Workshop (Machinery) (non-self-propelled)
Full load displacement: 750 tons
Length overall: 151'
Extreme beam: 35'
Propulsion: None
Screws/max. speed: None
Accommodations: 47
Units: YRDM-1, 2, 5, 7. **Summary:** Active: 1; Reserve: 3.
Comments: Identical to YRDHs but with a different mission. Also used as companion craft for Dry Docks. Only active unit, YRDM-5, has been in service since 6/73. All were completed between 12/43 and 5/44. YRDM-1, 2 are ex-YRs.

YRR—Radiological Repair Barge (non-self-propelled)
Full load displacement: 590 tons/990 tons
Length overall: 110'/153'
Extreme beam: 32'/43'
Propulsion: None
Screws/max. speed: None
Accommodations: 47
Units: YRR-1/14. **Summary:** Active: 14; Reserve: 0.
Comments: YRR-1, 2, 6/10 are ex-YRs, YRR-11, 12 are ex-YRDHs, and YRR-5, 13, 14 are ex-YRDMs. All were completed between 1937 and 11/45.

YRST—Salvage Craft Tender (non-self-propelled)
Full load displacement: 225 tons/2,700 tons
Length overall: 110'/261'
Extreme beam: 34'/61'
Propulsion: None
Screws/max. speed: None
Accommodations: 17/49
Units: YRST-1/3, 5, 6. **Summary:** Active: 3; Reserve: 2.
Comments: Used as tenders in salvage operations. YRST-1/3 are former YDTs and 5 and 6 are former YFNXs. All active units are "in service." Completed between 6/41 and 4/47.

YSD—Seaplane Wrecking Derricks (self-propelled)
Full load displacement: 270 tons
Length overall: 104'
Extreme beam: 31'
Propulsion: Two diesels
Screws/max. speed: 1/10 kts.
Accommodations: 13/15
Units: YSD-34, 39, 42, 53, 60, 63, 72, 74, 77. **Summary:** Active: 9; Reserve: 0.
Comments: All are YSD-11 class and were completed between 5/41 and 6/45. They are primarily employed as mobile cranes.

YSR—Sludge Removal Barge (non-self-propelled)
Full load displacement: 300 tons/1,270 tons
Length overall: 80'/165'
Extreme beam: 30'/35'
Propulsion: None
Screws/max. speed: None
Accommodations: 2 (YSR-4), None (remainder)
Units: YSR-1, 4, 6, 7, 11, 17/20, 22, 23, 26/33, 37/40, 45. **Summary:** Active: 18; Reserve: 5; Loan: 1.
Comments: These barges are used to remove liquid wastes/sludge dredged up by dredges (YM) to dumping grounds. YSR-45 is a former Army craft. Completed between 1932 and 4/46.

YTB—Large Harbor Tugboat (self-propelled)
Full load displacement: 341 tons/409 tons
Length overall: 85'/109'
Extreme beam: 24'/31'
Propulsion: 2 diesels (761), 1 diesel (remainder)
Screws/max. speed: 11/12 kts.
Accommodations: 10 (756/759), 12 (remainder)
Units: *Edenshaw* (YTB-752), *Marin* (YTB-753), *Pontiac* (YTB-756), *Oshkosh* (YTB-757), *Paducah* (YTB-758), *Bogalusa* (YTB-759), *Natick* (YTB-760), *Ottumwa* (YTB-761), *Tuscumbia* (YTB-762), *Muskegon* (YTB-763), *Mishawaka* (YTB-764), *Okmulgee* (YTB-765), *Wapakoneta* (YTB-766), *Apalachicola* (YTB-767), *Arcata* (YTB-768), *Chesaning* (YTB-769), *Dahlonega* (YTB-770), *Keokuk* (YTB-771), *Nashua* (YTB-774), *Wauwatosa* (YTB-775), *Weehawken* (YTB-

776), *Nogales* (YTB-777), *Apopka* (YTB-778), *Manhattan* (YTB-779), *Saugus* (YTB-780), *Niantic* (YTB-781), *Manistee* (YTB-782), *Redwing* (YTB-783), *Kalispell* (YTB-784), *Winnemucca* (YTB-785), *Tonkawa* (YTB-786), *Kittanning* (YTB-787), *Wapato* (YTB-788), *Tomahawk* (YTB-789), *Monominee* (YTB-790), *Marinette* (YTB-791), *Antigo* (YTB-792), *Piqua* (YTB-793), *Mandan* (YTB-794), *Ketchikan* (YTB-795), *Saco* (YTB-796), *Tamaqua* (YTB-797), *Opelika* (YTB-798), *Natchitoches* (YTB-799), *Eufaula* (YTB-800), *Palatka* (YTB-801), *Cheraw* (YTB-802), *Nanticoke* (YTB-803), *Ahoskie* (YTB-804), *Ocala* (YTB-805), *Tuskegee* (YTB-806), *Massapequa* (YTB-807), *Wenatchee* (YTB-808), *Agawam* (YTB-809), *Anoka* (YTB-810), *Houma* (YTB-811), *Accomac* (YTB-812), *Poughkeepsie* (YTB-813), *Waxahachie* (ex-*Waxahatchie*) (YTB-814), *Neodesha* (YTB-815), *Campti* (YTB-816), *Hyannis* (YTB-817), *Mecosta* (YTB-818), *Ikuka* (YTB-819), *Wanamassa* (YTB-820), *Tontogany* (YTB-821), *Pawhuska* (YTB-822), *Canonchet* (YTB-823), *Santaquin* (YTB-824), *Wathena* (YTB-825), *Washtucna* (YTB-826), *Chetek* (YTB-827), *Catahecassa* (YTB-828), *Metacom* (YTB-829), *Pushmataha* (YTB-830), *Dekanawida* (YTB-831), *Petalesharo* (YTB-832), *Shabonee* (YTB-833), *Negwagon* (YTB-834), *Skenandoa* (YTB-835), *Pokagon* (YTB-836). **Summary:** Active: 81; Reserve: 0.

Comments: Small coastal and harbor tugs for towing non-self-propelled harbor service craft, aiding large ships in mooring, etc. All YTBs below YTB-752 that were still extant, were reclassified YTMs in mid-1960s. *Anoka* (YTB-810) was rammed and sunk on 1–17–72 by *Nashville* (LPD-13) while aiding the LPD to dock at Norfolk. Raised 1–21–72, repaired and returned to service. First unit completed 1/46 (YTB-762). Units of this type are still under construction. YTB-752/759 are of YTB-752 class. Remainder are YTB-760 class. YTB-837 and 838 are building for Saudi Arabia at Marinette Marine Corp.

YTL—Small Harbor Tugboat (self-propelled)

Full load displacement: 80 tons
Length overall: 66'
Extreme beam: 18'
Propulsion: One diesel
Screws/max. speed: 1/10 kts.
Accommodations: 5
Units: YTL-211, 422, 425/427, 431, 434, 435, 438, 439, 441, 443/445, 448, 550, 558, 567, 583, 588, 591, 594, 600, 602. **Summary:** Active: 10; Reserve: 2; Loan: 2; ILP: 11.
Comments: Smaller versions of YTBs. All are of the YTL-422 class except YTL-211. Completed between 9/42 and 11/45.

YTM—Medium Harbor Tugboat (self-propelled)

Full load displacement: 205 tons/390 tons
Length overall: 85'/107'
Extreme beam: 23'/28'
Propulsion: 2 diesels (760/779), 1 diesel (remainder)
Screws/max. speed: 1 or 2/11 to 14 kts.
Accommodations: 9/23

Units: *Hoga* (YTM-146), *Toka* (YTM-149), *Konoka* (YTM-151), *Junaluska* (YTM-176), *Black Fox* (YTM-177), *Dekaury* (YTM-178), *Madokawando* (YTM-180), *Mazapeta* (YTM-181), *Nepanet* (YTM-189), *Sassacus* (YTM-193), *Dekanisora* (YTM-252), *Hiawatha* (YTM-265), *Red Cloud* (YTM-268), *Satanta* (YTM-270), *Olathe* (YTM-273), *Pawtucket* (YTM-359), *Sassaba* (YTM-364), *Waubansee* (YTM-366), *Smohalla* (YTM-371), *Chepanoc* (YTM-381), *Coatopa* (YTM-382), *Cochali* (YTM-383), *Wannalancet* (YTM-385), *Washakie* (YTM-386), *Connewango* (YTM-388), *Ganadoga* (YTM-390), *Itara* (YTM-391), *Mecosta* (YTM-392), *Nakarna* (YTM-393), *Winamac* (YTM-394), *Wingina* (YTM-395), *Yanegua* (YTM-397), *Natahki* (YTM-398), *Numa* (YTM-399), *Otokomi* (YTM-400), *Panameta* (YTM-402), *Pitamakan* (YTM-403), *Coshecton* (YTM-404), *Cusseta* (YTM-405), *Kittaton* (YTM-406), *Minniska* (YTM-408), *Anamosa* (YTM-409), *Porobago* (YTM-413), *Satago* (YTM-414), *Secota* (YTM-415), *Taconnet* (YTM-417), *Tensaw* (YTM-418), *Topawa* (YTM-419), *Wallacut* (YTM-420), *Windigo* (YTM-421), *Abinago* (YTM-493), *Barboncito* (YTM-495), *Unnamed* (YTM-496), *Hisada* (YTM-518), *Mahoa* (YTM-519), *Nabigwon* (YTM-521), *Sagawamick* (YTM-522), *Senasqua* (YTM-523), *Tutahaco* (YTM-524), *Wabanaquot* (YTM-525), *Wahaka* (YTM-526), *Wahpeton* (YTM-527), *Ocmulgee* (YTM-532), *Nadli* (YTM-534), *Nahoke* (YTM-536), *Chegodega* (YTM-542), *Etawina* (YTM-543), *Yatanocas* (YTM-544), *Accohanoc* (YTM-545), *Takos* (YTM-546), *Yanaba* (YTM-547), *Matunak* (YTM-548), *Migadan* (YTM-549), *Acoma* (YTM-701), *Arawak* (YTM-702), *Moratoc* (YTM-704), *Manktao* (YTM-734), *Yuma* (YTM-748), *Hackensack* (YTM-750), *Manteo* (YTM-751), *Kewaunee* (YTM-752), *Woonsocket* (YTM-754), *Waukegan* (YTM-755), *Unnamed* (YTM-759), *Mascoutah* (YTM-760), *Menasha* (YTM-761), *Cholocco* (YTM-764), *Chiquito* (YTM-765), *Chohonaga* (YTM-766), *Ankachak* (YTM-767), *Apohola* (YTM-768), *Mimac* (YTM-770), *Chilkat* (YTM-773), *Hastwiana* (YTM-775), *Hiamonee* (YTM-776), *Lelaka* (YTM-777), *Oswegatchie* (YTM-778) and *Pocasset* (YTM-779). **Summary:** Active: 76; Reserve: 17; Loan: 1; ILP: 5.

Comments: Medium-size versions of the YTB, they perform similar duties. All are ex-YTBs except YTM-748, 750/752, 754, 755, 759 which are former Army tugs. YTMs are gradually being replaced by YTBs. YTM-800/802 were authorized under FY 1973, but deferred in favor of YTB construction. While under tow to Bremerton by *Takelma* (ATF-113), *Nanigo* (YTM-537) parted her tow in heavy seas and disappeared and was presumed sunk at sea as of 4–7–73. Completed between 3/40 and 1/65.

YW—Water Barge (self-propelled)

Full load displacement: 1,390 tons
Length overall: 174'
Extreme beam: 33'
Propulsion: One diesel
Screws/max. speed: 1/11 kts. (YW-128, 157), 7 kts. (remainder)
Accommodations: 23
Units: YW-83, 84, 86, 89, 90, 98, 101, 103, 108, 111, 113, 119, 122, 123, 126/128, 131, 157. **Summary:** Active: 4; Reserve: 13; ILP: 2.
Comments: These craft duplicate the YO/YOG design, but are used to resupply ships moored in harbors, roadsteads, or at piers where access to fresh water is not available. They can also be used in places like Guam and Wake to supply stations where there are no evaporators. YW-157 is ex-YOG-32. All completed between 7/43 and 11/45.

YWN—Water Barge (non-self-propelled)
Full load displacement: 710 tons/1,460 tons
Length overall: 86'/165'
Extreme beam: 20'/42'
Propulsion: None
Screws/max. speed: None
Accommodations: None
Units: YWN-66, 67, 70, 71, 78, 79, 82, 147, 154, 156. **Summary:** Active: 8; Reserve: 2.
Comments: Non-self-propelled, barge-like versions of the YWs. They perform the same mission, but have to be towed from place to place. YWN-147 and 156 are ex-Army craft and YWN-156 is ex-YOGN-116. Completed between 10/41 and 10/52.

GLOSSARY:

Lifting capacity (nominal): Normal lifting capacity is with an 18″ pontoon freeboard for capacities greater than 12,000 tons and with a 12″ pontoon freeboard for 12,000 tons or less than otherwise noted.

Maximum draft: Draft, maximum when submerged, is determined by full load conditions, the use of emergency ballast tanks, if any, and trim.

Light draft: Draft, light, is based upon stripped ballast tanks and light load conditions.

Over blocks draft: Average draft 4'0″ high blocks for same conditions as for maximum draft.

Inside width: Width clear inside is between permanent obstructions.

Active: All units that are active or schedule to be activated.

Reserve: All units that are in reserve or are scheduled to be inactivated.

Loan: All units on loan to non-government/government institutions or agencies, such as schools and the Department of the Interior.

ILP: All units transferred to foreign countries whether it be under the International Logistics Program (ILP) or not.

Richland (AFDM-8). **AFDM-3** class.

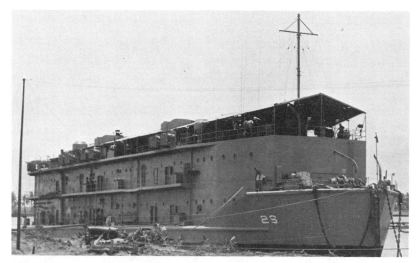

APL-25. Since stricken, but typical in appearance. **APL-17** class.

DSRV-1. Note bow propulsion unit. 1–70.

DSRV-2. Within the outer formed fiber-glass hull are three interconnected spheres. The one forward contains the control unit and two pilots; the middle and after spheres accommodate a third crew member and up to 24 passengers. 8–72.

SERVICE CRAFT

Windsor (ARD-22). 1967. **ARD-12** class.

Trieste II (DSV-1). Note propulsion units forward and aft. 3–72.

Turtle (DSV-3). Note propeller pods on sides and twin-arm manipulators well forward. 4–69.

Alvin (DSV-2). Accidentally sunk in over 5,000′ water 16 October 1968. Raised in August 1969 and refurbished.

SERVICE CRAFT

IX-306. Torpedo Research ship. Note torpedo tube just aft of hull number. 10–69.

Sea Cliff (DSV-4) on board her support vessel *Maxine D.* 10–71.

Elk River (IX-501). Support vessel for deep submergence activities. 9–68.

Elk River (IX-501). Note prominent gantry crane. 9–68.

Constitution (IX-21) under way on her annual turn-around cruise. 6–70.

NR-1. Has no periscopes, but is fitted with external television cameras. 8–69.

YFB-87. 3–70.

George Eastman (YAG-39).

YFRT-520. 2–69.

YFU-72. Commercial lighter design.

YFU-83. Same design as LCU-1646.

YP-669. 10–71. **YP-254** class.

YR-29.

YRST-1, a former YDT. 7–71.

YSD-64. Since stricken, but represents the class.

Edenshaw (YTB-752). **Edenshaw** class.

SERVICE CRAFT

Wenatchee (YTB-808). 4–74. **Natick** class.

Ahoskie (YTB-804). 6–70. **Natick** class.

Red Cloud (YTM-268).

SEVEN: NAVAL RESERVE TRAINING SHIPS

This section lists 73 ships and some 153 riverine craft and patrol boats assigned to Naval Reserve Training duty as of 1 May 1975. Data on these ships and craft can be found in Sections 1 through 4 of this publication. In these sections (except Section 4), NRT ships are identified by "NRT" in the fleet status column. The status of NRT ships varies. DDs and MSOs are in full commission; MSCs are "in service, active" and all PTFs and Riverine Craft have no status at all. These craft are not on the Naval Vessel Register and are rated as "floating equipment." All NRT ships are operational and are capable of getting underway for training at sea or in rivers.

Name/Classification	NRT Homeport	Effective Date of Assignment	Remarks
William R. Rush (DD-714)	Brooklyn, N.Y.	7-2-73	Replaced Moale (DD-693)
Wiltsie (DD-716)	San Francisco, Calif.	3-18-73	
Hamner (DD-718)	San Francisco, Calif.	7-2-73	Replaced James C. Owens (DD-776)
Epperson (DD-719)	Seattle, Wash.	9-10-73	Replaced Bridget (DE-1024)
Southerland (DD-743)	San Diego, Calif.	7-2-73	Replaced Buck (DD-761)
William C. Lawe (DD-763)	New Orleans, La.	8-31-73	Replaced Putnam (DD-757)
McKean (DD-784)	Long Beach, Calif.	7-1-72	Replaced Maddox (DD-731)
McKean (DD-784)	Seattle, Wash.	10-1-75	Replaced Theodore E. Chandler (DD-717)
Henderson (DD-785)	Long Beach, Calif.	10-1-73	Replaced Arnold J. Isbell (DD-869)
Hollister (DD-788)	Long Beach, Calif.	7-2-73	Replaced Hooper (DE-1026)
Higbee (DD-806)	Long Beach, Calif.	10-1-73	Replaced De Haven (DD-727)
Higbee (DD-806)	Portland, Ore.	7-1-75	Replaced Ozbourn (DD-846)
Corry (DD-817)	Philadelphia, Pa.	8-31-73	Replaced Lowry (DD-770)
Holder (DD-819)	Boston, Mass.	7-1-72	Replaced Harlan R. Dickson (DD-708)
Holder (DD-819)	Newport, R.I.[1]	2-1-74	
Rich (DD-820)	Philadelphia, Pa.	8-31-73	Replaced Charles S. Sperry (DD-697)
Johnston (DD-821)	Philadelphia, Pa.	7-1-72	Replaced Hank (DD-702)
Robert H. McCard (DD-822)	Tampa, Fla.	8-1-72	Replaced Beatty (DD-756)
Carpenter (DD-825)	San Francisco, Calif.	1-15-73	Replaced Perkins (DD-877)
Robert A. Owens (DD-827)	Norfolk, Va.	7-2-73	Replaced Henley (DD-762)
Robert A. Owens (DD-827)	Galveston, Tex.	11-30-74	Replaced Charles R. Ware (DD-865)
Myles C. Fox (DD-829)	New York City, N.Y.	7-2-73	Replaced John R. Pierce (DD-753)
Charles P. Cecil (DD-835)	New London, Conn.	7-2-73	Replaced Gearing (DD-710)
Power (DD-839)	Fort Schuyler, N.Y.	8-31-73	Replaced Massey (DD-778)
Fiske (DD-842)	Bayonne, N.J.	8-31-73	Replaced Robert K. Huntington (DD-781)
Vogelgesang (DD-862)	Newport, R.I.	3-1-74	
Steinaker (DD-863)	Baltimore, Md.	7-2-73	Replaced Allen M. Sumner (DD-692)
Harold J. Ellison (DD-864)	Norfolk, Va.	7-1-72	Replaced Willard Keith (DD-775)
Harold J. Ellison (DD-864)	Philadelphia, Pa.	11-30-74	Replaced Robert L. Wilson (DD-847)

Name/Classification	NRT Homeport	Effective Date of Assignment	Remarks
Cone (DD-866)	Charleston, S.C.	8-31-73	Replaced Strong (DD-758)
Damato (DD-871)	Boston, Mass.	9-27-72	Replaced Compton (DD-705)
Damato (DD-871)	Newport, R.I.[1]	2-1-74	
Rogers (DD-876)	Portland, Oreg.	10-1-73	Replaced Wallace L. Lind (DD-703)
Dyess (DD-880)	Brooklyn, N.Y.	2-16-71	Replaced Zellars (DD-777)
Newman K. Perry (DD-883)	Fall River, Mass.	7-2-73	Replaced Purdy (DD-734)
John R. Craig (DD-885)	San Diego, Calif.	8-26-73	Replaced Bauer (DE-1025)
Orleck (DD-886)	Tacoma, Wash.	10-1-73	Replaced Brinkley Bass (DD-887)
Meredith (DD-890)	Mayport, Fla.	8-31-73	Replaced Waldron (DD-699)
Tulare (LKA-112)	San Francisco, Calif.	7-1-75	
Paul Revere (LPA-248)	Long Beach, Calif.	7-1-75	Replaced Higbee (DD-806) and McKean (DD-784)
Francis Marion (LPA-249)	Norfolk, Va.	11-14-75	
Peacock (MSC-198)	Long Beach, Calif.	3-1-71	
Phoebe (MSC-199)	Long Beach, Calif.	12-15-70	
Shrike (MSC-201)	Wilmington, N.C.	9-3-68	Replaced Plover (MSCO-33)
Thrasher (MSC-203)	San Francisco, Calif.	12-31-59	Longest serving NRT ship
Thrush (MSC-204)	Miami, Fla.	8-8-62	
Vireo (MSC-205)	Seattle, Wash.	10-1-70	
Warbler (MSC-206)	Seattle, Wash.	10-1-70	
Whippoorwill (MSC-207)	San Francisco, Calif.	12-15-70	
Woodpecker (MSC-209)	Seattle, Wash.	12-15-70	Replaced Cormorant (MSC-122)
Constant (MSO-427)	Long Beach, Calif.	7-1-72	Replaced Embattle (MSO-434)
Dash (MSO-428)	Fall River, Mass.	9-1-71	Replaced Jacana (MSC-193)
Detector (MSO-429)	Portsmouth, N.H.	9-1-71	Replaced Frigate Bird (MSC-191)
Direct (MSO-430)	Perth Amboy, N.J.	9-1-71	Replaced Limpkin (MSC-195) and Meadowlark (MSC-196)
Dominant (MSO-431)	St. Petersburg, Fla.	9-1-71	
Engage (MSO-433)	St. Petersburg, Fla.	8-1-74	
Enhance (MSO-437)	San Diego, Calif.	7-1-74	
Esteem (MSO-438)	Pearl Harbor, Hawaii	8-31-73	
Excel (MSO-439)	San Francisco, Calif.	7-1-72	
Exploit (MSO-440)	Little Creek, Va.	6-30-73	

Name/Classification	NRT Homeport	Effective Date of Assignment	Remarks
Exultant (MSO-441)	Perth Amboy, N.J.	7-1-72	
Fearless (MSO-442)	Charleston, S.C.	7-1-74	
Fortify (MSO-446)	Little Creek, Va.	8-1-74	
Impervious (MSO-449)	Mayport, Fla.	8-1-74	
Implicit (MSO-455)	Tacoma, Wash.	7-1-72	
Inflict (MSO-456)	Portland, Me.	8-1-74	
Pluck (MSO-464)	San Diego, Calif.	7-1-72	
Conquest (MSO-488)	Pearl Harbor, Hawaii	8-31-73	
Gallant (MSO-489)	San Francisco, Calif.	7-1-72	Replaced *Reaper* (MSO-467)
Pledge (MSO-492)	Long Beach, Calif.	7-1-72	
Adroit (MSO-509)	Fall River, Mass.	9-29-73	
Adroit (MSO-509)	Newport, R.I.	6-30-74	
Affray (MSO-511)	Portland, Me.	6-30-73	
Coastal River Squadron 2	Little Creek, Va.	4-1-71	

Craft Assigned: *Tacoma* (PG-92), *Welch* (PG-93), *Chehalis* (PG-94), 3 *Nasty* class PTFs, 2 *Osprey* class PTFs, 2 PBS, 1 LCU, 2 LCM, 5 PBR (MK II), 1 mini-ATC and 38 miscellaneous craft

Coastal River Division 22   New Orleans, La.   7-1-72

Craft Assigned: 4 *Nasty* class PTFs, 1 PCF (MK I), 2 PCF (MK II) and 5 PBR (MK II)

Coastal River Squadron 1   San Diego, Calif.   7- -73

Craft Assigned: *Gallup* (PG-85), *Cannon* (PG-90). 3 *Trumpy* class PTFs, 2 *Osprey* class PTFs, 2 LCUs, 2 STABs and 46 miscellaneous craft

Coastal River Division 11   Mare Island, Calif.   7-1-72

Craft Assigned: 9 PBR (MK II), 9 mini-ATC, 1 CCB and 7 miscellaneous craft

Coastal River Division 21   Great Lakes, Ill.   7-1-72

Craft Assigned: *Asheville* (PG-84), *Crockett* (PG-88), *Marathon* (PG-89), and 3 *Trumpy* class PTFs.

[1] Holder *(DD-819)* and Damato *(DD-871)* were shifted to Newport, R.I., on indicated date as a result of the closing of Boston Naval Shipyard, where they had previously been berthed.

EIGHT: MILITARY SEALIFT COMMAND

The Military Sealift Command was established on 1 October 1949 as the Military Sea Transportation Service. It combined all the functions of the Naval Overseas Transportation Service and the Army Overseas Transportation Service. On 1 August 1970, the name Military Sea Transportation Service was changed to the Military Sealift Command. As part of the Navy Department and the Navy's operational forces, the MSC fleet is made up of naval vessels that are carried on the NVR. All such ships serve in a noncommissioned, unarmed status and are manned by civilian crews. However, each ship has a small Navy detachment aboard under the command of a naval officer. As noncommissioned ships, they have USNS vice USS in front of their names. Also, the letter "T" is placed in front of their classifications to indicate that they are under the administrative control of MSC ("T" is not a formal part of the ship's classification, however). For example, a regular commissioned ship is referred to as the USS *Comet* (AKR-7). A noncommissioned ship under MSC control would be referred to as the USNS *Comet* (T-AKR-7). The MSC fleet has three main duties. The first consists of operating cargo ships and oilers that carry bulk goods, equipment and petroleum products from point to point in support of Navy operations. This is called the "nucleus fleet." The second duty of MSC consists of operating research ships and special mission ships of all types. Normally, these ships are under the administrative control of MSC, but under the operational control of the Navy or a Navy office, such as the Oceanographer's Office, or a private organization that is doing research for the Navy (such as Woods Hole Institute). These are called "special projects ships." On 17 July 1972, the Military Sealift Command took on an additional duty, that of Fleet support, and commenced operating ships in support of the oceangoing forces of the U.S. Navy. Administrative control is under MSC, but operational control rests with the Navy. These ships are unarmed, manned by civilians, serve in a noncommissioned status, and have a Navy detachment aboard. Their sole purpose is to support fleet operations. As of this writing, there are 4 AOs, 1 AF, 3 ARCs and 4 ATFs operating with MSC in support of the fleet. At present it is planned to additionally transfer 9 AOs of the AO-105 and AO-143 classes to MSC for further service in support of the operational fleet. It should be noted that for the purposes of this introductory chapter, the editors have arbitrarily divided MSC into three groups. This was done to more easily explain the varied missions that the Military Sealift Command has. In actuality, MSC is not divided into three groups and operates as one homogenous "fleet" with one commander, who is the Commander of the Military Sealift Command. For all practical purposes, MSC is the "fifth fleet" of the Navy's operational forces. Data on the ships in the following table can be found in the Auxiliary and Amphibious sections of the main text. Ships assigned to MSC have the prefix "MSC" in the fleet status column.

Name and Hull Classification	MSC F/S
USNS *Denebola* (T-AF-56)	TAA
USNS *Kingsport* (T-AG-164)	TAA
USNS *Wheeling* (T-AGM-8)	TPR
USNS *General H. H. Arnold* (T-AGM-9)	TPA
USNS *General Hoyt S. Vandenberg* (T-AGM-10)	TPA
USNS *Vanguard* (T-AGM-19)	TAA
USNS *Redstone* (T-AGM-20)	TAA
USNS *Range Sentinel* (T-AGM-22)	TAA
USNS *Lynch* (T-AGOR-7)	TAA
USNS *Mizar* (T-AGOR-11)	TAA
USNS *De Steiguer* (T-AGOR-12)	TPA
USNS *Bartlett* (T-AGOR-13)	TPA
USNS *Hayes* (T-AGOR-16)	TAA
USNS *Bowditch* (T-AGS-21)	TAA
USNS *Dutton* (T-AGS-22)	TAA
USNS *Silas Bent* (T-AGS-26)	TPA

Name and Hull Classification	MSC F/S
USNS *Kane* (T-AGS-27)	TAA
USNS *Chauvenet* (T-AGS-29)	TPA
USNS *Harkness* (T-AGS-32)	TAA
USNS *Wilkes* (T-AGS-33)	TAA
USNS *Wyman* (T-AGS-34)	TPA
USNS *Greenville Victory* (T-AK-237)	TAA
USNS *Pvt. John R. Towle* (T-AK-240)	TAA
USNS *Sgt. Andrew Miller* (T-AK-242)	TAA
USNS *Sgt. Truman Kimbro* (T-AK-254)	TPA
USNS *Pvt. Leonard C. Brostrom* (T-AK-255)	TPA
USNS *Mirfak* (T-AK-271)	TAA
USNS *Lt. James E. Robinson* (T-AK-274)	TAA
USNS *Schuyler Otis Bland* (T-AK-277)	TPA
USNS *Norwalk* (T-AK-279) (FBM)	TAA
USNS *Furman* (T-AK-280) (FBM)	TPA
USNS *Victoria* (T-AK-281)	TAA

Name and Hull Classification	MSC F/S	Name and Hull Classification	MSC F/S
USNS Marshfield (T-AK-282)	TAA	USNS Neptune (T-ARC-2)	TAA
USNS Wyandot (T-AK-382)	TPA	USNS Aeolus (T-ARC-3)	TPA
USNS Comet (T-AKR-7)	TAA	USNS Thor (T-ARC-4)	TPR
USNS Sea Lift (T-AKR-9)	TPA	USNS Albert J. Meyer (T-ARC-6)	TPA
USNS Tallulah (T-AO-50)[1]	TWWR	USNS Ute (T-ATF-76)	TPA
USNS Marias (T-AO-57)	TAA	USNS Lipan (T-ATF-85)	TPA
USNS Taluga (T-AO-62)	TPA	USNS Atakapa (T-ATF-149)	TAA
USNS Millicoma (T-AO-73)[1]	TWWR	USNS Mosopelea (T-ATF-158)	TAA
USNS Schuylkill (T-AO-76)[1]	TWWR	USNS LST-47 (T-LST-47)	TPA
USNS Mispillion (T-AO-105)	TPA	USNS LST-230 (T-LST-230)[2]	TPR
USNS Passumpsic (T-AO-107)	TPA	USNS LST-287 (T-LST-287)	TPA
USNS Waccamaw (T-AO-109)	TAA	USNS LST-491 (T-LST-491)[2]	TPR
USNS Maumee (T-AO-149)[1]	TWWR	USNS LST-579 (T-LST-579)[2]	TPR
USNS Shoshone (T-AO-150)[1]	TWWR	USNS LST-607 (T-LST-607)[2]	TPR
USNS Yukon (T-AO-151)[1]	TWWR	USNS LST-613 (T-LST-613)[2]	TPR
USNS American Explorer (T-AO-165)[1]	TWWR	USNS LST-623 (T-LST-623)[2]	TPR
USNS Sealift Pacific (T-AO-168)[4]	TWWR	USNS LST-629 (T-LST-629)	TPA
USNS Sealift Arabian Sea (T-AO-169)[4]	TWWR	USNS LST-649 (T-LST-649)	TPA
USNS Sealift Atlantic (T-AO-172)[4]	TWWR	USNS Davies County (T-LST-692)	TPA
USNS Sealift Mediterranean (T-AO-173)[4]	TWWR	USNS Harris County (T-LST-822)	TPA
USNS Sealift Caribbean (T-AO-174)[4]	TWWR	USNS Orleans Parish (T-LST-1069)[2]	TPR
USNS Rincon (T-AOG-77)	TPA	USNS LST-1072 (T-LST-1072)[2]	TPR
USNS Nodaway (T-AOG-78)	TPA	USNS YFNB-6 (T-YFNB-6)[3]	TPA
USNS Petaluma (T-AOG-79)	TPA	USNS YFNB-13 (T-YFNB-13)[3]	TPA

[1] Operated under charter by Hudson Waterways Corp. as point-to-point bulk carriers on worldwide routes.
[2] All LSTs in ready-reserve berthed at Sasebo, Japan, will remain there for a minimum of two years and will be disposed of in stages after that.

[3] Assigned to Commander, MSC Honolulu.
[4] Operated under charter by Marine Transport Lines as point-to-point bulk carriers on worldwide routes.

NINE: U.S. COAST GUARD

The United States Coast Guard was established by an Act of Congress on 28 January 1915. It combined the functions of the Revenue Cutter Service and the Lifesaving Service. On 1 July 1939, the Lighthouse Service was absorbed by the Coast Guard. Originally under Treasury Department control, the Coast Guard came under the control of the newly formed Department of Transportation on 1 April 1967. In time of national emergency, or when the President so directs, the Coast Guard operates under the operational control of the Navy.

At the end of FY 1975, the Coast Guard Register listed 276 vessels of various types, sizes, and shapes. A summary of these vessels follows:

Patrol Craft, Small	(WPB)	54		Buoy Tender, Inland	(WLI)	17
Harbor Tug, Medium	(WYTM)	13		Construction Tender, Inland	(WLIC)	10
Harbor Tug, Small	(WYTL)	15		Buoy Tender, River	(WLR)	22
Oceangraphic Cutter	(WAGO)	2		Lightship	(WLV)	6
Buoy Tender, Seagoing	(WLB)	35		Training Cutter	(WIX)	2
Buoy Tender, Coastal	(WLM)	16		Reserve Training Cutter	(WTR)	2

High Endurance Cutter	(WHEC)	27		Medium Endurance Cutter	(WMEC)	22
Icebreaker	(WAGB)	10		Patrol Craft, Large	(WPB)	23

Unlike the Navy, the Coast Guard officially refers to all classes by the vessel's length. In keeping with conformity in this publication, the classes have been listed by the name of the ship that has the lowest number within the class. Because of their inland stations, river buoy tenders (WLR) will carry the status symbol "IW, A," in the Fleet Status column in the text, to signify "Inland Waters, Active." This is not to be confused with inland waterways.

Class	Number	No. in Class	Full Load Displ.	Length Overall	Max. Draft	Ext. Beam	Number and Type Boilers/Engines	Screws/ SHP	Max. Speed (Kts.)	Allowance Officers	Allowance Enlisted	Armament
Hamilton	WHEC-715	12	3,050	378'	20'	42'	2 P.W. FT4 Gas Turbines and 2D(F.M.)	2/36,000	29.0	15	149	1 single 5"/38 cal. mt., 2 81mm mortars, 4 .50 cal. mg., 2 triple MK 32 torpedo tubes.
Bibb	WHEC-31	6	2,656	327'	15'	41'	2B(B.W.)/GT(West.)	2/6,200	19.8	13	131	1 single 5"/38 cal. mt., 2 81 mm mortars, 4 .50 cal. mg.
Owasco	WHEC-39	9	1,913	254'	17'	43'	2B(F.W.)/Turbine Electric (West.)	1/4,000	18.4	13	127	1 single 5"/38 cal. mt., 2 81mm mortars, 4 .50 cal. mg.
Polar Star	WAGB-10	2	12,000	399'	28'	83'6"	3 P.W. FT4A Gas Turbines and 6 D	3/78,000 (combined)	17.0	13	125	None
Glacier	WAGB-4	1	8,449	310'	29'	74'	10D(F.M.)/2 EM(West.)	2/21,000	17.6	15	226	4 .50 cal. mg.
Mackinaw	WAGB-83	1	5,252	290'	19'	74'	6D(F.M.)/3 EM(West.)	3/10,000	18.7	10	117	None
"Wind-R"	WAGB-281	2	6,515	269'	29'	64'	4D(Enterprise)/2 EM(West.)	2/10,000	16.0	14	167	4 .50 cal. mg.
"Wind"	WAGB-278	4	6,515	269'	29'	64'	6D(F.M.)/2 EM(West.)	2/10,000	16.0	14	167	4 .50 cal. mg.
Storis	WMEC-38	1	1,925	230'	15'	43'	3D(C.B.)/1 EM(West.)	2/1,800	14.0	10	96	1 single 3"/50 cal. mt., 2 .50 cal. mg.
Yocona	WMEC-168	1	1,745	213'	15'	41'	2D(C.B.)(#GSB-8)	2/3,000	15.5	7	65	2 .50 cal. mg.
Resolute	WMEC-620	11	1,007	211'	10'	34'	2D(Alco)	2/5,000	18.0	7	54	1 single 3"/50, 2 .50 cal. mg.
Reliance	WMEC-615	5	970	211'	10'	34'	2 Solar Gas Turbines/2D(Alco)	2/5,000	18.0	7	54	1 single 3"/50, 2 .50 cal. mg.
"Avoyel"	WMEC-150	3	1,731	205'	17'	39'	1D(Cleveland)(#12-278A)	1/3,000	16.2	7	65	1 single 3"/50, 2 .50 cal. mg.
Modoc	WMEC-194	2	860	143'	14'	34'	1D(Cleveland)(#12-278A)	1/1,500	13.5	5	42	2 .50 cal. mg.
"Cape" (C)	WPB-95321	6	105	95'	6'	20'	4D(Cummins)(#VT12-600M)	2/2,324	21.0	1	13	1 81mm mortar, 1 .50 cal. mg. (#95326, 28 have 2 .50 cal. mg.).
"Cape" (B)	WPB-95312	8	105	95'	6'	20'	4D(Cummins)(#VT12-600M)	2/2,324	20.0	1	13	1 81mm mortar, 1 .50 cal. mg. (#95314, 18, 19 have 2 .50 cal. mg.).

Class	Number	No. in Class	Full Load Displ.	Length Overall	Max. Draft	Ext. Beam	Number and Type Boilers/Engines	Screws/ SHP	Max. Speed (Kts.)	Allowance Officers	Enlisted	Armament
"Cape" (A)	WPB-95300	9	105	95'	6'	20'	4D(Cummins)(#VT12-600M)	2/2,324	20.0	1	13	1 81mm mortar, 1 .50 cal. mg. (#95300/02, 04 have 2 .50 cal. mg.).
"Point" (D)	WPB-82371	9	69	83'	6'	18'	2D(Cummins)(#VT12-900M)	2/1,600	22.6	0	8	2 .50 cal. mg.
"Point" (C)	WPB-82318	40	66	83'	6'	18'	2D(Cummins)(#VT12-900M)	2/1,600	23.7	0	8	1 81mm mortar, 1 .50 cal. mg. (#82318, 34, 35, 38/40, 43 have 2 .50 cal. mg.).
"Point" (A)	WPB-82302	4	67	83'	6'	18'	2D(Cummins)(#VT12-900M)	2/1,600	23.5	0	8	1 81mm mortar, 1 .50 cal. mg.
Arundel	WYTM-90	4	370	110'	11'	27'	Ingersoll-Rand Type S	1/1,000	11.2	0	10	None
Manitou	WYTM-60	8	370	110'	11'	27'	Ingersoll-Rand Type S	1/1,000	11.2	1	19	None
Messenger	WYTM-85009	1	230	85'	9'	23'	Enterprise DMG-38	1/700	9.5	0	10	None
Bitt	WYTL-65613	3	72	65'	6'	19'	1D(Caterpiller)(#D379-D)	1/400	9.8	0	10	None
Hawser	WYTL-65610	3	72	65'	6'	19'	1D(Waukesha)(#LRD-BSM)	1/400	9.8	0	10	None
Bridle	WYTL-65607	3	72	65'	6'	19'	1D(Waukesha)(#LRD-BSM)	1/400	9.8	0	10	None
Capstan	WYTL-65601	6	72	65'	6'	19'	1D(Caterpiller)(#D375-D)	1/400	10.5	0	10	None
Acushnet	WAGO-167	1	1,745	213'	15'	41'	2D(C.B.)(#GSB8 Stand.)	2/3,000	15.5	7	57	2 .50 cal. mg.
Evergreen	WAGO-295	1	1,025	180'	13'	37'	2D(C.B.)(#GN8-600)/1 EM(West.)	1/1,000	12.9	6	51	2 .50 cal. mg.
Basswood	WLB-388	19	1,025	180'	13'	37'	2D(C.B.)(#GN8-700)/1 EM(West.)	1/1,200	13.0	6	47	2 .50 cal. mg. (394 has 1 single 3"/50 cal. mt., 392, 404, 406, 407 are unarmed, 402 has 2 .40 cal mg.)
Ironwood	WLB-297	6	1,025	180'	13'	37'	2D(C.B.)(#GN8-700)/1 EM(West.)	1/1,200	13.0	6	47	2 .50 cal. mg. (305 is unarmed).
Balsam	WLB-62	10	1,025	180'	13'	37'	2D(C.B.)(#GN8-600)/1 EM(West.)	1/1,000	12.8	6	47	2 .50 cal. mg. (296, 300 have 1 single 3"/50)
Juniper	WLM-224	1	794	177'	9'	33'	2D(C.B.)(#GN-6)	2/900	10.8	4	34	None
Fir	WLM-212	3	989	175'	12'	34'	2D(F.M.)(#38D8-1/8)	2/1,350	12.0	5	35	None
Red Wood	WLM-685	5	512	157'	6'	33'	2D(Caterpiller)(#D398A)	2/1,800	12.8	4	27	None
White Sumac	WLM-540	7	600	133'	9'	31'	2D(Union) Model 06	2/600	9.8	1	20	None
Buckthorn	WLI-642	1	200	100'	4'	24'	2D(Caterpiller)(#D353)	2/600	10.9	1	13	None
Azalea	WLI-641	1	200	100'	5'	25'	2D (G.M.)	2/440	9.0	1	13	None
Cosmos	WLI-293	6	178	100'	5'	24'	2D(Caterpiller)(#D353)	2/600	10.5	1	14	None
Tern	WLI-80801	1	168	80'	5'	25'	2D (G.M.)	2/450	10.0	0	7	None
Clematis	WLI-74286	2	93	74'	4'	19'	2D (G.M.)(#6-71)	2/330	8.0	0	9	None
Bayberry	WLI-65400	2	68	65'	4'	17'	2D (G.M.)(#6-110)	2/400	11.3	0	5	None
Blackberry	WLI-65303	3	68	65'	4'	17'	2D (G.M.)(#6-110)	1/220	9.0	0	5	None
Blueberry	WLI-65302	1	45	65'	4'	15'	2D (G.M.)(#6-71)	2/330	10.5	0	5	None
Pamlico	WLIC-800	2		160'10"	4'	30'	2D	2/1,000	9.3	13 total		None
Clamp	WLIC-75306	5	145	76'	4'	22'	2D(Waukesha)(#F1905-DSIM)	2/600	10.2	0	9	None
Sledge	WLIC-75303	3	145	75'	4'	22'	2D(Waukesha)(#F1905-DSIM)	2/600	10.0	1	9	None
Anvil	WLIC-75301	2	145	75'	4'	22'	2D(Caterpiller)(#D-353)	2/600	10.0	0	9	None
Sumac	WLR-311	1	478	115'	8'	30'	3D(Caterpiller)(#D-379)	2/1,695	10.6	1	22	None
Forsythia	WLR-63	4	280	114'	5'	26'	2D(G.M.)(#8-268)	2/800	11.0	1	19	None
Lantana	WLR-80310	1	235	80'	6'	30'	3D(Cummins)(#VLA525)	3/945	10.0	1	19	None
Gasconade	WLR-75401	9	141	75'	4'	22'	2D(Caterpiller)(#D-353)	2/600	10.8	0	12	None
Oleander	WLR-73264	1	105	73'	5'	18'	2D(G.M.)(#8V-71N)	2/492	12.0	0	10	None
Ouachita	WLR-65501	6	139	66'	5'	21'	2D(Waukesha)(#6NKD)	2/630	12.5	0	10	None
"Nantucket"	WLV-534	1	1,100	149'	16'	32'	1D(C.B.)(#GSB-8)	1/900	9.0	1	19	None
"Boston"	WLV-189	5	600	128'	11'	30'	1D(G.M.)(#6-278A)	1/600	9.0	1	15	None
Eagle	WIX-327	1	1,784	295'	17'	40'	Sail and aux. diesel	1/700	10.5	280 total		None
Cuyahoga	WIX-157	1	290	125'	8'	24'	Diesels	1/800	13.2	1	10	None
Unimak	WTR-379	1	2,800	311'	14'	41'	4D(F.M.)(#38D81)	2/6,080	19.0	12	79	1 single 5"/38 cal. mt., 2 81mm mortars, 4 .50 cal. mg.

12 HIGH ENDURANCE CUTTERS, *HAMILTON (378') CLASS*

Name	Number	F/S
Midgett	WHEC-726	PA
Jarvis	WHEC-725	PA
Munroe	WHEC-724	PA
Rush	WHEC-723	PA
Morgenthau	WHEC-722	AA
Gallatin	WHEC-721	AA
Sherman	WHEC-720	AA
Boutwell	WHEC-719	PA
Chase	WHEC-718	AA
Mellon	WHEC-717	PA
Dallas	WHEC-716	AA
Hamilton	WHEC-715	AA

Authorized as WPGs; reclassed WHECs on 5–1–66. They replaced the *"Casco"* class cutters (ex-USN/AVPs). Built 1967–72 by Avondale Shipyards. They have oceanographic research and meteorological data-collecting facilities. The *Hamiltons* have controllable pitch propellers and 350 SHP bow thruster. They have long range and fair seakeeping qualities. Flight deck aft is 80 ft. long for the SAR helicopter. Largest cutters to be fitted with gas turbine propulsion. On 15 November 1972, during stormy seas in Iliuliuk Bay, Alaska, *Jarvis* dragged anchor and struck a reef. Sonar dome and both transducers were sheared off. She flooded, lost power, and almost sank. She was salvaged and repaired.

6 HIGH ENDURANCE CUTTERS, *BIBB (327') CLASS*

Name	Number	F/S
Taney (ex-Roger B.)	WHEC-37	AA
Spencer (ex-John C.)	WHEC-36	AR*
Ingham (ex-Samuel D.)	WHEC-35	AA
Duane (ex-William J.)	WHEC-33	AA
Campbell (ex-George W.)	WHEC-32	PA
Bibb (ex-George W.)	WHEC-31	AA

This class was completed 1936/37 as WPGs; to WHEC on 5–1–66. Originally named with full name of Treasury Secretary; but first name and middle initial dropped soon after completion. Seventh ship of class, *Hamilton* (ex-*Alexander*) (WPG-34), was lost in WW II. *Taney* is the world's only Pearl Harbor attack survivor in commissioned service. WHEC-36 decommissioned 2–1–74.

9 HIGH ENDURANCE CUTTERS, *OWASCO (255') CLASS*

Name	Number	F/S
Ponchartrain (ex-Okeechobee)	WHEC-70	AR*
Mendota	WHEC-69	AR*
Androscoggin	WHEC-68	DAR*
Minnetonka (ex-Sunapee)	WHEC-67	PR*
Winona	WHEC-65	PR*
Escanaba	WHEC-64	DAR*
Chautauqua	WHEC-41	AR*
Winnebago	WHEC-40	DAR*
Owasco	WHEC-39	DAR*

Completed 1945–46 as WPGs, there were originally 13 vessels in class. *Iroquois* (WPG-43), *Sebago* (WHEC-42), *Klamath* (WHEC-66), and *Wachusett* (WHEC-44) have been disposed of. WHEC-39, 40, 64 and 68 are for disposal.

2 ICEBREAKERS, *POLAR STAR (400') CLASS*

Name	Number	F/S
Polar Sea	WAGB-11	Bldg.
Polar Star	WAGB-10	PA

Built by Lockheed SB and Construction Company, Seattle. The *"Polar"* class will be the world's most powerful icebreakers. Powered by combined gas turbines (60,000 SHP) and diesels (18,000 BHP). Capable of breaking ice 6' thick at 3 knots, or ice up to 21' thick by ramming. Able to cruise around the world on one fueling. They are roll stabilized and have stainless steel, controllable pitch propellers; carry two HH-52A helicopters. They are equipped for scientific activities. *Polar Star* to commission in fall 1975; *Polar Sea* will follow in 12 months.

1 ICEBREAKER, *GLACIER (310') CLASS*

Name	Number	F/S
Glacier (ex-USN AGB-4)	WAGB-4	PA

Commissioned in USN as USS *Glacier* (AGB-4) on 5–27–55. Stricken from the NVR and transferred to USCG 6–30–66 as part of plan to consolidate icebreaking under one organization. Has heavily armored bow, helicopter deck aft, and small hangar.

1 ICEBREAKER, *MACKINAW (290') CLASS*

Name	Number	F/S
Mackinaw	WAGB-83	GLA

Built for Great Lakes service. Commissioned 12–20–44. Reclassified from WAG on 5–1–66.

2 ICEBREAKERS, "WIND-R" (269') CLASS

Name	Number	F/S
Northwind	WAGB-282	PA
Westwind	WAGB-281	AA

Redesignated "Wind-R" class upon installation of new propulsion system. Ships originally "Wind" class. WAGB-281 served in Russian Navy in the late 1940s.

4 ICEBREAKERS, "WIND" (269') CLASS

Name	Number	F/S
Edisto (ex-USN AGB-2)	WAGB-284	AR*
Burton Island (ex-USN AGB-1)	WAGB-283	PA
Southwind (ex-USN Atka, AGB-3)	WAGB-280	DAR*
Staten Island (ex-USN Northwind, AGB-5)	WAGB-278	PR*

Designed and built as heavy duty icebreakers 1943–47. All have helicopter decks and telescopic hangars. WAGB-278, 280 served in Russian Navy in 1940s. Acquired from USN 1965–66 and struck from the NVR. Originally 7 ships in class. Eastwind (WAGB-279) has been disposed of; two sisters form "Wind-R" class. Edisto was seriously damaged while trying to free another ship from Arctic icepack, about 600 miles south of North Pole; repaired and returned to service 3/73. Southwind decommissioned 5/74. Staten Island and Edisto decommissioned 11-15-74. Burton Island to lay up in spring of 1976.

1 MEDIUM ENDURANCE CUTTER, STORIS (230') CLASS

Storis (ex-Eskimo)	WMEC-38	PA

Built in 1942 and stationed at Kodiak, Alaska, Storis serves primarily as search-rescue, supply, and law enforcement vessel. Reclassified from WAG to WAGB on 5-1-66, and to WMEC on 7-1-72.

1 MEDIUM ENDURANCE CUTTER, YOCONA (213') CLASS

Yocona	WMEC-168	PA

Built as USS Seize (ARS-26) of USN Escape class; commissioned 11-3-44. Transferred to USCG, permanently after WW II. Reconfigured as tug and reclassed WAT. To WMEC in 1968. Sister ship Acushnet (WAT-167) was rerated WAGO at the same time.

11 MEDIUM ENDURANCE CUTTERS, RESOLUTE (210') B CLASS

Name	Number	F/S
Alert	WMEC-630	AA
Decisive	WMEC-629	AA
Durable	WMEC-628	AA
Vigorous	WMEC-627	AA
Dependable	WMEC-626	AA
Venturous	WMEC-625	PA
Dauntless	WMEC-624	AA
Steadfast	WMEC-623	AA
Courageous	WMEC-622	AA
Valiant	WMEC-621	AA
Resolute	WMEC-620	PA

Completed 1967–69; same as A class, less gas turbines. Diesels are marine versions of modern locomotive engines.

4. MEDIUM ENDURANCE CUTTERS/1 TRAINING CUTTER, RELIANCE (210') A CLASS

Confidence	WMEC-619	PA
Active	WMEC-618	AA
Vigilant	WMEC-617	AA
Diligence	WMEC-616	AA
Reliance	WTR-615	AA

Completed 1964–66. Originally rated WPC; reclassed WMEC on 5-1-66. Design requirements were for a vessel able to steam 750 miles, search for 7 days at 10/12 knots, and return to base with tow. Provisions for fire-fighting, pumping, and fuel-transfer capabilities. Ships have helicopter deck aft; no hangar. Wheelhouse has 360° visibility; no funnels. Powered by either gas turbines or diesels. Exhaust vented out the stern. Reliance reclassified WTR 6-27-75 as replacement for Unimak (WTR-379).

3 MEDIUM ENDURANCE CUTTERS, "AVOYEL" (205') CLASS

Tamaroa (ex-USN Zuni, ATF-95)	WMEC-166	AA
Cherokee (ex-USN ATF-66)	WMEC-165	AA
Chilula (ex-USN ATF-153)	WMEC-153	AA

Former Cherokee class ATFs. Commissioned in USN 1940–45. WMEC-165/66 to USCG 6–29–46; WMEC-153 in 1956. Permanently transferred 6-1-69. Original USCG rating was WAT; to WMEC 1968. Sister Avoyel (WMEC-150) decommissioned 9-30-69 and leased to a private research concern for further service.

2 MEDIUM ENDURANCE CUTTERS, *MODOC (143') CLASS*

Name	Number	F/S
Comanche (ex-USN ATA-202)	WMEC-202	PA
Modoc (ex-USN Bagaduce, ATA-194)	WMEC-194	PA

Former USN *Sotoyomo* class ATAs; commissioned 1944–45. *Modoc* is ex-USNS (T-ATA). Acquired by USCG in 1959 from MarAd. WMEC-202 acquired on loan from USN 2–25–59; acquired permanently 6–1–69, when she was stricken from the NVR. Both vessels were originally rated as WAT; reclassified WMEC in 1968.

6 PATROL CRAFT, LARGE, *"CAPE" (95') C* CLASS

Cape York	WPB-95332	AA
Cape Henlopen	WPB-95328	PA
Cape Corwin	WPB-95326	PA
Cape Shoalwater	WPB-95324	AA
Cape Horn	WPB-95322	AA
Cape Cross	WPB-95321	AA

Constructed 1958–59. 9 units of this class were transferred to South Korea. 3 units of a new class of WPB will be requested under FY 1975.

8 PATROL CRAFT, LARGE, *"CAPE" (95') B* CLASS

Cape Starr	WPB-95320	AA
Cape Romain	WPB-95319	PA
Cape Newagen	WPB-95318	PA
Cape Jellison	WPB-95317	PA
Cape Fox	WPB-95316	AA
Cape Fairweather	WPB-95314	AA
Cape Morgan	WPB-95313	AA
Cape Knox	WPB-95312	AA

Built in 1955. Similar to *A* and *C* classes.

9 PATROL CRAFT, LARGE, *"CAPE" (95') A* CLASS

Cape Hedge	WPB-95311	PA
Cape Wash	WPB-95310	PA
Cape Carter	WPB-95309	PA
Cape Strait	WPB-95308	AA
Cape Current	WPB-95307	AA
Cape George	WPB-95306	AA
Cape Gull	WPB-95304	AR*

Name	Number	F/S
Cape Coral	WPB-95301	PA
Cape Small	WPB-95300	PA

Constructed in 1953; all *Capes* built by Curtis Bay Yard, Maryland. Primary duties are search-rescue and port security. Three sisters (WPB-95302, 03, 05) are in reserve and are being cannibalized. The residue hulks will then be scrapped.

9 PATROL CRAFT, SMALL, *"POINT" (82') D* CLASS

Point Martin	WPB-82379	AA
Point Jackson	WPB-82378	AA
Point Hobart	WPB-82377	PA
Point Harris	WPB-82376	PA
Point Doran	WPB-82375	PA
Point Carrew	WPB-82374	PA
Point Camden	WPB-82373	PA
Point Brower	WPB-82372	PA
Point Barnes	WPB-82371	AA

"Point" classes were built at the Curtis Bay Yard, Maryland; *A* 1960–61, *C* 1961–67, *D* 1970. Designed for search-rescue and law enforcement. They are steel-hulled; engine room unmanned and controlled from the bridge. Originally unnamed, they were assigned names January 1964. In 1965, 26 units deployed to Vietnam under the operational control of the Navy. They were later transferred to Vietnam and replaced in USCG with new construction. *A* class consisted of 82301/82317; *B* class of 82318/82331. *Point Thatcher* was used for experiments with gas turbines and controllable pitch propeller propulsion.

40 PATROL CRAFT, SMALL, *"POINT" (82') C* CLASS

Point Richmond	WPB-82370	PA
Point Heyer	WPB-82369	PA
Point Warde	WPB-82368	AA
Point Knoll	WPB-82367	AA
Point Lobos	WPB-82366	AA
Point Turner	WPB-82365	AA
Point Whitehorn	WPB-82364	AA
Point Nowell	WPB-82363	AA
Point Brown	WPB-82362	AA
Point Charles	WPB-82361	AA
Point Winslow	WPB-82360	PA
Point Steele	WPB-82359	AA
Point Stuart	WPB-82358	PA
Point Huron	WPB-82357	AA
Point Franklin	WPB-82350	AA

Name	Number	F/S
Point Spencer	WPB-82349	AA
Point Barrow	WPB-82348	PA
Point Bonita	WPB-82347	AA
Point Arena	WPB-82346	AA
Point Judith	WPB-82345	PA
Point Estero	WPB-82344	AA
Point Wells	WPB-82343	AA
Point Baker	WPB-82342	AA
Point Lookout	WPB-82341	AA
Point Batan	WPB-82340	AA
Point Chico	WPB-82339	PA
Point Bridge	WPB-82338	PA
Point Divide	WPB-82337	PA
Point Francis	WPB-82356	AA
Point Hannon	WPB-82355	AA
Point Evans	WPB-82354	PA
Point Monroe	WPB-82353	AA
Point Sal	WPB-82352	AA
Point Bennett	WPB-82351	PA
Point Glass	WPB-82336	PA
Point Countess	WPB-82335	PA
Point Ledge	WPB-82334	PA
Point Highland	WPB-82333	AA
Point Roberts	WPB-82332	AA
Point Herron	WPB-82318	AA

4 PATROL CRAFT, SMALL, "POINT" (82') A CLASS

Point Thatcher	WPB-82314	AA
Point Swift	WPB-82312	AA
Point Verde	WPB-82311	AA
Point Hope	WPB-82302	AA

4 HARBOR TUGS, MEDIUM, ARUNDEL (110') B CLASS

Raritan	WYTM-93	GLA
Naugatuck	WYTM-92	GLA
Mahoning	WYTM-91	AA
Arundel	WYTM-90	GLA

Built in 1939.

8 HARBOR TUGS, MEDIUM, MANITOU (110') A CLASS

Name	Number	F/S
Sauk	WYTM-99	AA
Snohomish	WYTM-98	AR
Ojibwa	WYTM-97	GLA
Chinook	WYTM-96	AA
Mohican	WYTM-73	AA
Yankton	WYTM-72	AA
Apalachee	WYTM-71	AA
Kaw	WYTM-61	GLA
Manitou	WYTM-60	AA

Built in 1943.

1 HARBOR TUG, MEDIUM, MESSENGER (85') CLASS

Name	Number	F/S
Messenger	WYTM-85009	AA

Built in 1944. Stationed at Coast Guard Yard, Curtis Bay, Maryland.

3 HARBOR TUGS, SMALL, BITT (65') D CLASS

Cleat	WYTL-65615	AA
Bollard	WYTL-65614	AA
Bitt	WYTL-65613	PA

Built in 1966–67. Vessels stationed at Bellingham, Washington (Bitt), Governors Island, New York (Bollard), and Gloucester, New Jersey (Cleat).

3 HARBOR TUGS, SMALL, HAWSER (65') C CLASS

Wire	WYTL-65612	AA
Line	WYTL-65611	AA
Hawser	WYTL-65610	AA

Built in 1963. This class stationed at Governors Island, New York.

U.S. COAST GUARD

3 HARBOR TUGS, SMALL, *BRIDLE (65') B* CLASS

Name	Number	F/S
Shackle	WYTL-65609	AA
Pendant	WYTL-65608	AA
Bridle	WYTL-65607	AA

Built in 1963. *Bridle* and *Shackle* are stationed in Maine; *Pendant* in Boston, Mass.

6 HARBOR TUGS, SMALL, *CAPSTAN (65') A* CLASS

Catenary	WYTL-65606	AA
Towline	WYTL-65605	AA
Tackle	WYTL-65604	AA
Swivel	WYTL-65603	AA
Chock	WYTL-65602	AA
Capstan	WYTL-65601	AA

Built in 1961–62. Provide towing, assistance, boarding, firefighting, and icebreaking.

1 OCEANOGRAPHIC CUTTER, *ACUSHNET (213')* CLASS

Acushnet (ex-USN ARS-9)	WAGO-167	AA

Built as USS *Shackle* (ARS-9) of *Escape* class and commissioned 2–5–44. Decommissioned after WW II; transferred to USCG permanently. Reconfigured as tug and classified as WAT-167; rerated WAGO 1968. She is stationed at Gulfport, Mississippi, in support of the National Data Buoy Project.

1 OCEANOGRAPHIC CUTTER, *EVERGREEN (180')* CLASS

Evergreen	WAGO-295	AA

Built in 1943 as *Balsam* class seagoing buoy tender. Reconfigured to oceanographic cutter in February 1973. She has bow thruster. Ship has been extensively rebuilt. Stationed at New London, Connecticut.

19 BUOY TENDERS, SEAGOING, *BASSWOOD (180') C* CLASS

Woodrush	WLB-407	GLA
Acacia	WLB-406	GLA
Sweetbrier	WLB-405	AA
Sundew	WLB-404	GLA
Spar	WLB-403	AA

Name	Number	F/S
Sedge	WLB-402	AA
Sassafras	WLB-401	AA
Salvia	WLB-400	AA
Sagebrush	WLB-399	AA
Mariposa	WLB-397	AA
Mallow	WLB-396	PA
Iris	WLB-395	PA
Hornbeam	WLB-394	AA
Firebrush	WLB-393	AA
Bramble	WLB-392	GLA
Blackthorn	WLB-391	AA
Blackhaw	WLB-390	PA
Bittersweet	WLB-389	PA
Basswood	WLB-388	PA

Built in 1943–44. WLB-390, 392, and 402/404 are ice reinforced. WLB-389, 394, 402, and 405 have bow thruster. A twentieth unit, *Redbud* (WLB-398), was transferred to the Philippine Islands after serving with the U.S. Navy. *Hornbeam* was damaged in a collision with a Brazilian freighter 5–24–72. Her bow was gashed and she received other minor damage. All *B* and *C* class tenders will be renovated by 1979 to improve habitability and extend service life. WLB-397, 402 and 405 are currently being renovated at Curtis Bay. Will take approximately 9 months.

6 BUOY TENDERS, SEAGOING, *IRONWOOD (180') B* CLASS

Sweetgum	WLB-309	AA
Papaw	WLB-308	AA
Planetree	WLB-307	PA
Buttonwood	WLB-306	PA
Mesquite	WLB-305	GLA
Ironwood	WLB-297	PA

Built in 1943–44; WLB-297 overhauled 4/74 to 4/75 at Curtis Bay.

10 BUOY TENDERS, SEAGOING, *BALSAM (180') A* CLASS

Tupelo	WLB-303	PA
Madrona	WLB-302	AA
Conifer	WLB-301	AA
Citrus	WLB-300	PA
Sorrel	WLB-296	PA
Clover	WLB-292	PA

Name	Number	F/S
Laurel	WLB-291	AA
Gentian	WLB-290	AA
Cowslip	WLB-277	DAR*
Balsam	WLB-62	PR*

Built in 1942–44. WLB-62, 296, and 300 are ice reinforced. WLB-277 has bow thruster. *Woodbine* (289) and the damaged *Cactus* (270) have been disposed of. *Balsam* decommissioned 2/75 at Bremerton. WLB-292, 296, 300 will decommission prior to FY 1978.

1 BUOY TENDER, COASTAL, *JUNIPER (177')* CLASS

Juniper	WLM-224	AA

Built in 1941. Reclassed from WAGL on 1-1-65. Stationed at St. Petersburg, Florida.

3 BUOY TENDERS, COASTAL, *FIR (175')* CLASS

Walnut	WLM-252	PA
Hollyhock	WLM-220	AA
Fir	WLM-212	PA

Built 1937–38. Reclassed from WAGL on 1-1-65.

5 BUOY TENDERS, COASTAL, *RED WOOD (157')* CLASS

Red Oak	WLM-689	AA
Red Cedar	WLM-688	AA
Red Birch	WLM-687	PA
Red Beech	WLM-686	AA
Red Wood	WLM-685	AA

Built in 1964–71 at Curtis Bay Yard, Maryland. Steering/engine controls from bridge wings and pilot house. This class has improved maneuverability and is highly suited for maintaining aids to navigation in coastal waters, performing SAR, law enforcement duties, and special assignments.

7 BUOY TENDERS, COASTAL, *WHITE SUMAC (133')* CLASS

White Pine	WLM-547	AA
White Lupine	WLM-546	AA
White Heath	WLM-545	AA
White Sage	WLM-544	AA
White Holly	WLM-543	AA
White Bush	WLM-542	PA
White Sumac	WLM-540	AA

Built in 1942–44, these tenders are former USN YFs. Scheduled for machinery modernization by 1977. An eighth ship, *White Alder* (WLM-541) was sunk by collision 12–7–68.

1 BUOY TENDER, INLAND, *BUCKTHORN (100')* C CLASS

Name	Number	F/S
Buckthorn	WLI-642	GLA

Built in 1963. Pilothouse and upper deckhouse are constructed of aluminum. Steering and engines are operated from console panels located in pilothouse and each bridge wing. The five-ton boom rotates 360° and is located at forward end of the buoy deck. A centerline spud can assist in holding the vessel while it is working on an aid.

1 BUOY TENDER, INLAND, *AZALEA (100')* B CLASS

Azalea	WLI-641	AA

Built in 1958. Pile driver equipped. Stationed at Charleston, South Carolina.

6 BUOY TENDERS, INLAND, *COSMOS (100')* A CLASS

Verbena	WLI-317	AA
Primrose	WLI-316	AA
Smilax	WLI-315	AA
Bluebell	WLI-313	PA
Rambler	WLI-298	AA
Cosmos	WLI-293	AA

Built in 1942–45. *Cosmos* and *Smilax* have construction barges assigned. *Primrose* and *Verbena* have pile driver installed. *Barberry* (WLI-294) has been disposed of.

1 BUOY TENDER, INLAND, *TERN (80')* CLASS

Tern	WLI-80801	AA

Built in 1969, this is a prototype design with the first USCG gantry crane installed. Has bow thruster. The crane lifts buoys from the stern; moves on rails from edge of stern to deckhouse.

2 BUOY TENDERS, INLAND, *CLEMATIS (74')* CLASS

Shadbush	WLI-74287	AA
Clematis	WLI-74286	AA

Built in 1944. *Clematis* homeports at Corpus Christi; *Shadbush* at New Orleans. Latter has construction barge assigned.

2 BUOY TENDERS, INLAND, *BAYBERRY (65400)* CLASS

Name	Number	F/S
Elderberry	WLI-65401	PA
Bayberry	WLI-65400	PA

Built in 1954. Stationed at Petersburg, Alaska, and Seattle, Washington, respectively.

3 BUOY TENDERS, INLAND, *BLACKBERRY (65303)* CLASS

Name	Number	F/S
Loganberry	WLI-65305	AA
Chokeberry	WLI-65304	AA
Blackberry	WLI-65303	AA

Built in 1946. Stationed at New Orleans, Hatteras Inlet, and Southport, North Carolina, respectively.

1 BUOY TENDER, INLAND, *BLUEBERRY (65302)* CLASS

Name	Number	F/S
Blueberry	WLI-65302	PA

Built in 1942. Has construction barge assigned. Homeports at Kennewick, Station, Washington.

2 CONSTRUCTION TENDERS, INLAND, *PAMLICO (160')* CLASS

Name	Number	F/S
Hudson	WLIC-801	Bldg.
Pamlico	WLIC-800	Bldg.

Building at Curtis Bay. Scheduled completion late 1975. Replaces old towboat/barge type. New vessels will be single-hull construction. Assigned to New Orleans.

5 CONSTRUCTION TENDERS, INLAND, *CLAMP (75')* D CLASS

Name	Number	F/S
Axe	WLIC-75310	AA
Hatchet	WLIC-75309	AA
Spike	WLIC-75308	AA
Wedge	WLIC-75307	AA
Clamp	WLIC-75306	AA

Built in 1964–65. Though actual hull length is 76', they are regarded as 75' class. Hull numbers of five digits usually indicate the vessel's length in the first two digits. *Clamp* and *Hatchet* stationed at Galveston, Texas; *Axe* at Mobile, Alabama; *Spike* at Mayport, Florida; *Wedge* at New Orleans, Louisiana. Construction barge assigned.

3 CONSTRUCTION TENDERS, INLAND, *SLEDGE (75')* B CLASS

Name	Number	F/S
Vise	WLIC-75305	AA
Mallet	WLIC-75304	AA
Sledge	WLIC-75303	AA

Built in 1962. Stationed at Portsmouth, Virginia (75303), Corpus Christi, Texas (75304), and St. Petersburg, Florida (75305). Construction barge assigned.

2 CONSTRUCTION TENDERS, INLAND, *ANVIL (75')* A CLASS

Name	Number	F/S
Hammer	WLIC-75302	AA
Anvil	WLIC-75301	AA

Built in 1962. Stationed in Florida. Construction barge assigned.

1 BUOY TENDER, RIVER, *SUMAC (115')* CLASS

Name	Number	F/S
Sumac	WLR-311	IW,A

Built in 1943. Stationed at Keokuk, Iowa. *Fern* (WLR-304) has been disposed of.

4 BUOY TENDERS, RIVER, *FORSYTHIA (114')* CLASS

Name	Number	F/S
Foxglove	WLR-285	IW,A
Sycamore	WLR-268	IW,A
Dogwood	WLR-259	IW,A
Forsythia	WLR-63	IW,A

Built in 1940–45. *Foxglove* displaces 350 tons, has 6' draft; engine provides 1200 SHP (3 screws), and has greater range and speed. *Dogwood* and *Sycamore* displace 230 tons. *Forsythia* has less boom capacity.

1 BUOY TENDER, RIVER, *LANTANA (80')* CLASS

Name	Number	F/S
Lantana	WLR-80310	IW,A

Built in 1943. Stationed at Owensboro, Kentucky.

9 BUOY TENDERS, RIVER, *GASCONADE (75')* CLASS

Name	Number	F/S
Chena	WLR-75409	IW,A
Patoka	WLR-75408	IW,A
Kanawha	WLR-75407	IW,A
Kickapoo	WLR-75406	IW,A
Cheyenne	WLR-75405	IW,A
Chippewa	WLR-75404	IW,A
Wyaconda	WLR-75403	IW,A
Muskingum	WLR-75402	IW,A
Gasconade	WLR-75401	IW,A

Built 1964–70. Stationed at Omaha, Nebraska (75401), Memphis, Tennessee (75402, 75407), Dubuque, Iowa (75403), Hickman, Kentucky (75404), St. Louis, Missouri (75405), Pine Bluff, Arkansas (75406), Sallisaw, Oklahoma (75408), and Natchez, Mississippi (75409). Assigned buoy handling barge.

1 BUOY TENDER, RIVER, *OLEANDER (73')* CLASS

Oleander	WLR-73264	IW,A

Built in 1940. Stationed at Point Pleasant, West Virginia.

6 BUOY TENDERS, RIVER, *OUACHITA (65')* CLASS

Sangamon	WLR-65506	IW,A
Osage	WLR-65505	IW,A
Scioto	WLR-65504	IW,A
Obion	WLR-65503	IW,A
Cimarron	WLR-65502	IW,A
Ouachita	WLR-65501	IW,A

Built in 1960–62. Class has 3-ton crane barge assigned. Stationed at East Chattanooga, Tennessee (65501), Paris Landing, Tennessee (65502), Memphis, Tennessee (65503), Leavenworth, Kansas (65504), Sheffield, Alabama (65505), and Peoria, Illinois (65506). Buoy handling barge assigned.

1 LIGHTSHIP, "*NANTUCKET*" (149') CLASS

Nantucket	WLV-534	AA

Built in 1936. Names of lightships refer to their stations. All units being phased out in favor of large, automated buoys.

5 LIGHTSHIPS, "*BOSTON*" (128') CLASS

Name	Number	F/S
Relief	WLV-613	AA
Portland	WLV-612	AA
Relief	WLV-605	PA
Columbia River	WLV-604	PA
Boston	WLV-189	AA

Built in 1946–52. WLV-605 and 613 relieve the normal station ship for yard period or repairs.

1 TRAINING CUTTER, *EAGLE (295')* CLASS

Eagle	WIX-327	AA

Built in 1936 by Blohm and Voss, Hamburg, Germany. Served as German Navy training ship. Awarded to USN as war prize January 1946. Transferred to USCG July 1946 for use as Coast Guard training vessel. Stationed at New London. Square sails on fore and main mast; fore and aft sails on mizzen mast. Can reach 18 knots with full sail. Bark-rigged, has 21,351 square feet of sail.

1 TRAINING CUTTER, *CUYAHOGA (125')* CLASS

Cuyahoga (ex WPC-157)	WIX-157	AA

Last survivor of the *Alert* class cutters. Completed 1926 as WPC-157. Re-engined late 1930s. Became training cutter at Yorktown, Virginia, in late 1950s.

1 RESERVE TRAINING CUTTER, *UNIMAK (311')* CLASS

Unimak (ex WHEC, WAVP, USN AVP-31)	WTR-379	DAR*

Completed as a *Barnegat* class AVP; commissioned 12–31–43 in USN. Transferred to Coast Guard 9–14–48 as WAVP-379. Rerated WHEC on 5–1–66, and again as WTR in 1969. Homeports at Yorktown, Virginia. Lone AVP survivor in American service. The exceptionally large fuel capacity gave these cutters a cruising range of 22,000 miles. *Unimak* decommissioned 5–30–75 at Baltimore. Replaced by *Reliance* (WTR-615).

COAST GUARD AIRCRAFT IN SERVICE AS OF JULY 1974

Model	Year Ordered/ Delivered	Number In Service	Crew-Type	Lbs. Gross Weight	LOA	Dimensions Span	Height	Number	Engine Model	Thrust in Lbs. or HP (each)	Performance Max. Speed/Range (Kts.)/(nm)
VC-11A		1	4-L	59,500	79'11"	68'10"	24'6"	2	MK511-8	11,400	511/2930
VC-4A	1963	1	3-L	36,000	63'9"	78'4"	23'4"	2	MK529-8	2,210HP	350/2621
HC-130B	1958	12	7-L	135,000	97'9"	132'7"	38'3"	4	T56-A-7A	4,050HP	320/3500
EC-130E	1965	1	7-L	135,000	97'9"	132'7"	38'3"	4	T56-A-7A	4,050HP	330/3600
HC-130H	1968	8	7-L	155,000	100'6"	132'7"	38'3"	4	T56-A-15	4,910HP	335/4650
HH-52A	1962	72	3-L	8,100	44'7"	1–53'	16'0"	1	T58-GE-8B	1,250HP	90/474
HH-3F	1963	39	4-L	22,050	57'3"	1–62'	18'1"	2	T58-GE-5	1,500HP	140/683
HU-16E	1958	31	6-A		62'10"	80'0"	24'3"	2	R1820-76A	1,425HP	200/2200

GULFSTREAM II, VC-11A Long-range staff/administration aircraft. Turbofan jet with 25° swept wing with Rolls Royce engines. A T-type empennage consists of a swept vertical fin with a swept horizontal tail mounted atop the fin. Carries 12 passengers.

GULFSTREAM I, VC-4A Medium-range staff personnel transport. Engines manufactured by Rolls Royce (Dart).

HERCULES, C-130 Series HC-130B: Similar to C-130B except has special equipment for SAR missions. **EC-130E:** Similar to C-130E except modified with the deletion of external pylon tanks and the addition of a radio operator and alternate navigator positions, electronic

calibration aircraft for worldwide calibration of LORAN. **HC-130H:** Similar to USAF HC-130H, used for SAR missions.

SEAGUARD, HH-52A Amphibious SAR type designed to operate equally well at high altitudes or sea level in Arctic or tropical regions.

PELICAN, HH-3F Non-combat SAR. No armor, armament, or self-sealing tanks; sonar equipment removed. Modified version of USAF CH-3C/D.

ALBATROSS, HU-16E Amphibious SAR. Similar to USN HU-16D; obtained from USN/USAF.

USCGC *Dallas* (WHEC-716). 1972. HH-52A landing aboard.

USCGC *Dallas* (WHEC-716). 4–25–70.

USCGC *Taney* (WHEC-37). Last active Pearl Harbor veteran. Special storm tracking radar housing located in dome mounted on top of her bridge. 8–8–73.

USCGC *Minnetonka* (WHEC-67). 4–5–70.

USCGC *Polar Star* (WAGB-10). Artist's conception. 10–31–71.

USCGC *Glacier* (WAGB-4) at Juneau. 7–6–72.

USCGC *Mackinaw* (WAGB-83). "Big Mac" on the Great Lakes. Undated.

USCGC *Staten Island* (WAGB-278). 12–29–71.

USCGC *Storis* (WAGB-38) at Kodiak, Alaska. Undated.

USCGC *Yocona* (WMEC-168). 6–3–70.

USCGC *Venturous* (WMEC-625) refueling HH-3F helicopter. 10–23–72.

USCGC *Vigilant* (WMEC-617). 8–4–69.

USCGC *Tamaroa* (WMEC-166). 12–1–70.

USCGC *Comanche* (WMEC-202). 10–13–69.

USCGC *Cape Cross* (WPB-95321). 8–5–69. **C** class.

USCGC *Cape Jellison* (WPB-95317). 6–20–68. **B** class.

USCGC *Cape Carter* (WPB-95309). 11–2–68. **A** class.

USCGC *Point Hobart* (WPB-82377). 4–19–71. **D** class.

USCGC *Point Bonita* (WPB-82347). 8–5–69. **C** class.

USCGC *Mahoning* (WYTM-91). 7–70.

USCGC *Yankton* (WYTM-72). 1–12–69.

USCGC *Messenger* (WYTM-85009). 11–20–69.

USCGC *Bollard* (WYTL-65614). 11–25–69. **D** class.

USCGC *Line* (WYTL-65611). Undated. **C** class.

USCGC *Shackle* (WYTL-65609). 1–12–69. **B** class.

USCGC *Towline* (WYTL-65605). 2–17–67. **A** class.

USCGC *Acushnet* (WAGO-167). Undated.

USCGC *Evergreen* (WAGO-295) with new superstructure. 2–28–73.

USCGC *Spar* (WLB-403). 10–3–68. **C** class.

USCGC *Ironwood* (WLB-297). 12–1–70. **B** class.

USCGC *Clover* (WLB-292). 10–31–72. **A** class.

USCGC *Juniper* (WLM-224). 6–29–71.

USCGC *Fir* (WLM-212). Undated.

USCGC *Red Birch* (WLM-687). Undated.

USCGC *White Sage* (WLM-544). 3–11–69.

USCGC *Buckthorn* (WLI-642). 4–30–70. **C** class.

USCGC *Azalea* (WLI-641). 1–20–71. **B** class.

USCGC *Smilax* (WLI-315). 1–20–71. **A** class.

USCGC *Tern* (WLI-80801). Note gantry crane. 5–26–69.

USCGC *Clematis* (WLI-74286). 8–25–70.

USCGC *Elderberry* (WLI-65401). 9–10–68.

USCGC *Loganberry* (WLI-65305). 4–13–71.

U.S. COAST GUARD

USCGC *Spike* (WLIC-75308). 1–20–71. **D** class.

USCGC *Sledge* (WLIC-75303). 8–21–69. **B** class.

USCGC *Hammer* (WLIC-75302). 1973. **A** class.

USCGC *Foxglove* (WLR-285) with construction barge. Undated.

USCGC *Lantana* (WLR-80310). Undated.

USCGC *Cheyenne* (WLR-75405). 6–1–71.

USCGC *Oleander* (WLR-73264). 1972.

USCGC *Osage* (WLR-65505). 1972.

USCGC *Nantucket* (WLV-534). Undated.

USCGC *"Relief"* (WLV-605). 1–8–74.

USCGC *Eagle* (WIX-327). Undated.

USCGC *Cuyahoga* (WIX-157). Undated.

USCGC *Unimak* (WTR-379). Last active **Barnegat** class AVP in U.S. service. Undated.

GULFSTREAM II, VC-11A. Undated.

GULFSTREAM I, VC-4A. 3–23–73.

HERCULES, HC-130B. Undated.

HERCULES, EC-130E. Undated.

HERCULES, HC-130H. Undated.

SEAGUARD, HH-52A. Undated.

PELICAN, HH-3F. Undated.

TEN: AIRCRAFT

All Department of Defense aircraft are assigned designations to conform to the Joint Regulations as of 9-18-62. The uniform identification system is a combination of a number and letters that identifies any given model of aircraft.

EXPLANATION OF AIRCRAFT LETTERS AND NUMBERS

BASIC DESIGNATION—the basic-mission letter, a dash, and a design number (A-5).
BASIC MISSION SYMBOL—a letter indicating the basic intended function or capability (A-5, attack).
DESIGN NUMBER—the sequence number indicating a new design of the same basic mission or type (A-5, 5th attack design).
SERIES SYMBOL—the letter *A* is placed to the right of a new design number. Letters in alphabetical order (except *I* or *O*) indicate improvements or modifications on the same design (A-5B, second series of the fifth design).
MODIFIED MISSION SYMBOL—prefix letter indicating the type of mission a design has been modified for other than the original and intended purpose (RA-5C, *R* is reconnaissance).
STATUS SYMBOL—prefix letter that indicates the aircraft is being used for special or service test and experimentation. Also, aircraft is in planning or is a prototype.
In addition, a popular name is usually assigned to an aircraft. The RA-5C is *VIGILANTE*.

NOTES

1. Except for those which are prototypes, tables list operational aircraft only.
2. Nonoperational aircraft do not appear in the tables, but are indicated under respective notes and comments. Because of security, it is impossible to comment on each model modified for special test or experimentation, even though some modifications are unclassified in nature.
3. Speed given in characteristics tables is in knots.
4. In the column headed "Thrust in lbs. or HP each," the figure given is thrust unless otherwise indicated. Further, all figures given, be it HP or thrust, are for *each* engine.

SYMBOLS
BASIC MISSION

A. Attack	H. Helicopter	U. Utility
C. Cargo/transport	O. Observation	V. VTOL/STOL; vertical/
E. Airborne early warning	P. Patrol	or short takeoff and landing
F. Fighter	S. Antisubmarine	X. Research
	T. Trainer	

MODIFIED MISSION

A. Attack	K. Tanker; inflight refueling	S. Antisubmarine
C. Cargo/transport	L. Cold weather; Arctic/Antarctic	T. Trainer
D. Directs or controls drones, aircraft, or missiles	M. Missile carrier	U. Utility; small payload; tows targets, etc.
E. Special electronic installation	Q. Drone aircraft	V. Staff
H. Search and rescue	R. Reconnaissance	W. Weather, meteorology

STATUS PREFIX

G. Permanently grounded	N. Special test; perm.	Y. Prototype
J. Special test; temp.	X. Experimental	Z. Planning

ABBREVIATIONS

AEW	Airborne early warning
ASW	Antisubmarine warfare
ATDS	Airborne Tactical Data System
A/W	All weather
B/N	Bombardier/navigator
C	Carrier-based (tables)
COD	Carrier on-board delivery
DIANE	Digital integrated attack navigation equipment
ECM	Electronic countermeasures
F/W	Fair weather
ILP	International Logistics Program
JL	JULIE (active, acoustic)
JL/JZ	JULIE/JEZEBEL
JZ	JEZEBEL (passive, acoustic)
L	Land-based (tables)
L-A/W	Limited all weather
LORAN	Long range aid to navigation
MAD	Magnetic anomaly detector
MCM	Mine countermeasures
RAG	Replacement air group
REINS	Radio equipped inertial navigation system
TRIM	Trails, roads, interdiction, multisensor
VERTREPS	Vertical replenishment

AIRBORNE EARLY WARNING

Model	Year Ordered/ Delivered	Number Proc.	Crew- Type	Lbs. Gross Weight	LOA	Dimensions Span	Height	Number	Engine Model	Thrust in Lbs. or HP (each)	Performance Max. Speed/Range (Kts.)/(nm)
E-2B	67/69	52	5-C	49,500	56'4"	80'7"	18'4"*	2	T56-A-8B	4,050 HP	368/1654
E-2C	68/73	28	5-C	51,550	57'6"	80'7"	18'4"*	2	T56-A-422	4,050 HP	368/1654
E-1B	56/58	88	4-C	27,000	45'3½"	72'5"	16'10"*	2	R1820-82A	1,525 HP	250/2000

* with rotor extended.

HAWKEYE, E-2 Series (W2F) Aircraft with primary mission to maintain a duty station at some distance from a task force, to provide early warning of approaching enemy aircraft, and to vector suitable aircraft into intercept position. HAWKEYE is the focal point of ATDS and is linked to the basic NTDS. **E-2B:** E-2As remaining were retrofitted with the B model computer and redesignated E-2B (49). Has improved electronics, including a new micro-miniaturized general-purpose computer. **E-2C:** First flight 23 September 1972. Has improved overland capabilities, an updated computer, a new inertial guidance system and a passive detection system. The 24' diameter APA-171 rotodome rotates at a speed of 6 rpm. Nose

extension of 21" accommodates the passive system antenna, in addition to the existing E-2B liquid oxygen converter. **TE-2A:** Two conversions; similar to E-2A except has ATDS removed. Further modified for training purposes only.

TRACER, E-1B (WF-2) Design based on C-1A TRADER. "WILLIE FUDD" is being phased out. As of 25 May 1973, all E-1 training has been terminated. Identification of this craft is unmistakable; twin rudders and large, circular rotodome extended above the fuselage. The projected E-1C avionics modification of E-1B was cancelled.

ANTISUBMARINE WARFARE

Model	Year Ordered/ Delivered	Number Proc.	Crew- Type	Lbs. Gross Weight	LOA	Dimensions Span	Height	Number	Engine Model	Thrust in Lbs. or HP (each)	Performance Max. Speed/Range (Kts.)/(nm)
S-3A	69/72	187	4-C	42,500	53'4"	68'8"	22'9"	2	TF34-GE-2	9,275	447/3370
S-2D	57/59	100	4-C	29,934	43'6"	72'7"	16'7½"	2	R1820-82	1,525 HP	210/1200
S-2E	62/62	252	4-C	29,934	43'6"	72'7"	16'7½"	2	R1820-82A	1,525 HP	210/1130
S-2G		50	4-C		43'6"	72'7"	16'7½"	2	R1820-82	1,525 HP	210/1130

VIKING, S-3A New carrier-based ASW aircraft, replacing S-2 TRACKER. Has all-weather search and destroy capabilities. Armed with homing torpedoes, mines, depth charges, rockets, and missiles. Designed to counter the nuclear submarine threat. Eight prototypes for R & D with option for production models. First flight was 21 January 1972. The fifth R & D model was reconfigured for feasibility tests as aerial tanker. A COD version is under consideration. The five R & D aircraft will be reconditioned following tests for use as RAG transition trainers. Will not have full avionics suit. The eighth S-3 produced was accidentally lost. VIKING was introduced to the Fleet with VS-41 (North Island) on 20 February 1974.

TRACKER, S-2 Series (S2F) Search and attack aircraft armed with bombs, torpedoes, and rockets; has searchlight. Of 755 S-2A produced, 207 were converted in 1957 to TS-2A; ASW systems removed. **US-2A:** 51 converted for limited target towing/utility; JULIE equipment removed. The one aircraft converted in 1962 to RS-2C has been deleted. 66 S-2Bs were pro-

cured, but were modified 1966 to US-2B along with 66 S-2A; JULIE equipment removed and 5 passenger seats added. Of 60 S-2C procured, 48 were modified in 1966 to US-2C for target towing operations. 43 S-2s are on loan to California Division of Forestry for aerial fire fighting. S-2D and onward have increase of wingspan and nose lengthened by 18". Improved version of S-2A/B. ES-2D/US-2D are operational models. The number modified is not known at this time, but the characteristics are very similar to S-2D. **S-2E:** Improved S-2D with ASW Tactical Navigation System (AN/ASN-30). Has improved ECM. Fin is 18" longer, nacelles revised, has wider tail, and round wing tips. **S-2F:** Was S2F-1S1; improved JL/JZ installation. None in USN inventory. **S-2G:** Interim aircraft for the S-3 VIKING. Primary mission is development of tactics and equipment for the VIKING. Has AN/AQA-7 DIFAR processing equipment used in P-3 ORION, and BULLPUP missile control. Essentially an improved S-2E. Will operate from fleet carriers for about two years after introduction of the VIKINGs. Will then give reserve units the latest sonobuoy sensors.

Model	Year Ordered/ Delivered	Number Proc.	Crew-Type	Lbs. Gross Weight	Dimensions LOA	Span	Height	Engine Number	Model	Thrust in Lbs. or HP (each)	Performance Max. Speed/Range (Kts.)/(nm)
A-7A	64/66	199	1-C	38,000	46'2"	38'9"	16'0"	1	TF30-P-6	11,350	595/4100
A-7B	67/68	196	1-C	38,000	46'2"	38'9"	16'0"	1	TF30-P-8	12,200	598/3800+
A-7C	68/69	67	1-C	42,000	46'2"	38'9"	16'0"	1	TF30-P-8	12,200	598/3800+
A-7E	68/69	398	1-C	42,000	46'2"	38'9"	16'0"	1	TF41-A-2	15,000	562/2800
YA-7H		1	2-C	42,657	48'2"	38'9"	16'5"	1	TF41-A-2	15,000	537/1970
A-6A	58/60	488	2-C	60,626	54'7"	53'0"	15'7"	2	J52-P-8A	9,300	600/3225
A-6B	66/67	19	2-C	60,626	54'7"	53'0"	15'7"	2	J52-P-8A	9,300	600/3225
A-6C	68/70	12	2-C	60,626	54'7"	53'0"	15'7"	2	J52-P-8A	9,300	600/3225
EA-6A	62/65	27	2-C	56,500	55'3"	53'0"	16'4"	2	J52-P-8A	9,300	620/2995
EA-6B	66/71	54	4-C	65,000	59'5"	53'0"	16'4"	2	J52-P-408	11,200	620/2995
KA-6D	69/71	62	2-C	60,626	54'7"	53'0"	15'7"	2	J52-P-8A	9,300	600/3225
A-6E	71/71	89+	2-C	60,626	54'7"	53'0"	15'7"	2	J52-P-8A	9,300	600/3225
RA-5C	60/63	140	2-C	66,800	75'10"	53'0"	19'5"	2	J79-GE-8/10	17,859	M2/2650
A-4C	57/59	638	1-C	22,500	40'4"	27'6"	15'0"	1	J65-W-16A/20	7,700	577/1740
A-4E	60/62	500	1-C	24,500	40'4"	27'6"	15'0"	1	J52-P-6/8A	8,500	588/1700+
A-4F	65/66	146	1-C	24,500	40'4"	27'6"	15'0"	1	J52-P-8A	9,300	588/1700+
TA-4F	65/66	139	2-C	24,500	42'7"	27'6"	15'2"	1	J52-P-6/8A	9,300	588/1700+
TA-4J	67/68	185	2-C	24,500	42'7"	27'6"	15'2"	1	J52-P-6/8A	9,300	588/1700+
A-4L	Mod.	100	1-L	22,500	40'1"	27'6"	15'0"	1	J65-W-20	8,400	560/1500
A-4M	/70	60+	1-L	25,500	40'4"	27'6"	15'0"	1	J52-P-408A	11,200	597/1600
A-3A	51/54	45	3-C	78,000	74'8"	72'6"	23'10"	2	J57-P-6B	8,500	540/2500
A-3B	55/56	164	3-C	78,000	74'8"	72'6"	23'10"	2	J57-P10	10,500	558/2200
EA-3B	55/59	25	7-C	78,000	74'8"	72'6"	23'10"	2	J57-P10	10,500	558/2200
KA-3B	/66	50	3-C	78,000	74'8"	72'6"	23'10"	2	J57-P10	10,500	558/2200
EKA-3B	/67	39	3-C	78,000	74'8"	72'6"	23'10"	2	J57-P10	10,500	558/2200
RA-3B	55/59	30	3-C	78,000	74'8"	72'6"	23'10"	2	J57-P10	10,500	558/2200
TA-3B	/59	12	8-C	78,000	74'8"	72'6"	23'10"	2	J57-P10	10,500	558/2200

CORSAIR II, A-7 Series A-7A: All-weather, carrier-based, light attack aircraft. Primarily used for tactical strike, close support, and interdiction type missions. Designed based on F-8 CRUSADER. Can deliver a maximum ordnance payload of 19,940 pounds. First flight on 27 September 1965. Has six wing pods plus one pylon each side of fuselage for SIDE-WINDERs. A-7A/B armed with two 20mm cannons; A-7C, E with M61 Gatling gun. Protection includes cockpit armor, two backup power systems. A/B models are being phased out of the Fleet to reserve squadrons. The first 67 A-7E built had B engine. To eliminate confusion with the follow-on A-7E, the 67 planes were redesignated A-7C in 1971. NA-7A and NA-7C are operational models. **TA-7C:** 40 A-7B and 41 A-7C will be modified to TA-7C, beginning early 1975 and completed mid-1979. The two-seat configuration will be fitted with M61 20mm gun, external underwing stores pylons, and weapons delivery system; also will have tactical capability. **A-7D:** 387 units produced for USAF. **A-7E:** features HUD (Head Up Display), projected map display, digital computer, Doppler radar, computer-directed avionics system, and strike assessment camara. A-7E production model #68 and up have improved engine. **YA-7H:** Prototype two-seat CORSAIR II. The first production A-7E with TF41 engine (BuNo. 156801) was modified to study potential as ordnance trainer or new operational configuration for

tactical use. (Equipped with parabrake for use in short-field operations for combat crew or instrument training or combat.) To make room for the two-seat arrangement, the nose section was re-faired to just forward of the wing and "stretched" 16". An 18" insert was added just aft of the wing, and the aft section of the plane was tilted upward about 1.2° to retain the aircraft's no-damage ground line. Second cockpit has primary and secondary controls for take-off, navigation, and landing on carriers. First flight was 29 August 1972.

INTRUDER/PROWLER, A-6 Series (A2F) Primarily an all-weather, twin-engine attack bomber for low level penetration and close support missions. INTRUDERs also provide the best "eyes" in the worst weather for other attack planes. The overall function which makes INTRUDER "all weather" is DIANE. The A-6 has two prime ordnance stores under each wing and a centerline weapon station for a payload of 18,000 pounds. **A-6B:** Same as A-6A except configured for the STANDARD ARM missile system. **A-6C:** TRIM version of the A-6A by the addition of a beacon receiver system, multisensor displays, and a removable centerline pod containing DIANE in a gimballed turret. The pod differs in this model from A-6A/B. Some are reconfigured A-6As; some are production models. **A-6E:** Main feature is TRAM (Target Recognition Attack Multisensor). Configuration adds a turreted electro-optical sensor package, containing infrared and lasar equipment for lasar-guided weapons delivery. Has new radar systems with "track while scan" and the first HUD for a production A-6. The CONDOR missile system is externally mounted. As of 5/74, 43 A-6Es have been produced and 46 converted from early A-6 models. **EA-6A:** USMC; configured for tactical ECM. Thirty different antennas provide electronic intelligence capability instantly in combat areas. Retains attack capability. **EA-6B:** Similar to A-6A except has increased length, higher data rate, more versatile electronic surveillance system, and more powerful jammers. Originally named INTRUDER, but because of different mission, was renamed PROWLER in 1972. Has a four-man crew and increased wing strength because of its higher combat weight. To replace EKA-3Bs. **KA-6D:** Tanker version of the basic A-6 airframe. All conversions. DIANE system removed; internal aerial refueling system was installed. Retains visual attack capability. Hose and reel replaces avionics "birdcage" aft and bottom of fuselage.

VIGILANTE, RA-5C (A3J-3) Carrier-based, all-weather tactical reconnaissance aircraft. Two-man crew, tandem seating, internal linear bomb bay for carriage of fuel tanks and/or reconnaissance equipment. The last production of RA-5Cs are fitted with J79-GE-10 engines. They were initially designed as carrier-based A/W attack aircraft, utilizing special and conventional ordnance. Internal ordnance ejected rearward out the tail from the linear bomb bay. Hopefully, the following will clarify the VIGILANTE program. For the aviation historian, Bureau Numbers are included: Originally, 77 A-5A were ordered, but only 59 were built (145157/8, 146694/702, 147850/863, 148924/933, 149276/299). The remaining 18 aircraft were re-ordered as A-5B (149300/317); only 6 were built (149300/305). These were delivered to Sanford NAS between 5/63 and 4/64. Parts of the remaining 12 aircraft were stored unassembled at the Columbus plant. The 6 A-5B were not considered operational or fleet aircraft, as they were sent to Sanford specifically to train crews for transition to the RA-5C aircraft. On 8 August 1963, the 6 A-5Bs were redesignated A-5C (Limited) and eventually returned to Columbus for conversion to RA-5C; they were delivered May/August 1965. BuNos. 149306/317 were built to RA-5C design. RA-5C: 43 A-5A converted (BuNos. 145157, 146695/6, 146698, 146701/2, 147850, 147852/54, 147856/61, 148925/6, 148928/9, 148932/3). 18 A-5B became RA-5C (149300/317). 79 newly built RA-5C as follows: (BuNos. 150823/842, 151615/634, 151726/728, 156608/643).

Although the primary mission is tactical reconnaissance, external ordnance carriage attack capability is retained. Image-forming reconnaissance equipment is in a ventral pod, at bottom of fuselage; includes frame/panoramic cameras, side-looking radar, and infrared mapping set. Electronic emitter signal collection equipment, AN/ALQ-61, in internal linear bomb bay.

The complete reconnaissance system consists of RA-5C and an integrated operational intelligence center (IOIC) installed aboard an aircraft carrier (mobility) or a shore base.

SKYHAWK, A-4 Series (A4D) The U.S. Navy's smallest attack plane; a high-performance, non-folding delta wing, carrier-based craft with low-level and long-range capability. Engine has no afterburner. Tricycle landing gear retracts forward; unusually long stroke permits a wide variety of stores. Has 3000-lb. centerline weapon rack and two 1000-lb. wing pods. Outer racks can carry SIDEWINDER, BULLPUP, large rockets, and rocket packages. Armed with two 20mm guns (fuselage wing joint). **A-4C:** An improved A-4B, having a longer nose, uprated engine, and limited weather capability. **A-4E:** Equipped with improved engine for 27% increased range. Two wing pods added (increased 4500-lb. payload), seat ejection (zero altitude/90-knot speed). **A-4F:** Improved controls/armament flexibility. Avionics compartment added to top of fuselage, aft of cockpit, alters appearence. Seat ejection (zero altitude/speed). **TA-4F:** Formerly designated TA-4E. Has fuselage extended 28" for second seat/dual set of controls. **EA-4F:** Four TA-4F modified to perform specific ECM application. Addition of target missile-launching capability. **TA-4J:** Light version of TA-4F. Air-to-air ground launcher system removed, except for basic wiring provisions. **A-4L:** A-4C aircraft configured with uprated engine, wing lift spoilers, WALLEYE and SHRIKE capability; upper avionics compartment has changed with improved avionics. For Naval Reserve—**A-4M:** Similar to A-4F except fitted with an engine with 20% more thrust, enlarged canopy, increased ammunition capacity, improved weapons delivery system, and employs drag chute for short-field landings. For USMC—**Special versions of A-4:** NA-4C/F are operational; NTF-4F is nonoperational. A-4G/TA-4G built for Australia; A-4H (90) and TA-4H (10) for Israel; A-4K/TA-4K built for New Zealand; A-4N (50/100) for Israel; A-4P/Q (48) are A-4Bs rebuilt for Argentina; A-4S are 40 refurbished A-4Bs for Singapore; A-4T for possible purchase by French Navy. In addition, about 20 A-4s in reserve are set aside for possible sale to Chile as well as 30 models for Thailand.

SKYWARRIOR, A-3 Series (A3D) Largest carrier-based attack bomber. Radar bombing system for A/W missions. Weapons bay for bombs, torpedoes, mines, and nuclear bombs. Tail-mounted barbette with two 20mm guns removed from later models. Limited number of A-3A/B remain; no EA-3A/RA-3A/VA-3A. **A-3A:** swept wing, high performance attack aircraft with tricycle landing gear. **A-3B:** Improved A-3A; adaptable to mining missions. **EA-3B:** Equipped for countermeasures. **EKA-3B:** Configured for the TACOS (Tanker Aircraft/Countermeasures, or Strike) mission. **KA-3B:** A-3B modified to a tanker capability. **RA-3B:** Equipped for photography. **TA-3B:** Equipped for bombardier/navigation training. **VA-3B:** Modified for staff use; nonoperational. ERA-3B model is operational; equipped for ECM missions.

CARGO TRANSPORT

Model	Year Ordered/ Delivered	Number Proc.	Crew Type	Lbs. Gross Weight	LOA	Dimensions Span	Height	Engine Number	Engine Model	Thrust in Lbs. or HP (each)	Performance Max. Speed/Range (Kts.)/(nm)
C-9B	72/73	8	3-L	108,000	119'4"	93'4"	27'6"	2	JT8-D-9	14,500	495/2000
TC-4C	66/68	9	2-L	36,000	67'11"	78'4"	22'9"	2	MK529-8X	2,210 HP	350/2621

continued

Model	Year Ordered/ Delivered	Number Proc.	Crew-Type	Lbs. Gross Weight	LOA	Dimensions Span	Height	Number	Engine Model	Thrust in Lbs. or HP (each)	Performance Max. Speed/Range (Kts.)/(nm)
C-2A	62/64	19	3-C	54,830	56'8"	80'7"	15'11"	2	T56-A-8A	4,050 HP	352/1650
C-1A	53/55	87	2-C	27,000	42'0"	69'8"	16'3½"	2	R1820-82	1,525 HP	290/1200
EC-1A	55/57	4	5-C	26,000	42'0"	69'8"	16'3½"	2	R1820-82	1,525 HP	275/2000
C-131F	54/55	36	3-L	53,200	79'2"	105'4"	28'0"	2	R2800-52W	2,500 HP	275/2000
C-131G	56/58	2	3-L	53,200	79'2"	105'4"	28'0"	2	R2800-52W	2,500 HP	275/2000
DC-130A	/70	2	12-L	124,200	97'9"	132'7"	38'3"	4	T56-A-9	3,750 HP	310/2900
C-130F	60/62	7	4-L	135,000	97'9"	132'7"	38'3"	4	T56-A-16	4,910 HP	335/3950
KC-130F	58/62	5	7-L	135,000	97'9"	132'7"	38'3"	4	T56-A-16	4,910 HP	335/3700
EC-130G	63/64	4	4-L	155,000	97'9"	132'7"	38'3"	4	T56-A-16	4,910 HP	335/3950
EC-130Q	67/74	10	4-L	155,000	97'9"	132'7"	38'3"	4	T56-A-16	4,910 HP	335/5100
KC-130R	74/75	4	7-L	155,000	97'9"	132'7"	38'3"	4	T56-A-16	4,910 HP	335/4600
LC-130R	68/74	4	4-L	155,000	97'9"	132'7"	38'3"	4	T56-A-16	4,910 HP	330/4600
C-121J	50/52	50	8-L	140,000	116'2"	123'5"	24'10"	4	R3350-34	3,250 HP	285/3500
EC-121K	51/53	142	26-L	120,000	116'2"	123'5"	24'10"	4	R3350-34/-42	3,250 HP	285/3850
C-119F	52/53	58	5-L	72,800	86'6"	109'3"	26'6"	2	R3350-36W	3,500 HP	255/2350
C-118B	50/52	61	6-L	112,000	107'0"	117'6"	28'8"	4	R2800-52W	2,500 HP	270/1870
VC-118B	50/53	4	5-L	112,000	107'0"	117'6"	28'8"	4	R2800-52W	2,500 HP	270/1870
C-117D	50/51	101	3-L	31,000	67'9"	90'0"	18'3"	2	R1820-80A	1,475 HP	250/2500

SKYTRAIN II, C-9B Navy version of commercial DC-9. To replace C-118, C-121, C-131. Carries 90 passengers or cargo. Has large cargo door on port side of fuselage. Program objective is 34 planes: 27 for USN and 7 for USMC. First aircraft delivered 8 May 1973. First 8 aircraft serve with VR-1 and VR-30.

ACADEME, TC-4C Basic configuration of Grumman GULFSTREAM I with an A-6 nose radome added to house the INTRUDER/PROWLER search and track installation. Engine manufactured by Rolls-Royce (Dart). Aircraft outfitted with a complete A-6 weapons system, lacking only the release capabilities. TC-4C contains an A-6 cockpit and four additional repeater scopes. Configuration permits a simultaneous instruction of up to six B/N plus one instructor. Conversion of GULFSTREAM I to navigation trainer (TC-4B) cancelled in 1963. VC-4A is USCG staff version.

GREYHOUND, C-2A All-weather, carrier-based, land plane to provide logistic support for Fleet and Marine operations (COD). Design based on E-2A. Can carry 39 troops, 28 passengers, 20 litters, or a cargo. Has four vertical tail surfaces, three of which have rudders.

TRADER, C-1A (TF-1) All-weather instrument flight trainer and light COD. Has tricycle landing gear. Similar to S-2A; wide tail as S-2C. Can carry nine passengers. **EC-1A:** C-1A modified for special purpose ECM (active/passive).

SAMARITAN, C-131 Series (R4Y) Cargo/personnel transport version of Convair 340 (C-131F) and Convair 440 (C-131G). Can carry 44 passengers, cargo, or 21 litters plus 3 attendants.

HERCULES, C-130 Series (GV) A high-wing, medium-range, land-based monoplane, basically for transportation of personnel, cargo, or troops. **DC-130A:** Conversions from USAF C-130A. Launch and control platforms for target drones. Can carry and operate four drones for training purposes. **KC-130F:** Similar to C-130B, but with aerial refueler kit (pods and cargo compartment) added. **C-130F:** Similar to C-130B. Tactical cargo/personnel/evacuation transport. **EC-130G:** Similar to C-130E. Has permanently installed TACOMO III system and up-rated electronics. **EC-130Q:** Similar to EC-130G. Has permanently installed VLF radio transmitter systems used to supplement shore-based communications facilities. **KC-130R:** Similar to USAF C-130H; has aerial refueler kit added. Six additional KC-130R approved for FY-1975. **LC-130R:** Similar to USAF C-130F aircraft except has improved engine, Navy special equipments, cold weather modifications, and skis. JEC-130G is a nonoperational version of C-130 series.

C-121 Series (R7V/WV) SUPER CONSTELLATION, C-121J: Cargo, personnel evacuation, transport. Can carry 92 passengers, or 62 litters, or equivalent cargo. **WARNING STAR, EC-121K:** "Super Snooper" is equivalent to Russian BADGER/BEAR eavesdroppers. EC-121K has plastic radar domes top and bottom of fuselage. **EC-121M:** Data not in above tables, but similar to EC-121K. Modified to countermeasures aircraft with an electronic configuration and a mission capability differing in many details from EC-121K.

FLYING BOXCAR, C-119F (R4Q-2) Twin boom, high wing, land monoplane. Tricycle landing gear with a steerable nose gear. Can carry 42 troops or 35 litters. Fairchild model M-110.

LIFTMASTER, C-118B Series (R6D) **C-118B:** Commercial model DC-6A. Cargo transport for 79 troops, or 76 passengers, or 60 litters and 6 attendants, or equivalent cargo. **VC-118B:** Commercial version of DC-6B; a C-118B modified for administrative operations; 30 passengers.

SKYTRAIN, C-117D Series (R4D-8) **C-117D:** Commercial model SUPER DC-3. Can carry 35 troops, or 30 passengers, or 27 litters or equivalent cargo. **VC-117D:** C-117D equipped for administrative operations; 16 passengers.

SKYMASTER, C-54Q (R5D-3) The last C-54 of any version, BuNo. 56501, was retired 1974 at Patuxent.

SKYTRAIN, C-47 Series (R4D) Of over 10,000 models produced for the military, only a few C-47H/SC-47H remain as nonoperational models.

NAVIGATOR, C-45 Series (SNB) The last aircraft were retired at Pensacola July 1972. A C45-H version remains as a nonoperational model.

FIGHTER

Model	Year Ordered/ Delivered	Number Proc.	Crew-Type	Lbs. Gross Weight	Dimensions LOA	Span	Height	Engine Number	Model	Thrust in Lbs. or HP (each)	Performance Max. Speed/Range (Kts.)/(nm)
F-14A	69/70	189+	2-C	55,000	61'10"	62'10"	16'0"	2	TF30-P-412	20,000	M2+/2000+
QF-9J	conv.	30	1-L	21,000	40'10"	34'6"	12'4"	1	J48-P-8/A	7,250	562/810
TF-9J	56/60	257	2-C	21,000	42'2"	34'6"	12'4"	1	J48-P-8/A	7,250	400/810
RF-8G	cv/65	73	1-C	29,000	54'6"	35'8"	15'9"	1	J57-P-20/A	16,900	870/1000+
F-8H	cv/68	89	1-C	30,000	54'3"	35'8"	15'9"	1	J57-P-420	18,500	886/1000+
F-8J	cv/68	136	1-C	31,000	54'6"	35'8"	15'9"	1	J57-P-420	18,500	943/1000+
F-8K	cv/69	87	1-C	29,000	54'3"	35'8"	15'9"	1	J57-P-16A	16,900	960/1000+
F-8L	cv/69	63	1-C	27,500	54'3"	35'8"	15'9"	1	J57-P-4A	16,000	880/1500
F-4B	59/61	649	2-C	54,600	58'3"	38'5"	16'3"	2	J79-GE-8A/B	17,000	M2+/1800+
RF-4B	63/65	46	2-C	54,500	62'11"	38'5"	16'3"	2	J79-GE-8A/B	17,000	M2+/1520
F-4J	64/66	522	2-C	56,000	58'3"	38'5"	16'3"	2	J79-GE-10	17,900	M2,2+/1800+

F-111B (unnamed) This ill-fated Navy fighter was cancelled 1968. F-111B was an A/W, twin jet-engine, fighter weapon system with variable sweep wing. Armed with six PHOENIX missiles and AWG-9 system. Main fault was excessive weight. Of approximately 30 units ordered, 7 were produced, and of these, 3 were lost. The last two aircraft were stricken 1971: BuNo. 152715 on 15 June and BuNo. 151972 on 14 December.

SABRE, F-86 F-86H is nonoperational; QF-86H is an operational drone aircraft. No details available.

TOMCAT, F-14 Series Eventually to replace F-4. Twin-tail, long-range, A/W fighter plane. Podded engines, improved A-6 INTRUDER-type landing gear, nose-tow catapult system. Armed with PHOENIX missiles (6) and AWG-9 fire control system, M-61 Vulcan 20mm on left side of fuselage just aft of the radome. Four SPARROWs carried semisubmerged in bottom of fuselage. F-14 can carry six SPARROWs and four SIDEWINDERs, or six PHOENIX. Variable geometrical wing note: extended—high lift/high load; partially swept—long range/efficient; delta wing—supersonic dash. Original plan called for a total of 722 USN/USMC purchases. Escalating costs, largely because of reduction in planned buy, revises plan to 500/600 units, including at least 80 for Iran. Purchases in Lots 1/4 are 134 F-14, including 12 for R&D. First flight was 21 December 1971. Nine days later, the plane crashed due to complete failure of flight control hydraulic systems. Aircraft #10 crashed in Chesapeake Bay 30 June 1972. In

June 1973, an F-14 was shot down by a SPARROW missile it had just launched. The missile failed to clear the plane and struck the fuselage, setting it on fire. However, trials and tests have been most encouraging. TOMCATs are now operational with VF-1/2 on CVAN-65. **F-14B:** Was to be of light weight with improved engine. First F-14B is aircraft #7; first flight was 12 September 1973. Engine is F401-PW-400(28,000#). No procurement is planned.

TIGER, F-11 Series (F11F-1) High-performance, sweptback wings, "coke bottle"-shaped fighter. As of January 1975, the last two F-11A remaining in flight status in test programs were sent to Litchfield Park for storage. **TF-11A:** Remains on the list in nonoperational status.

COUGAR, F-9J Series (F9F-8) **QF-9J:** Drone configuration of F-9J; modified for operational employment on RDT&E missions. Only two remain, these at Point Mugu, California. **TF-9J/NTF-9J:** An F-9J with extended front fuselage for two-crew in tandem. A few models remain, but not likely for long.

CRUSADER, F-8 Series (F8U) 1261 built, including two XF-8A (one converted to 2-seat TF-8A, Bu No. 143710). 448 CRUSADERS were rebuilt. Two-position wing angles 7° on take-off. Retractable refueling probe on left side of fuselage. Reworked F-8s included new wing for attack, long-range capability, strengthened fuselage, landing and arresting gear, and improved avionics. Original armament included four 20mm guns, two SIDEWINDERs on fuselage pylons, and retractable rocket pack in fuselage (later removed). **RF-8G:** Reconnaissance version of F-8. Modernized RF-8A to extend service life and reconnaissance capabilities. Added ventral fins, wing hard points, Doppler radar, IF scanner, external stores capability. Has 6 cameras. **F-8H:** Modernized F-8Ds; has external wing stores, increased armament capability with incorporation of SEAM (SIDEWINDER Extended Acquisition Mode). **F-8J:** Modernized F-8Es; pulse Doppler mode added to radar, BLC, improved landing characteristics. Carries extra fuel tanks, enlarged tail surfaces. About 100 models retrofitting with TF30-P-420 engines (19,600 lbs.). **F-8K:** Modernized F-8Cs; has fuselage, wing, landing gear structural changes, and miscellaneous modifications. **F-8L:** Modernized F-8Bs; similar to F-8K. Version is on the list as nonoperational. **DF-8L:** F-8Ls configured for remote control of drones and drone aircraft. Details of characteristics not available at this time. **F-8M:** Conversion of six F-8A cancelled.

PHANTOM, F-4 Series (F4H-1) All-weather weapons system fighter-attack and interceptor. Detects incoming enemy aircraft at extreme ranges with largest fighter craft radar antenna (APQ-72 auto fire control in the nose). Armament: six SPARROW III or four SPARROW III and four SIDEWINDERs. For attack: 8 ton payload in 5 weapon mounts with SPARROWs for protection. The 45° swept-back wing and horizontal stabilizer, which slopes downward 23°, provides unmistakable recognition. **F-4B:** Improved F-4A. **QF-4B:** 44 converted from F-4B. Supersonic drone configuration. Weapons system replaced by radio and telemetry equipment. Can be remotely controlled. No details for data tables. **RF-4B:** Photo reconnaissance version of F-4B; has 2/3 camera stations; no armament. Configurations differ for high/low altitudes and day/night missions. **F-4G** (historical note): 12 modified on assembly line to special configuration. Had AN/ASW-21 two-way data link system. First unit delivered May 1963. BuNos. 150481, 150484, 150485, 150487, 150489, 150492, 150625, 150633, 150636, 150639, 150642, 150645. Those surviving redesignated F-4B. **F-4J:** Higher performance, improved combat capabilities than earlier F-4s. AWG-10 pulse Doppler radar fire control system, AJB bombing system, improved engine, and improved control surfaces. **F-4N:** 178 F-4Bs updated and modified; interim fighter for F-14. Life of aircraft extended for 6 years. First delivered early 1973. Insufficient data for characteristics tables as of this writing. Other versions: F-4C, D, E and RF-4C for USAF. F-4K, M for England.

HELICOPTERS

Model	Year Ordered/ Delivered	Number Proc.	Crew-Type	Lbs. Gross Weight	LOA	Dimensions Span	Height	Number	Engine Model	Thrust in Lbs. or HP (each)	Performance Max. Speed/Range (Kts.)/(nm)
TH-57A	68/68	40	2-L	2,900	28'8"	1–33'4"	9'6½"	1	250-C18	317 HP	119/345
CH-53A	62/66	141	3-L	35,000	67'2"	1–72'3"	24'11"	2	T64-GE-6A/B	2,850 HP	170/245
CH-53D	68/69	124	3-L	36,573	67'2"	1–72'3"	24'11"	2	T64-GE-413	3,925 HP	164/242
RH-53D	72/72	30	6-L	41,304	67'6"	1–72'3"	24'11"	2	T64-GE-415	4,330 HP	165/596
CH-53E	/74	2	3-L	56,000	71'2"	1–79'	27'9"	3	T56-GE-413A	3,975 HP	180/1200
XH-51A	62/63	2	2-L	4,700	41'0"	1–35'	8'1"	1	T74-P	500	178/300
CH-46A	61/62	159	3-L	19,000	45'8"	2–50'	16'11"	2	T58-GE-8B/F	1,250 HP	140/200
CH-46D	66/66	267	3-L	23,000	45'8"	2–51'	16'11½"	2	T58-GE-10	1,400 HP	147/200
UH-46D	65/66	10	3-L	23,000	45'8"	2–51'	16'11½"	2	T58-GE-10	1,400 HP	147/200
CH-46E	/75	292+	3-L	23,500	45'8"	2–51'	16'11½"	2	T58-GE-16	1,870 HP	147/200
CH-46F	67/68	174	3-L	23,000	36'11"	2–51'	16'11½"	2	T58-GE-10	1,400 HP	147/200
UH-34D	56/57	626	2-L	13,300	44'2"	1–56'	15'10"	1	R1820-84A/C	1,525 HP	150/435
HH-3A	cv/68	12	4-L	20,050	54'9"	1–62'	16'10"	2	T58-GE-8B/F	1,250 HP	144/540
SH-3A	57/59	255	4-L	20,050	54'9"	1–62'	16'10"	2	T58-GE-8B/F	1,250 HP	144/540
VH-3A	61/62	8	4-L	20,050	54'9"	1–62'	16'10"	2	T58-GE-8C	1,250 HP	144/595
SH-3D	63/66	90	4-L	20,500	54'9"	1–62'	16'10"	2	T58-GE-10	1,400 HP	144/540
SH-3H	71/72	21	4-L	21,000	54'9"	1–62'	16–10"	2	T58-GE-10	1,400 HP	134/415
UH-2C	67/68	57	2-L	11,614	40'6"	1–44'	14'8"	2	T58-GE-8B	1,250 HP	140/425
HH-2D	69/70	67	3-L	12,500	40'6"	1–44'	14'8"	2	T58-GE-8B	1,250 HP	140/425
SH-2D	70/71	20	3-L	12,500	40'6"	1–44'	13'5"	2	T58-GE-8B	1,250 HP	143/422
SH-2F	cv/73	30+	3-L	12,800	40'6"	1–44'	13'7"	2	T58-GE-8F	1,350 HP	143/422
UH-1D	Army loan	45	2-L	9,500	42'7"	1–48'	12'8½"	1	T53-L-11/13B	1100/1400 HP	120/299
UH-1E	62/64	209	2-L	9,500	42'7"	1–44'	12'8½"	1	T53-L-11/13B	1100/1400 HP	129/314
AH-1G	66/67	38	2-L	9,500	44'5"	1–44'	13'5"	1	T53-L-13A/B	1,400 HP	153/370

Model	Year Ordered/ Delivered	Number Proc.	Crew- Type	Lbs. Gross Weight	Dimensions LOA	Dimensions Span	Height	Engine Number	Engine Model	Thrust in Lbs. or HP (each)	Performance Max. Speed/Range (Kts.)/(nm)
AH-1J	68/69	49	2-L	10,000	53'4"	1–44'	13'5"	2	T400-CP-400	900 HP	148/342
HH-1K	68/70	27	3-L	9,500	42'7"	1–44'	12'8½"	1	T53-L-13A/B	1,400 HP	129/314
TH-1L	68/69	45	2-L	9,500	42'7"	1–44'	12'8½"	1	T53-L-13A/B	1,400 HP	129/314
UH-1L	68/69	8	2-L	9,500	42'7"	1–44'	12'8½"	1	T53-L-13A/B	1,400 HP	129/314
UH-1N	70/71	77	2-L	10,000	45'11"	1–48'	13'5"	2	T400-CP-400	900 HP	126/277

SEARANGER, TH-57A Trainer helicopter with skid-type landing gear. Has single two-bladed main rotor, turboshaft engine, dual flight controls, and seats for five personnel, including the crew. Engine manufactured by Allison. UH-57A is a nonoperational version.

SEA STALLION, CH-53 Series CH-53A is USMC assault cargo helicopter for equipment or troops (38 troops and 20 litters). Has six-bladed main rotor. **CH-53D:** Similar to CH-53A except for engines. **RH-53D:** Airborne Mine Countermeasures (AMCM) helicopter. Optimized to tow existing and future gear used to sweep mines. (1) MK103, gear used for moored-mine sweeping. Cutters are attached to sweep cables that are towed by the helo at a length of cable to buoyant floats. (2) MK104, sweep gear that is normally pulled behind the MK105 and sets off acoustic mines. Both MK103 and MK104 are carried on board the helo. (3) MK105 is a sled on hydrofoils and is fitted with a turbogenerated and magnetic cable. This device is transferred by ship to the helicopter. An air-to-air refueling probe is located on the right side of the RH-53D fuselage. Two 550-gallon fuel tanks are carried externally, and mission-type modifications have been made. **CH-53E:** Basic H-53 airframe with addition of 3rd engine. Has a seven-bladed main rotor. Tail rotor is canted to offset the center of gravity shift caused by the installation of a third engine. Landing gear has been strengthened, sponsons have been lengthened, and mission-type modifications have been made. Load lift limit is 16 tons. **CH-53G:** Modified for sale to West Germany; similar to CH-53D.

XH-51A (unnamed) Single lifting rotor research helicopter to test and evaluate the rigid-rotor concept. Incorporates a gyroscopic system for inherent stability. Follow-on versions were compounded with wings and added T-60 engine.

SEA KNIGHT, H-46 Series (HRB) A/W troop or cargo carrier with emergency water-landing capabilities. Has three-bladed rotors. Can carry 25 troops, or 15 litters and 2 attendants, or cargo. **CH-46A:** USMC version. **UH-46A:** 14 procured. Modified for Navy VERTREP mission. Presently nonoperational. **CH-46D:** Similar to CH-46A, but with uprated engines. 61 CH-46As will be retrofitted to HH-46A for search and rescue role. **UH-46D:** Uprated engines, otherwise similar to UH-46A. **CH-46E:** Navy plans to modify 292 CH-46D/F in an update program to the E configuration. Would receive T58-GE-16 (1870 SHP) engines, new navigation system to permit SAR, plus other improvements. **CH-46F:** Similar to CH-46D except for modifications to the electrical system and instrumentation. Boeing Vertol is modifying one D and one F to E configuration. They will receive the uprated engines, a crash-resistant fuel system, crash-attenuating cockpit seats, improved rescue system, and a new navigation system.

SEAHORSE, UH-34D (HUS-1) Utility version of the basic CH-34A; 12 passengers. H-34s are phased out of active USN/USMC squadrons.

SEA KING, H-3 Series (HHS-2) Twin-turbine, amphibious A/W ASW helicopter. Five-blade main and tail rotors. **HH-3A:** SH-3A conversion with sonar equipment removed. Has armor, deck-edge refueling capability, external fuel tanks, two 7.62mm minigun turret, and other modifications. **SH-3A:** Search and attack ASW configuration. **VH-3A:** Executive transport version of SH-3A. **SH-3D:** Similar to SH-3A except for improved power plant, internally mounted fuel tanks, and general improvements. Ten SH-3D for Iran as ASH-3D. **VH-3D:** Presidential helicopters. No details available. HH-3F is USCG version (SAR). **SH-3G:** Reconfiguration of SH-3A to perform ASW/logistics support missions. **SH-3H:** Initial contract called for modification of 11 existing SH-3A, G. Provisions for Anti-Ship Missile Defense (ASMD), and additional ASW equipment. New light-weight sonar and increased sensor capability.

SEASPRITE, H-2 Series (HU2K-1) UH-2A (88 built) and UH-2B (102 built) were single-engine models that were converted to two-engine configuration, some to HH-2C/Ds and most to UH-2C. **HH-2C:** Armed and armored version of UH-2C for SAR. Chin-mounted minigun turret, waist-mounted machine gun, four-blade tail rotor, dual wheels on the main landing gear. Six were converted for operations off Vietnam aboard frigates. All later converted to SH-2s. **UH-2C:** Inflatable sponsons in wheel-well fairings form the flotation hull. **HH-2D:** Similar to HH-2C, but armor and armament deleted. Two modified as LAMPS prototypes. Two others modified for ASW tests aboard frigates. **SH-2D:** For ASW; carries a mix of 15 sonobuoys (ASQ-41 passive or ASQ-47 active), which are launched from a rack on the left side of the fuselage. The ASQ-81 MAD is deployed on a cable from a pylon-mounted winch on the right side of the fuselage. Also has MK25 marine markers. Can carry one or two MK44 or MK46 ASW homing torpedoes. The MK I LAMPS carries a radome under the nose, which houses the search radar antenna. Uses LN-66 search radar to search for surface targets. Converted from UH-2A/B/,D and HH-2C/D. **YSH-2E:** Two HH-2D modified for LAMPS (MK II) role and testing aboard FOX (DLG-33). Delivered March 1972. Following tests, will probably be recycled into MK III program. **SH-2F:** MK III LAMPS. Incorporates a new rotor system and changes in location of tail wheel for easier landings aboard destroyers. All remaining UH-2C and HH-2D are being modified and converted to SH-2F. 80+ Fs and the rest Ds delivered 1971–72. Modification program continues to the end of 1975.

IROQUOIS/HUEYCOBRA/"SEACOBRA," H-1 Series (HU-1E) UH is IROQUOIS; AH is HUEYCOBRA, except AH-1J, which is "SEACOBRA." **UH-1B,D:** Loaned by Army. Tactical utility and assault helicopter. Has ski gear, single rotor, and turbine engine. Armament: four 7.62mm externally mounted guns, two 2.75" rocket packages, two MK79 grenade launchers. UH-1B is on the list, but nonoperational. **UH-1D:** Similar to UH-1B except has a single 48' two-bladed main rotor, provisions for two external ferry tanks; 11 passengers or 6 litters. **UH-1E:** Similar to UH-1B except for improved electronic installations and fitting of cargo/rescue hoist and rotor brake. Chin-mounted minigun turret has been removed. **AH-1G:** Army-diverted production model. An attack helicopter incorporating dynamic components of UH-1B, but modified with new rotor system, reduced cabin frontal area with tandem seating for pilot and co-pilot/gunner, intregal chin-mounted turret, and provisions for external armament on the stub wing. Armament: four 19-shot 2.75" rockets, or four 7-shot rocket launchers, two 7.62mm gun pods, and two bomb racks. **UH-1H:** No details available. **AH-1J:** "SEACOBRA" is unofficial name.

Has two engines. Similar to AH-1G except has AC electrical system, USMC avionics, rotor brake, and new armament system. Has turreted 3-barrel 20mm cannon, 7.62mm minigun pod attached to wing pylons (or 2.75" folded fin aerial rocket pods). **HH-1K:** Similar to UH-1E except for engine; SAR missions. Has improved avionics. **TH-1L:** Similar to UH-1E; has different engine; armor and armament deleted. **UH-1L:** Similar to UH-1E except for engine; armor and armament deleted; 7 passengers. **UH-1N:** Two engines. Basic UH-1H reconfigured to transport special teams, crews, equipment service between medical installations where facilities for fixed-wing aircraft are not available, and to deliver protective weapons fire when operating in a hostile environment. Can carry up to 14 passengers.

PATROL

Model	Year Ordered/ Delivered	Number Proc.	Crew-Type	Lbs. Gross Weight	LOA	Dimensions Span	Height	Engine Number	Model	Thrust in Lbs. or HP (each)	Performance Max. Speed/Range (Kts.)/(nm)
P-3A	59/62	157	10-L	127,500	116'10"	99'8"	33'8½"	4	T56-A-10W/A	4,500 HP	368/3500
P-3B	65/66	144	10-L	135,000	116'10"	99'8"	33'8½"	4	T56-A-14	4,910 HP	380/4860
P-3C	68/69	115	10-L	135,000	116'10"	99'8"	33'8½"	4	T56-A-14	4,910 HP	380/4860
RP-3D		1	17-L	141,500	116'10"	99'8"	33'8½"	4	T56-A-14	4,910 HP	380/5500
DP-2E	conv.	10	9-L	80,000	98'8"	104'0"	29'4"	2	R3350-36W/32W	3,500 HP	314/3500
SP-2H	conv.		10-L	80,000	91'8"	101'4"	29'4"	2	R3350-32W	3,500 HP	310/3685

ORION, P-3 Series (P3V) **P-3A:** Developed from Lockheed ELECTRA design. Antisubmarine patrol aircraft, replacing the P-2 NEPTUNE series. Armament: bombs, mines, nuclear depth charges, and up to 18 ASW torpedoes in 10 mounts. **WP-3A:** Converted from P-3A. Modified to perform weather reconnaissance missions. Certain ASW equipment removed; radome reconfigured. Has shorter tail boom and a large bubble under the nose wheel. Also, EP-3A and RP-3A version; no details available at this time. **P-3B:** Similar to P-3A except for improved engines and armed with BULLPUP missiles. One P-3B was converted to YP-3C. **EP-3B:** Two P-3B modified in 1969 to electronic reconnaissance configuration (see EP-3E). **P-3C:** Production version of YP-3C. Airframe houses more than 385 pieces of avionics equipment, comprising the A-NEW system. It includes ASQ-114 General Purpose Digital computer and integrated display. Low Light Level TV (LLLTV) pod installed for visual observation of low visible targets, replacing searchlights on earlier models. Has AQA-7 DIFAR sonar computer. FLIR pod installed with planned retrofit for P-3A/B. Computer update program now underway. **RP-3D:** A P-3D configured for PROJECT MAGNET mission, mapping the earth's magnetic field. ASW equipment removed; added fuel tank in the bomb bay to increase range. **WP-3D:**

One ordered 1974 for service with National Oceanographic and Atmospheric Agency. **EP-3E:** Two EP-3B and 10 P-3A reconfigured for electronic reconnaissance missions, complete with solid state signal intelligence suite. MAD "stinger" was removed. Large canoe-radar on top and bottom of aircraft plus ventral radome on the bottom. **P-3F:** For sale to Iran. P-3 airframe, lacking sophisticated ASW equipment for long range surveillance missions. Six on order.

NEPTUNE, P-2 Series (P2V) In February 1970, NEPTUNEs were retired from active USN service; some remain with the Reserves. Originally armed with sixteen 5" rockets in two weapons mounts. Two jet pods (J34-WE-34) to assist in take-offs. **DP-2E:** Modified to launch and control aerial targets. **EP-2H:** SP-2H modified with UHF telemetry equipment installed and ASW equipment removed. Utilized to perform data relay mission. **SP-2H:** On the list, but not operational. P-2Hs modified to JL/JZ configuration. **NP-2H:** The last production model of the 1167 NEPTUNEs built. Modified for use as electro-optical systems test and development vehicle.

RESEARCH

X-26A	/69	4	2-L	1,340	26'9"	57'0"	9'0"	0	None	None	
X-26B	/69	2	2-L	2,430	30'9"	57'0"	9'0"	1	0-200A	100 HP	144/375
X-25A	66/68	2	1-L	500	11'4"	5'6"	6'3"	1	431G/E	72/90 HP	75.5/300

X-26 Series **X-26A:** Schweitzer 2-32 sailpane. A two-place, dual-control, high-performance craft used at Navy test pilot school flight syllabus for test pilot training. Delivered 1969 to Patuxent to inaugurate a course in soaring. An inexpensive instructional plane. **X-26B:** Powered version of X-26A with a Continental engine. Patuxent Test Pilot School obtained two of the QT-2PC II gliders modified by Lockheed to incorporate an engine with an additional shaft to a wooden propeller. The QT model is noisy in the cockpit, but cannot be heard from the ground at cruising altitudes because of the slow-turning propeller and a muffling system for the exhaust. Being phased out.

X-25A Rotor diameter is 16'8"; powered by McCulloch engine. A powered gyrocopter used to demonstrate the escape system concept. One manned and one drone configuration each.

TRAINER

Model	Year Ordered/ Delivered	Number Proc.	Crew- Type	Lbs. Gross Weight	Dimensions LOA	Dimensions Span	Height	Engine Number	Engine Model	Thrust in Lbs. or HP (each)	Performance Max. Speed/Range (Kts.)/(nm)
T-39D	61/63	42	5-L	17,760	44'0"	44'6"	16'0"	2	J60-P3A	3,000	497/2500
CT-39E	68/	7	2-L	18,650	44'0"	44'6"	16'0"	2	JT12-A-6A/8	3,000	497/2100
T-38A	/69	6	2-L	12,000	46'4"	25'3"	12'11"	2	J85-GE-5A/J	3,850	M1.6/950
T-34B	54/55	423	2-L	2,985	25'11"	32'10"	9'7"	1	0-470-4	225 HP	162/755
YT-34C	conv.	2	2-L	4,000	28'9"	33'4"	9'11"	1	PT6A-25	715 HP	240+/1000+
T-29B	tr/62	12	3-L	43,575	74'8"	91'9"	27'3"	2	R2800-97	2,400 HP	266/2000
T-28B	52/53	489	2-L	8,038	32'11"	40'7"	12'7"	1	R1820-86A	1,425 HP	290/901
T-28C	55/56	299	2-C	8,216	34'6"	40'7"	12'7"	1	R1820-86A	1,425 HP	286/743
T-2B	64/65	97	2-C	13,307	38'3"	38'2"	14'10"	2	J60-P6A	2,905	472/966
T-2C	67/69	231	2-C	13,179	38'3"	38'2"	14'10"	2	J85-GE-4	2,950	466/930

SABRELINER, T-39 Series (T3J-1) **T-39D:** Swept back, low wing, jet-powered trainer. Engines are mounted on pylons on each side of the fuselage, just aft and above the wing trailing edge. Equipped with APQ-94 radar set for sub-sonic radar training for Fleet pilots and crew. **CT-39E:** Redesignated from VT-39E in 1968. Used for rapid-response airlift of high priority passengers, ferry of pilots, and cargo. Commercial Series 40. **CT-39G:** Lengthened version of Series 40 (series 60). Seven in service with USN.

TALON, T-38A All-metal, low-wing monoplane, advanced supersonic jet pilot trainer. Used in U.S. Naval Test Pilot syllabus. Some on loan from USAF to Fighter Weapons School. Four being droned.

MENTOR, T-34 Series **T-34B:** Modified USAF primary trainer with Continental engine. An all-metal, low wing, semi-monocoque construction, two-place tandem monoplane. Has sectionalized cockpit canopy. Easily distinguished from USAF counterpart by presence of a notch at the trailing edge base of the rudder. **YT-34C:** Modified T-34B to determine feasibility of upgrading the airplane and equipment to conform more closely with current Fleet aircraft. Turboprop power plant, all new solid state avionics, wings, increased gross weight, and fuel capacity. High speed not necessary requirement for training; a torque limiter restricts engine operation to 400 SHP.

SHOOTING STAR, T-33 Series (TV-2) **QT-33A:** All-metal, full cantilever, low wing, two-seat, high-performance aircraft designed for training. Was similar to USAF T-33A, except now has primary mission of operational employment as RDT&E aircraft. **T-33B:** Not listed in characteristics table; phasing out. Similar to T-33A except for engine and minor changes.

FLYING CLASSROOM, T-29B Transferred from USAF. Similar to T-29A except for installation of cabin pressurization, periscopic sextant window, deletion of one astrodome, and addition of a hydraulic system, driving an alternator and generator. Ten students. Derived from Convair model #240.

TROJAN, T-28 Series **T-28B:** Prop-driven basic trainer; improved USAF T-28A. Two-spar, straight low wing, aluminum alloy skin and ribs. Tricycle landing gear. Armament: accessory kit 2.25" SCA rockets and .50 caliber gunpods. **DT-28B:** Converted for target aircraft control. **T-28C:** Modified T-28B incorporating redesigned rudder and lower fuselage, arresting hook, reduced propeller diameter. Suitable for carrier operations.

BUCKEYE, T-2 Series (T2J) Basic, carrier-based jet trainer. Two-place, low wing aircraft. **T-2B:** Similar to T-2A except for dual engine installation, reinforced wing structure, and modernized avionics equipment. **T-2C:** Improved engines and avionics. Armament: two 320-pound capacity underwing store stations, .50 caliber gun package, bomb racks, rocket packets, tow target containers, and fire control package (baggage compartment). **T-2D:** 12 built for Venezuela. **T-2E:** 40 ordered 1974 for Greek Air Force. A T-2C was the test vehicle used for the first flight test of the new generation of airfoils termed "supercritical." The airfoil, 40% thicker than the production model airfoil, was installed over the existing wing. These airfoils are designed to operate efficiently at transonic conditions. The drag was no more than the thinner wing and buffeting characteristics were improved and lift increased.

UTILITY

Model	Year Ordered/ Delivered	Number Proc.	Crew-Type	Lbs. Gross Weight	Dimensions LOA	Span	Height	Number	Engine Model	Thrust in Lbs. or HP (each)	Performance Max. Speed/Range (Kts.)/(nm)
HU-16D	Mod/59	31	6-A	32,000	62'10"	96'8"	24'3"	2	R1820-76A/B	1,425 HP	200/2200
U-11A	60/61	22	1-L	4,800	30'2½"	37'2"	10'3½"	2	0-540-A-1A	250 HP	191/1250
U-6A	60/60	2	1-L	5,100	30'4"	48'0"	9'0"	1	R985-AN-39A	450 HP	139/470
U-1B	55/55	17	2-L	8,000	41'10"	58'0"	13'0"	1	R1340	600 HP	140/830

ALBATROSS, HU-16 Series (UF-1) HU-16D: Improved version of HU-16C; rebuilt with a new wing 1959. Carries 12 litters. **HU-16E:** USCG SAR, similar to HU-16D.

AZTEC, U-11A (UO-1) Engine manufactured by Lycoming. Light logistics support aircraft for CONUS; carries 4 passengers.

BEAVER, U-6A (L-20A) A high wing, all-metal monoplane; has fixed landing gear, throw-over controls, dual rudder controls. For general utility mission. STOL aircraft, De Havilland model DHC-2. Carries 5 passengers. Obtained from USAF. Three additional units obtained for MAP Philippines and never in USN custody.

U-3A Two-engine Cessna, 5-place, low wing monoplane. Light utility. Other details not available at this time.

OTTER, U-1B (UC-1) STOL polar transport with ski landing gear. De Havilland DHC-3. For DEEP FREEZE operations in Antarctic. Operational as NU-1B. 14 models accepted by USN, including one under British contract. Three were borrowed from aircraft/Canada 1955, but replaced with new production in 1956.

V/STOL

Model	Year Ordered/ Delivered	Number Proc.	Crew-Type	Lbs. Gross Weight	Dimensions LOA	Span	Height	Number	Engine Model	Thrust in Lbs. or HP (each)	Performance Max. Speed/Range (Kts.)/(nm)
XFV-12A	72/74	2	1-C	19,500	43'9"	28'5"	9'1"	1	F401-PW-400	21,800	M2+/
YOV-10A	64/65	7	2-L	13,800	40'0"	34'0"	15'1"	2	T76-G-6/8	650 HP	240/1240
OV-10A	66/67	114	2-L	14,466	41'7"	40'0"	15'1"	2	T76-G-10/12	715 HP	244/1208
YOV-10D	70/71	2	2-L	13,200	44'1"	40'0"	15'1"	2	T76-G-10/12	715 HP	200/1200+
OV-10D	74/	24	2-L	14,300	44'1"	40'0"	15'1"	2	T76-G-420/421	1,000 HP	220/1200+
AV-8A	69/71	100+	1-L	25,000	45'8"	25'3"	11'3"	1	PEGASUS 103	21,500	625/1800
TAV-8A		8+	2-L	25,000	45'8"	25'3"	11'3"	1	PEGASUS 103	21,500	635/1800

AV-16A (unnamed) Advanced HARRIER configuration. Planned modification of an existing aircraft rather than a long-range program, which would include a prototype. McDonnell Douglas design with Hawker Siddeley. Funds deleted FY-1975 due to rising costs (British withdrew from program).

XFV-12A (unnamed) Two, single-seat, single-engine prototypes; one to develop flight characteristics and the other to have a thrust-augmented wing design. Two additional prototypes proposed; to be armed with General Electric M61 Gatling 20mm guns. XFV-12A features the Thrust-Augmented Wing Concept to achieve vertical lift. Ordnance: in addition to an internal gun, the lower fuselage may carry SPARROW missiles, a variety of air-to-ground missiles, or free-fall bombs. The outer wing tips may be configured to carry SIDEWINDER missiles or ZUNI rockets.

BRONCO, OV-10 Series OV-10A: U.S. Government procured 271 OV-10s; 114 for USN and 157 for USAF. Two-place tandem, lightweight, multipurpose armed reconnaissance aircraft with Garrett-AiResearch engines. BRONCO features a high shoulder wing and a short pod-type fuselage/utility bay with a landing gear system for operation from unimproved runways. Armament: centerline station for 20mm gun pod or external fuel tank, four 7.62mm machine guns in sponsons, four sponson stations for rockets, flares and miniguns, optical wing stations for rockets/missiles. **OV-10B:** 18 built for West Germany. OV-10B(Z) has third engine (jet pod located on upper surface of the center wing section). **OV-10C:** 32 built for Thailand. **OV-10E:** 16 built for Venezuela. **YOV-10D:** Prototype model of the Night Observation Gunship System (NOGS) version of OV-10A. **OV-10D:** Production configuration of OV-10 modified to NOGS version. Has stabilized FLIR sensor mounted in the nose assembly with a 20mm gun turret slaved to the FLIR sensor. Fuselage sponsons are removed to clear the field of fire.

HARRIER, AV-8 Close support aircraft capable of shipboard operations and operations from natural or roughly prepared areas of limited size. Equipped with inertial navigation attack system and HUD. Has wing-mounted outrigger landing gear and two centerline wheels. AV-8 was formerly designated AV-6B. The first HARRIERs delivered were retrofitted with engines as indicated. HARRIER carries seven weapon mounts, including two 30mm guns and SIDEWINDER. **TAV-8A:** Two-seat training version. **AV-8C:** USMC seeking to develop improved follow-on aircraft.

Aircraft Notes

1. STRATOJET (EB-47E/NB-47E): Six-engine (J47-GE-25A) Boeing aircraft. Two acquired for special test purposes. Similar to USAF B-47E except modified for addition of special electronic equipment. Used as ECM test bed for surface missile system testing, training, and evaluation. Since February 1971, development models of VIKING TF34-GE-2 engine has been test flown on a modified B-47. Engine is installed on the left wing between inboard and outboard nacelles.

2. F-5E (5): Obtained by USN for Fighter Weapons School, replacing USAF T-38s.

3. Lockheed is testing an EPX designated version (Electronics Patrol, Experimental) of the high altitude U-2 aircraft. Configured to the Navy's ocean surveillance missions. Tests to determine effectiveness of several sensors, including radar, electronic intelligence receivers, and FLIR to monitor maritime and naval ship movements from high altitudes.

AIRCRAFT TAIL MARKINGS OF CURRENT ACTIVE AIR WINGS (A—ATLANTIC, N—PACIFIC)

CAW	ID Letters	Aircraft Carrier	CAW	ID Letters	Aircraft Carrier
CVW-1	AB	CV-67	CVW-9	NG	CV-64
CVW-2	NE	CVA-61	CVW-11	NH	CV-63
CVW-3	AC	CV-60	CVW-14	NK	CVAN-65
CVW-5	NF	CVA-41	CVW-15	NL	CVA-43
CVW-6	AE	CVA-42	CVW-17	AA	CVA-59
CVW-7	AG	CV-62	CVW-19	NM	CVA-34
CVW-8	AJ	CV-66	CVW-21	NP	CVA-19

AIRCRAFT MANUFACTURERS' CODE

Code	Manufacturer and Location	Code	Manufacturer and Location
BF	Bell Helicopter, Fort Worth, Texas.	KA	Kaman AC Corp., Bloomfield, Connecticut.
BH	Beech AC Corp., Wichita, Kansas.	LM	Lockheed AC Corp., Marietta, Ga.
BV	Boeing Co. (Vertol), Morton, Pa.	LO	Lockheed AC Corp., Burbank, Cal.
CE	Cessna AC Company, Wichita, Kansas.	MC	McDonnell-Douglas, St. Louis, Mo.
CV	Ling Temco Vought, Dallas, Texas.	NA	North American Aviation, Inglewood, California.
DH	De Havilland AC, Toronto, Canda.	NH	North American Aviation, Columbus, Ohio.
DO	McDonnell-Douglas, Santa Monica, California.	NO	Northrop Corporation, Hawthorne, California.
FA	Fairchild AC Div., Hagerstown, Maryland.	PA	Piper AC Corp., Lockhaven, Pa.
GR	Grumman AC Div., Bethpage, Long Island, N.Y.	SI	Sikorsky Aircraft Division, Stratford, Connecticut.

POPULAR NAMES/SERIES/BUILDER

Name	Series	Builder	Name	Series	Builder
ACADEME	TC-4C	GR	BEAVER	U-6	DH
ALBATROSS	HU-16	GR	BRONCO	OV-10	NH
AZTEC	U-11	PA	BUCKEYE	T-2	NH

continued

Name	Series	Builder	Name	Series	Builder
CORSAIR II	A-7	CV	SEA KING	H-3	SI
COUGAR	F-9	GR	SEA KNIGHT	H-46	BV
CRUSADER	F-8	CV	SEA STALLION	H-53	SI
			SEABAT	H-34G	SI
FLYING BOXCAR	C-119	FA	SEACOBRA	AH-1J	BF
FLYING CLASSROOM	T-29	CO	SEAGUARD	H-52	SI
			SEAHORSE	H-34	SI
GREYHOUND	C-2	GR	SEARANGER	TH-57	BF
GULFSTREAM I	C-4	GR	SEASPRITE	H-2	KA
GULFSTREAM II	C-11	GR	SEASTAR	T-1	LO
			SHOOTING STAR	T-33	LO
HARRIER	AV-8	MC	SIOUX	H-13	BF
HAWKEYE	E-2	GR	SKYHAWK	A-4	DO
HERCULES	C-130	LM	SKYKNIGHT	F-10	DO
HUEYCOBRA	AH-1	BF	SKYMASTER	C-54	DO
			SKYRAIDER	A-1	DO
INTRUDER	A-6	GR	SKYRAY	F-6	DO
IROQUOIS	UH-1	BF	SKYTRAIN	C-47	DO
			SKYTRAIN	C-117	DO
LIFTMASTER	C-118	DO	SKYTRAIN II	C-9B	DO
			SKYWARRIOR	A-3	DO
MENTOR	T-34	BH	SUPER CONSTELLATION	C-121	LO
NAVIGATOR	C-45	BH	TALON	T-38	NO
NEPTUNE	P-2	LO	TIGER	F-11	GR
			TOMCAT	F-14	GR
ORION	P-3	LO	TRACER	E-1	GR
OTTER	U-1	DH	TRACKER	S-2	GR
			TRADER	C-1	GR
PANTHER	QF-9E	GR	TROJAN	T-28	NH
PHANTOM II	F-4	MC			
PROVIDER	C-123	FA	VIGILANTE	A-5	NH
PROWLER	EA-6B	GR	VIKING	S-3	LO
SABRELINER	T-39	NA	WARNING STAR	C-121	LO
SAMARITAN	C-131	CO			

NEW/OLD AIRCRAFT DESIGNATIONS (Recent Types)

Note: The following is a complete list of designation changes, effective in 1962. While most of the models are no longer in service, their photos exist indicating the old designations only. The table will assist the researcher and student.

New	Old	New	Old	New	Old	New	Old
Attack		A-1H	AD-6	A-3A	A3D-1	EA-3B	A3D-2Q
A-1E	AD-5	A-1J	AD-7	YEA-3A	Y/A3D-1Q	YRA-3B	Y/A3D-2P
EA-1E	AD-5W	A-2A	AJ-1	EA-3A	A3D-1Q	RA-3B	A3D-2P
EA-1F	AD-5Q	A-2B	AJ-2	YPA-3A	Y/A3D-1P	TA-3B	A3D-2T
A-1G	AD-5N	YA-3A	Y/A3D-1	A-3B	A3D-2	YA-4A	Y/A4D-1

New	Old	New	Old	New	Old	New	Old
A-4A	A4D-1	WC-121N	WV-3	YF-8D	Y/F8U-2N	YSH-34J	Y/HSS-1N
A-4B	A4D-2	EC-121L	WV-2E	F-8D	F8U-2N	SH-34J	HSS-1N
YA-4C	Y/A4D-2N	EC-121M	WV-2Q	YF-8E	Y/F8U-2NE	CH-37C	HR2S-1
A-4C	A4D-2N	TC-117D	R4D-8T	F-8E	F8U-2NE	UH-43C	HUK-1
A-4E	A4D-5	C-130F	GV-1U	DF-9E	F9F-5KD	CH-43D	HOK-1
YA-5A	Y/A3J-1	KC-130F	GV-1	F-9F	F9F-6	CH-46A	HRB-1
A-5A	A3J-1	LC-130F	C-130BL	DF-9F	F9F-6D	QH-50A	DSN-1
A-5B	A3J-2	C-131F	R4Y-1	QF-9F	F9F-6K	QH-50B	DSN-2
RA-5C	A3J-3	C-131G	R4Y-2	QF-9G	F9F-6K2	QH-50C	DSN-3
A-6A	A2F-1	C-140C	UV-1	F-9H	F9F-7	XH-51A	(New)
EA-6A	A2F-1H	C-1A	TF-1	F-9J	F9F-8		
		EC-1A	TF-1Q	YAF-9J	Y/F9F-8B		
Bomber		C-2A	(New)	AF-9J	F9F-8B	*Observation*	
UB-26J	JD-1			YTF-9J	Y/F9F-8T	O-1B	OE-1
DB-26J	JD-1D	*AEW*		TF-9J	F9F-8T	O-1C	OE-2
		E-1B	WF-2	RF-9J	F9F-8P		
Cargo-Transport		E-2A	W2F-1	F-10A	F3D-1		
RC-45J	SNB-5P			F-10B	F3D-2	*Patrol*	
TC-45J	SNB-5	*Fighter*		EF-10B	F3D-2Q	P-2D	P2V-4
C-47H	R4D-5	F-111B	TFX	MF-10B	F3D-2M	P-2E	P2V-5F
EC-47H	R4D-5Q	F-1C	FJ-3	TF-10B	F3D-2T2	DP-2E	P2V-5FD
LC-47H	R4D-5L	DF-1C	FJ-3D	YF-11A	Y/F11F-1	EP-2E	P2V-5FE
SC-47H	R4D-5S	MF-1C	FJ-3M	F-11A	F11F-1	SP-2E	P2V-5FS
TC-47H	R4D-5R	DF-1D	FJ-3D2			P-2F	P2V-6
VC-47H	R4D-5Z	YF-1E	Y/FJ-4	*Helicopter*		MP-2F	P2V-6M
C-47J	R4D-6	F-1E	FJ-4	UH-1E	HU-1E	TP-2F	P2V-6T
EC-47J	R4D-6Q	YAF-1E	YFJ-4B	UH-2A	HU2K-1	P-2G	P2V-6F
LC-47J	R4D-6L	AF-1E	FJ-4B	UH-2B	HU2K-1U	YP-2H	Y/P2V-7
SC-47J	R4D-6S	F-2C	F2H-3	YSH-3A	Y/HSS-2	P-2H	P2V-7
TC-47J	R4D-6R	F-2D	F2H-4	SH-3A	HSS-2	SP-2H	P2V-7S
VC-47J	R4D-6Z	YF-3B	Y/F3H-2	VH-3A	HSS-2Z	LP-2J	P2V-7LP
TC-47K	R4D-7	F-3B	F3H-2	TH-13L	HTL-4	YP-3A	Y/P3V-1
VC-54N	R5D-1Z	MF-3B	F3H-2M	TH-13M	HTL-6	P-3A	P3V-1
C-54P	R5D-2	F-3C	F3H-2N	TH-13N	HTL-7	QP-4B	P4Y-2K
VC-54P	R5D-2	F-4A	F4H-1F	UH-13P	HUL-1	P-5A	P5M-1
C-54Q	R5D-3Z	F-4B	F4H-1	HH-13Q	HUL-1G	SP-5A	P5M-1S
VC-54Q	R5D-3Z	RF-4B	F4H-1P	UH-13R	HUL-1M	TP-5A	P5M-1T
C-54R	R5D-4R	YF-6A	Y/F4D-1	CH-19E	HRS-3	P-5B	P5M-2
C-54S	R5D-5	F-6A	F4D-1	UH-19F	HO4S-3	SP-5B	P5M-2S
VC-54S	R5D-5Z	YF-7A	Y/F2Y-1	HH-19G	HO4S-3G		
C54T	R5D-5R	YF-8A	Y/F8U-1	UH-25B	HUP-2		
C-117D	R4D-8	F-8A	F8U-1	UH-25C	HUP-3	*ASW*	
LC-117D	R4D-8L	DF-8A	F8U-1D	LH-34D	HUS-1L	S-2A	S2F-1
VC-117D	R4D-8Z	QF-8A	F8U-1KD	YSH-34G	Y/HSS-1	YS-2A	Y/S2F-1
C-118B	R6D-1	YRF-8A	Y/F8U-1P	SH-34G	HSS-1	TS-2A	S2F-1T
VC-118B	R6D-1Z	RF-8A	F8U-1P	UH-34D	HUS-1	S-2B	S2F-1S
C-119F	R4Q-2	TF-8A	F8U-1T	VH-34D	HUS-1Z	S-2C	S2F-2
C-121J	R7V-1	F-8B	F8U-1E	UH-34E	HUS-1A	RS-2C	S2F-2P
EC-121K	WV-2	YF-8C	Y/F8U-2	HH-34F	HUS-1G	S-2D	S2F-3
YEC-121K	Y/WV-2	F-8C	F8U-2	SH-34H	HSS-1F	S-2E	S2F-3S

continued

AIRCRAFT

New	Old	New	Old	New	Old	New	Old
Trainer		T-28C	T-28C	*Utility*		HU-16D	UF-2
T-1A	T2V-1	T-33B	TV-2	U-1B	UC-1	HU-16E	UF-2G
YT-2A	Y/T2J-1	DT-33B	TV-2D	U-6A	L-20A		
T-2A	T2J-1	DT-33C	TV-2KD	U-11A	UO-1	*Airship*	
T-2B	T2J-2	T-34B	T-34B	HU-16C	UF-1	EZ-1B	ZPG-2W
T-28A	T-28A	YT-34B	Y/T-34B	LU-16C	UF-1L	SZ-1B	ZPG-2
T-28B	T-28R	T-39D	T3J-1	TU-16C	UF-1T	EZ-1C	ZPG-3W
DT-28B	T-28BD						

E-1B TRACER, VAW-88. (Photo: R. L. Lawson.)

US-2B TRACKER, NATC Patuxent River. (Photo: Jim Sullivan.)

E-2B HAWKEYE, VAW-116. (Photo: R. L. Lawson.)

E-2C improved HAWKEYE, VAW-123. Note extended nose.

US-2C TRACKER, VC-3. (Photo: R. L. Lawson.)

S-2D TRACKER.

S-2E TRACKER, CVSG-50, lands aboard *Lexington* (CVT-16).

S-2G TRACKER, VS-31.

TS-2A. One of 42 US-2A/TS-2A TRACKERS on lease to California Division of Forestry for fire-fighting. (Photo: R. L. Lawson.)

S-3A VIKING, NATC Patuxent River. (Photo: Jim Sullivan.)

A-7A CORSAIR II, VA-125.

A-7B CORSAIR II, VA-46. (Photo: R. L. Lawson.)

A-7C CORSAIR II, VA-174 of RCVW-4, Cecil Field. (Photo: Ling Temco Vought.)

A-7E CORSAIR II, VA-192, CVW-11.

YA-7H CORSAIR II; two-place version. (Photo: Ling Temco Vought.)

A-6B INTRUDER, VA-165.

A-6C INTRUDER.

A-6E INTRUDER, VA-175.

EA-6A INTRUDER, VMCJ-3, USMC. (Photo: R. L. Lawson.)

EA-6B PROWLER, VAQ-129.

KA-6D. Tanker version of INTRUDER, VA-165. Assigned to *Constellation* (CVA-64).

RA-5C VIGILANTE, RVAH-13. (Photo: R. L. Lawson.)

Rarely published photo of A-5B VIGILANTE. (Photo: North American Rockwell.)

A-4C SKYHAWK, VC-7. (Photo: R. L. Lawson.)

A-4F SKYHAWK, VA-144. Note enlarged avionics compartment.

EA-4F SKYHAWK, VAQ-33.

TA-4F SKYHAWK, VA-127, RCVW-12.

TA-4J SKYHAWK, VT-21. Markings on nose, wing tips, and rudder are orange.

A-4L SKYHAWK, VA-205, CVWR-20.

A-4M SKYHAWK, VMA-324, USMC. (Photo: General Electric Company.)

A-3B SKYWARRIOR, VAQ-130, over *Enterprise* (CVAN-65).

EA-3B SKYWARRIOR, VAQ-208, CVWR-20. (Photo: R. L. Lawson.)

KA-3B SKYWARRIOR, VAQ-130, CVW-6.

EKA-3B SKYWARRIOR, VAQ-135, DET. 1 (CVW-11). (Photo: R. L. Lawson.)

F-14A TOMCAT, VF-2, NAS Miramar. (Photo: R. L. Lawson.)

F-14A TOMCAT, VF-1, CVW-14. (Photo: USS *Enterprise* (CVAN-65).)

Fully armed F-14A TOMCAT.

TF-9J COUGAR, one of few remaining. VT-10, NAS Miramar. (Photo: R. L. Lawson.)

RF-8G CRUSADER, VFP-63, NAS Miramar. (Photo: R. L. Lawson.)

F-8H CRUSADER, VF-202, CVWR-20. (Photo: R. L. Lawson.)

F-8J CRUSADER, VF-194, CVW-19. (Photo: R. L. Lawson.)

F-8K CRUSADER, VF-302, NAS Miramar. (Photo: R. L. Lawson.)

F-4B PHANTOM II, VF-302, CVWR-30, NAS Miramar. (Photo: R. L. Lawson.)

RF-4B PHANTOM II, VMCJ-2, MCAS Cherry Point. (Photo: Jim Sullivan.)

AIRCRAFT

F-4J PHANTOM II, VF-142, CVW-8. (Photo: R. L. Lawson.)

F-4J PHANTOM II, VF-31, CVW-3. (Photo: USS *Saratoga* (CV-60).)

F-4N PHANTOM II, VF-161, CVW-5, at NAS Miramar. (Photo: R. L. Lawson.)

C-1A TRADER. (Photo: USS *Ranger* (CVA-61).)

C-2A GREYHOUND, VRC-50, NAS North Island. (Photo: R. L. Lawson.)

TC-4C ACADEME, VA-128, RCVW-12, NAS Whidbey Island (Photo: Harry Gann.)

C-9B SKYTRAIN II, VR-30. (Photo: R. L. Lawson.)

C-131F SAMARITAN, VR-30, at Nellis AFB. (Photo: R. L. Lawson.)

DC-130A HERCULES, VC-3, NAS North Island. (Photo: R. L. Lawson.)

C-130F HERCULES, VMGR-352, MCAS El Toro. (Photo: R. L. Lawson.)

KC-130F HERCULES, refueling OV-1 MOHAWK.

LC-130R HERCULES, VXE-6. Note ski/wheel landing gear.

EC-121K WARNING STAR, VT-86, at Nellis AFB. (Photo: R. L. Lawson.)

C-119F FLYING BOXCAR. (Photo: Fairchild.)

C-118B LIFTMASTER, VR-52, Detached. Detroit. (Photo: R. L. Lawson.)

C-117D SKYTRAIN, NAS Norfolk. (Photo: R. L. Lawson.)

C-54Q SKYMASTER, Test Pilot School, Patuxent River. Last active C-54, since retired. (Photo: R. L. Lawson.)

C-47J SKYTRAIN, NARF El Centro. Over 10,000 were built for the military. Very few remain. (Photo: R. L. Lawson.)

TH-57A SEARANGER, HT-8. (Photo: PAO NAS Whiting Field.)

CH-53A SEA STALLION during a minesweeping operation.

AIRCRAFT

MARK 105 minesweeping unit being towed by CH-53 SEA STALLION.

CH-53 SEA STALLION with 3rd MarDiv, Vietnam. (Photo: USMC.)

CH-46A SEA KNIGHT, HC-6.

CH-46D SEA KNIGHT, HMM-164, NAS Hospital, Da Nang. (Photo: R. L. Lawson.)

UH-34D SEAHORSE, HMM-362, Da Nang. (Photo: R. L. Lawson.)

SH-3A SEA KING, HS-6. (Photo: R. L. Lawson.)

SH-3D SEA KING, HS-4, USS *Hornet* (CVS-12). (Photo: R. L. Lawson.)

SH-3H SEA KING, HS-7.

UH-2C SEASPRITE, modified with SPARROW III missile.

SH-2D SEASPRITE, HSL-31 landing aboard *Harold E. Holt* (DE-1074). Note MAD device on side rack. (Photo: Kaman Aerospace.)

HH-2D SEASPRITE with inflatable radome dish antenna. (Photo: Kaman Aerospace.)

YSH-2E SEASPRITE. Modified HH-2D to LAMPS MK. II configuration. (Photo: Kaman Aerospace.)

SH-2F SEASPRITE, MK. III LAMPS. Note relocation of tail wheel. (Photo: Kaman Aerospace.)

UH-1E IROQUOIS, HML-167, Da Nang. (Photo: R. L. Lawson.)

AH-1J "SEACOBRA", HML-267. Twin engine configuration. Note 20mm cannon under the nose. (Photo: R. L. Lawson.)

TH-1L HUEYCOBRA. (Photo: PAO NAS Whiting Field.)

P-3A ORION, VP-44, observing Soviet vessels.

P-3B ORION, VP-9, with BULLPUP missiles.

P-3C ORION. Note absence of searchlights under wings.

DP-2E NEPTUNE with BQM-34A FIREBEE. (Photo: Teledyne Ryan Aeronautical.)

SP-2H NEPTUNE, VP-65, NAS Miramar. (Photo: R. L. Lawson.)

X-26A. Schweitzer 2-32 sailplane. (Photo: NAS Patuxent River.)

X-26B. Powered version of X-26A. (Photo: NAS Patuxent River.)

X-25A. Bensen gyrocopter. (Photo: Bensen Aircraft.)

T-39D SABRELINER, NAS Pensacola, at North Island. (Photo: R. L. Lawson.)

T-39D SABRELINER, USMC, Nellis AFB. (Photo: R. L. Lawson.)

T-38A TALON, Fighter Weapons School. USAF aircraft on loan to Navy. (Photo: R. L. Lawson.)

YT-34C MENTOR. Uprgraded version of T-34B. (Photo: Beech Aircraft.)

T-34B MENTOR, NAS Corpus Christi. (Photo: Beech Aircraft.)

T-33B SHOOTING STAR, HQ USMC, at North Island. (Photo: R. L. Lawson.)

T-29B FLYING CLASSROOM, VT-29.

T-28C TROJAN, NAS North Island. (Photo: R. L. Lawson.)

T-28B TROJAN, VT-2. (Photo: NAS Whiting Field.)

T-2C BUCKEYE, VT-26, NAS Miramar. (Photo: R. L. Lawson.)

T-2B BUCKEYE, VT-9, landing aboard *Lexington*. (Photo: USS *Lexington* (CVT-16).)

HU-16C ALBATROSS.

U-11A AZTEC, NAS North Island. (Photo: R. L. Lawson.)

U-6A BEAVER, Test Pilot School. (Photo: NAS Patuxent River.)

U-1B OTTER. (Photo: NAS Patuxent River.)

XFV-12A, prototype. (Photo: North American.)

OV-10D BRONCO, USMC, at North Island. (Photo: R. L. Lawson.)

OV-10A BRONCO, VMO-8, MCAS El Toro. (Photo: R. L. Lawson.)

OV-10A BRONCO, VMO-1.

AV-8A HARRIER, VMA-513, USMC.

AV-8A HARRIER, VMA-513, USMC. (Photo: Marine Corps.)

ELEVEN: MISSILES AND CONVENTIONAL ORDNANCE

All DOD rockets and guided missiles, like aircraft, are assigned official designations, which are the minimum combination of letters and numbers to identify the vehicle.

Example of symbols: SIDEWINDER, AIM-9D.
SIDEWINDER is the popular name assigned to that missile family. *A* is the launch environment (Air); *I* is the mission (Intercept, aerial); *M* is the vehicle type (Guided Missile); *9* is the design number (9th Missile); *D* is the series symbol (4th Version of AIM-9). If designated YAIM-9D, *Y* would be the status prefix symbol (Prototype).

Symbols

LAUNCH ENVIRONMENT
A   Air
B   Multiple
C   Coffin
F   Individual
M   Mobile
P   Soft Pad
R   Ship
U   Underwater

MISSION
D   Decoy
E   Special Electronic
G   Surface Attack
I   Intercept, Aerial
Q   Drone
T   Training
U   Underwater Attack
W   Weather

TYPE VEHICLE
M   Guided Missile
N   Probe
R   Rocket

STATUS
J   Special Test, Temporary
N   Special Test, Permanent
X   Experimental
Y   Prototype
Z   Planning

Abbreviations

ARM	Antiradiation missile
ER	Extended range
IR	Infrared homing
HVAR	High velocity antiaircraft rocket
LPR	Liquid propellant rocket
MR	Medium range
N/A	Not available
F/S	Cognizant service
SAR	Semiactive, radar homing
SPR	Solid propellant rocket

AIR-AIR MISSILES

Number	Name	Manufacturer	Guidance	Type Engine
AIM-7D	SPARROW III	Raytheon	SAR	SPR
AIM-7E	SPARROW IIIB	Raytheon	SAR	SPR
AIM-7F	SPARROW MK58, 65	Raytheon	SAR	SPR
AIM-9B	SIDEWINDER 1A	Philco/G.E.	IR	SPR
AIM-9D	SIDEWINDER 1C-IR	Raytheon/Philco	IR	SPR
AIM-9G	SIDEWINDER	Raytheon	IR	SPR
AIM-9H	SIDEWINDER	Raytheon	IR	SPR
ZAIM-9K	SIDEWINDER	Raytheon	IR	SPR
ZAIM-9L	SIDEWINDER	Raytheon	IR	SPR
AIM-54A	PHOENIX	Hughes	SAR	SPR
AIM-95A	AGILE	Hughes	Cross Array	SPR

SPARROW (AIM-7): SPARROW I became operational in 1956, but was later replaced by SPARROW III. SPARROW II was part of the Navy's development program and was not intended for operational use. AIM-7D is a solid fuel, radar homing missile with a high explosive warhead. AIM-7E is an improved version. AIM-7E-2 was developed into SEA SPARROW (BPDMS). AIM-7F is an advanced solid state version of AIM-7E; has greater range, performance, maneuverability, reliability, and larger warhead. AIM-7G is USAF version. RIM-7H-1 is SEA SPARROW (see SURFACE-AIR MISSILES).

SIDEWINDER (AIM-9): A supersonic homing weapon employing passive infrared target detection, proportional navigation guidance, and torque balance control. AIM-9D is SIDE-WINDER 1C, IRAH (infrared alternate head). ATM-9D is used for captive flight target acquisition training. ATM-9G is an improved ATM-9D. AIM-9G is similar to AIM-9D except for SEAM (SIDEWINDER expanded acquisition mode) with improved lock-on and tracking prior to launch. AIM-9H is AIM-9G with solid state guidance control group (GCG). ZAIM-9K is a modified version of AIM-9H (GCG). ZAIM-9L is super SIDEWINDER with infrared seekers for use in TOMCAT (F-14A), with PHOENIX (AIM-54A). AIM-9E and AIM-9J are USAF versions.

PHOENIX (AIM-54): Originally intended for the ill-fated F-111B aircraft, but is now employed by TOMCAT (F-14A). Has high explosive warhead and proximity fuse. Also has active radar terminal homing. The PHOENIX system consists of the AWG-9 Airborne Missile Control System (AMCS), launchers, and the missiles. TOMCAT set a record by hitting a supersonic FIREBEE II at 126 miles range.

AGILE (AIM-95): A thrust-vectored control, dogfight missile in RDT&E. It was to replace SIDEWINDER when development was completed and production begun, but the project was cancelled by Congress in FY 1975 after it had begun to show great promise.

AIR-SURFACE MISSILES

Number	Name	Manufacturer	Guidance	Type Engine
AGM-12B	BULLPUP A	Martin/Maxson	Radio	LPR
AGM-12C	BULLPUP B	Martin Marietta	Radio	LPR
AGM-45A	SHRIKE	Texas Inst.	ARM	SPR
AGM-45B	SHRIKE	Texas Inst.	ARM	SPR
AGM-53A	CONDOR	No. American	TV	SPR
AGM-62A	WALLEYE I	Martin/Hughes	TV	None
AGM-78A	STANDARD ARM	G.D., Pomona	Passive Homing	SPR
AGM-78B	STANDARD ARM	G.D., Pomona	Passive Homing	SPR
AGM-83A	BULLDOG	Texas Inst/NWC	Laser	LPR
AGM-84A	HARPOON	McDonnell Douglas	Active Radar	SPR
AGM-87A	FOCUS I	G.E./NWC	Infrared Homing	SPR
AGM-88A	HARM	Texas Inst./NWC		SPR

BULLPUP (AGM-12): AGM-12B is a short range guided missile used against comparatively small, defended targets. Has radio-link command guidance, nose-mounted control planes, and a 250-lb. warhead. AGM-12C is an improved version with a 1000-lb. warhead. AGM-12E and AEM-12F are USAF versions. ATM-12A (BULLPUP TRAINER) radio-guided training missile built around a standard 5″ HVAR. ATM-12B is AGM-12B with an inert warhead.

SHRIKE (AGM-45): A four-section missile consisting of a guidance control, warhead, and solid rocket motor. Missile senses and homes on radiation targets. AGM-45B has improved operational characteristics. ATM-45A/B are practice guided missiles; warhead section is inert.

CONDOR (AGM-53): A rocket-powered, conventional warhead weapon with television guidance for "fire, then aim" capability. Has launch-and-leave capability before target lock-on; has hit target 60 miles from launch aircraft. The TURBO CONDOR is fitted with underslung, semisubmerged turbojet engine in place of solid rocket motor; extends range to 280 miles. Designation of missile not available.

WALLEYE (AGM-62): A TV-guided glide bomb. WALLEYE II (FAT ALBERT) is larger and heavier with a larger warhead and improved guidance package. Designation not known. Further development of the WALLEYE smart bomb is an extended range-data link WALLEYE II. Has bigger wings and a data link that stretches effective range to as much as 35 miles. Has launch weight of 2000 lb.

STANDARD ARM (AGM-78): A tactical antiradiation missile configured with a smoke device. AGM-78B/C are improved versions. AGM-78D is a further improved version. ATM-78C/D are training missiles used for captive flight and classroom training.

BULLDOG (AGM-83): Modified BULLPUP for more effective close air support (USMC). Missile has laser guidance system. Scheduled for limited production to take advantage of obsolete BULLPUP airframes available. Has 250 lb. warhead.

HARPOON (AGM-84): Antiship missile with active radar terminal guidance system. Wave-skimming HARPOON pitches up in the last few seconds before target impact, thus avoiding ship's point defense. (See RGM-84A-1 for surface and sub-surface version).

FOCUS I (AGM-87): Modified SIDEWINDER under test and evaluation. Configuration classified. Uses a laser-seeker guidance system.

HARM (AGM-88): High-speed, antiradiation, tactical missile for suppressing and destroying enemy radar air defense systems. A four-section missile; warhead, guidance, control, and solid propellant rocket engine.

SURFACE TO AIR/SURFACE MISSILES

Number	Name	Manufacturer	Guidance	Type Engine
RIM-2D	TERRIER	G.D., Pomona	Beam Rider	SPR
RIM-2E	TERRIER	G.D., Pomona	SAR	SPR
RIM-2F	TERRIER	G.D., Pomona	SAR	SPR
RIM-7H	SEA SPARROW	Raytheon	SAR	SPR
RIM-8G	TALOS	Bendix	SAR	RJ/SPR
RGM-8H	TALOS	Bendix	SAR	RJ/SPR
RIM-24B	TARTAR	G.D., Pomona	SAR	SPR
RIM-24C	TARTAR	G.D., Pomona	SAR	SPR
RIM-66A	STANDARD MR	G.D., Pomona	SAR	SPR
RIM-66B/C	STANDARD MR	G.D., Pomona	SAR	SPR
RIM-67A	STANDARD ER	G.D., Pomona	SAR	SPR
RGM-84A-1	HARPOON	McDonnell Douglas	Active Radar	SPR

TERRIER (RIM-2): Supersonic, solid fuel, radar guided missile for ship's inner defense against surface and air targets. Armed with nuclear or conventional warhead.

SEA SPARROW (RIM-7): Surface-air version of AIM-7E. Configured with folded wings for use in shipboard launcher. Has improved guidance and clipped wings. Also can be employed against ships. YRIM-7H-1 is AIM-7E-2, modified to provide a shorter commitment time.

TALOS (RIM-8): Long range, two-stage supersonic missile using mid-course beam-riding and semiactive Continuous Wave Interferometer (CWI) homing. Launched by a solid propellant booster and is ramjet-propelled after missile-booster separation. Can be used against single or massed groups of high-speed aircraft, or against surface targets. RGM-8H is similar to the preceding RIM-8G except employs advanced terminal guidance system, which changes the design mission and/or function. TALOS phase-out has begun.

MISSILES AND CONVENTIONAL ORDNANCE

TARTAR (RIM-24): Developed because solid fuel boosters made missiles too long for use aboard destroyer types. The booster and rocket engine were combined into one unit. RIM-24C is similar to RIM-24B except for increase in operating characteristic modes.

ZRGM-59A (no name assigned): A ship-launched, rocket-propelled, surface-to-surface weapon for landing support. Details not available.

STANDARD MR (RIM-66): YRIM-66A is a medium range, surface-to-air weapon with surface-to-surface capability for shipboard use. Solid state guidance with continuous wave and semi-active homing system. Missile is roll stabilized. Replaces TARTAR (RIM-24B). RIM-66B is similar to RIM-66A except has longer range and improved performance. RIM-66C is adaptable to AEGIS missile system. RGM-66D is similar to RIM-66B but modified as surface-to-surface ARM. RTM-66D is exercise version of RGM-66D. RGM-66E is similar to RGM-66D but adapted to ASROC launcher.

STANDARD ER (RIM-67): Extended range version of RIM-66; replaces TERRIER (RIM-2E). Difference between ER and MR is the propulsion system. ER has a separable booster and a sustainer rocket motor. MR has an integral dual-thrust level rocket motor.

HARPOON (RGM-84): Ship-launched version of AGM-84. Not for air launch, but can be launched from submarines or surface ships (ASROC, TERRIER, TARTAR, or MARK 26 launchers). Adding a SPR booster increases the overall length over the AGM version. Has folded fins to fit into the launchers.

ZRIM-85A (no name assigned): Medium range, all-weather missile for use against attack aircraft, air-to-surface and surface-to-surface missiles, and surface targets. Details not available.

ZRIM-101A (no name assigned): Surface-to-air weapon. Tube-launched by a solid propellant ejector with subsequent sustainer motor ignition. Initial guidance is in the passive I-band RF mode with terminal guidance in the passive IR mode.

CRUISE MISSILES PLANNED

General Dynamics (ZBGM-109) and LTV Aerospace (ZBGM-110) have been selected for competitive fly-off of new cruise missile. Winner to be selected 6/76. Missiles will use captive flight guidance system. ZBGM-109 will be loaded encapsulated into torpedo tubes of SSNs, and ejected like torpedoes. Further details not available at this time.

GROUND-LAUNCHED MISSILES

Number	Name	Manufacturer	Guidance	Type Engine
MIM-23A	HAWK	Raytheon	SAR	SPR
MIM-43A	REDEYE	G.D., Pomona	IR	SPR
XFIM-92A	STINGER	G.D., Pomona	IR	SPR

HAWK (MIM-23): USMC low altitude air defense weapon. Also has antimissile capability.

REDEYE (MIM-43): USMC hand-carried, shoulder-fired air defense weapon system.

STINGER (XFIM-92): Improved REDEYE. Passive infrared homing, proportional navigation with head-on launch capability. Missile has a dual-thrust rocket. STINGER is propelled from a launcher tube by an ejector booster for safe separation prior to rocket motor ignition.

SUBMARINE-LAUNCHED MISSILES

Number	Name	Manufacturer	Guidance	Type Engine
UGM-27B	POLARIS A2	Lockheed	Inertial	SPR
UGM-27C	POLARIS A3	Lockheed	Inertial	SPR
UUM-44A	SUBROC	Goodyear	Inertial	SPR
UGM-73A	POSEIDON C3	Lockheed	Inertial	SPR
UGM-84A	HARPOON	McDonnell Douglas	Active Radar	SPR
UGM-96A	TRIDENT I C4	Lockheed	Inertial	SPR
ZUGM-96B	TRIDENT II D5	Lockheed	Inertial	SPR

POLARIS (UGM-27): Deterrent missiles launched from SSBN at enemy land targets. POLARIS A2 replaced by POLARIS A3 on SSBN-598 class. UGM-27B being retained in *Ethan Allen* SSBN class. A1 (UGM-27A) phased out.

SUBROC (UUM-44): Submarine-launched nuclear depth bomb, using standard submarine torpedo tubes and conventional targeting methods.

POSEIDON (UGM-73): Back-fitted on all SSBN-616 and SSBN-640 class submarines. Has double the POLARIS A3 payload. Each missile capable of distributing no less than ten warheads, each one programmed to hit a different target (MIRV: Multiple Independently targetable Re-entry Vehicle).

HARPOON (UGM-84): Third version of antiship missile; contained in a special capsule designed for underwater launching at a surface target. Otherwise details same as RGM-84A-1.

TRIDENT (UGM-96): C4 is an improved POSEIDON, earlier referred to as EXPO (extended range POSEIDON). Program for 1977/78 with option to backfit C4 in SSBN-616 and SSBN-640 class submarines, as well as the new SSBN-726 class. D5 is planned for early 1980s with longer range, for SSBN-726 submarines only.

TARGET MISSILES/DRONES

Number	Name	Manufacturer	Guidance	Type Engine
BQM-34A	FIREBEE I	Teledyne Ryan	Radio	Jet
BQM-34E	FIREBEE II	Teledyne Ryan	Radio	Jet
MQM-36A	(none)	Northrop	Radio	Prop.
AQM-37A	(none)	Beech	Program	LPR
AQM-38B	(none)	Northrop	Radio	SPR
MQM-74A	CHUKAR	Northrop	Radio	Jet
MQM-74C	CHUKAR	Northrop	Radio	Jet

BOMARC (CQM-10A): Largest aerial target in Navy's inventory. Derived from obsolete USAF system, IM-99A INTERCEPTOR. Originally a long range, surface-to-air, area defense guided missile. Modified to drone configuration. Details N/A.

FIREBEE (BQM-34): FIREBEE I (BQM-34A) is a jet-powered, swept wing, subsonic aircraft target system. Air or ground launched, and recoverable. FIREBEE II (BQM-34E) is a high altitude, supersonic version, capable of simulating enemy aircraft. BQM-34T is a modified BQM-34E to incorporate transponder set and auto pilot with the integrated target control system. Many versions in this series for USN/USAF.

MQM-36A (no name assigned): Details not available.

AQM-37A (no name assigned): Decoy and target missile with limited reconnaissance capability. Recoverable.

AQM-38B (no name assigned): Details not available.

CHUKAR (MQM-74): MQM-74A is a recoverable gunnery aircraft/missile target drone. High-midwing monoplane, medium performance. Launched by JATO from shore or ship-based launchers. MQM-74C has a larger engine, improved flight control system, larger wings, and longer fuselage. Can be modified to act as decoy aircraft, or to carry chaff pods.

ZBQM-90A (no name assigned): Remotely controlled high-low altitude supersonic aerial target, replacing HAST/LAST. Details not available.

Numerous targets and drones are employed by USN/USMC. DOD designations are either not assigned or are not known at this time. A partial listing follows.

HAST (Beech): High Altitude Supersonic Target drone. High swept, clipped delta wing drone designed for launching from F-4 and F-15 (USAF). Powered by 13″ hybrid rocket motor. Programmed/ground command guidance.

LAST (Bendix): Low Altitude Supersonic Target drone counterpart of HAST. Ramjet power plant. Radio command/radar altimeter guidance. For test and evaluation of SAM-D and AEGIS system.

GUNRUNNER (Celesco): Rocket propelled (5″ HVAR), molded foam ballistic missile target for conventional antiaircraft gunnery and for REDEYE missile (USMC).

SHARK (Developmental Sciences): Recoverable, yawed-wing drone capable of supersonic sprint. Programmed guidance with one Williams WR24-17 powerplant. Currently in development. Projected to outperform FIREBEE II (BQM-34E), although it is somewhat smaller.

LOOK OUT (Fairchild): Ship-launched recoverable drone with radio command guidance.

MINI POP (Fairchild): Programmed guidance decoy drone with SPR power plant.

QH-50 SERIES: COAXIAL DRONE HELICOPTERS

Model	ORD/DEL	No. Proc.	Crew-Type	Lbs. Weight	Length	Span	Height	Number	Model	SHP Each, or Thrust #	Performance Max. Speed/Range
						Dimensions			**Engine**		
QH-50C	60/62-65	373	0/On Board	Wooden Blades 2285	AF—12′9.83″ Rotor—20′	AF—5′1″	9′8½″	1	T50-BO-8	Mil. Rated 300 SHP S.L. STD. Day	80KTS/82 N.M. Lateral SPD—35KTS AFT SPD 35 KTS
QH-50D	64/65-69	377	0/On Board	Fiberglass Blades 2328	AF—7′3½″ Rotor—20′	AF—5′1″	9′8½″	1	T50-BO-12	Mil. Rated 365 SHP S.L. STD. Day	83KTS/141 N.M. AFT—55 KTS LAT—74 KTS

Design mission was ASW torpedo carrier from destroyer decks. Twelve QH-50 A/B drones were built for research and development tests. The QH-50C was a larger drone than the A/B versions and incorporated a turboshaft engine. This production version was capable of carrying two Mark 44 homing torpedoes. The QH-50D was similar to the QH-50C, except for a new higher shaft horsepower engine, increased fuel capacity, fiberglass rotor blades, improved heading control, tail removal and relocation of avionic provided improved symmetry, with resultant lateral and aft flight performance improvements. The QH-50D equipped with a 30-300mm Zoom Lens TV camera in a single axis mount attached directly to the transmission and with associated electronics was utilized extensively in Vietnam for reconnaissance and gun-fire spotting in Project Snoopy. The attrition rate per flight hour surpassed all other drone operations. Reliability for Navy training operations of the QH-50D was 99.5% using telemetry, and 97.8% without telemetry in Fleet operations (1.5 hour mission). Over 300 QH-50C/D vehicles are still in the Navy inventory. The system was phased out of the Fleet in 1971 after nine years of operations from over 100 destroyers. The U.S. Army and the Japanese Navy are still using them. The Japanese Navy has achieved 8 times the Mean Time Between Loss of the U.S. Navy. Extensive development work was accomplished under ARPA/Navy sponsorship in evaluation of drones for reconnaissance, target designation and weapon delivery systems feasibility studies. DASH retains DOD designation as Drone Helicopter, but is listed under DRONES/RPV/TARGETS.

TARGETS BY CELESCO INDUSTRIES INC.

FIGAT: FiberGlass Aerial Target. 30′ long × 9′ high. Air-to-air gunnery tow target.

LOFAT: LOw altitude Fiberglass Aerial Tow Target constructed with foam/fiberglass. 10′ long × 30″ diameter. Bomb-like configuration. Takeoff weight is 300 lbs.

VASTT: Versatile Aerial Simulation Tow Target of foam/fiberglass construction. Length, 21′, diameter, 27″, and weight, 600 lbs. A solid propellant gas generator is capable of producing a tailored IR plume. Missile target.

TMT: Tactical Missile Target. GABRIEL (U.S. only) is a single stage subsonic cruise missile with cruciform configuration; powered by SPR. Used in ASMD programs.

FSMT: Full Size Maneuvering Target. Realistic simulation of a tactical fighter capable of .95 MACH speed for air-to-air gunnery and missile training. Tow target constructed of foam/fiberglass. Length = 52′; diameter = 6′. Weight = 4,000 lbs.

SEPTAR TARGET BOAT (MARK 35): Expendable, high-speed target boat. Glass-reinforced plastic hull, 27.2 heavy tons, 55′ OAL, 14′ beam. Launch platform primarily for BQM-34 aerial targets, simulating an attacking Soviet OSA or KOMAR missile boat.

RCST: Radio Controlled Surface Target. Basic vehicle is fitted over with foam target envelopes such as tanks, trucks, etc.

AIR-LAUNCHED ROCKETS

Number	Name	Manufacturer	Guidance	Type Engine
XAGR-14A	ZAP	Martin Marietta		

ZAP (AGR-14): Zero Anti-Aircraft Potential. Configuration classified at this time.

ANTISUBMARINE ROCKETS

Number	Name	Manufacturer	Guidance	Type Engine
RUR-5A	ASROC	Honeywell	(none)	SPR

ASROC (RUR-5): Has function selection as homing torpedo or nuclear depth bomb. Modified ASROC can be fired from Mark 10, Mod 7/8 TERRIER and Mark 26 STANDARD launchers.

GROUND-LAUNCHED ROCKETS

Number	Name	Manufacturer	Guidance	Type Engine
MGR-1A	HONEST JOHN	McDonnell Douglas	(none)	SPR
MGR-1B	HONEST JOHN	McDonnell Douglas	(none)	SPR
MGR-3A	LITTLE JOHN	Emerson	(none)	SPR

HONEST JOHN (MGR-1) and **LITTLE JOHN (MGR-3):** Unguided artillery rockets.

MQR-16A (no name assigned): Inexpensive aerial target with IR augmentation, providing a ballistic flight profile within REDEYE performance characteristics.

MISSILE DATA

Number	Name	OAL	Span Fins	Body Diam.	Launch Weight	Range/Miles	Max. Speed
AIR-TO-AIR MISSILES							
AIM-7D	SPARROW III	12′0″	3′2″	8″	350	5+	M3
AIM-7E	SPARROW IIIB	12′0″	3′4″	8″	450	12	M2.5
AIM-7F	SPARROW MK58, 65	12′0″	3′4″	8″	500	24+	M2+
AIM-9B	SIDEWINDER 1A	9′5″	2′0″	5″	160	2	M2+
AIM-9D	SIDEWINDER IC-IR	9′6″	2′2″	5″	185	15	M2+
AIM-9G	SIDEWINDER	9′6″	2′2″	5″	185	15	M2+
AIM-9H	SIDEWINDER	9′6″	2′2″	5″	185		M2+
ZAIM-9K	SIDEWINDER	9′6″	2′2″	5″	185		M2+
ZAIM-9L	SIDEWINDER	9′6″	2′2″	5″	185		M2+
AIM-54A	PHOENIX	13′0″	3′0″	1′3″	838	30+	M2+
AIM-95A	AGILE	7′10″		8″		2	M3
AIR-TO-SURFACE MISSILES							
AGM-12B	BULLPUP A	10′6″	3′2″	1′0″	570	8	M2+
AGM-12C	BULLPUP B	13′5″	3′8″	1′5″	1,790	10	M2+
AGM-45A	SHRIKE	10′0″	3′0″	8″	390	8+	M2+

Number	Name	OAL	Span Fins	Body Diam.	Launch Weight	Range/Miles	Max. Speed
AGM-45B	SHRIKE	10'0"	3'0"	8"	390	8+	M2+
AGM-53A	CONDOR	13'10"	4'5"	1'5"	2,104	60+	Subsonic
AGM-62A	WALLEYE I	11'4"	3'9"	1'9"	1,100	16	
AGM-78A	STANDARD ARM	15'0"	3'7"	1'1½"	1,350	35	M1+
AGM-78B	STANDARD ARM	15'0"	3'7"	1'1½"	1,350	35	M1+
AGM-78C	STANDARD ARM	15'0"	3'7"	1'1½"	1,350	35	M1+
AGM-78D	STANDARD ARM	15'0"	3'7"	1'1½"	1,350	35	M1+
AGM-83A	BULLDOG	10'6"	3'2"	1'0"	570	7+	M1+
AGM-84A	HARPOON	12'7"		1'2"	1,100	35+	
AGM-87A	FOCUS I	9'6"	3'1"	5'0"	187	15	M3
ZAGM-88A	HARM	13'0"		10"	670		

SURFACE-TO-AIR MISSILES

Number	Name	OAL	Span Fins	Body Diam.	Launch Weight	Range/Miles	Max. Speed
RIM-2D	TERRIER	26'6"	5'3"	1'1½"	3,070	20+	M2.5
RIM-2E	TERRIER	26'6"	5'3"	1'1½"	3,070	20+	M2.5
RIM-2F	TERRIER	26'6"	5'3"	1'1½"	3,070	20+	M2.5
RIM-7H	SEA SPARROW	12'0"	3'4"	8"	450	12	M2.5
RIM-8G	TALOS	33'0"	9'0"	2'6"	7,800	70+	M2.5+
RGM-8H	TALOS (ARM)	33'0"	9'0"	2'6"	7,800	70+	M2.5+
RIM-24B	TARTAR	14'10"	3'6"	1'1½"	1,425	10+	M2.5+
RIM-24C	TARTAR	14'10"	3'6"	1'1½"	1,425	10+	M2.5+
RIM-66A	STANDARD MR	14'0"	3'0"	1'1½"	1,300	12+	M2+
RIM-66B/C	STANDARD MR	14'0"	3'0"	1'1½"	1,300	12+	M2+
RIM-67A	STANDARD ER	21'0"	3'0"	1'1½"	3,000	30+	M2.5+
RGM-84A-1	HARPOON	15'0"		1'1½"	1,400	50+	

GROUND-LAUNCHED MISSILES

Number	Name	OAL	Span Fins	Body Diam.	Launch Weight	Range/Miles	Max. Speed
MIM-23A	HAWK	16'6"	3'11"	1'2"	1,295	22	M2.5
MIM-43A	REDEYE	4'2"	4"	2¾"	29*	1.0	M1+
XFIM-92A	STINGER	6'0"	6½"		30*	3.0	

SUBMARINE-BASED MISSILES

Number	Name	OAL	Span Fins	Body Diam.	Launch Weight	Range/Miles	Max. Speed
UGM-27B	POLARIS A2	31'0"	none	4'6"	30,000	1,725	M5/10
UGM-27C	POLARIS A3	32'0"	none	4'6"	35,000	2,880	M5/10
UUM-44A	SUBROC	20'6"	none	1'9"	4,000		25+
UGM-73A	POSEIDON C3	34'0"	none	6'2"	65,000	2,900+	
UGM-84A	HARPOON	15'0"		1'2"	1,400	50+	
UGM-96A	TRIDENT I C4	34'0"	none	6'2"		4,500+	
ZUGM-96B	TRIDENT II D5	45'0"	none	8'4"		6,000	

TARGET MISSILES/DRONES

Number	Name	OAL	Span Fins	Body Diam.	Launch Weight	Range/Miles	Max. Speed
BQM-34A	FIREBEE I	22'11"	12'11"	3'10"	2,500	900	M.96
BQM-34E	FIREBEE II	28'3"	9'2"	2'1"	2,350	805	M1.8
MQM-36A	(none)	13'7"	13'3"	2'7"	327	90	272
AQM-37A	(none)	13'6"	3'4"	1'1"	565	100+	M3+
AQM-38B	(none)	9'8"	5'0"	1'0"	301	30	M1+
MQM-74A	CHUKAR	11'4"	5'7"	1'3"	322	385	506
MQM-74C	CHUKAR	12'7"	5'7"	1'3"	365	640	575

UNDESIGNATED TARGETS/DRONES

Number	Name	OAL	Span Fins	Body Diam.	Launch Weight	Range/Miles	Max. Speed
	HAST	16'9"	3'4"	1'2"	1,145		M4

continued

MISSILES AND CONVENTIONAL ORDNANCE

Number	Name	OAL	Span Fins	Body Diam.	Launch Weight	Range/Miles	Max. Speed
	LAST	21'0"	9'3"	2'5"	7,800		M2.2
	GUNRUNNER	16'6"	3'6"	1'6"	235	400+	
	SHARK	14'0"	7'7"	1'3"	345		M1.2
	LOOK OUT	12'9"	14'7"	2'0"	195		83
	MINI POP	7'0"	6'0"	6"	50		
AIR-LAUNCHED ROCKETS							
XAGM-14A	ZAP	8'9"	1'2"	6"	170		
ANTISUBMARINE ROCKETS							
RUR-5A	ASROC	15'0"	2'6"	1'0"	1,000		M1
BATTLEFIELD SUPPORT ROCKETS							
MGR-1A	HONEST JOHN	27'3"	9'1"	2'6"	5,820	10	M1.5
MGR-1B	HONEST JOHN	26'0"	4'6"	2'6"	4,719	10+	M1.5
MGR-3A	LITTLE JOHN	14'5"	1'11"	1'1½"	780	10+	

* Includes launcher

ROCKET SERIES—DESIGN NUMBER AND POPULAR NAMES

No.	F/S*	Name	No.	F/S*	Name	No.	F/S*	Name	No.	F/S*	Name
1	M/A	HONEST JOHN	5	N	ASROC	9	F		13	A	none
2	F	GENIE	6	F	none	10	F		14	N	ZAP
3	M/A	LITTLE JOHN	7	F		11	F		15	A	none
4	N	WEAPON ALPHA	8	F	none	12	F		16	N	none

MISSILE SERIES—DESIGN NUMBER AND POPULAR NAMES

No.	F/S	Name	No.	F/S	Name	No.	F/S	Name	No.	F/S	Name
1	F	MATADOR	17	F	THOR	33	A/F	(drone)	49	A	NIKE ZEUS
2	N	TERRIER	18	A	LACROSSE	34	N/F	FIREBEE	50	N	TYPHON LR
3	A	NIKE AJAX	19	F	JUPITER	35	N/F	TALOS TRAINER	51	A	SHILLELAGH
4	F	FALCON	20	F	QUAIL	36	N	(drone)	52	A	LANCE
5	A	CORPORAL	21	A	SS-10	37	N	(drone)	53	N	CONDOR
6	N	REGULUS I	22	A	SS-11	38	N/F/A	(drone)	54	N	PHOENIX
7	N/F	SPARROW	23	M/A	HAWK	39	N/F/A	CARDINAL	55	N	TYPHON MR
8	N	TALOS	24	N	TARTAR	40	N	(drone)	56	N	(drone)
9	N/F	SIDEWINDER	25	F	TITAN	41	N	PETREL	57	A	(drone)
10	F/N	BOMARC	26	F	FALCON	42	A/M	REDHEAD/ROADRUNNER	58	A	OVERSEER
11	A	REDSTONE	27	N	POLARIS	43	M/A	REDEYE	59	N	(support)
12	N/F	BULLPUP	28	F	HOUND DOG	44	N	SUBROC	60	A	KINGFISHER
13	F	MACE	29	A	SERGEANT	45	N/F	SHRIKE	61	A	CARDINAL
14	A	NIKE HERCULES	30	F	MINUTEMAN	46	N/A	MAULER (SEA)	62	N	WALLEYE
15	N	REGULUS II	31	A	PERSHING	47	F	FALCON	63	N	
16	F	ATLAS	32	A	ENTAC	48	F	SKYBOLT	64	F	HORNET

No.	F/S*	Name	No.	F/S*	Name	No.	F/S*	Name	No.	F/S*	Name
65	F	MAVERICK	77	A	DRAGON	89			101	N	(RIM)
66	N	STANDARD MR	78	M/F	STANDARD ARM	90	N	(vehicle)	102	F	(drone)
67	N	STANDARD ER	79	F	BLUE EYE	91	F	(drone)	103		
68			80	F	VIPER	92	M	STINGER	104	A	SAM D
69	F	SRAM	81	F	(XAQM)	93	F	(drone)	105		
70			82	F	(ZAIM)	94	F	(vehicle)	106		
71	A	TOW	83	M	BULLDOG	95	N	AGILE	107		
72	M/A	CHAPARRAL	84	N	HARPOON	96	N	TRIDENT	108		
73	N	POSEIDON	85	N	(none assigned)	97	F	SEEKBAT	109	N	(ZBGM)
74	N	CHUKAR	86	F	SCAD	98	F	(vehicle)	110	N	(ZBGM)
75			87	N	FOCUS I	99			111		
76	F		88	N	HARM	100					

* A—Army, F—Air Force, N—Navy/Marines, M—Marines

POPULAR NAMES—CURRENT MISSILES/ROCKETS

Name	Designation	Name	Designation	Name	Designation	Name	Designation
AGILE	AIM-95	HARM	AGM-88	REDEYE	MIM-43	STINGER	FIM-92
ASROC	RUR-5	HARPOON	AGM-84	SEA SPARROW	RIM-7	SUBROC	UUM-44
BOMARC	CQM-10	HAWK	MIM-23	SHRIKE	AGM-45	TALOS	RIM-8
BULLDOG	AGM-83	HONEST JOHN	MGR-1	SIDEWINDER	AIM-9	TARTAR	RIM-24
BULLPUP	AGM-12	LITTLE JOHN	MGR-3	SPARROW	AIM-7	TERRIER	RIM-2
CHUKAR	MQM-74	PHOENIX	AIM-54	STANDARD ARM	AGM-78	TRIDENT	UGM-96
CONDOR	AGM-53	POLARIS	UGM-27	STANDARD ER	RIM-67	WALLEYE	AGM-62
FIREBEE	AQM-34	POSEIDON	UGM-73	STANDARD MR	RIM-66	ZAP	AGR-14
FOCUS I	AGM-87						

CONVENTIONAL ORDNANCE

A: Table lists gun data only. Abbreviations: AP = armor-piercing; HC = high capacity; N/A = not available.

Guns	Mark/Mod.	Gun Weight in Pounds	Barrel Length in Inches	Range in Yards	Feet Max. Altitude	Muzzle Velocity Feet/Second	Guns	Mark/Mod.	Gun Weight in Pounds	Barrel Length in Inches	Range in Yards	Feet Max. Altitude	Muzzle Velocity Feet/Second
16"/50	7/0	239,156	800.0	40.185 (AP 45° elv.)	N/A (AP proj.)	2425 (AP projectile)	8"/55	15/0	37,280	440.0	30,100 (AP 41° elv.)	24,770 (AP proj.)	2500 (AP projectile)
				41,622 (HC 45° elv.)	38,049 (HC proj.)	2690 (HC projectile)		12/1	34,147	440.0	31,350 (HC 41° elv.)	27,860 (HC proj.)	2700 (HC projectile)
8"/55	16/0	37,370	440.0	30,100 (AP 41° elv.)	24,770 (AP proj.)	2500 (AP projectile)	6"/47	16/0	9,632	282.0	26,118 (AP 47° elv.)	N/A (AP proj.)	2500 (AP projectile)
				31,350 (HC 41° elv.)	27,860 (HC proj.)	2700 (HC projectile)					22,992 (HC 45° elv.)	34,077 (HC proj.)	2590 (HC projectile)

continued

Guns	Mark/Mod.	Gun Weight in Pounds	Barrel Length in Inches	Range in Yards	Feet Max. Altitude	Muzzle Velocity Feet/Second
5"/54	18/0	5,615	270.0	25,909	48,700	2650
5"/54	16/0	5,361	270.0	25,183	48,657	2500
5"/38	12/1	3,990	190.0	17,306	32,250	2500
3"/50	21/0,2 22/0-9	1,242	150.0	14,041 (45° elv.)	29,367	2650
40mm 60 cal. (quad)	1/0	202	90.8	11,189 (40° elv.)	21,768	2800
40mm 60 cal. (twin)	1/0	202	90.8	11,189 (40° elv.)	21,633	2800

Guns	Mark/Mod.	Gun Weight in Pounds	Barrel Length in Inches	Range in Yards	Feet Max. Altitude	Muzzle Velocity Feet/Second
40mm 60 cal. (single)	1/0	202	90.8	10,850 (40° elv.)	21,633	2800
20mm 70 cal.	2/ 4/0,1	150	51.7	4,800 (35° elv.)	10,000	2730
6 pounder (saluting)	9/1	860	103.3	N/A (20°)	N/A	N/A
6 pounder (saluting)	3/0	800	108.9	N/A (20°)	N/A	N/A
40mm (saluting)	11/0	150	72.0	N/A (5°)	N/A	N/A

B: List of turrets/mounts (current).

Turrets

16"/50 Mark 7/Mod. 0, triple.   8"/55 Mark 15, 16/Mod. 0, triple.   6"/47 Mark 16/Mod. 0, triple.

Mounts

5"/54 single.   Mark 39/Mod. 0; Mark 42/Mod. 3, 4, 7/10; Mark 45/Mod. 0.
5"/38 twin, enclosed. Mark 28/Mod. 0,2; Mark 32/Mod. 0,2/4, 11/13; Mark 38/Mod. 0,1,4,11.
5"/38 single, open. Mark 24/Mod. 9, 11.
5"/38 single, enclosed. Mark 30/Mod. 6, 12, 13, 18, 19, 21, 24, 30, 31, 41/44, 60, 61, 65, 70, 71, 73, 75/77, 90, 93/95; Mark 37/Mod. 13.
3"/50 twin, open. Mark 27/Mod. 3; Mark 33/Mod. 0.
3"/50 twin enclosed. Mark 33/Mod. 12, 13.
3"/50 single, open. Mark 22/Mod. 0, 3, 4; Mark 26/Mod. 0/2; Mark 34/Mod. 0/1.
3"/50 single, enclosed. Mark 34/Mod. 2.
3"/50 single, N/A. Mark 34/Mod. 3, 5.
40mm quad. Mark 2/Mod. 10, 14, 16, 18, 20, 36.
40mm twin. Mark 1/Mod. 2, 6.
40mm single. Mark 3/Mod. 0, 4, 6; M3 (modified Army model).
20mm twin. Mark 24/Mod. 4, 5.
20mm single. Mark 10/Mod. 1, 3, 23, 29.

Saluting Guns

Six pounder. Mark 3/Mod. 0 is 45 caliber.
Six pounder. Mark 9/Mod. 1 is 42 caliber.
40mm. Mark 11/Mod. 0 is modified Mark 1.

Notes: New 8" Mark 71 lightweight gun is being tested aboard *Hull* (DD-945) mid-1975. Fully automatic mount configured to operate with Mark 86 gunfire control system. Total weight is 172,000 pounds; fires 12 rounds per minute. Designed for *Spruance* destroyers.

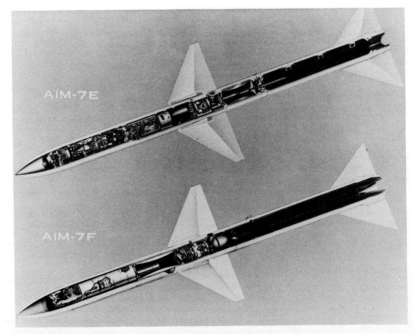

Interior views of AIM-7E and AIM-7F SPARROW missiles. 1973.

MISSILES AND CONVENTIONAL ORDNANCE

AIM-7 SPARROW III launched by PHANTOM II. 2–15–71.

AIM-54A PHOENIX launched from F-14 TOMCAT. 10–72. (Photo: Hughes Aircraft Company.)

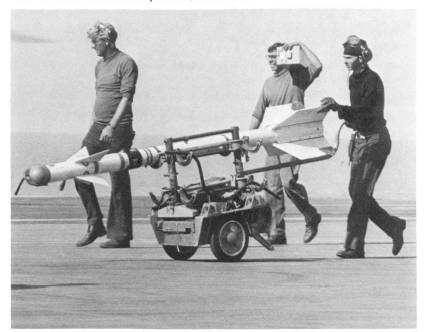

AIM-9 SIDEWINDER, deck of *Ranger* (CVA-61). 12–13–67.

AIM-54A PHOENIX with F-14 TOMCAT in background. 10–72. (Photo: Hughes Aircraft Company.)

MISSILES AND CONVENTIONAL ORDNANCE

AIM-95A AGILE mockup on A-6 INTRUDER. 11–17–70.

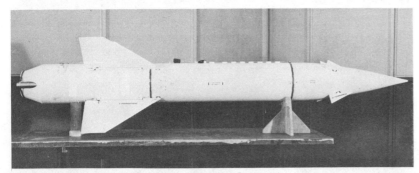

AGM-12B BULLPUP A. (Photo: Maxson Electronics Corp.)

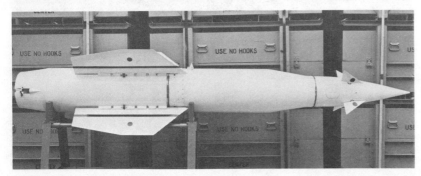

AGM-12C BULLPUP B. Note tapered nose section compared to AGM-12B. (Photo: Maxson Electronics Corp.)

BRAZO (undesignated). Nation's first air-to-air radiation missile. See addenda for data. 5–74. (Photo: Hughes Aircraft Company.)

AGM-45A SHRIKE mounted on A-7E CORSAIR II. 1972. (Photo: NWC, China Lake, California.)

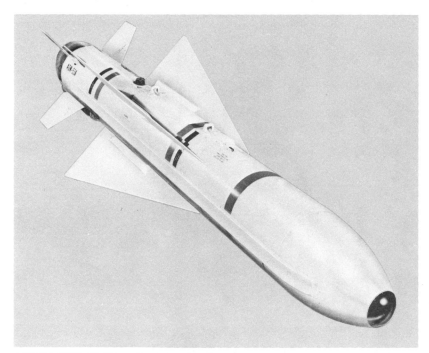

AGM-53A CONDOR. (Photo: North American Rockwell.)

AGM-62A WALLEYE I. (Photo: Martin Marietta.)

AGM-53A CONDOR attached to A-6 INTRUDER. 4–25–69. (Photo: NWC, China Lake.)

WALLEYE II. 10–13–72. (Photo: NWC, China Lake, California.)

AGM-78 STANDARD ARM. (Photo: General Dynamics, Pomona Division.)

AGM-78 STANDARD ARM aboard *Ready* (PG-87). (Photo: General Dynamics, Pomona Division.)

AGM-83A BULLDOG mounted on A-4 SKYHAWK. 3–3–71.

MISSILES AND CONVENTIONAL ORDNANCE

AGM-84A HARPOON loaded on P-3 ORION. 3–20–72.

RIM-7H SEA SPARROW launched from *Okinawa* (LPH-3). Forward fins still folded. 1–6–70.

RIM-2 TERRIER in launcher aboard *William H. Standley* (DLG-32). 2–21–72.

RIM-7H SEA SPARROW fired from *John F. Kennedy* (CV-67). 5–19–70.

RIM-8 TALOS. Undated.

RIM-24 TARTAR. (Photo: General Dynamics, Pomona Division.)

RIM-67 STANDARD ER, *Fox* (DLG-33). (Photo: General Dynamics, Pomona Division.)

MISSILES AND CONVENTIONAL ORDNANCE

RIM-66A STANDARD MR, *Buchanan* (DDG-14). 1–30–68.

RGM-84A HARPOON. Undated.

RGM-84 HARPOON. 9–1–72. (Photo: NWC, Point Mugu, California.)

MISSILES AND CONVENTIONAL ORDNANCE

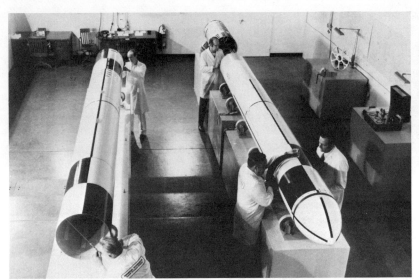

ZBGM-109 sub-launched cruise missile. (Photo: General Dynamics, Convair Division.)

MIM-23A HAWK with launcher. 4–2–73. (Photo: USMC.)

UUM-44A SUBROC. Undated.

MISSILES AND CONVENTIONAL ORDNANCE

MIM-43A REDEYE and launcher. 1967. (Photo: General Dynamics, Pomona Division.)

XFIM-92A STINGER, advanced version of REDEYE. (Photo: General Dynamics, Pomona Division.)

UGM-27C POLARIS A-3. Undated.

MISSILES AND CONVENTIONAL ORDNANCE

UGM-73A POSEIDON C-3, sequence views. 8–16–71.

BQM-34A FIREBEE I. Note wing-mounted towbees. (Photo: Teledyne Ryan Aeronautical.)

MQM-36A. (Photo: Northrop Ventura.)

MISSILES AND CONVENTIONAL ORDNANCE

BQM-34 FIREBEE II launched from DC-130 HERCULES. (Photo: Teledyne Ryan Aeronautical.)

AQM-37A. 1967. (Photo: Beech Aircraft Corporation.)

MQM-74A CHUKAR, San Clemente Island. (Photo: R. L. Lawson.)

MQM-74C CHUKAR. (Photo: Northrop Ventura.)

GUNRUNNER, ballistic missile target. (Photo: Celesco Industries, Inc.)

QH-50 DASH, in better days. 1963.

RUR-5A. ASROC fired from *Brooke* (DEG-1). 1969.

MGR-1 HONEST JOHN launched. 1970. (Photo: McDonnell Douglas.)

RUR-5A ASROC with nuclear warhead, fired from *Agerholm* (DD-826), explodes underwater. 1970.

MISSILES AND CONVENTIONAL ORDNANCE

TWELVE: FOREIGN TRANSFERS

This section comprises a list of ships and craft, arranged alphabetically by classification, transferred to foreign countries since 1 July 1971. All transfers, except where noted, were accomplished under the International Logistics Program (formerly the Military Defense Assistance Pact). The seven methods of transfer are as follows:

SALE—The recipient buys the vessel(s) and receives the title(s). Most all ship sales usually fall in this category.

SALE (B)—The recipient contracts with a U.S. firm for the construction of a ship(s). In some cases the U.S. pays part of the costs as an ILP commitment. However, the U.S. always provides technical assistance and/or equipment. USN hull numbers are assigned for accounting purposes.

LOAN—Vessel(s) is loaned to recipient. USN retains title; recipient pays operating and maintenance costs.

GRANT AID—The recipient receives the vessel(s) in lieu of a grant of money. U.S. does not retain title, but pays for activation (if needed), modernization, and all other costs to make the vessel(s) suitable for transfer. After the transfer, the recipient country assumes all costs.

LEASE—Similar to a loan, only the navy of the recipient country, rather than its government, makes the request to lease a vessel(s) directly to the U.S. Navy rather than to the U.S. government.

OFF-SHORE PROCUREMENT (OSP)—Vessel(s) are built in a foreign yard (usually in a yard in country of the recipient) and the U.S. pays half the costs of construction and/or provides equipment and technical assistance. U.S. Navy hull numbers are assigned for accounting purposes.

SPECIAL—Vessel(s) transferred under methods other than the six listed above will be listed in the "Mode" column as *Special*.

Currently, it is the policy of the U.S. Navy, whenever possible, to sell ships and craft rather than lease or loan them. Congress originally did not have the power to approve or disapprove of the sale of former U.S. Navy ships to foreign countries. However, under a law that became effective on 5 August 1974 this "loophole" was plugged. In essence the law states the following: ". . . no naval vessels in excess of 2,000 tons or less than 20 years of age may be sold, leased, granted, loaned, bartered, transferred or otherwise disposed of to another nation unless the disposition thereof has been approved by law enacted after such date of enact-ment." Further, "after the date of enactment . . . any naval vessel not subject to the provisions of paragraph (1) [preceding sentence] may be sold, leased, granted, loaned, bartered, transferred or otherwise disposed of to another nation in accordance with applicable provisions of law only after the Secretary of the Navy, or his designee, has notified the committees on armed services of the Senate and the House of Representatives in writing of the proposed disposition and 30 days of continuous session of Congress have expired following the date on which notice was transmitted to such committees. . . ." Finally, "the effect of the Byrd Amendment will be to reduce the Administration's flexibility in administering the ship transfer program, particularly with regard to 'Hot Ship Transfers.' We intend to continue the policy of selling ships now on loan/lease status as existing agreements expire. The Byrd Amendment is not expected to affect the substance of this policy, but will require planning for such sales to begin well in advance of the anticipated sale date." The sale of vessels and craft to foreign countries works to the advantage of the recipient country. Until recently, most ships were either loaned or leased. Under these two methods of transfer the U.S. could recall the vessel for use by the U.S. Navy in cases of national emergency. As a result, the recipient would spend only enough money to keep the ship operating. However, under a sales agreement, the recipient receives the ship outright and can do anything it wants with it. It should be pointed out that the chance of a country being asked to return a ship is virtually nonexistent unless the U.S. goes to war. However, the possibility is there and to most recipients this is enough to prevent expenditures for improvement or modernization of the vessel.

Notes: In the following list double entries appear for certain ships. In these cases, the first entry gives the date the ship was transferred to the recipient country. Then, if the ship was sold to the recipient country (since 1 July 1971), the second entry gives the date it was sold. If the foreign name appears in the "Foreign Name and Hull Number" column of the second entry, the ship was sold to the recipient for further service. If the comment "(For cannibalization and scrapping)" appears in the same column of the second entry, the ship in question was sold to the country as a source of spare parts and eventual scrapping. If an entry has no date in the "Date of Transfer" column, the ship is scheduled for transfer, but has not yet been handed over to the recipient. Finally, if there is no foreign name and/or hull number in the "Foreign Name and Hull Number" column the foreign name and/or hull number is unknown as of writing.

Hull No.	Name	Date of Transfer	Recipient	Foreign Name and Hull Number	Mode
AFDL-11	Unnamed	6–20–72	Khmer Republic	DF-2	Lease
AFDL-22	Unnamed	9–30–71	South Vietnam	HQ-9604	Lease

Hull No.	Name	Date of Transfer	Recipient	Foreign Name and Hull Number	Mode
AFDL-28	Unnamed	1-23-73	Mexico		Sale
AGOR-1	*Josiah Willard Gibbs*	12-7-71	Greece	*Hephaístos* (A-413)	Lease
AGOR-6	*Sands*	7-1-74	Brazil	*Almirante Camara* (H-41)	Lease
AGOR-8	*Eltanin*	2-19-74	Argentina	*Islas Orcades* (Q-9)	Lease
AGP-838	*Hunterdon County*	7-1-71	Malaysia	*Sri Langkawi* (A-1500)	Lease
AGP-838	*Hunterdon County*	8-1-74	Malaysia	*Sri Langkawi* (A-1500)	Sale
AGS-25	*Kellar*	1-21-72	Portugal	*Commandante Almeida Carvalho* (A-527)	Lease
AGS-35	*Sgt. George D. Keathley*	3-29-72	Taiwan	*Chu Hwa* (AGS-564)	Lease
AKA-91	*Whitley*	2- -62	Italy	*Etna* (A-5328)	Lease
AKA-91	*Whitley*	2-23-74	Italy	*Etna* (L-9870)	Sale
AKL-10	*Sharps*	4- -56	South Korea	*Kun San* (AKL-908)	Loan
AKL-10	*Sharps*	11-15-74	South Korea	*Kun San* (AKL-908)	Sale
AKL-12	*Mark*	7-1-71	Taiwan	*Yung Kang* (AKL-514)	Lease
AKL-28	*Brule*	11-1-71	South Korea	*Ulsan* (AKL-910)	Lease
AKL-28	*Brule*	11-15-74	South Korea	*Ulsan* (AKL-910)	Sale
AKL-35	Unnamed	9- -56	South Korea	*Ma San* (AKL-909)	Loan
AKL-35	Unnamed	11-15-74	South Korea	*Ma San* (AKL-909)	Sale
AO-132	*Mission Santa Clara*	1-17-63	Pakistan	*Dacca* (A-41)	Loan
AO-132	*Mission Santa Clara*	5-31-74	Pakistan	*Dacca* (A-41)	Sale
AOG-7	*Elkhorn*	7-1-72	Taiwan	*Hsing Lung* (AOG-517)	Lease
AOG-8	*Genesee*	7-5-72	Chile	*Beagle* (AOG-54)	Lease
AOG-11	*Tombigbee*	7-7-72	Greece	*Ariadni* (A-414)	Lease
APD-128	*Cavallaro*	10-15-59	South Korea	*Kyong Nam* (APD-81)	Loan
APD-128	*Cavallaro*	11-15-74	South Korea	*Kyong Nam* (APD-81)	Sale
APL-26	Unnamed	3- -71	South Vietnam	HQ-9050	Special
APL-27	Unnamed	3- -71	South Vietnam	HQ-9051	Special
APL-47	Unnamed	12-1-71	Turkey	*Denizal Ti Barci* (Y-1204)	Lease
APL-53	Unnamed	12-6-74	Turkey		Loan
AR-13	*Amphion*	10-1-71	Iran	*Chah Bahar* (A-41)	Lease
AR-14	*Cadmus*	1-31-74	Taiwan	*Yu Tai* (AR-521)	Sale
ARD-11	Unnamed	6-17-74	Mexico		Sale
ARD-12	Unnamed	11-18-71	Turkey	*Havuz #7* (Y-1087)	Lease
ARD-25	Unnamed	8-20-73	Chile	*Ingeniero Mery* (ARD-131)	Sale
ARD-29	*Arco*	11-1-71	Iran	FD-4	Lease
ARG-4	*Tutuila*	2-21-72	Taiwan	*Pien Tai* (ARG-516)	Sale
ARL-23	*Satyr*	9-30-71	South Vietnam	*Vinh Long* (HQ-802)	Loan
ARL-30	*Askari*	8-31-71	Indonesia	*Djaja Widjaja* (9017)	Lease
ARL-38	*Krishna*	10-30-71	Philippines	*Narra* (AR-88)	Lease
ARVA-6	*Megara*	10-1-73	Mexico	*General Vicinte Guerrero* (IA-05)	Sale
ASR-10	*Greenlet*	6-12-70	Turkey	*Akin* (A-585)	Lease
ASR-10	*Greenlet*	2-15-73	Turkey	*Akin* (A-585)	Sale
ASR-20	*Skylark*	6-30-73	Brazil	*Gastao Moutinho* (R-60)	Sale
ATA-184	*Kalmia*	7-1-71	Columbia	*Bahia Utria* (RM-75)	Lease
ATA-186	*Cahokia*	4-14-72	Taiwan	*Ta An* (ATA-550)	Lease
ATA-187	*Salish*	2-10-72	Argentina[1]	*Alfrez Sobral* (A-9)	Lease
ATA-187	*Salish*	-75	Argentina[1]	*Alfrez Sobral* (A-9)	Sale
ATA-192	*Tillamook*	8-9-71	South Korea[2]	*Tan Yung*	Lease
ATA-196	*Mahopac*	7-1-71	Taiwan	*Ta Peng* (ATA-549)	Lease
ATA-208	*Sagamore*	2-1-72	Dom. Republic	*Caomabo* (RM-18)	Lease

continued

Hull No.	Name	Date of Transfer	Recipient	Foreign Name and Hull Number	Mode
ATA-209	*Umpqua*	7–1–71	Columbia	*Bahia Honda (RM-74)*	Lease
ATA-210	*Catawba*	2–10–72	Argentina[1]	*Commodore Somellera (A-10)*	Lease
ATA-210	*Catawba*	–75	Argentina[1]	*Commodore Somellera (A-10)*	Sale
ATF-67	*Apache*	6–30–74	Taiwan	*ATF-551*	Sale
ATF-72	*Kiowa*	10–16–72	Dom. Republic	*Macorix (RM-21)*	Lease
ATF-75	*Sioux*	10–30–72	Turkey	*Gazal (A-587)*	Lease
ATF-75	*Sioux*	8–15–73	Turkey	*Gazal (A-587)*	Sale
ATF-90	*Pinto*	12–31–60	Peru	*Rios (123)*	Loan
ATF-90	*Pinto*	5–17–74	Peru	*Rios (123)*	Sale
ATF-98	*Arikara*	7–1–71	Chile	*Sargento Aldea (ATF-63)*	Lease
ATF-163	*Utina*	9–3–71	Venezuela	*Felipe Larrazabal (R-21)*	Lease
AVT-3	*Cabot*	8–30–67	Spain	*Dedalo (PH-01)*	Loan
AVT-3	*Cabot*	12–5–72	Spain	*Dedalo (PH-01)*	Sale
DD-421	*Benson*	2–26–54	Taiwan	*Lo Yang (DD-14)*	Loan
DD-421	*Benson*	11–1–74	Taiwan	(For cannibalization and scrapping)	Sale
DD-427	*Hilary P. Jones*	2–26–54	Taiwan	*Han Yang (DD-15)*	Loan
DD-427	*Hilary P. Jones*	11–1–74	Taiwan	(For cannibalization and scrapping)	Sale
DD-431	*Plunkett*	2–16–59	Taiwan	*Nan Yang (DD-17)*	Loan
DD-431	*Plunkett*	11–1–74	Taiwan	(For cannibalization and scrapping)	Sale
DD-448	*La Vallette*	7–26–74	Peru	(For cannibalization and scrapping)	Sale
DD-472	*Guest*	6–5–59	Brazil	*Para (D-27)*	Loan
DD-472	*Guest*	8–1–73	Brazil	*Para (D-27)*	Sale
DD-473	*Bennett*	12–15–59	Brazil	*Paraiba (D-28)*	Loan
DD-473	*Bennett*	8–1–73	Brazil	*Paraiba (D-28)*	Sale
DD-500	*Ringgold*	7–14–59	Germany	*Z-2 (D-171)*	Loan
DD-500	*Ringgold*	–74	Germany	*Z-2 (D-171)*	Sale
DD-509	*Converse*	7–1–59	Spain	*Almirante Valdes (D-23)*	Loan
DD-509	*Converse*	10–1–72	Spain	*Almirante Valdes (D-23)*	Sale
DD-513	*Terry*	7–26–74	Peru	(For cannibalization and scrapping)	Sale
DD-515	*Anthony*	1–17–58	Germany	*Z-1 (D-170)*	Loan
DD-515	*Anthony*	6–27–72	Germany	(For cannibalization and scrapping)	Sale
DD-516	*Wadsworth*	10–6–59	Germany	*Z-3 (D-172)*	Loan
DD-516	*Wadsworth*	–74	Germany	*Z-3 (D-172)*	Sale
DD-520	*Isherwood*	10–8–61	Peru	*Guise (DD-72)*	Loan
DD-520	*Isherwood*	1–15–74	Peru	*Guise (DD-72)*	Sale
DD-521	*Kimberly*	6–1–67	Taiwan	*An Yang (DD-18)*	Loan
DD-521	*Kimberly*	1–25–74	Taiwan	*An Yang (DD-18)*	Sale
DD-528	*Mullany*	10–6–71	Taiwan	*Ching Yang (DD-9)*	Sale
DD-540	*Twining*	8–16–71	Taiwan	*Kwei Yang (DD-8)*	Sale
DD-541	*Yarnall*	6–10–68	Taiwan	*Kun Yang (DD-19)*	Loan
DD-541	*Yarnall*	1–25–74	Taiwan	*Kun Yang (DD-19)*	Sale
DD-547	*Cowell*	8–17–71	Argentina	*Almirante Storni (D-24)*	Sale
DD-550	*Capps*	5–15–57	Spain	*Lepanto (D-21)*	Loan
DD-550	*Capps*	10–1–72	Spain	*Lepanto (D-21)*	Sale
DD-551	*David W. Taylor*	5–15–57	Spain	*Almirante Ferrandiz (D-22)*	Loan
DD-551	*David W. Taylor*	10–1–72	Spain	*Almirante Ferrandiz (D-22)*	Sale
DD-556	*Hailey*	7–20–61	Brazil	*Pernambuco (D-30)*	Loan
DD-556	*Hailey*	8–1–73	Brazil	*Pernambuco (D-30)*	Sale
DD-571	*Claxton*	12–15–59	Germany	*Z-4 (D-178)*	Loan
DD-571	*Claxton*	–75	Germany	*Z-4 (D-178)*	Sale

Hull No.	Name	Date of Transfer	Recipient	Foreign Name and Hull Number	Mode
DD-572	*Dyson*	2–23–60	Germany	*Z-5* (D-179)	Loan
DD-572	*Dyson*	–75	Germany	*Z-5* (D-179)	Sale
DD-596	*Shields*	7–1–72	Brazil	*Maranhao* (D-33)	Sale
DD-630	*Braine*	8–17–71	Argentina	*Almirante Domecq Garcia* (D-25)	Sale
DD-656	*Van Valkenburg*	2–28–67	Turkey	*Izmir* (D-341)	Loan
DD-656	*Van Valkenburg*	2–15–73	Turkey	(For cannibalization and scrapping)	Sale
DD-657	*Charles J. Badger*	5–17–74	Chile	(For cannibalization and scrapping)	Sale
DD-663	*Heywood L. Edwards*	3–10–59	Japan	*Ariake* (DD-183) (Returned 3–9–74)	Loan
DD-663	*Heywood L. Edwards*	–75	South Korea	(For cannibalization and scrapping)	Sale
DD-664	*Richard P. Leary*	3–10–59	Japan	*Yugure* (DD-184) (Returned 3–9–74)	Loan
DD-664	*Richard P. Leary*	–75	South Korea	(For cannibalization and scrapping)	Sale
DD-668	*Clarence K. Bronson*	1–14–67	Turkey	*Istanbul* (D-340)	Loan
DD-668	*Clarence K. Bronson*	2–15–73	Turkey	(For cannibalization and scrapping)	Sale
DD-675	*Lewis Hancock*	8–2–67	Brazil	*Piaui* (D-31)	Loan
DD-675	*Lewis Hancock*	4–11–73	Brazil	(For cannibalization and scrapping)	Sale
DD-678	*McGowan*	11–30–60	Spain	*Jorge Juan* (D-25)	Loan
DD-678	*McGowan*	10–1–72	Spain	*Jorge Juan* (D-25)	Sale
DD-694	*Ingraham*	7–16–71	Greece	*Miaoulis* (D-211)	Sale
DD-697	*Charles S. Sperry*	1–8–74	Chile	*Ministro Zenteno* (DD-16)	Sale
DD-699	*Waldron*	10–30–73	Columbia	*Santander* (D-03)	Sale
DD-702	*Hank*	7–1–72	Argentina	*Segui* (D-25)	Sale
DD-703	*Wallace L. Lind*	12–4–73	South Korea	*Dae Gu* (DD-97)	Sale
DD-704	*Borie*	7–1–72	Argentina	*Bouchard* (D-26)	Sale
DD-705	*Compton*	9–27–72	Brazil	*Mato Grosso* (D-34)	Sale
DD-709	*Hugh Purvis*	7–1–72	Turkey	*Zafer* (D-356)	Lease
DD-709	*Hugh Purvis*	2–15–73	Turkey	*Zafer* (D-356)	Sale
DD-711	*Eugene A. Greene*	8–31–72	Spain	*Churruca* (D-61)	Loan
DD-713	*Kenneth D. Bailey*	1–13–75	Iran	(For cannibalization and scrapping)	Sale
DD-727	*De Haven*	12–5–73	South Korea	*In Cheon* (DD-98)	Sale
DD-728	*Mansfield*	6–4–74	Argentina	(For cannibalization and scrapping)	Sale
DD-729	*Lyman K. Swenson*	5–6–74	Taiwan	(For cannibalization and scrapping)	Sale
DD-730	*Collett*	6–4–74	Argentina	(For cannibalization and scrapping)	Sale
DD-731	*Maddox*	7–6–72	Taiwan	*Po Yang* (DD-10)	Sale
DD-746	*Taussig*	5–6–74	Taiwan	*Lo Yang* (DD-14)	Sale
DD-755	*John A. Bole*	5–6–74	Taiwan	(For cannibalization and scrapping)	Sale
DD-756	*Beatty*	7–14–72	Venezuela	*Carabobo* (D-41)	Sale
DD-758	*Strong*	10–31–73	Brazil	*Rio Grande Do Norte* (D-37)	Sale
DD-759	*Lofberg*	5–6–74	Taiwan	(For cannibalization and scrapping)	Sale
DD-760	*John W. Thomason*	5–6–74	Taiwan	*Nan Yang* (DD-17)	Sale
DD-761	*Buck*	7–16–73	Brazil	*Alagoas* (D-36)	Sale
DD-764	*Lloyd Thomas*	10–12–72	Taiwan	*Dang Yang* (D-11)	Sale
DD-765	*Keppler*	7–1–72	Turkey	*Tinaztepe* (D-355)	Sale
DD-770	*Lowry*	10–29–73	Brazil	*Espirito Santo* (D-38)	Sale
DD-775	*Willard Keith*	7–1–72	Columbia	*Caldas* (D-41)	Sale
DD-776	*James C. Owens*	7–16–73	Brazil	*Sergipe* (D-35)	Sale
DD-779	*Douglas H. Fox*	1–8–74	Chile	*Ministro Portales* (DD-17)	Sale
DD-780	*Stormes*	2–16–72	Iran	*Palang* (D-9)	Sale
DD-781	*Robert K. Huntington*	10–31–73	Venezuela	*Falcon* (D-51)	Sale
DD-787	*James E. Kyes*	4–18–73	Taiwan	*Chien Yang* (DD-12)	Sale

continued

Hull No.	Name	Date of Transfer	Recipient	Foreign Name and Hull Number	Mode
DD-789	*Eversole*	7–11–73	Turkey	*Gayret* (D-352)	Sale
DD-790	*Shelton*	4–18–73	Taiwan	*Lao Yang* (DD-20)	Sale
DD-794	*Irwin*	5–10–68	Brazil	*Santa Catarina* (D-32)	Loan
DD-794	*Irwin*	4–11–73	Brazil	(For cannibalization and scrapping)	Sale
DD-796	*Benham*	12–15–60	Peru	*Villar* (DD-71)	Loan
DD-796	*Benham*	1–15–74	Peru	*Villar* (DD-71)	Sale
DD-797	*Cushing*	7–20–61	Brazil	*Parana* (D-29)	Loan
DD-797	*Cushing*	8–1–73	Brazil	*Parana* (D-29)	Sale
DD-799	*Jarvis*	11–3–60	Spain	*Alcala Galiano* (D-24)	Loan
DD-799	*Jarvis*	10–1–72	Spain	*Alcala Galiano* (D-24)	Sale
DD-805	*Chevalier*	7–5–72	South Korea	*Chung Buk* (DD-95)	Lease
DD-830	*Everett F. Larson*	10–30–72	South Korea	*Jeon Buk* (DD-96)	Loan
DD-831	*Goodrich*	–75	Venezuela	(For cannibalization and scrapping)	Sale
DD-832	*Hanson*	4–18–73	Taiwan	*Liao Yang* (DD-21)	Sale
DD-833	*Herbert J. Thomas*	5–6–74	Taiwan	*Han Yang* (DD-15)	Sale
DD-841	*Noa*	10–31–73	Spain	*Blas De Lezo* (D-65)	Loan
DD-843	*Warrington*	4–24–73	Taiwan	(For cannibalization of bow and scrapping of the remainder)	Sale
DD-851	*Rupertus*	7–10–73	Greece	*Kountouriotis* (D-213)	Sale
DD-853	*Charles H. Roan*	9–21–73	Turkey	*M. F. Cakmak* (D-351)	Sale
DD-859	*Norris*	7–7–74	Turkey	*Kocatepe* (D-354)	Sale
DD-861	*Harwood*	12–17–71	Turkey	*Kocatepe* (D-354)	Loan
DD-861	*Harwood*	2–15–73	Turkey	*Kocatepe* (D-354)	Sale
DD-869	*Arnold J. Isbell*	12–4–73	Greece	*Sachtouris* (D-214)	Loan
DD-869	*Arnold J. Isbell*	2–1–74	Greece	(Sale of ship cancelled 1–74. Remains on loan)	Sale
DD-872	*Forrest Royal*	3–27–71	Turkey	*Adatepe* (D-353)	Loan
DD-872	*Forrest Royal*	2–15–73	Turkey	*Adatepe* (D-353)	Sale
DD-875	*Henry W. Tucker*	12–3–73	Brazil	*Marcilio Dias* (D-25)	Sale
DD-877	*Perkins*	1–15–73	Argentina	*Py* (D-27)	Sale
DD-879	*Leary*	10–31–73	Spain	*Langara* (D-64)	Loan
DD-882	*Furse*	8–31–72	Spain	*Gravina* (D-62)	Loan
DD-887	*Brinkley Bass*	12–3–73	Brazil	*Mariz E. Barros* (D-26)	Sale
DD-888	*Stickell*	7–1–72	Greece	*Kanaris* (D-212)	Sale
DD-889	*O'Hare*	10–31–73	Spain	*Mendez Nunez* (D-63)	Loan
DE-250	*Hurst*	10–1–73	Mexico	*Commodore Manuel Azueta* (IA-06)	Sale
DE-579	*Riley*	7–10–68	Taiwan	*Tai Yuan* (DE-27)	Loan
DE-579	*Riley*	1–25–74	Taiwan	*Tai Yuan* (DE-27)	Sale
DE-706	*Holt*	6–19–63	South Korea	*Chung Nam* (DE-73)	Loan
DE-706	*Holt*	11–15–74	South Korea	*Chung Nam* (DE-73)	Sale
DE-746	*Hemminger*	7–22–59	Thailand	*Pin Klao* (DE-1)	Loan
DE-746	*Hemminger*	–75	Thailand	*Pin Klao* (DE-3)	Sale
DE-770	*Muir*	2–2–56	South Korea	*Kyong Ki* (DE-71)	Loan
DE-770	*Muir*	11–15–74	South Korea	*Kyong Ki* (DE-71)	Sale
DE-771	*Sutton*	2–2–56	South Korea	*Kang Won* (DE-72)	Loan
DE-771	*Sutton*	11–15–74	South Korea	*Kang Won* (DE-72)	Sale
DE-1006	*Dealey*	7–28–72	Uruguay	*18 De Julio* (DE-3)	Sale
DE-1029	*Hartley*	7–8–72	Columbia	*Boyaca* (DE-16)	Sale
DE-1033	*Claud Jones*	12–16–74	Indonesia	*Mongisidi* (343)	Sale
DE-1034	*John R. Perry*	2–20–73	Indonesia	*Samadikun* (341)	Sale
DE-1035	*Charles Berry*	1–31–74	Indonesia	*Martadainata* (342)	Sale
DE-1036	*McMorris*	12–16–74	Indonesia	*Ngurah Rai* (344)	Sale

Hull No.	Name	Date of Transfer	Recipient	Foreign Name and Hull Number	Mode
DEG-7	Unnamed	9–24–73	Spain	*Baleares* (F-71)	OSP
DEG-8	Unnamed	6– –74	Spain	*Andalucia* (F-72)	OSP
DEG-9	Unnamed	1– –75[3]	Spain	*Cataluna* (F-73)	OSP
DER-326	*Thomas J. Gary*	10–22–73	Tunisia	*President Bourguiba* (E-7)	Sale
FFR-334	*Forester*	9–25–71	South Vietnam	*Tran Khanh Du* (HQ-04)	Loan
IX-311	*Benewah*	5–22–74	Philippines[4]		Grant Aid
LCU-1471	Unnamed	6–28–72	Spain		Lease
LCU-1481	Unnamed	1– –72	South Vietnam	HQ-547	Special
LCU-1491	Unnamed	6–28–72	Spain		Lease
LCU-1498	Unnamed	1– –72	South Vietnam	HQ-548	Special
LSD-13	*Casa Grande*	–75	Israel	(For use as ARD for *Saar* class PTFGs)	Sale
LSD-22	*Fort Marion*	–75	Taiwan		Sale
LSD-25	*San Marcos*	7–1–71	Spain	*Galicia* (TA-31)	Lease
LSD-25	*San Marcos*	8–1–74	Spain	*Galicia* (TA-31)	Sale
LSM-17	Unnamed	10– –56	South Korea	*Ul Rung* (LSM-613)	Loan
LSM-17	Unnamed	11–15–74	South Korea	*Ul Rung* (LSM-613)	Sale
LSM-19	Unnamed	7– –56	South Korea	*Ki Rin* (LSM-610)	Loan
LSM-19	Unnamed	11–15–74	South Korea	*Ki Rin* (LSM-610)	Sale
LSM-30	Unnamed	4– –56	South Korea	*Ko Mun* (LSM-606)	Loan
LSM-30	Unnamed	11–15–74	South Korea	*Ko Mun* (LSM-606)	Sale
LSM-54	Unnamed	5– –56	South Korea	*Pung To* (LSM-608)	Loan
LSM-54	Unnamed	11–15–74	South Korea	*Pung To* (LSM-608)	Sale
LSM-57	Unnamed	5– –56	South Korea	*Wol Mi* (LSM-609)	Loan
LSM-57	Unnamed	11–15–74	South Korea	*Wol Mi* (LSM-609)	Sale
LSM-84	Unnamed	7– –56	South Korea	*Nung Ra* (LSM-611)	Loan
LSM-84	Unnamed	11–15–74	South Korea	*Nung Ra* (LSM-611)	Sale
LSM-96	Unnamed	4– –56	South Korea	*Pian* (LSM-607)	Loan
LSM-96	Unnamed	11–15–74	South Korea	*Pian* (LSM-607)	Sale
LSM-268	Unnamed	2–16–55	South Korea	*Tyo To* (LSM-602)	Loan
LSM-268	Unnamed	11–15–74	South Korea	*Tyo To* (LSM-602)	Sale
LSM-316	Unnamed	10– –56	South Korea	*Sin Mi* (LSM-612)	Loan
LSM-316	Unnamed	11–15–74	South Korea	*Sin Mi* (LSM-612)	Sale
LSM-462	Unnamed	2–16–55	South Korea	*Ka Tok* (LSM-605)	Loan
LSM-462	Unnamed	11–15–74	South Korea	*Ka Tok* (LSM-605)	Sale
LSM-546	Unnamed	2–16–55	South Korea	*Tae Cho* (LSM-601)	Loan
LSM-546	Unnamed	11–15–74	South Korea	*Tae Cho* (LSM-601)	Sale
LST-117	USNS LST-117	6–27–74	Singapore		Sale
LST-218	Unnamed	5–3–55	South Korea	*Bi Bong* (LST-809)	Loan
LST-218	Unnamed	11–15–74	South Korea	*Bi Bong* (LST-809)	Sale
LST-222	USNS LST-222	7–15–72	Philippines	*Mindoro Occidental* (LT-93)	Lease
LST-227	Unnamed	3–29–55	South Korea	*Duk Bong* (LST-808)	Loan
LST-227	Unnamed	11–15–74	South Korea	*Duk Bong* (LST-808)	Sale
LST-276	USNS LST-276	6–27–74	Singapore		Sale
LST-277	USNS LST-277	2–2–73	Chile	*Commandante Toro* (LST-97)	Sale
LST-288	*Berkshire County*	3– –56	South Korea	*Kae Bong* (LST-810)	Loan
LST-288	*Berkshire County*	11–15–74	South Korea	*Kae Bong* (LST-810)	Sale
LST-488	USNS LST-488	7–15–72	Philippines	*Suriago Del Norte* (LT-94)	Lease
LST-532	USNS *Chase County*	6–27–74	Singapore		Sale
LST-546	USNS LST-546	7–15–72	Philippines	*Suriago Del Sur* (LT-95)	Lease

continued

Hull No.	Name	Date of Transfer	Recipient	Foreign Name and Hull Number	Mode
LST-602	USNS *Clearwater County*	5-30-72	Mexico	*Manzanillo* (IA-02)	Sale
LST-735	*Dukes County*	5- -57	Taiwan	*Chung Hsi* (LST-219)	Loan
LST-735	*Dukes County*	11-1-74	Taiwan	*Kaoshiung* (AGC-1)	Sale
LST-836	*Holmes County*	7-1-71	Singapore	*Endurance* (A-82)	Lease
LST-1010	Unnamed	3-22-55	South Korea	*Un Pong* (LST-807)	Loan
LST-1010	Unnamed	11-15-74	South Korea	*Un Pong* (LST-807)	Sale
LST-1066	USNS *New London County*	8-29-73	Chile	*Commandante Hemmerdinger* (LST-88)	Sale
LST-1067	USNS *Nye County*	8-29-73	Chile	*Commandante Araya* (LST-89)	Sale
LST-1073	*Outagamie County*	5-21-71	Brazil	*Garcia D'Avila* (G-28)	Lease
LST-1073	*Outagamie County*	12-1-73	Brazil	*Garcia D'Avila* (G-28)	Sale
LST-1077	*Park County*	9-20-71	Mexico	*Rio Panuco* (IA-01)	Sale
LST-1141	*Stone County*	3-12-70	Thailand	*Lanta* (LST-4)	Lease
LST-1141	*Stone County*	3-20-74	Thailand	*Lanta* (LST-4)	Lease (renewed)
LST-1156	*Terrebonne Parish*	10-29-71	Spain	*Velasco* (L-11)	Lease
LST-1159	*Tom Green County*	1-5-72	Spain	*Conde Del Venadito* (L-13)	Lease
LST-1161	*Vernon County*	6-29-73	Venezuela	*Amazonas* (T-21)	Loan
LST-1167	*Westchester County*	8-27-74	Turkey	*Serdar* (L-402)	Loan
LST-1168	*Wexford County*	10-29-71	Spain	*Martin Alvarez* (L-12)	Lease
LST-1170	*Windham County*	6-1-73	Turkey	*Ertugrul* (L-401)	Loan
LST-1171	*De Soto County*	7-17-72	Italy	*Grado* (L-9890)	Lease
LST-1174	*Grant County*	1-15-73	Brazil	*Duque De Caxias* (G-26)	Lease
LST-1175	*York County*	7-17-72	Italy	*Caorle* (L-9891)	Lease
MMD-33	*Gwin*	10-22-71	Turkey	*Muavenet* (DM-357)	Sale
MSC-121	*Bluebird*	-75	Thailand		Sale
MSC-191	*Frigate Bird*	8-11-71	Indonesia	*Pulau Antung* (721)	Lease
MSC-196	*Hummingbird*	7-12-71	Indonesia	*Pulau Ampalasa* (720)	Lease
MSCO-8	*Curlew*	1-6-56	South Korea	*Kum Hwa* (MSCO-519)	Loan
MSCO-8	*Curlew*	11-15-74	South Korea	*Kum Hwa* (MSCO-519)	Sale
MSCO-22	*Kite*	1-6-56	South Korea	*Kim Po* (MSCO-520)	Loan
MSCO-22	*Kite*	11-15-74	South Korea	*Kim Po* (MSCO-520)	Sale
MSCO-27	*Mockingbird*	1-6-56	South Korea	*Ko Chang* (MSCO-521)	Loan
MSCO-27	*Mockingbird*	11-15-74	South Korea	*Ko Chang* (MSCO-521)	Sale
MSF-64	*Starling*	2-16-73	Mexico	*Valentin Gomez Farias* (IG-11)	Sale
MSF-101	*Herald*	4-11-73	Mexico	*Mariano Matamores* (IG-17)	Sale
MSF-104	*Pilot*	4-11-73	Mexico	*Juan Aldama* (IG-18)	Sale
MSF-105	*Pioneer*	9-19-72	Mexico	*Leandro Valle* (IG-01)	Sale
MSF-111	*Sage*	4-11-73	Mexico	*Hermenegildo Galeana* (IG-19)	Sale
MSF-120	*Sway*	2-16-73	Mexico	*Ignacio Altamirano* (IG-12)	Sale
MSF-123	*Symbol*	9-19-72	Mexico	*Guillermo Prieto* (IG-02)	Sale
MSF-124	*Threat*	2-16-73	Mexico	*Francisco Zarco* (IG-13)	Sale
MSF-128	*Velocity*	2-16-73	Mexico	*Ignacio L. Vallarta* (IG-14)	Sale
MSF-306	*Specter*	4-11-73	Mexico	*DM-04* (ID-04)	Sale
MSF-314	*Champion*	9-19-72	Mexico	*Mariano Escobedo* (IG-03)	Sale
MSF-315	*Chief*	2-16-73	Mexico	*Jesus Gonzales Ortega* (IG-15)	Sale
MSF-316	*Competent*	9-19-72	Mexico	*Ponciano Arriaga* (IG-04)	Sale
MSF-317	*Defense*	9-19-72	Mexico	*Manual Doblado* (IG-05)	Sale
MSF-318	*Devastator*	9-19-72	Mexico	*Sebastian Lerdo De Tejada* (IG-06)	Sale
MSF-319	*Gladiator*	9-19-72	Mexico	*Santos Degollado* (IG-07)	Sale
MSF-322	*Spear*	9-19-72	Mexico	*Ignacio De La Llave* (IG-08)	Sale
MSF-340	*Ardent*	9-19-72	Mexico	*Juan N. Alvarez* (IG-09)	Sale

Hull No.	Name	Date of Transfer	Recipient	Foreign Name and Hull Number	Mode
MSF-379	Roselle	2–16–73	Mexico	Melchor Ocampo (IG-16)	Sale
MSF-380	Ruddy	11–1–60	Peru	Galvez (68)	Loan
MSF-380	Ruddy	3–1–74	Peru	Galvez (68)	Sale
MSF-381	Scoter	9–19–72	Mexico	Manuel Gutierrez Zamora (IG-10)	Sale
MSF-382	Shoveler	11–1–60	Peru	Diez Canseco (69)	Loan
MSF-382	Shoveler	5–17–74	Peru	Diez Canseco (69)	Sale
MSO-422	Aggressive	–75	Peru		Sale
MSO-424	Bold	–75	Taiwan		Sale
MSO-425	Bulwark	–75	Taiwan		Sale
MSO-432	Dynamic	7–1–71	Spain	Guadalete (M-41)	Lease
MSO-432	Dynamic	8–1–74	Spain	Guadalete (M-41)	Sale
MSO-434	Embattle	–75	Peru		Sale
MSO-436	Energy	7–5–72	Philippines	Davao Del Norte (PM-91)	Lease
MSO-444	Firm	7–5–72	Philippines	Davao Del Sur (PM-92)	Lease
MSO-463	Pivot	7–1–71	Spain	Guadalmednia (M-42)	Lease
MSO-463	Pivot	8–1–74	Spain	Guadalmednia (M-42)	Sale
MSO-466	Prime	–75	Thailand		Sale
MSO-467	Reaper	–75	Thailand		Sale
MSO-473	Vigor	4–5–72	Spain	Guadiana (M-44)	Lease
MSO-473	Vigor	8–1–74	Spain	Guadiana (M-44)	Sale
MSO-491	Persistent	7–1–71	Spain	Guadalquivir (M-43)	Lease
MSO-491	Persistent	8–1–74	Spain	Guadalquivir (M-43)	Sale
PCE-873	Unnamed	9–2–55	South Korea	Han San (PCEC-53)	Loan
PCE-873	Unnamed	11–15–74	South Korea	Han San (PCEC-53)	Sale
PCE-882	Unnamed	2–14–55	South Korea	Ro Ryang (PCEC-51)	Loan
PCE-882	Unnamed	11–15–74	South Korea	Ro Ryang (PCEC-51)	Sale
PCE-896	Unnamed	2–14–55	South Korea	Myong Ryang (PCEC-52)	Loan
PCE-896	Unnamed	11–15–74	South Korea	Myong Ryang (PCEC-52)	Sale
PCE-898	Unnamed	9–2–55	South Korea	Ok Po (PCEC-55)	Loan
PCE-898	Unnamed	11–15–74	South Korea	Ok Po (PCEC-55)	Sale
PF-3	Tacoma	10–8–51	South Korea	Tae Tong (PF-63)	Loan
PF-3	Unnamed (ex-Tacoma)	7–12–73	South Korea	(For use as naval museum and non-op. naval reserve training ship)	Sale
PF-4	Sausalito	9–3–52	South Korea	Imchin (PF-66)	Loan
PF-4	Sausalito	9–1–72	South Korea	(For cannibalization and scrapping)	Sale
PF-5	Hoquiam	10–8–51	South Korea	Naktong (PF-65)	Loan
PF-5	Hoquiam	8–1–72	South Korea	(For cannibalization and scrapping)	Sale
PF-49	Muskogee	10–23–50	South Korea	Duman (PF-61)	Loan
PF-49	Muskogee	9–15–72	South Korea	(For cannibalization and scrapping)	Sale
PF-107	Unnamed	11–13–71	Thailand	Tapi (PF-5)	Sale (B)
PF-108	Unnamed	8–10–74	Thailand	Khirirat (PF-6)	Sale (B)
PG-95	Defiance	6–11–73	Turkey	Yildirim (P-338)	Loan
PG-96	Benicia	10–15–71	South Korea	Paekku (PGM-11)	Lease
PG-97	Surprise	2–28–73	Turkey	Bora (P-339)	Loan
PGM-79	Unnamed	11– –66	Thailand	T-12	Loan
PGM-79	Unnamed	10–3–71	Thailand	T-12	Grant Aid
PGM-111	Unnamed	6–30–72	Peru	Rio Chira (PC-12)	OSP
PGM-119	Unnamed	7–29–71	Brazil	Parati (P-13)	OSP
PGM-120	Unnamed	9–30–71	Brazil	Penedo (P-14)	OSP

continued

Hull No.	Name	Date of Transfer	Recipient	Foreign Name and Hull Number	Mode
PGM-121	Unnamed	10–29–71	Brazil	Poti (P-15)	OSP
SS-319	Becuna	7–31–74	Peru	(For cannibalization and scrapping)	Sale
SS-320	Bergall	10–18–58	Turkey	Turgut Reis (S-342)	Lease
SS-320	Unnamed (ex-Bergall)	2–15–73	Turkey	(For cannibalization and scrapping)	Sale
SS-323	Caiman	6–30–72	Turkey	Dumlupinar (S-339)	Sale
SS-339	Catfish	7–1–71	Argentina	Santa Fe (S-21)	Sale
SS-340	Entemedor	7–31–72	Turkey	Preveze (S-345)	Lease
SS-340	Entemedor	8–15–73	Turkey	Preveze (S-345)	Sale
SS-341	Chivo	7–1–71	Argentina	Santiago Del Estero (S-22)	Sale
SS-343	Clamagore	–75	Turkey		Sale
SS-344	Cobbler	11–21–73	Turkey	Canakkale (S-341)	Sale
SS-346	Corporal	11–21–73	Turkey	Inonu II (S-333)	Sale
SS-347	Cubera	1–5–72	Venezuela	Tiburon (S-12)	Sale
SS-350	Dogfish	7–28–72	Brazil	S. Guanabara (S-10)	Sale
SS-351	Greenfish	12–19–73	Brazil	Amazonas (S-16)	Sale
SS-363	Guitarro	8–7–54	Turkey	Preveze (S-340)	Loan
SS-363	Unnamed (ex- Guitarro)	1–30–72	Turkey	(For cannibalization and scrapping)	Sale
SS-364	Hammerhead	10–23–54	Turkey	Cerbe (S-341)	Loan
SS-364	Unnamed (ex-Hammerhead)	1–30–72	Turkey	(For cannibalization and scrapping)	Sale
SS-365	Hardhead	7–26–72	Greece	Papanikolis (S-114)	Sale
SS-366	Hawkbill	4–21–53	Netherlands	Zeeleeuw (S-803)	Loan
SS-366	Unnamed (ex-Hawkbill)	4–3–70	Netherlands	(For cannibalization and scrapping)	Sale
SS-368	Jallao	6–26–74	Spain	Submarino (S-35)	Sale
SS-370	Kraken	10–17–58	Spain	Almirante Garcia De Los Reyes (S-31)	Loan
SS-370	Kraken	11–18–74	Spain	Almirante Garcia De Los Reyes (S-31)	Sale
SS-372	Lamprey	7–21–60	Argentina	Santa Fe (S-11)	Loan
SS-372	Lamprey	9–1–71	Argentina	(For cannibalization and scrapping)	Sale
SS-375	Macabi	8–11–60	Argentina	Santiago Del Estero (S-12)	Loan
SS-375	Macabi	9–1–71	Argentina	(For cannibalization and scrapping)	Sale
SS-376	Mapiro	3–18–60	Turkey	Piri Reis (S-343)	Loan
SS-376	Mapiro	8–15–73	Turkey	Piri Reis (S-343)	Sale
SS-378	Mero	4–20–60	Turkey	Hizir Reis (S-344)	Loan
SS-378	Mero	8–15–73	Turkey	Hizir Reis (S-344)	Sale
SS-381	Sand Lance	9–7–63	Brazil	Rio Grande Do Sul (S-11)	Loan
SS-381	Unnamed (ex-Sand Lance)	10–12–72	Brazil	(For use as non-op. dockside trainer, cannibalization and ultimate scrapping)	Sale
SS-382	Picuda	10–1–72	Spain	Narciso Monturiol (S-33)	Loan
SS-382	Picuda	11–18–74	Spain	Narciso Monturiol (S-33)	Sale
SS-385	Bang	10–1–72	Spain	Cosme Garcia (S-34)	Loan
SS-385	Bang	11–18–74	Spain	Cosme Garcia (S-34)	Sale
SS-391	Pomfret	7–1–71	Turkey	Oruc Reis (S-337)	Loan
SS-391	Pomfret	8–15–73	Turkey	Oruc Reis (S-337)	Sale
SS-396	Ronquil	7–1–71	Spain	Issac Peral (S-32)	Sale
SS-403	Atule	7–31–74	Peru	Pacocha (SS-48)	Sale
SS-406	Sea Poacher	7–1–74	Peru	Pabellon De Pica[5] (SS-49)	Sale
SS-410	Threadfin	8–18–72	Turkey	I. Inonu (S-346)	Lease
SS-410	Threadfin	8–15–73	Turkey	I. Inonu (S-346)	Sale
SS-414	Springer	1–23–61	Chile	Thompson (S-20)	Loan
SS-414	Springer	9–1–72	Chile	(For cannibalization and scrapping)	Sale
SS-416	Tiru	–75	Turkey		Sale

Hull No.	Name	Date of Transfer	Recipient	Foreign Name and Hull Number	Mode
SS-418	*Thornback*	7-1-71	Turkey	*Uluc Ali Reis* (S-338)	Lease
SS-418	*Thornback*	8-15-73	Turkey	*Uluc Ali Reis* (S-338)	Sale
SS-421	*Trutta*	7-1-72	Turkey	*Cerbe* (S-340)	Sale
SS-425	*Trumpetfish*	10-15-73	Brazil	*Goias* (S-15)	Sale
SS-426	*Tusk*	10-18-73	Taiwan	*Hai Pao* (SS-92)	Sale
SS-478	*Cutlass*	4-12-73	Taiwan	*Hai Shih* (SS-91)	Sale
SS-483	*Sea Leopard*	3-27-73	Brazil	*S. Bahia* (S-12)	Sale
SS-484	*Odax*	7-8-72	Brazil	*S. Rio De Janeiro* (ex-*S. Guanabara*) (S-13)	Sale
SS-487	*Remora*	10-29-73	Greece	*Katsonis* (S-115)	Sale
SS-490	*Volador*	8-18-72	Italy	*Gianfranco Gazzana Priaroggia* (S-502)	Loan
SS-522	*Amberjack*	10-17-73	Brazil	*Ceara* (S-14)	Sale
SS-523	*Grampus*	5-13-72	Brazil	*Rio Grande Do Sul* (S-11)	Sale
SS-524	*Pickerel*	8-18-72	Italy	*Primo Longobardo* (S-501)	Loan
SS-525	*Grenadier*	5-15-73	Venezuela	*Picua* (S-13)	Sale
SS-564	*Trigger*	7-10-73	Italy	*Livio Piomarta* (S-515)	Sale
SS-568	*Harder*	2-20-74	Italy	*Romeo Romei* (S-516)	Sale
YC-1402	Unnamed	8- -71	Philippines	YU-227	Lease
YD-183	Unnamed	7- -71	Mexico		Lease
YD-191	Unnamed	8- -71	Philippines	YU-207	Lease
YD-195	Unnamed	6-30-72	South Vietnam	HQ-9651	Special
YD-230	Unnamed	9- -71	South Vietnam	HQ-9650	Lease
YFR-889	Unnamed	5- -71	South Vietnam	HQ-490	Special
YFU-56	Unnamed	5-19-72	Khmer Republic	T-918	Lease
YFU-68	Unnamed	5-19-72	Khmer Republic	T-919	Lease
YFU-73	Unnamed	11-15-73	Khmer Republic	*Skilak* (T-920)	Loan
YFU-90	Unnamed	7- -71	South Vietnam	HQ-546	Special
YO-179	Unnamed	9- -71	South Korea	(YO-6)	Lease
YO-221	Unnamed	-75	Peru		Sale
YO-226	Unnamed	8-2-62	Denmark	*Rimfaxe* (A-568)	Loan
YO-226	Unnamed	7-1-74	Denmark	*Rimfaxe* (A-568)	Sale
YO-229	Unnamed	8-2-62	Denmark	*Skinfaxe* (A-569)	Loan
YO-229	Unnamed	7-1-74	Denmark	*Skinfaxe* (A-569)	Sale
YOG-56	Unnamed	6-30-72	South Vietnam	HQ-475	Grant Aid
YR-40	Unnamed	7- -62	Guatamala	YR-44	Lease
YR-40	Unnamed	-75	Guatamala	YR-44	Sale
YRBM-16	Unnamed	1-3-72	South Vietnam	HQ-9612	Special
YRBM-16	Unnamed	10-2-73	South Vietnam	HQ-9612	Grant Aid
YRBM-17	Unnamed	4-15-71	South Vietnam	HQ-9610	Special
YRBM-17	Unnamed	7-15-71	South Vietnam	HQ-9610	Grant Aid
YRBM-18	Unnamed	11-10-72	South Vietnam		Special
YRBM-21	Unnamed	1- -72	South Vietnam	HQ-9613	Special
YTL-425	Unnamed	8- -71	Philippines	*Tasaday* (YQ-226)	Lease
YTL-433	Unnamed	11-5-73	Khmer Republic	R-915	Loan
YTL-452	Unnamed	10- -69	South Vietnam	HQ-9508	Special
YTL-452	Unnamed	7-15-71	South Vietnam	HQ-9508	Grant Aid
YTL-456	Unnamed	10- -69	South Vietnam	HQ-9509	Special
YTL-456	Unnamed	7-15-71	South Vietnam	HQ-9509	Grant Aid
YTL-457	Unnamed	2- -71	South Vietnam	HQ-9511	Special
YTL-457	Unnamed	7-15-71	South Vietnam	HQ-9511	Grant Aid

continued

Hull No.	Name	Date of Transfer	Recipient	Foreign Name and Hull Number	Mode
YTL-567	Unnamed	4–1–74	Paraguay		Loan
YTL-586	Unnamed	4– –71	South Vietnam	HQ-9510	Special
YTL-586	Unnamed	7–15–71	South Vietnam	HQ-9510	Grant Aid
YTM-762	Pokanoket	6–30–72	South Vietnam	HQ-9550	Grant Aid
YTM-767	Ankachak	7–1–72	Greece	Aias (A-412)	Lease
YTM-769	Hombro	6–30–72	South Vietnam	HQ-9551	Grant Aid
YTM-771	Nootka	6–30–72	South Vietnam	HQ-9552	Grant Aid
WAK-186	Kukui	3–1–72	Philippines	Mactan (TK-90)	Lease
WHEC-374	Absecon	7–15–72	South Vietnam	Tham Ngu Lao (HQ-15)	Special
WHEC-375	Chincoteague	6–21–72	South Vietnam	Ly Thoung Kiet (HQ-16)	Special
WHEC-383	Castle Rock	12–21–71	South Vietnam	Tran Vinh Trong (HQ-05)	Special
WHEC-384	Cook Inlet	12–21–71	South Vietnam	Tran Quoc Toan (HQ-06)	Special
WHEC-386	McCulloch	6–21–72	South Vietnam	Ngo Quyen (HQ-17)	Special
WLB-398	Redbud	3–1–72	Philippines	Kalinga (AG-89)	Grant Aid
WLV-523	Unnamed	9– –71	South Vietnam	Ba Dong (DBK-304)	Special

[1] Leased to Argentina Navy, but manned by Argentine Coast Guard.

[2] Leased to the Korean Coast and Geodetic Survey via the U.S. State Department. Not transferred under ILP. Not part of the Korean Navy.

[3] Completed 1–1–75.

[4] Transferred to the Philippine government for service as a civilian hospital ship. Not part of Philippine Navy.

[5] Name changed to La Pedrera on 7–15–74.

THIRTEEN: STRIKE LIST

This section comprises a list of U.S. Navy ships and craft stricken from the U.S. Naval Vessel Register and a list of ships disposed of by the U.S. Coast Guard since 1 July 1971. For easy reference, this section is divided into three parts. The first part comprises all ships of the U.S. Navy that have been stricken, the second part comprises a list of U.S. Navy service craft that have been stricken, and the third consists of ships disposed of by the Coast Guard. In each part, ships are arranged alphabetically by classification and within each classification by hull number. All data is arranged in table form. As stated in previous chapters, all ships transferred to the permanent custody of the Maritime Administration (MarAd), but not

stricken from the Naval Vessel Register, have been counted as stricken ships. These ships have been excluded from their respective sections in the main text and are only included in this section. Such ships are indicated with an asterisk immediately before the date in the "Date Stricken" column. This date is also the date they were transferred to the permanent custody of MarAd. Finally, for all ships indicated as "Trans./MarAd for layup" in the "Comments" column, consult Section 14 for pertinent data relating to the individual ship after it was transferred to MarAd.

A. COMMISSIONED NAVY SHIPS

Hull No.	Name	Date Stricken	Comments
AD-16	Cascade	11–23–74	Only ship of class. Trans./MarAd for disposal.
AD-23	Arcadia	7–1–73	Trans./MarAd for layup 6–30–69. Later scrapped.
AD-25	Frontier	12–1–72	Trans./MarAd for layup 8–31–69. Later scrapped.
AD-27	Yellowstone	9–12–74	Trans./MarAd for disposal.
AD-29	Isle Royale	*9–1–71	Trans./MarAd permanently for layup.
ADG-8	Lodestone	2–21–75	Ex-PCE. Scrapped.
ADG-9	Magnet	2–21–75	Ex-PCE. Scrapped.
ADG-10	Deperm	2–21–75	Ex-PCE. Scrapped.
ADG-383	Surfbird	2–21–75	Ex-MSF. Last AUK Class MSF type on the NVR. Scrapped.
AE-8	Mauna Loa	*9–1–71	Trans./MarAd permn. for layup.
AE-15	Vesuvius	8–14–73	Trans./MarAd for disposal. Scrapped.
AE-16	Mount Katmai	8–14–73	Trans./MarAd for disposal. Scrapped.
AE-17	Great Sitkin	7–2–73	Trans./MarAd for disposal. Scrapped.
AE-18	Paricutin	6–1–73	Trans./MarAd for layup 7–29–71. Later scrapped.
AE-19	Diamond Head	3–1–73	Trans./MarAd for disposal. Scrapped.
AE-31	Chara	3–10–72	Ex AKA-58. Trans./MarAd for disposal. Scrapped.
AF-10	Aldebaran	6–1–73	Trans./MarAd for layup 6–30–69. Later scrapped.
AF-28	Hyades	*9–1–71	Trans./MarAd permn. for layup.
AF-42	USNS Bondia	5–1–73	Last of class on NVR. Trans./MarAd for disposal. Scrapped.
AF-49	Zelima	9–1–71	Trans./MarAd permn. for layup.
AF-50	USNS Bald Eagle	10–19–71	Trans./MarAd for disposal. Sold.
AF-51	USNS Blue Jacket	10–19–71	Trans./MarAd for disposal. Sold.
AF-57	Regulus	9–10–71	Irreparably damaged by typhoon and grounding in Hong Kong Harbor on 8–16–71. Beyond economical salvage and repair. Scrapped "in place".
AF-63	USNS Asterion	6–15–73	Trans./MarAd for disposal. Scrapped.
AF-64	USNS Perseus	6–15–73	Trans./MarAd for disposal. Scrapped.
AG-162	USNS Mission Capistrano	10–19–71	Ex AO-112. Trans./MarAd for disposal. Sold.
AG-169	USNS Pvt. Jose E. Valdez	*9–1–71	Trans./MarAd permn. for layup.
AG-172	USNS Phoenix	6–15–73	Trans./MarAd for disposal. Scrapped.
AG-173	USNS Provo	6–15–73	Trans./MarAd for disposal. Scrapped.

continued

Hull No.	Name	Date Stricken	Comments
AG-174	USNS *Cheyenne*	6–15–73	Trans./MarAd for disposal. Scrapped.
AG-191	*Spokane*	4–15–72	Ex CLAA-120. Last of class on NVR. Conversion to AG never undertaken. Scrapped.
AGF-1	*Valcour*	1–15–73	Ex AVP-55. Last AVP type on the NVR. Test Hulk NWL Dahlgren (1973 to present).
AGM-3	USNS *Longview*	11–1–74	Ex AK-238. Trans./MarAd for disposal.
AGM-5	USNS *Sunnyvale*	12–15–74	Trans./MarAd for disposal. Scrapped.
AGM-6	USNS *Watertown*	2–16–73	Trans./MarAd for disposal. Scrapped.
AGM-7	USNS *Huntsville*	11–8–74	Trans./MarAd for disposal.
AGM-11	USNS *Twin Falls*	9–1–72	Conversion to AGS-37 cancelled. Trans./New York City, via the Dept. of Commerce, on 11–6–72 for use as a non-operable trade school, replacing the Liberty Ship SS *John Brown*.
AGP-838	*Hunterdon County*	8–1–74	Ex-LST-838. Sold/Malaysia.
AGSS-318	*Baya*	10–30–72	Ex-SS. Scrapped.
AGSS-419	*Tigrone*	6–30–75	Ex-SSR, SS. Scrapped.
AGSS-479	*Diablo*	12–4–71	Trans./Pakistan 6–1–64 as *Ghazi* (S-130) (Loan). Sunk 12–5–71 (Pakistani time) off East Pakistan in 110' of water, by internal explosion or depth charges, with all hands during the Indo-Pakistani War.
AH-15	*Consolation*	9–16–74	Served as the private AH SS *Hope* from 3–16–60 until return to USN on 9–16–74. Trans./MarAd for disposal.
AH-16	*Repose*	3–15–74	Trans./MarAd for disposal.
AK-180	*Fentress*	10–15–73	Trans./MarAd for disposal 11–21–73, but acquired by Dept. of Interior on 7–9–74 for further service in the Pacific Trust Territories.
AK-188	USNS *Herkimer*	6–15–73	Trans./Dept. of Interior 10–3–73 for service in the Pacific Trust Territories.
AK-198	USNS *Muskingum*	6–10–73	Trans./Dept. of Interior 10–3–73 for service in the Pacific Trust Territories.
AK-241	USNS *Pvt. Francis X. McGraw*	5–15–74	Trans./MarAd for disposal. Scrapped.
AK-243	USNS *Sgt. Archer T. Gammon*	5–1–73	Trans./MarAd for disposal. Scrapped.
AK-246	USNS *Col. William J. O'Brien*	9–1–73	Trans./MarAd for disposal. Scrapped.
AK-249	USNS *Short Splice*	6–15–73	Trans./MarAd for disposal. Scrapped.
AK-250	USNS *Pvt. Frank J. Petrarca*	10–15–73	Trans./MarAd for disposal.
AK-251	USNS *Lt. George W. G. Boyce*	7–15–73	Trans./MarAd for disposal. Sold.
AK-252	USNS *Lt. Robert Craig*	7–10–73	Trans./MarAd for disposal. Sold.
AK-260	*Betelgeuse*	2–1–74	Disposition pending.
AK-275	USNS *Pvt. Joseph E. Merrell*	1–31–74	Ex AKV-4. Irreparably damaged in collision on 12–29–73 off coast of California. Beyond economical repair. Trans./MarAd for disposal. Scrapped.
AK-276	USNS *Sgt. Jack J. Pendleton*	2–15–74	Ex AKV-5. Irreparably damaged when she ran aground on 9–25–73 on Triton Island, Paracel Islands, South China Sea. Beyond economical repair and salvage. Attempts were made to refloat the ship and tow her to sea for scuttling, but in 1/74, the Paracel islands were seized from the South Vietnamese by the Communist Chinese. As a result of this seizure, the disposition of the hulk is unknown.
AKA-91	*Whitley*	5–1–73	Sold/Italy.
AKL-10	*Sharps*	11–15–74	Sold/South Korea.
AKL-28	*Brule*	11–15–74	Sold/South Korea.
AKL-35	Unnamed	11–15–74	Sold/South Korea.
AKS-32	*Altair*	6–1–73	Ex AK-257. Trans./MarAd for layup on 5–21–69. Later scrapped.
AKV-21	*Rabaul*	9–1–71	Ex CVE-121. Last CVE on the NVR. Scrapped.
AKV-42	USNS *Breton*	8–6–71	Ex CVE-23. Last of its class on the NVR. Trans./MarAd for disposal. Scrapped.
ANL-78	*Cohoes*	6–30–72	Ex AN-78. Last of its class and last AN/ANL type on the NVR. Scrapped.
AO-25	*Sabine*	*9–1–71	Trans./MarAd permanently for layup.
AO-32	*Guadalupe*	5–15–75	Trans./MarAd for disposal.
AO-36	*Kennebec*	*9–1–71	Trans./MarAd permanently for layup.
AO-39	*Kankakee*	6–1–73	Trans./MarAd for layup 6–30–69. Sold.
AO-43	*Tappahannock*	*9–1–71	Trans./MarAd permanently for layup.
AO-49	*Suamico*	11–15–74	Trans./MarAd for disposal.
AO-52	*Cacapon*	8–14–73	Trans./MarAd for disposal. Sold.
AO-53	*Caliente*	12–1–73	Trans./MarAd for disposal. Sold.

Hull No.	Name	Date Stricken	Comments
AO-58	*Manatee*	8–14–73	Trans./MarAd for disposal.
AO-60	*Nantahala*	7–2–73	Hulk used as Fuel Oil Storage Depot at Philadelphia Naval Shipyard.
AO-61	*Severn*	7–1–74	Trans./MarAd for disposal. Sold.
AO-63	*Chipola*	8–14–73	Trans./MarAd for disposal. Sold.
AO-65	USNS *Pecos*	10–1–74	Trans./MarAd for disposal. Sold.
AO-67	USNS *Cache*	*5–6–72	Trans./MarAd permanently for layup.
AO-77	USNS *Cossatot*	9–18–74	Trans./MarAd for disposal. Sold.
AO-78	USNS *Chepachet*	*3–13–72	Trans./MarAd permanently for layup.
AO-79	USNS *Cowanesque*	6–1–72	Irreparably damaged on 4–23–72 when she ran aground in Kin Bay, Okinawa. Beyond economical repair. Trans./MarAd for disposal. Scrapped.
AO-97	*Allagash*	6–1–73	Trans./MarAd for layup. Later sold.
AO-100	*Chukawan*	7–1–72	Trans./MarAd for layup. Scrapped.
AO-111	USNS *Mission Buenaventura*	3–31–72	Trans./MarAd for disposal. Sold.
AO-132	*Mission Santa Clara*	5–31–74	Sold/Pakistan.
AO-140	USNS *Pioneer Valley*	8–15–72	Trans./MarAd for disposal. Sold.
AO-142	USNS *Shawnee Valley*	2–29–72	Trans./MarAd for disposal. Sold.
AOG-1	*Patapsco*	8–1–74	Trans./MarAd for disposal.
AOG-9	*Kishwaukee*	8–1–74	Trans./MarAd for disposal.
AOG-55	*Nespelen*	7–1–75	Trans./MarAd for disposal.
AOG-80	USNS *Piscataqua*	8–1–74	Trans./MarAd for disposal.
AP-116	*General M. C. Meigs*	1–9–72	Originally stricken 10–1–58 and trans./MarAd for layup at their reserve fleet at Olympia, Wash. While under tow from Olympia to the MarAd Reserve Fleet at Suisun Bay, Calif., by *Gear* (ARS-34), the ship parted her tow line in heavy seas and grounded on a rocky beach just south of the entrance to Juan de Fuca Straits, Puget Sound, on 1–9–72. Heavy seas caused her to break up on the beach. The AP was carrying YTL-432 as deck cargo at the time. Since the ship had never been reinstated on the NVR since 10–1–58 strike, *Meigs* is the only USN ship to be stricken twice without being first reinstated on the NVR.
AP-196	USNS *Barrett*	7–1–73	Trans./New York Maritime Academy, via MarAd, on 9–5–73 for service as its training ship SS *Empire State V.*
AP-198	USNS *Upshur*	4–2–73	Trans./Maine Maritime Academy, via MarAd, on 4–2–73 for service as its training ship SS *State of Maine.*
APB-36	*Colleton*	6–1–73	Sold.
APB-46	*Dorchester*	6–1–73	Ex AKS-17, LST-1112. Sold.
APB-48	*Vanderburgh*	4–1–72	Ex AKS-19, LST-1114. Sold.
AR-14	*Cadmus*	1–15–74	Reacquired from MarAd 1/74. Sold/Taiwan.
AR-22	*Klondike*	9–15–74	Ex AD-22. Trans./MarAd for disposal.
ARB-4	*Zeus*	6–1–73	Ex LST-132. Scrapped.
ARB-8	*Telamon*	6–1–73	Ex LST-976. Scrapped.
ARG-4	*Tutuila*	2–21–72	Last of class on the NVR. Sold/Taiwan.
ARL-1	*Achelous*	6–1–73	Ex LST-10. Sold.
ARL-7	*Atlas*	6–1–72	Ex LST-231. Sold.
ARL-9	*Endymion*	6–1–72	Ex LST-513. Sold.
ARS-22	*Current*	6–1–73	Scrapped.
ARSD-1	*Gypsy*	6–1–73	Ex LSM-549. Scrapped.
ARSD-2	*Mender*	6–1–73	Ex LSM-550. Scrapped.
ARST-1	*Laysan Island*	6–1–73	Ex LST-1098. Scrapped.
ARST-3	*Palmyra*	6–1–73	Ex LST-1100. Scrapped.
ARVA-5	*Fabius*	6–1–73	Ex LST-1093. Scrapped.
ARVA-6	*Megara*	6–1–73	Ex LST-1094. Sold/Mexico.
ARVE-4	*Chloris*	6–1–73	Ex LST-1095. Scrapped.
ARVH-1	USNS *Corpus Christi Bay*	12–31–74	Ex-*Albemarle* (AV-5). Trans/MarAd for disposal. Possible memorial at Corpus Christi, Texas.
AS-13	*Griffin*	8–1–72	Last of class on NVR. Trans./MarAd for disposal. Sold.

continued

STRIKE LIST

Hull No.	Name	Date Stricken	Comments
AS-14	Pelias	8-1-71	Trans./MarAd for disposal. Sold.
AS-22	Euryale	12-1-71	Trans./MarAd for disposal. Sold.
ASR-7	Chanticleer	6-9-73	Scrapped.
ASR-10	Greenlet	2-1-73	Sold/Turkey.
ASR-20	Skylark	6-30-73	Ex-*Yustaga* (ATF-165). Last of class on NVR. Sold/Brazil.
ATA-185	Koka	12-3-73	Trans./Dept. of HEW on 12-3-73 for further service in American Samoa.
ATA-187	Salish	2-1-75	Sold/Argentina.
ATA-190	Samoset	*9-1-71	Trans./MarAd permanently for layup.
ATA-193	Stallion	*9-1-71	Trans./MarAd permanently for layup.
ATA-204	Wandank	8-1-73	Trans./Dept. of Interior as loan on 7-1-71. Returned to USN 5-22-73. Trans./Dept. of Interior permanently on 8-1-73 for further service in the Pacific Trust Territories.
ATA-210	Catawba	2-1-75	Sold/Argentina.
ATA-213	Keywadin	*9-1-71	Trans./MarAd permanently for layup.
ATA-240	Unnamed	8-4-71	Trans./Army for cannibalization and scrapping.
ATF-67	Apache	3-30-74	Sold/Taiwan.
ATF-75	Sioux	8-15-73	Sold/Turkey.
ATF-90	Pinto	5-17-74	Sold/Peru.
AVT-3	Cabot	8-1-72	Ex CVL-28, CL-79. Last of class on NVR. Sold/Spain.
CA-69	Boston	1-4-74	Ex CAG-1, CA-69. Scrapped.
CA-71	Quincy	10-1-73	Scrapped.
CA-72	Pittsburgh	7-1-73	Scrapped.
CA-75	Helena	1-1-74	Scrapped.
CA-124	Rochester	10-1-73	Scrapped.
CA-130	Bremerton	10-1-73	Scrapped.
CA-133	Toledo	1-1-74	Scrapped.
CA-135	Unnamed (ex-*Los Angeles*)	1-1-74	Possible memorial at Los Angeles, Calif.
CLG-3	Galveston	12-21-73	Ex CLG-93, CL-93. Scrapped.
CLG-8	Topeka	12-1-73	Ex CL-67. Sunk as target.
CVS-9	Essex	6-1-73	Ex CVA, CV. Disposition pending.
CVS-10	Yorktown	6-1-73	Ex CVA, CV. Memorial at Patriots Point, S.C.
CVS-14	Ticonderoga	11-16-73	Ex CVA, CV. Scrapped.
CVS-15	Randolph	6-1-73	Ex CVA, CV. Disposition pending.
CVS-18	Wasp	7-1-72	Ex CVA, CV. Scrapped.
CVS-33	Kearsarge	5-1-73	Ex CVA, CV. Scrapped.
CVS-36	Antietam	5-1-73	Ex CVA, CV. Scrapped.
DD-421	Benson	11-1-74	SoldTaiwan.
DD-427	Hilary P. Jones	11-1-74	Sold/Taiwan.
DD-431	Plunkett	11-1-74	Sold/Taiwan.
DD-437	Woolsey	7-1-74	Scrapped.
DD-448	La Vallette	2-1-74	Sold/Peru.
DD-456	Rodman	11-1-72	Ex DMS-21, DD-456. While on loan to Taiwan, ship was irreparably damaged by grounding on 5-22-70. Beyond economical repair. Scrapped in Taiwan.
DD-462	Fitch	7-1-71	Sunk as target.
DD-472	Guest	8-1-73	Sold/Brazil.
DD-473	Bennett	8-1-73	Sold/Brazil.
DD-475	Hudson	12-1-72	Scrapped.
DD-479	Stevens	12-1-72	Scrapped.
DD-490	Quick	1-15-72	Ex DMS-32, DD-490. Scrapped.
DD-493	Carmick	7-1-71	Ex DMS-33, DD-493. Scrapped.
DD-494	Doyle	7-1-71	Ex DMS-34, DD-494. Scrapped.

Hull No.	Name	Date Stricken	Comments
DD-496	McCook	1–15–72	Ex DMS-36, DD-496. Scrapped.
DD-500	Ringgold	10–1–74	Sold/West Germany.
DD-501	Schroeder	10–1–72	Scrapped.
DD-502	Sigsbee	12–1–74	Last Fletcher class DD in its original configuration on the NVR. Scrapped.
DD-509	Converse	10–1–72	Sold/Spain.
DD-511	Foote	10–1–72	Scrapped.
DD-513	Terry	4–1–74	Sold/Peru.
DD-515	Anthony	4–15–72	Sold/West Germany.
DD-516	Wadsworth	10–1–74	Sold/West Germany.
DD-519	Daly	12–1–74	Scrapped.
DD-520	Isherwood	1–15–74	Sold/Peru.
DD-521	Kimberly	1–25–74	Sold/Taiwan.
DD-528	Mullany	10–1–71	Sold/Taiwan.
DD-530	Trathen	11–1–72	Sunk as target.
DD-531	Hazelwood	12–1–74	Served as test ship for ill-fated DASH system. Scrapped.
DD-534	McCord	10–1–72	Scrapped.
DD-535	James Miller	12–1–74	Ex-Miller. Scrapped.
DD-536	Owen	4–15–73	Scrapped.
DD-537	The Sullivans	12–1–74	Ex-Putnam. Possible memorial.
DD-538	Stephen Potter	12–1–72	Scrapped.
DD-540	Twining	7–1–71	Sold/Taiwan.
DD-541	Yarnall	1–25–74	Sold/Taiwan.
DD-547	Cowell	8–17–71	Sold/Argentina.
DD-550	Capps	10–1–72	Sold/Spain.
DD-551	David W. Taylor	10–1–72	Sold/Spain.
DD-554	Franks	12–1–72	Scrapped.
DD-556	Hailey	8–1–73	Sold/Brazil.
DD-558	Laws	4–15–73	Scrapped.
DD-562	Robinson	12–1–74	Scrapped.
DD-563	Ross	12–1–74	Scrapped.
DD-564	Rowe	12–1–74	Scrapped.
DD-567	Watts	2–1–74	Scrapped.
DD-568	Wren	12–1–74	Scrapped.
DD-571	Claxton	10–1–74	Sold/West Germany.
DD-572	Dyson	10–1–74	Sold/West Germany.
DD-575	McKee	10–1–72	Scrapped.
DD-578	Wickes	11–1–72	Sunk as target 4–8–74 by aircraft south of Santa Rosa Island, Calif., after being irreparably damaged by a HARPOON missile.
DD-585	Haraden	11–1–72	Sunk as target.
DD-587	Bell	11–1–72	Sunk as target.
DD-588	Burns	11–1–72	Sunk as target 6–20–74.
DD-594	Hart	4–15–73	Scrapped.
DD-596	Shields	7–1–72	Only Fletcher class DD to see continuous service from 1st commissioning until strike. Sold/Brazil.
DD-604	Parker	7–1–71	Scrapped.
DD-606	Coghlan	7–1–71	Scrapped.
DD-607	Frazier	7–1–71	Scrapped.
DD-608	Gansevoort	7–1–71	Sunk as target 3–23–72 by aircraft and naval gunfire.
DD-609	Gillespie	7–1–71	Sunk as target.
DD-610	Hobby	7–1–71	Sunk as target 6–28–72 by missiles, aircraft and surface gunfire.

continued

STRIKE LIST

Hull No.	Name	Date Stricken	Comments
DD-613	Laub	7-1-71	Scrapped.
DD-614	MacKenzie	7-1-71	Sunk as target 5/74.
DD-615	McLanahan	7-1-71	Scrapped.
DD-617	Ordronaux	7-1-71	Scrapped.
DD-618	Davison	1-15-72	Ex DMS-37, DD-618. Scrapped.
DD-619	Edwards	7-1-71	Scrapped.
DD-621	Jeffers	7-1-71	Ex DMS-27, DD-621. Scrapped.
DD-627	Thompson	7-1-71	Ex DMS-38, DD-627. Scrapped.
DD-629	Abbot	12-1-74	Scrapped.
DD-630	Braine	8-17-71	Sold/Argentina.
DD-634	Doran	1-15-72	Ex DMS-41, DD-634. Scrapped.
DD-638	Herndon	7-1-71	Sunk as target 5-23-74 by aircraft and missiles.
DD-642	Hale	6-2-75	Sold/Columbia.
DD-643	Sigourney	12-1-74	Scrapped.
DD-646	Stockton	7-1-71	Scrapped.
DD-647	Thorn	7-1-71	Sunk as target 8/74.
DD-650	Caperton	12-1-74	Scrapped.
DD-653	Knapp	3-6-72	Scrapped.
DD-654	Bearss	12-1-74	Scrapped.
DD-655	John Hood	12-1-74	Scrapped.
DD-656	Van Valkenburg	2-1-73	Scrapped.
DD-657	Charles J. Badger	2-1-74	Sold/Chile.
DD-659	Dashiell	12-1-74	Scrapped.
DD-660	Bullard	12-1-72	Scrapped.
DD-661	Kidd	12-1-74	Possible memorial.
DD-663	Heywood L. Edwards	3-18-74	Ret'd from loan to Japan 3-9-74. Sold/South Korea.
DD-664	Richard P. Leary	3-18-74	Ret'd from loan to Japan 3-9-74. Sold/South Korea.
DD-667	Chauncey	10-1-72	Scrapped.
DD-668	Clarence K. Bronson	2-1-73	Sold/Turkey.
DD-669	Cotten	12-1-74	Scrapped.
DD-671	Gatling	12-1-74	Possible memorial.
DD-672	Healy	12-1-74	Scrapped.
DD-674	Hunt	12-1-74	Scrapped.
DD-675	Lewis Hancock	3-15-73	Sold/Brazil.
DD-678	McGowan	10-1-72	Sold/Spain.
DD-679	McNair	12-1-74	Scrapped.
DD-680	Melvin	12-1-74	Scrapped.
DD-683	Stockham	12-1-74	Scrapped.
DD-687	Uhlmann	7-15-72	Last active Fletcher class in USN. Scrapped.
DD-688	Remey	12-1-74	Scrapped.
DD-690	Norman Scott	4-15-73	Scrapped.
DD-692	Allen M. Sumner	8-15-73	FRAM II. Scrapped.
DD-693	Moale	7-2-73	FRAM II. Scrapped.
DD-694	Ingraham	7-16-71	FRAM II. Sold/Greece.
DD-697	Charles S. Sperry	12-15-73	FRAM II. Sold/Chile.
DD-698	Ault	7-16-73	FRAM II. Scrapped.
DD-699	Waldron	10-30-73	FRAM II. Sold/Columbia.
DD-702	Hank	7-1-72	FRAM II. Sold/Argentina.
DD-703	Wallace L. Lind	12-4-73	FRAM II. Sold/South Korea.
DD-704	Borie	7-1-72	FRAM II. Sold/Argentina.

Hull No.	Name	Date Stricken	Comments
DD-705	Compton	9-27-72	Sold/Brazil.
DD-708	Harlan R. Dickson	7-1-72	Scrapped.
DD-709	Hugh Purvis	2-1-73	FRAM II. Sold/Turkey.
DD-710	Gearing	7-2-73	FRAM I. Scrapped.
DD-713	Kenneth D. Bailey	2-1-74	FRAM II. Ex-DDR. Sold/Iran.
DD-723	Walke	2-1-74	FRAM II. Scrapped.
DD-724	Laffey	3-29-75	FRAM II. Last of class on the NVR. Possible memorial at Alexandria, Va.
DD-725	O'Brien	2-18-72	FRAM II. Sunk as target 7-13-72.
DD-727	De Haven	12-5-73	FRAM II. Sold/South Korea.
DD-728	Mansfield	2-1-74	FRAM II. Sold/Argentina.
DD-729	Lyman K. Swenson	2-1-74	FRAM II. Sold/Taiwan.
DD-730	Collett	2-1-74	FRAM II. Sold/Argentina.
DD-731	Maddox	7-6-72	Sold/Taiwan.
DD-734	Purdy	7-2-73	Scrapped.
DD-744	Blue	2-1-74	FRAM II. Sunk as target.
DD-746	Taussig	2-1-74	FRAM II. Sold/Taiwan.
DD-752	Alfred A. Cunningham	2-1-74	FRAM II. Sunk as target.
DD-753	John R. Pierce	7-2-73	Scrapped.
DD-755	John A. Bole	2-1-74	FRAM II. Sold/Taiwan.
DD-756	Beatty	7-14-56	Sold/Venezuela.
DD-757	Putnam	8-6-73	FRAM II. Scrapped.
DD-758	Strong	10-31-73	FRAM II. Sold/Brazil.
DD-759	Lofberg	2-1-74	FRAM II. Sold/Taiwan.
DD-760	John W. Thomason	2-1-74	FRAM II. Sold/Taiwan.
DD-761	Buck	7-16-73	FRAM II. Sold/Brazil.
DD-762	Henley	7-2-73	Scrapped.
DD-764	Lloyd Thomas	10-12-72	FRAM II. Ex-DDE. Sold/Taiwan.
DD-765	Keppler	7-1-72	FRAM II. Ex-DDE. Sold/Turkey.
DD-770	Lowry	10-29-73	FRAM II. Sold/Brazil.
DD-775	Willard Keith	7-1-72	Sold/Columbia.
DD-776	James C. Owens	7-16-73	FRAM II. Sold/South Korea.
DD-778	Massey	9-17-73	FRAM II. Scrapped.
DD-779	Douglas H. Fox	12-15-73	FRAM II. Sold/Chile.
DD-780	Stormes	2-16-72	FRAM II. Sold/Iran.
DD-781	Robert K. Huntington	10-31-73	FRAM II. Sold/Venezuela.
DD-787	James E. Kyes	3-31-73	FRAM I. Sold/Taiwan.
DD-789	Eversole	7-11-73	FRAM I. Sold/Turkey.
DD-790	Shelton	3-31-73	FRAM I. Sold/Taiwan.
DD-793	Cassin Young	12-1-74	Scrapped.
DD-794	Irwin	3-15-73	Sold/Brazil.
DD-796	Benham	1-15-74	Sold/Peru.
DD-797	Cushing	8-1-73	Sold/Brazil.
DD-799	Jarvis	10-1-72	Sold/Spain.
DD-800	Porter	10-1-72	Scrapped.
DD-807	Benner	2-1-74	FRAM II. Ex-DDR. Scrapped.
DD-808	Dennis J. Buckley	7-2-73	FRAM II. Ex-DDR. Scrapped.
DD-831	Goodrich	2-1-74	FRAM II. Ex-DDR. Sold/Venezuela.
DD-832	Hanson	3-31-73	FRAM I. Sold/Taiwan.
DD-833	Herbert J. Thomas	2-1-74	FRAM I. Sold/Taiwan.

continued

Hull No.	Name	Date Stricken	Comments
DD-843	Warrington	10-1-72	FRAM I. Irreparably damaged by two mines on 7-17-72 while on patrol off the coast of North Vietnam. Beyond economical repair. Hulk sold/Taiwan.
DD-844	Perry	7-2-73	FRAM I. Scrapped.
DD-847	Robert L. Wilson	9-30-74	FRAM I. Ex-DDE. Scrapped.
DD-850	Joseph P. Kennedy, Jr.	7-2-73	FRAM I. Memorial at Fall River, Mass.
DD-851	Rupertus	7-10-73	FRAM I. Sold/Greece.
DD-853	Charles H. Roan	9-21-73	FRAM I. Sold/Turkey.
DD-859	Norris	2-1-74	FRAM II. Ex-DDE. Sold/Turkey.
DD-860	McCaffery	9-30-73	FRAM II. Ex-DDE. Scrapped.
DD-861	Harwood	2-1-73	FRAM II. Ex-DDE. Sold/Turkey. Accidentally sunk by Turkish Air Force on 7-22-74 during the Turkish invasion of Cyprus.
DD-865	Charles R. Ware	12-12-74	FRAM I. Scrapped.
DD-872	Forrest Royal	2-1-73	FRAM I. Sold/Turkey.
DD-874	Duncan	9-1-73	FRAM II. Ex-DDR. Replaced ex-Ingersoll (DD-652) as target ship at Pacific Missile Range, Point Mugu, Calif.
DD-875	Henry W. Tucker	12-3-73	FRAM I. Sold/Brazil.
DD-877	Perkins	1-15-73	FRAM II. Ex-DDR. Sold/Argentina.
DD-884	Floyd B. Parks	7-2-73	FRAM I. Scrapped.
DD-887	Brinkley Bass	12-3-73	FRAM I. Sold/Brazil.
DD-888	Stickell	7-1-72	FRAM I. Ex-DDR. Sold/Greece.
DE-131	Hammann	10-1-72	Ex-Langley. Scrapped.
DE-137	Herbert C. Jones	7-1-72	Scrapped.
DE-138	Douglas L. Howard	10-1-72	Scrapped.
DE-139	Farquhar	10-1-72	Scrapped.
DE-141	Hill	10-1-72	Scrapped.
DE-145	Huse	8-1-73	Scrapped.
DE-146	Inch	10-1-72	Scrapped.
DE-149	Chatelain	8-1-73	Scrapped.
DE-150	Neunzer	7-1-72	Scrapped.
DE-152	Peterson	8-1-73	Scrapped.
DE-162	Levy	8-1-73	Scrapped.
DE-163	McConnell	10-1-72	Scrapped.
DE-164	Osterhaus	11-1-72	Scrapped.
DE-165	Parks	7-1-72	Scrapped.
DE-167	Acree	7-1-72	Scrapped.
DE-172	Cooner	7-1-72	Scrapped.
DE-180	Trumpeter	8-1-73	Scrapped.
DE-181	Straub	8-1-73	Ship had title role in movie "Enemy Below." Scrapped.
DE-191	Coffman	7-1-72	Scrapped.
DE-202	Eichenberger	12-1-72	Scrapped.
DE-217	Coolbaugh	7-1-72	Scrapped.
DE-220	Francis M. Robinson	7-1-72	Scrapped.
DE-231	Hodges	12-1-72	Scrapped.
DE-238	Stewart	10-1-72	Memorial at Galveston, Texas, as of 2-22-74.
DE-240	Moore	8-1-73	Sunk as target.
DE-241	Keith	11-1-72	Scrapped.
DE-242	Tomich	11-1-72	Scrapped.
DE-248	Swasey	11-1-72	Scrapped.
DE-250	Hurst	12-1-72	Sold/Mexico.
DE-253	Pettit	8-1-73	Sunk as target 9-30-74.

Hull No.	Name	Date Stricken	Comments
DE-254	Ricketts	11-1-72	Scrapped.
DE-340	O'Flaherty	12-1-72	Scrapped.
DE-341	Raymond	7-1-72	Sunk as target 1-22-74.
DE-342	Richard W. Suesens	3-15-72	Scrapped.
DE-346	Edwin A. Howard	12-1-72	Scrapped.
DE-348	Key	3-1-72	Scrapped.
DE-349	Gentry	1-15-72	Scrapped.
DE-353	Doyle C. Barnes	12-1-72	Scrapped.
DE-354	Kenneth M. Willett	7-1-72	Sunk as target 3-5-74 off Puerto Rico.
DE-356	Lloyd E. Acree	1-15-72	Scrapped.
DE-357	George E. Davis	12-1-72	Scrapped.
DE-358	Mack	3-15-72	Scrapped.
DE-360	Johnnie Hutchins	7-1-72	Scrapped.
DE-362	Rolf	12-1-72	Scrapped.
DE-363	Pratt	3-15-72	Scrapped.
DE-364	Rombach	3-1-72	Scrapped.
DE-367	French	5-15-72	Scrapped.
DE-394	Swenning	7-1-72	Scrapped.
DE-395	Willis	7-1-72	Scrapped.
DE-396	Janssen	7-1-72	Scrapped.
DE-398	Cockrill	8-1-73	Sunk as target.
DE-399	Stockdale	7-1-72	Sunk as target on 5-26-74.
DE-405	Dennis	12-1-72	Scrapped.
DE-406	Edmonds	5-15-72	Scrapped.
DE-409	La Prade	1-15-72	Scrapped.
DE-411	Stafford	3-15-72	Scrapped.
DE-414	Leray Wilson	5-15-72	Scrapped.
DE-415	Lawrence C. Taylor	12-1-72	Scrapped.
DE-416	Melvin R. Nawman	7-1-72	Scrapped.
DE-417	Oliver Mitchell	3-15-72	Scrapped.
DE-418	Tabberer	7-1-72	Scrapped.
DE-419	Robert F. Kellar	7-1-72	Scrapped.
DE-420	Leland Thomas	12-1-72	Scrapped.
DE-421	Chester T. O'Brien	7-1-72	Scrapped.
DE-423	Dufilho	12-1-72	Scrapped.
DE-438	Corbesier	12-1-72	Scrapped.
DE-441	William Seiverling	12-1-72	Scrapped.
DE-443	Kendall C. Campbell	1-15-72	Scrapped.
DE-444	Goss	3-1-72	Scrapped.
DE-449	Hanna	12-1-72	Scrapped.
DE-508	Gilligan	3-1-72	Scrapped.
DE-531	Edward H. Allen	7-1-72	Scrapped.
DE-533	Howard F. Clark	5-15-72	Scrapped.
DE-534	Silverstein	12-1-72	Scrapped.
DE-537	Rizzi	8-1-72	Scrapped.
DE-538	Osberg	8-1-72	Scrapped.
DE-579	Riley	1-25-74	Last *Rudderow* class DE on NVR. Sold/Taiwan.
DE-580	Leslie L. B. Knox	1-15-72	Scrapped.
DE-581	McNulty	3-1-72	Sunk as target 11-16-72.

continued

Hull No.	Name	Date Stricken	Comments
DE-587	Thomas F. Nickel	12–1–72	Scrapped.
DE-589	Tinsman	5–15–72	Scrapped.
DE-639	Gendeau	12–1–72	Scrapped.
DE-640	Fieberling	3–1–72	Scrapped.
DE-641	William C. Cole	3–1–72	Scrapped.
DE-643	Damon M. Cummings	3–1–72	Scrapped.
DE-667	Wiseman	4–15–73	Scrapped.
DE-681	Gillette	12–1–72	Scrapped.
DE-696	Spangler	3–1–72	Scrapped.
DE-699	Marsh	4–15–73	Scrapped.
DE-701	Osmus	12–1–72	Scrapped.
DE-703	Holton	11–1–72	Scrapped.
DE-705	Frybarger	12–1–72	Ex-DEC, DE. Scrapped.
DE-706	Holt	11–15–74	Sold/South Korea.
DE-742	Hilbert	8–1–72	Scrapped.
DE-743	Lamons	8–1–72	Scrapped.
DE-744	Kyne	8–1–72	Scrapped.
DE-745	Snyder	8–1–72	Scrapped.
DE-746	Hemminger	9–3–74	Sold/Thailand.
DE-750	McClelland	8–1–72	Scrapped.
DE-765	Earl K. Olsen	8–1–72	Scrapped.
DE-767	Oswald	8–1–72	Scrapped.
DE-770	Muir	11–15–74	Sold/South Korea.
DE-771	Sutton	11–15–74	Sold/South Korea.
DE-795	Gunason	9–1–73	Last *Buckley* class and WW II DE (in USN) on the NVR. Sunk as target 7–28–74.
DE-796	Major	12–1–72	Scrapped.
DE-798	Varian	12–1–72	Scrapped.
DE-800	Jack W. Wilkie	8–1–72	Scrapped.
DE-1006	Dealey	7–28–72	Sold/Uruguay.
DE-1014	Cromwell	7–5–72	Scrapped.
DE-1015	Hammerberg	12–14–73	Scrapped.
DE-1021	Courtney	12–14–73	Scrapped.
DE-1022	Lester	12–14–73	Scrapped.
DE-1023	Evans	12–3–73	Scrapped.
DE-1024	Bridget	11–12–73	Scrapped.
DE-1025	Bauer	12–3–73	Scrapped.
DE-1026	Hooper	7–6–73	Ex-*Gatch*. Scrapped.
DE-1027	John Willis	7–14–72	Scrapped.
DE-1028	Van Voorhis	7–1–72	Scrapped.
DE-1029	Hartley	7–8–72	Sold/Columbia.
DE-1030	Joseph K. Taussig	7–1–72	Scrapped.
DE-1033	Claud Jones	12–16–74	Sold/Indonesia.
DE-1034	John R. Perry	2–20–73	Sold/Indonesia.
DE-1035	Charles Berry	1–31–74	Sold/Indonesia.
DE-1036	McMorris	12–16–74	Sold/Indonesia.
DER-147	Blair	12–1–72	Ex DE-147. Scrapped.
DER-239	Sturtevant	12–1–72	Ex DE-239. Scrapped.
DER-244	Otterstetter	8–1–74	Ex DE-244. Sunk as target.
DER-317	Joyce	12–1–72	Ex DE-317. Scrapped.
DER-318	Kirkpatrick	8–1–74	Ex DE-318. Last *Harveson* class DER on the NVR. Scrapped.

Hull No.	Name	Date Stricken	Comments
DER-326	Thomas J. Gary	10–22–73	Ex DE-326. Sold/Tunisia.
DER-328	Finch	2–1–74	Ex DE-328. Scrapped.
DER-329	Kretchmer	9–30–73	Ex DE-329. Scrapped.
DER-332	Price	8–1–74	Ex-DE-332. Scrapped.
DER-333	Strickland	12–1–72	Ex DE-333. Scrapped.
DER-336	Roy O. Hale	8–1–74	Ex DE-336. Scrapped.
DER-382	Ramsden	8–1–74	Ex DE-382. Sunk as target.
DER-383	Mills	8–1–74	Ex DE-383. Scrapped.
DER-384	Rhodes	8–1–74	Ex DE-384. Scrapped.
DER-388	Lansing	2–1–74	Ex DE-388. Scrapped.
DER-389	Durant	4–1–74	Ex DE-389. Scrapped.
DER-390	Calcaterra	7–2–73	Ex DE-390. Scrapped.
DER-539	Wagner	11–1–74	Ex DE-539. Sunk as target.
DER-540	Vandivier	11–1–74	Ex DE-540. Sunk as target.
DL-1	Norfolk	11–1–73	Ex CLK-1. Scrapped.
DL-4	Willis A. Lee	5–15–72	Ex DD-929. Scrapped.
DL-5	Wilkinson	5–1–74	Ex DD-930. Last DL on the NVR. Scrapped.
IX-311	Benewah	9–1–73	Ex APB-35. Trans./Philippines.
IXSS-224	Cod	12–15–71	Ex AGSS-224, SS-224. Possible memorial.
IXSS-240	Angler	12–15–71	Ex AGSS-240, SSK-240, SS-240. Scrapped.
IXSS-246	Croaker	12–20–71	Ex AGSS-246, SSK-246, SS-246. Memorial at Groton, Conn.
IXSS-269	Rasher	12–20–71	Ex AGSS-269, SSR-269, SS-269. Scrapped.
IXSS-287	Bowfin	12–1–71	Ex AGSS-287, SS-287. Memorial at Pearl Harbor, Hawaii.
IXSS-297	Ling	12–1–71	Ex AGSS-297, SS-297. Memorial at Hackensack, N.J.
IXSS-298	Lionfish	12–20–71	Ex AGSS-298, SS-298. Memorial at Fall River, Mass.
IXSS-301	Roncador	12–1–71	Ex AGSS-301, SS-301. Memorial at Canoga Park, Calif.
IXSS-313	Perch	12–1–71	Ex LPSS-313, APSS-313, ASSP-313, SSP-313, SS-313. Scrapped.
IXSS-328	Charr	12–20–71	Ex AGSS-328, SS-328. Scrapped.
IXSS-338	Carp	12–20–71	Ex AGSS-338, SS-338. Scrapped.
IXSS-342	Chopper	10–1–71	GUPPY II. Ex AGSS-342, SS-342. Replaced Hake (AGSS-256) as Salvage Training Hulk for Service Squadron 8.
IXSS-383	Pampanito	12–20–71	Ex AGSS-383, SS-383. Memorial at San Francisco, Calif.
IXSS-423	Torsk	12–15–71	Ex AGSS-423, SS-423. Memorial at Baltimore, Md. as of 9–26–72.
IXSS-476	Runner	12–15–71	Ex AGSS-476, SS-476. Scrapped.
IXSS-481	Requin	12–20–71	Ex AGSS-481, SS-481, SSR-481, SS-481. Memorial at Tampa, Fla.
LCC-7	Mount McKinley	*9–1–71	Trans./MarAd permanently for layup.
LCC-11	Eldorado	11–16–72	Trans./MarAd for disposal. Sold. Now a storage hulk at Kaoshiung, Taiwan.
LCC-12	Estes	*9–1–71	Trans./MarAd permanently for layup.
LCC-17	Taconic	*9–1–71	Trans./MarAd permanently for layup.
LFR-1	Carronade	5–1–73	Ex IFS-1. Scrapped.
LFR-401	Big Black River	5–1–73	Ex LSMR-401, LSM-401. Scrapped.
LFR-405	Broadkill River	5–1–73	Ex LSMR-405, LSM-405. Scrapped.
LFR-412	Des Plaines River	9–1–72	Ex LSMR-412, LSM-412. Scrapped.
LFR-512	Lamoille River	5–1–73	Ex LSMR-512, LSM-512. Scrapped.
LFR-513	Laramie River	5–1–73	Ex LSMR-513, LSM-513. Scrapped.
LFR-515	Owyhee River	5–1–73	Ex LSMR-515, LSM-515. Scrapped.
LFR-522	Red River	5–1–73	Ex LSMR-522, LSM-522. Scrapped.
LFR-531	Smoky Hill River	5–1–73	Ex LSMR-531, LSM-531. Scrapped.
LKA-19	Thuban	*9–1–71	Trans./MarAd permanently for layup.
LKA-54	Algol	*9–1–71	Trans./MarAd permanently for layup.

continued

STRIKE LIST

Hull No.	Name	Date Stricken	Comments
LKA-56	Arneb	8-13-71	Trans./MarAd for disposal. Sold.
LKA-57	Capricornus	*9-1-71	Trans./MarAd permanently for layup.
LKA-61	Muliphen	*9-1-71	Trans./MarAd permanently for layup.
LKA-106	Union	*9-1-71	Trans./MarAd permanently for layup.
LKA-108	Washburn	*9-1-71	Trans./MarAd permanently for layup.
LPA-38	Chilton	7-1-72	Trans./MarAd for disposal.
LPA-44	Fremont	6-1-73	Trans./MarAd for layup 10-10-69. Later scrapped.
LPA-45	Henrico	6-1-73	Trans./MarAd for layup 7-3-68. Later scrapped.
LPA-194	Sandoval	*9-1-71	Trans./MarAd permanently for layup.
LPA-199	Maggofin	*10-31-68	Trans./MarAd permanently for layup.
LPA-213	Mountrail	*9-1-71	Trans./MarAd permanently for layup.
LPA-215	Navarro	*9-1-71	Trans./MarAd permanently for layup.
LPA-220	Okanogan	6-1-73	Trans./MarAd for layup 4-20-71. Later scrapped.
LPA-222	Pickaway	*9-1-71	Trans./MarAd permanently for layup.
LPR-86	Hollis	9-15-74	Ex-APD, DE-794. Scrapped.
LPR-90	Kirwin	9-15-74	Ex-APD, DE-229. Scrapped.
LPR-100	Ringness	9-15-74	Ex-APD, DE-590. Scrapped.
LPR-101	Knudson	7-15-72	Ex-APD, DE-591. Scrapped.
I PR-119	Beverly W. Reid	9-15-74	Ex-APD, DE-722. Scrapped.
LPR-123	Diachenko	9-15-74	Ex-Alex Diachenko. Ex-APD, DE-690. Scrapped.
LPR-124	Horace A. Bass	9-15-74	Ex-APD, DE-691. Scrapped.
LPR-135	Weiss	9-15-74	Ex-APD, DE-719. Scrapped.
LSD-13	Casa Grande	*9-1-71	Trans./MarAd permanently for layup. Later sold/Israel.
LSD-15	Shadwell	*9-1-71	Trans./MarAd permanently for layup.
LSD-17	Catamount	10-31-74	Disposition pending.
LSD-18	Colonial	*9-1-71	Trans./MarAd permanently for layup.
LSD-22	Fort Marion	10-31-74	Sold/Taiwan.
LSD-25	San Marcos	8-1-74	Sold/Spain.
LSD-26	Tortuga	*9-1-71	Trans./MarAd permanently for layup.
LSD-27	Whetstone	*9-1-71	Trans./MarAd permanently for layup.
LSM-17	Unnamed	11-15-74	Sold/South Korea.
LSM-19	Unnamed	11-15-74	Sold/South Korea.
LSM-30	Unnamed	11-15-74	Sold/South Korea.
LSM-54	Unnamed	11-15-74	Sold/South Korea.
LSM-57	Unnamed	11-15-74	Sold/South Korea.
LSM-84	Unnamed	11-15-74	Sold/South Korea.
LSM-96	Unnamed	11-15-74	Sold/South Korea.
LSM-268	Unnamed	11-15-74	Sold/South Korea.
LSM-316	Unnamed	11-15-74	Sold/South Korea.
LSM-462	Unnamed	11-15-74	Sold/South Korea.
LSM-546	Unnamed	11-15-74	Sold/South Korea.
LST-117	USNS LST-117	6-10-73	Sold/Singapore.
LST-176	USNS LST-176	11-1-73	Sold.
LST-218	Unnamed	11-15-74	Sold/South Korea.
LST-227	Unnamed	11-15-74	Sold/South Korea.
LST-276	USNS LST-276	6-10-73	Sold/Singapore.
LST-277	USNS LST-277	2-1-73	Sold/Chile.
LST-288	Berkshire County	11-15-74	Sold/South Korea.
LST-344	Blanco County	9-15-74	Scrapped.
LST-399	USNS LST-399	11-1-73	Trans./MarAd for layup.

Hull No.	Name	Date Stricken	Comments
LST-456	USNS LST-456	6–15–73	Sold.
LST-525	Caroline County	9–15–74	Scrapped.
LST-530	USNS LST-530	6–15–73	Scrapped.
LST-532	USNS Chase County	6–10–73	Sold/Singapore.
LST-533	Cheboygan County	9–15–74	Scrapped.
LST-550	USNS LST-550	11–1–73	Scrapped.
LST-566	USNS LST-566	11–1–73	Trans./MarAd for layup.
LST-572	USNS LST-572	6–15–73	Sold.
LST-581	USNS LST-581	6–1–72	Scrapped.
LST-583	Churchill County	9–15–74	Scrapped.
LST-587	USNS LST-587	6–15–73	Scrapped.
LST-590	USNS LST-590	6–15–73	Scrapped.
LST-602	Clearwater County	5–1–72	Sold/Mexico.
LST-626	USNS LST-626	6–1–72	Scrapped.
LST-630	USNS LST-630	6–15–73	Scrapped.
LST-643	USNS LST-643	6–15–73	Scrapped.
LST-664	USNS LST-664	6–15–73	Scrapped.
LST-715	USNS De Kalb County	11–1–73	Trans./MarAd for layup.
LST-722	Dodge County	9–15–74	Disposition pending.
LST-735	Dukes County	11–1–74	Sold/Taiwan.
LST-983	Middlesex County	9–15–74	Disposition pending.
LST-1010	Unnamed	11–15–74	Sold/South Korea.
LST-1066	USNS New London County	6–10–73	Sold/Chile.
LST-1067	USNS Nye County	6–10–73	Sold/Chile.
LST-1073	Outagamie County	12–1–73	Sold/Brazil.
LST-1083	USNS Plumas County	6–1–72	Scrapped.
LST-1084	Polk County	9–15–74	FRAM II. Disposition pending.
LST-1088	USNS Pulaski County	11–1–73	Trans./MarAd for disposal.
LST-1122	San Joaquin County	5–1–72	Sold.
LST-1141	Stone County	8–15–73	FRAM II. Sold/Thailand.
LST-1148	Sumner County	9–15–74	FRAM II. Scrapped.
LST-1150	Sutter County	9–15–74	Disposition pending.
LST-1153	Talbot County	6–1–73	Last steam driven LST on NVR. Sold.
LST-1158	USNS Tioga County	11–1–73	Trans./MarAd for layup.
LST-1160	USNS Traverse County	11–1–73	Trans./MarAd for layup.
LST-1162	USNS Wahkiakum County	11–1–73	Trans./MarAd for layup.
LST-1163	USNS Waldo County	11–1–73	Trans./MarAd for layup.
LST-1164	USNS Walworth County	11–1–73	Trans./MarAd for layup.
LST-1165	USNS Washoe County	11–1–73	Trans./MarAd for layup.
MCS-2	Ozark	4–1–74	Trans./MarAd for layup.
MHC-43	Bittern	2–1–72	Last MHC on the NVR. Scrapped.
MMD-26	Harry F. Bauer	8–15–71	Ex DM-26, DD-738. Scrapped.
MMD-30	Shea	9–1–73	Ex DM-30, DD-750. Last MMD on NVR. Scrapped.
MMD-33	Gwin	8–15–71	Ex DM-33, DD-772. Sold/Turkey.
MSC-121	Bluebird	1–2–75	Disposition pending.
MSC-122	Cormorant	3–15–74	Scrapped.
MSC-194	Kingbird	7–1–72	Extensively damaged in collision on 5–12–71 with merchant containership at Pensacola, Florida. Beyond economical repair. Scrapped.
MSC-197	Parrot	8–1–72	Trans./Sea Cadets, Washington, D.C., on 8–23–73 for further service as their training ship.

continued

Hull No.	Name	Date Stricken	Comments
MSC-208	Widgeon	7–2–73	Scrapped.
MSCO-8	Curlew	11–15–74	Ex-AMS, YMS-218. Sold/South Korea.
MSCO-22	Kite	11–15–74	Ex-AMS, YMS-374. Sold/South Korea.
MSCO-27	Mockingbird	11–15–74	Ex-AMS, YMS-419. Sold/South Korea.
MSF-58	Broadbill	7–1–72	Scrapped.
MSF-64	Starling	7–1–72	Sold/Mexico.
MSF-101	Herald	7–1–72	Sold/Mexico.
MSF-104	Pilot	7–1–72	Sold/Mexico.
MSF-105	Pioneer	7–1–72	Sold/Mexico.
MSF-111	Sage	7–1–72	Sold/Mexico.
MSF-120	Sway	7–1–72	Sold/Mexico.
MSF-122	Swift	7–1–72	Scrapped.
MSF-123	Symbol	7–1–72	Sold/Mexico.
MSF-124	Threat	7–1–72	Sold/Mexico.
MSF-128	Velocity	7–1–72	Sold/Mexico.
MSF-165	Counsel	7–1–72	Scrapped.
MSF-215	Cruise	7–1–72	Scrapped.
MSF-306	Specter	7–1–72	Sold/Mexico.
MSF-311	Superior	7–1–72	Scrapped.
MSF-314	Champion	7–1–72	Sold/Mexico.
MSF-315	Chief	7–1–72	Sold/Mexico.
MSF-316	Competent	7–1–72	Sold/Mexico.
MSF-317	Defense	7–1–72	Sold/Mexico.
MSF-318	Devastator	7–1–72	Sold/Mexico.
MSF-319	Gladiator	7–1–72	Sold/Mexico.
MSF-320	Impeccable	7–1–72	Scrapped.
MSF-322	Spear	7–1–72	Sold/Mexico.
MSF-340	Ardent	7–1–72	Sold/Mexico.
MSF-379	Roselle	7–1–52	Sold/Mexico.
MSF-380	Ruddy	3–1–74	Sold/Peru.
MSF-381	Scoter	7–1–72	Sold/Mexico.
MSF-382	Shoveler	5–17–74	Sold/Peru.
MSF-384	Sprig	7–1–72	Scrapped.
MSF-386	Tercel	7–1–72	Salvage Training Hulk for SERVRON 8 as of 2/73 replacing Scurry (MSF-304).
MSF-390	Wheatear	7–1–72	Scrapped.
MSO-422	Aggressive	2–28–75	Disposition pending.
MSO-424	Bold	2–28–75	Disposition pending.
MSO-425	Bulwark	2–28–75	Disposition pending.
MSO-426	Conflict	6–9–72	Scrapped.
MSO-432	Dynamic	8–1–74	Sold/Spain.
MSO-434	Embattle	2–28–75	Disposition pending.
MSO-435	Endurance	7–1–72	Scrapped.
MSO-445	Force	4–24–73	Caught fire and sank 4–24–73 en route from Subic Bay, Philippines, to Guam.
MSO-447	Guide	6–9–72	Scrapped.
MSO-457	Loyalty	7–1–72	Scrapped.
MSO-463	Pivot	8–1–74	Sold/Spain.
MSO-466	Prime	2–28–75	Disposition pending.
MSO-467	Reaper	2–28–75	Disposition pending.
MSO-473	Vigor	8–1–74	Sold/Spain.
MSO-491	Persistent	8–1–74	Sold/Spain.

Hull No.	Name	Date Stricken	Comments
PCE-873	Unnamed	11–15–74	Sold/South Korea.
PCE-882	Unnamed	11–15–74	Sold/South Korea.
PCE-896	Unnamed	11–15–74	Sold/South Korea.
PCE-898	Unnamed	11–15–74	Sold/South Korea.
PF-3	Unnamed (ex-*Tacoma*)	4–2–73	Retained by South Korean Navy as Museum and non-op. dockside trainer.
PF-4	*Sausalito*	9–1–72	Sold/South Korea.
PF-5	*Hoquiam*	8–1–72	Sold/South Korea.
PF-49	*Muskogee*	9–15–72	Sold/South Korea.
SS-220	Unnamed (ex-*Barb*)	10–15–72	GUPPY IB. Ret'd from loan to Italy 7–1–74. Scrapped.
SS-247	Unnamed (ex-*Dace*)	10–15–72	GUPPY IB. Ret'd from loan to Italy 7–1–74. Scrapped.
SS-302	*Sabalo*	7–1–71	Sunk as target.
SS-319	*Becuna*	8–15–73	GUPPY IA. Sold/Venezuela.
SS-320	Unnamed (ex-*Bergall*)	2–1–73	Last Fleet Snorkle on the NVR. Sold/Turkey.
SS-322	*Blackfin*	9–15–72	GUPPY IA. Sunk as target.
SS-323	*Caiman*	6–30–72	GUPPY IA. Sold/Turkey.
SS-324	*Blenny*	8–15–73	GUPPY IA. Ex-AGSS, SS. Scrapped.
SS-339	*Catfish*	7–1–71	GUPPY II. Sold/Argentina.
SS-340	*Entemedor*	8–1–73	GUPPY IIA. Sold/Turkey.
SS-341	*Chivo*	7–1–71	GUPPY IA. Sold/Argentina.
SS-343	*Clamagore*	6–12–75	GUPPY III. Sold/Turkey.
SS-344	*Cobbler*	11–21–73	GUPPY III. Sold/Turkey.
SS-346	*Corporal*	11–21–73	GUPPY III. Sold/Turkey.
SS-347	*Cubera*	1–5–72	GUPPY II. Sold/Venezuela.
SS-350	*Dogfish*	7–28–72	GUPPY II. Sold/Brazil.
SS-351	*Greenfish*	12–19–73	GUPPY III. Sold/Brazil.
SS-352	*Halfbeak*	7–1–71	GUPPY II. Scrapped.
SS-363	Unnamed (ex-*Guitarro*)	1–1–72	Ret'd from loan to Turkey 1–1–72. Sold/Turkey.
SS-364	Unnamed (ex-*Hammerhead*)	1–1–72	Ret'd from loan to Turkey 1–1–72. Sold/Turkey.
SS-365	*Hardhead*	7–26–72	GUPPY II. Sold/Greece.
SS-367	*Icefish*	7–15–71	Ret'd from loan to Netherlands 7–15–71. Scrapped.
SS-368	*Jallao*	6–26–74	GUPPY IIA. Sold/Spain.
SS-370	*Kraken*	11–1–74	Sold/Spain.
SS-372	*Lamprey*	9–1–71	Ret'd from loan to Argentina 9–1–71. Sold/Argentina.
SS-375	*Macabi*	9–1–71	Ret'd from loan to Argentina 9–1–71. Sold/Argentina.
SS-376	*Mapiro*	8–1–73	Sold/Turkey.
SS-377	*Menhaden*	8–15–73	GUPPY IIA. Sunk as target.
SS-378	*Mero*	8–1–73	Sold/Turkey.
SS-381	Unnamed (ex-*Sand Lance*)	9–1–72	Ret'd from loan to Brazil 9–1–72. Sold/Brazil.
SS-382	*Picuda*	11–1–74	GUPPY IIA. Sold/Spain.
SS-385	*Bang*	11–1–74	GUPPY IIA. Sold/Spain.
SS-390	*Plaice*	4–1–73	Ret'd from loan to Brazil 4–1–73. Scrapped.
SS-391	*Pomfret*	8–1–73	GUPPY IIA. Sold/Turkey.
SS-396	*Ronquil*	7–1–71	GUPPY II. Sold/Spain.
SS-403	*Atule*	8–15–73	GUPPY IA. Sold/Peru.
SS-406	*Sea Poacher*	8–15–73	GUPPY IA. Ex-AGSS, SS. Sold/Peru.
SS-410	*Threadfin*	8–1–73	GUPPY IIA. Sold/Turkey.
SS-414	*Springer*	9–1–72	Ret'd from loan to Chile 9–1–72. Sold/Chile.
SS-416	*Tiru*	7–1–75	GUPPY III. Sold/Turkey.
SS-417	*Tench*	8–15–73	GUPPY IA. Ex-AGSS, SS. Scrapped.

continued

Hull No.	Name	Date Stricken	Comments
SS-418	*Thornback*	8–1–73	GUPPY IIA. Sold/Turkey.
SS-420	*Tirante*	10–1–73	GUPPY IIA. Scrapped.
SS-421	*Trutta*	7–1–72	GUPPY IIA. Scrapped.
SS-424	*Quillback*	3–23–73	GUPPY IIA. Scrapped.
SS-425	*Trumpetfish*	10–15–73	GUPPY III. Sold/Brazil.
SS-426	*Tusk*	10–18–73	GUPPY II. Sold/Taiwan.
SS-478	*Cutlass*	4–12–73	GUPPY II. Sold/Taiwan.
SS-483	*Sea Leopard*	3–27–73	GUPPY II. Sold/Brazil.
SS-484	*Odax*	7–8–72	GUPPY II. Sold/Brazil.
SS-485	*Sirago*	6–1–72	GUPPY II. Scrapped.
SS-487	*Remora*	10–29–73	GUPPY III. Sold/Greece.
SS-522	*Amberjack*	10–17–73	GUPPY II. Sold/Brazil.
SS-523	*Grampus*	5–13–72	GUPPY II. Sold/Brazil.
SS-525	*Grenadier*	5–15–73	GUPPY II. Sold/Venezuela.
SS-564	*Trigger*	7–10–73	Sold/Italy.
SS-568	*Harder*	2–20–74	Sold/Italy.
SS-T3	*Barracuda*	10–1–73	Ex SST-3, K-1 (SSK-1). Scrapped.
SST-1	*Mackerel*	1–31–73	Scrapped.
SST-2	*Marlin*	1–31–73	Memorial Omaha, Nebraska, as of 4/74.
SSX-1	*X-1*	2–16–73	Test Hulk at NRSD, Annapolis (1973-74). Memorial at Annapolis, Maryland.

B. NONCOMMISSIONED USN SERVICE CRAFT

Hull No.	Name	Date Stricken	Comments
AFDL-35	Unnamed	8–1–73	Ex-ARDC. Sold.
AFDL-42	Unnamed	5–1–74	Ex-ARDC. Sold.
AGDS-1	*White Sands*	4–1–74	Ex ARD-20. Sold.
APL-3	Unnamed	6–1–73	Sold.
APL-8	Unnamed	7–1–73	Sold.
APL-9	Unnamed	4–1–74	Sold.
APL-10	Unnamed	6–1–73	Sold.
APL-11	Unnamed	9–1–73	Sunk as target 5–18–74.
APL-20	Unnamed	6–1–73	Ex YF-631. Sold.
APL-21	Unnamed	4–1–72	Sold.
APL-23	Unnamed	6–1–73	Sold.
APL-25	Unnamed	6–1–73	Sold.
APL-26	Unnamed	11–1–71	Trans./South Vietnam.
APL-27	Unnamed	11–1–71	Trans./South Vietnam.
APL-30	Unnamed	6–15–74	Sold.
APL-41	Unnamed	4–1–72	Sold.
APL-45	Unnamed	11–1–72	Reinstated on the NVR in 1974 for further service.
ARD-10	Unnamed	7–1–72	Sold.
ARD-11	Unnamed	4–15–74	Sold/Mexico.
ARD-16	Unnamed	10–1–72	Sold.
ARD-25	Unnamed	4–1–73	Sold/Chile.
ARD-27	Unnamed	4–1–73	Sold.
ARD-31	Unnamed	4–1–74	Trans./Air Force permanently having been on loan since 6/66.
MSS-2	Unnamed	8–30–73	Ex-*Washtenaw County* (LST-1166). Scrapped.

Hull No.	Name	Date Stricken	Comments
PGH-2	*Tucumcari*	None	Craft not on the NVR. Placed out of service 11–3–73 for disposal having been irreparably damaged by grounding on 11-16-72. Test hulk (1973-present).
YAG-60	Unnamed	7-1-71	Ex-*Butternut* (ANL-9). Originally stricken 7–18–69 as an ANL. Reinstated 10–28–69 as YAG-60. Fire-fighting training hulk, Pearl Harbor, Hawaii. Replaced ex-*Kodiak* (LSM-161).
YAG-87	*Saluda*	4-15-74	Ex IX-87. Sold.
YC-302	Unnamed	3-1-72	Sold.
YC-703	Unnamed	2-1-74	Sold.
YC-710	Unnamed	2-1-74	Sold.
YC-744	Unnamed	9-1-73	Sold.
YC-750	Unnamed	4-1-74	Sold.
YC-762	Unnamed	4-1-72	Sold.
YC-776	Unnamed	6-1-72	Sold.
YC-790	Unnamed	10-1-71	Sold.
YC-791	Unnamed	5-1-72	Sold.
YC-797	Unnamed	5-1-72	Sold.
YC-801	Unnamed	3-1-72	Sold.
YC-806	Unnamed	5-1-72	Sold.
YC-807	Unnamed	5-1-72	Sold.
YC-808	Unnamed	10-1-71	Sold.
YC-982	Unnamed	9-1-73	Sold.
YC-1063	Unnamed	4-1-72	Sold.
YC-1108	Unnamed	5-1-72	Sold.
YC-1115	Unnamed	3-1-74	Sold.
YC-1320	Unnamed	5-1-72	Sold.
YC-1325	Unnamed	5-1-73	Sold.
YC-1370	Unnamed	7-1-73	Sold.
YC-1414	Unnamed	5-1-72	Sold.
YC-1415	Unnamed	5-1-72	Sold.
YC-1416	Unnamed	7-1-73	Trans./University of Hawaii on 2–19–74 for further service.
YC-1420	Unnamed	4-1-73	Sold.
YC-1422	Unnamed	11-15-73	Sold.
YC-1427	Unnamed	6-15-74	Sold.
YC-1452	Unnamed	4-1-72	Sold.
YD-33	Unnamed	7-1-73	Sold.
YD-72	Unnamed	10-15-74	Sold.
YD-76	Unnamed	11-1-74	Ex-YC. Sold.
YD-130	Unnamed	12-1-74	Sold.
YD-148	Unnamed	4-1-73	Sold.
YD-187	Unnamed	4-1-74	Sold.
YD-190	Unnamed	10-15-74	Sold.
YD-195	Unnamed	7-15-72	Trans./South Vietnam.
YD-221	Unnamed	1-1-74	Sold.
YDT-9	Unnamed	4-1-73	Ex-LCU. Accidentally sunk 6/74 in Chesapeake Bay. Raised and scrapped.
YF-861	Unnamed	9-10-73	Donated to private organization.
YF-863	Unnamed	6-1-74	Sold.
YF-864	*Little Compton*	11-1-73	Sold.
YF-867	Unnamed	6-1-74	Sold.
YF-869	Unnamed	2-1-74	Sold.
YF-871	Unnamed	4-1-74	Sold.
YF-872	Unnamed	4-1-74	Sold.

continued

Hull No.	Name	Date Stricken	Comments
YF-873	Unnamed	4–1–74	Sold.
YF-874	Unnamed	4–1–74	Sold.
YF-875	Unnamed	4–1–74	Sold.
YF-876	Unnamed	4–1–74	Sold.
YF-877	Unnamed	10–1–73	Trans./Cape Fear Technical Institute, Wilmington, N.C., on 2–1–74 for further service.
YF-878	Unnamed	4–1–74	Sold.
YF-879	Unnamed	4–1–74	Sold.
YF-880	Unnamed	9–15–74	Sold.
YF-883	Unnamed	4–1–74	Sold.
YF-884	Unnamed	4–1–74	Sold.
YF-886	Unnamed	9–15–74	Sold.
YF-887	Unnamed	9–15–74	Sold.
YFD-15	Unnamed	9–1–71	Sold.
YFD-55	Unnamed	2–15–73	Sold.
YFN-273	Unnamed	5–1–73	Sold.
YFN-302	Unnamed	5–1–72	Sold.
YFN-322	Unnamed	2–1–74	Sold.
YFN-710	Unnamed	11–1–71	Sold.
YFN 016	Unnamed	6–1–72	Sold.
YFN-950	Unnamed	7–1–72	Sold.
YFN-957	Unnamed	9–15–74	Sold.
YFN-995	Unnamed	10–1–71	Sold.
YFN-1182	Unnamed	9–15–74	Sold.
YFN-1185	Unnamed	10–1–71	Sold.
YFN-1201	Unnamed	9–15–74	Sold.
YFN-1210	Unnamed	8–1–74	Sold.
YFNB-18	Unnamed	6–1–72	Ex-YFN. Sold.
YFNB-27	Unnamed	11–8–72	Ex-YFN. Sold.
YFNB-28	Unnamed	6–1–72	Ex-YFN. Sold.
YFND-10	Unnamed	9–1–71	Sold.
YFND-28	Unnamed	5–1–73	Ex-YFN. Sold.
YFNX-8	Unnamed	10–1–72	Ex-YFN. Sold.
YFNX-14	Unnamed	7–15–74	Ex-YC. Sold.
YFNX-29	Unnamed	2–1–75	Ex-YFN. Sold.
YFP-1	Jacona	5–1–71	Trans./A.I.D. on 10–12–71 for further service.
YFP-10	Unnamed	9–1–74	Ex-Duval (AK-177). Scrapped.
YFR-889	Unnamed	11–1–71	Trans./South Vietnam.
YFRN-1236	Unnamed	10–15–74	Sold.
YFRT-257	Unnamed	9–1–73	Sold. Ex-YF.
YFRT-419	Unnamed	10–15–74	Sold.
YFRT-521	Unnamed	9–1–72	Sold.
YFRT-524	Unnamed	5–15–74	Ex-Range Recoverer (AGM-2), AG-161, FS-278. Sold.
YFU-4	Unnamed	10–1–74	Ex-LCU. Sold.
YFU-8	Unnamed	8–1–71	Ex-LCU. Sold.
YFU-18	Unnamed	7–1–72	Ex-LCU. Sold.
YFU-24	Unnamed	10–15–74	Ex-LCU. Salvage Training Hulk.
YFU-25	Unnamed	5–1–72	Ex-LCU. Sold.
YFU-37	Unnamed	12–1–71	Ex-LCU. Sold.
YFU-39	Unnamed	9–1–73	Ex-LCU. Sold.
YFU-47	Unnamed	8–1–71	Ex-LCU. Sold.

Hull No.	Name	Date Stricken	Comments
YFU-52	Unnamed	5-1-72	Ex-LCU. Sold.
YFU-54	Unnamed	7-1-72	Ex-LCU. Sold.
YFU-57	Unnamed	10-15-74	Ex-LCU. Sold.
YFU-58	Unnamed	12-1-71	Ex-LCU. Sold.
YFU-59	Unnamed	1-1-73	Ex-LCU. Sold.
YFU-60	Unnamed	12-1-71	Ex-LCU. Sold.
YFU-61	Unnamed	7-1-72	Ex-LCU. Sold.
YFU-64	Unnamed	7-1-72	Ex-LCU. Sold.
YFU-65	Unnamed	7-1-72	Ex-LCU. Sold.
YFU-66	Unnamed	7-1-72	Ex-LCU. Sold.
YFU-70	Unnamed	7-1-72	Ex-LCU. Sold.
YFU-87	Unnamed	2-1-72	Ex-LCU. Sold.
YFU-89	Unnamed	10-15-74	Ex-LCU. Sold.
YFU-90	Unnamed	11-1-71	Ex-LCU. Sold.
YFU-92	Unnamed	11-1-71	Ex-LCU. Sold.
YFU-96	Unnamed	12-1-74	Ex-LCU. Sold.
YG-22	Unnamed	5-15-74	Sold.
YG-23	Unnamed	11-15-73	Sold.
YG-24	Unnamed	5-15-74	Sold.
YG-29	Unnamed	7-1-72	Sold.
YG-30	Unnamed	5-1-72	Sold.
YG-31	Unnamed	7-1-71	Sold.
YG-33	Unnamed	11-15-73	Sold.
YG-35	Unnamed	7-1-72	Sold.
YG-37	Unnamed	11-15-73	Sold.
YG-46	Unnamed	4-1-74	Sold.
YG-48	Unnamed	7-1-72	Sold.
YG-49	Unnamed	8-1-74	Sold.
YG-50	Unnamed	4-1-74	Sold.
YG-51	Unnamed	10-1-74	Last YG on the NVR. Sold.
YG-53	Unnamed	8-15-74	Sold.
YG-54	Unnamed	8-15-74	Sold.
YG-55	Unnamed	5-15-74	Sold.
YGN-77	Unnamed	2-1-74	Sold.
YGN-78	Unnamed	5-15-74	Sold.
YLLC-1	Unnamed	7-15-71	Ex-LCU. Trans./South Vietnam.
YLLC-2	Unnamed	5-1-72	Ex-LCU. Sold.
YLLC-3	Unnamed	7-15-71	Ex-LCU. Trans./South Vietnam.
YLLC-5	Unnamed	7-15-71	Ex-LCU. Trans./South Vietnam.
YM-12	Unnamed	7-1-71	Sold.
YM-31	Sand Caster	9-1-72	Sold.
YMLC-3	Salvager	8-1-72	Ex-ARSD-3, LSM-551. Sold.
YMLC-4	Windlass	8-1-72	Ex-ARSD-4, LSM-552. Sold.
YNG-4	Unnamed	8-1-71	Sold.
YNG-5	Unnamed	5-15-74	Sold.
YNG-13	Unnamed	3-1-74	Sold.
YNG-15	Unnamed	12-1-73	Sold.
YNG-16	Unnamed	8-1-71	Sold.
YNG-23	Unnamed	5-15-74	Sold.

continued

Hull No.	Name	Date Stricken	Comments
YNG-25	Unnamed	12–1–73	Sold.
YNG-26	Unnamed	12–1–73	Sold.
YNG-27	Unnamed	5–15–74	Sold.
YNG-28	Unnamed	9–1–74	Sold.
YO-43	Unnamed	6–1–74	Sold.
YO-45	Unnamed	4–1–74	Sold.
YO-49	*Whipstock*	1–1–75	Sold.
YO-55	*Gauger*	4–1–74	Sunk as target.
YO-65	Unnamed	10–15–74	Sold.
YO-68	Unnamed	11–1–73	Trans./MarAd on 1–30–74 for further service.
YO-69	Unnamed	2–1–74	Sold.
YO-72	Unnamed	11–1–73	Sold.
YO-75	Unnamed	12–1–73	Sold.
YO-77	Unnamed	6–1–74	Sold.
YO-78	Unnamed	3–1–74	Sold.
YO-105	Unnamed	12–1–73	Sold.
YO-109	Unnamed	6–1–74	Sold.
YO-112	Unnamed	10–15–74	Sold.
YO-113	Unnamed	4–1–74	Sold.
YO-114	Unnamed	12–1–73	Sold.
YO-115	Unnamed	10–15–74	Sold.
YO-116	Unnamed	10–15–74	Sold.
YO-120	Unnamed	1–1–74	Sold.
YO-121	Unnamed	6–1–74	Sold.
YO-123	Unnamed	12–17–73	Sold.
YO-125	Unnamed	6–1–74	Sold.
YO-126	Unnamed	10–15–74	Sold.
YO-128	Unnamed	12–17–73	Sold.
YO-133	Unnamed	2–1–74	Sold.
YO-168	Unnamed	6–1–74	Sold.
YO-169	Unnamed	2–1–74	Sold.
YO-170	Unnamed	6–1–74	Sold.
YO-172	Unnamed	4–1–74	Sold.
YO-176	Unnamed	4–1–74	Sold.
YO-177	Unnamed	11–1–74	Sold.
YO-180	Unnamed	6–1–74	Trans./Dept. of Transportation for further service.
YO-190	Unnamed	6–1–74	Sold.
YO-191	Unnamed	4–1–74	Sold.
YO-192	Unnamed	1–1–75	Sold.
YO-193	Unnamed	11–1–74	Sold.
YO-201	Unnamed	6–1–74	Trans./Dept. of Transportation for further service.
YO-204	Unnamed	6–1–74	Sold.
YO-210	Unnamed	4–1–74	Sold.
YO-212	Unnamed	6–1–74	Trans./Dept. of Transportation for further service.
YO-221	Unnamed	2–1–74	Sold/Peru.
YO-226	Unnamed	7–1–74	Sold/Denmark.
YO-229	Unnamed	7–1–74	Sold/Denmark.
YO-263	Unnamed	10–1–73	Ex-YOG. Sold.
YOG-35	Unnamed	8–15–74	Sold.
YOG-36	Unnamed	7–15–74	Sold.

Hull No.	Name	Date Stricken	Comments
YOG-37	Unnamed	5–15–74	Sold.
YOG-56	Unnamed	7–15–72	Trans./South Vietnam.
YOG-57	Unnamed	10–15–74	Sunk as target.
YOG-59	Unnamed	11–1–74	Sold.
YOG-61	Unnamed	10–15–74	Sold.
YOG-63	Unnamed	5–15–74	Sold.
YOG-77	Unnamed	1–1–74	Sold.
YOG-90	Unnamed	5–15–74	Sold.
YOG-92	Unnamed	5–15–74	Sold.
YOG-131	Unnamed	7–15–71	Trans./South Vietnam.
YON-89	Unnamed	11–1–74	Sold.
YON-254	Unnamed	3–1–72	Accidentally sunk 1–14–71. Unsalvagable.
YOS-4	Unnamed	7–1–72	Sold.
YOS-13	Unnamed	2–1–72	Sold.
YP-584	Unnamed	5–1–74	Sold.
YP-585	Unnamed	5–1–74	Sold.
YP-586	Unnamed	10–1–74	Sold.
YP-588	Unnamed	2–1–72	Sold.
YPD-36	Unnamed	9–1–74	Sold.
YPD-44	Unnamed	8–1–71	Sold.
YR-40	Unnamed	4–1–74	Sold/Guatamala.
YR-71	Unnamed	11–1–71	Trans./South Vietnam.
YRB-6	Unnamed	9–1–71	Sold.
YRB-13	Unnamed	9–1–72	Sold.
YRB-16	Unnamed	10–15–74	Ex-YFN. Sold.
YRBM-16	Unnamed	10–2–73	Trans./South Vietnam.
YRBM-17	Unnamed	7–15–71	Trans./South Vietnam.
YRBM-18	Unnamed	11–27–72	Ex APL-55. Trans./South Vietnam.
YRDH-8	Unnamed	8–1–74	Donated to private organization.
YRST-4	*Naubec*	2–1–75	Ex AN-84. Sold.
YSD-25	Unnamed	5–1–74	Sold.
YSD-27	Unnamed	8–1–71	Sold.
YSD-33	Unnamed	6–1–74	Sold.
YSD-44	Unnamed	8–1–71	Sold.
YSD-46	Unnamed	3–1–74	Trans./MarAd on 3–14–74 for further service at the Suisun Bay Reserve Fleet.
YSD-51	Unnamed	5–1–74	Sold.
YSD-52	Unnamed	6–1–74	Sold.
YSD-54	Unnamed	6–1–74	Sold.
YSD-65	Unnamed	6–15–74	Sold.
YSD-66	Unnamed	10–15–74	Donated to private organization.
YSD-69	Unnamed	6–1–74	Sold.
YSR-22	Unnamed	9–1–74	Sold.
YSR-24	Unnamed	10–15–74	Sold.
YSR-35	Unnamed	9–1–74	Sold.
YSR-36	Unnamed	9–1–74	Sold.
YTL-423	Unnamed	8–15–72	Sold.
YTL-424	Unnamed	8–1–72	Sold.
YTL-428	Unnamed	8–15–72	Sold.

continued

Hull No.	Name	Date Stricken	Comments
YTL-432	Unnamed	2-1-72	Sank 1-9-72 off Cape Flattery, Wash., while being transported on ex-*General Meigs* (AP-116) to Suisun Bay, Calif. AP-116 broke her tow during transit and ran aground. When she broke up on the rocks YTL-432 sank.
YTL-440	Unnamed	10-15-74	Sold.
YTL-452	Unnamed	7-15-71	Trans./South Vietnam.
YTL-456	Unnamed	7-15-71	Trans./South Vietnam.
YTL-457	Unnamed	7-15-71	Trans./South Vietnam.
YTL-553	Unnamed	7-1-74	Sold.
YTL-557	Unnamed	8-15-72	Sold.
YTL-560	Unnamed	11-1-71	Sold.
YTL-571	Unnamed	7-15-74	Sold.
YTL-586	Unnamed	7-15-71	Trans./South Vietnam.
YTL-592	Unnamed	8-15-72	Sold.
YTL-601	Unnamed	11-1-73	Sold.
YTM-129	Osceola	2-15-73	Ex-YTB, YT. Sold.
YTM-131	Massasoit	4-1-72	Ex-YTB, YT. Sold.
YTM-140	Wahtah	10-15-74	Ex-YTB, YT. Sold.
YTM-142	Nokomis	5-1-73	Ex-YTB, YT. Sold.
YTM-145	Montezuma	10-15-74	Ex-YTB, YT. Sold.
YTM-147	Tazha	5-1-73	Ex-YTB, YT. Sold.
YTM-148	Wenonah	4-1-74	Ex-YTB, YT. Sold.
YTM-174	Allaquippa	6-1-73	Ex-YTB, YT. Sold.
YTM-175	Chekilli	5-1-73	Ex-YTB, YT. Sold.
YTM-182	Mawkaw	7-1-72	Ex-YTB, YT. Sold.
YTM-188	Negwagon	7-1-72	Ex-YTB, YT. Sold.
YTM-195	Yonaguska	8-15-74	Ex-YTB, YT. Sold.
YTM-266	Pocahontas	11-1-71	Ex-YTB, YT. Sold.
YTM-269	Sakarissa	1-15-74	Ex-YTB, YT. Trans./MarAd on 1-23-74 for further service.
YTM-272	Iwana	2-1-74	Ex-YTB, YT. Sold.
YTM-365	Segwarusa	1-1-74	Ex-YTB, YT. Sold.
YTM-367	Wawasee	5-1-74	Ex-YTB, YT. Trans./Mass. Maritime Academy for further service.
YTM-369	Shamokin	7-1-72	Ex-YTB, YT. Sold.
YTM-370	Skandawati	2-15-73	Ex-YTB, YT. Sold.
YTM-372	Tatarrax	5-1-73	Ex-YTB, YT. Trans./University of Hawaii on 3-8-74 for further service.
YTM-374	Vaga	10-1-72	Ex-YTB, YT. Sold.
YTM-384	Waneta	4-1-74	Ex-YTB, YT. Sold.
YTM-387	Watseka	7-1-72	Ex-YTB, YT. Sold.
YTM-396	Wovoka	6-1-74	Ex-YTB, YT. Sold.
YTM-401	Owachomo	5-15-74	Ex-YTB, YT. Sold.
YTM-407	Lonoto	8-1-73	Ex-YTB, YT. Sold.
YTM-412	Conchardee	9-1-71	Ex-YTB, YT. Sold.
YTM-416	Sonnicant	7-1-72	Ex-YTB, YT. Sold.
YTM-494	Alnaba	1-1-72	Ex-YTB, YT. Sold.
YTM-535	Nahasho	5-1-74	Ex-YTB, YT. Sold.
YTM-537	Nanigo	9-1-73	Ex-YTB, YT. Disappeared at sea on 4-7-73 when her tow line parted in heavy seas while she was under tow to Bremerton. Presumed sunk.
YTM-539	Sikis	5-15-74	Ex-YTB, YT. Sold.
YTM-540	Quileute	11-1-73	Ex-YTB, YT. Trans./Maine Maritime Academy for cannibalization in support of YTM-541. Returned to USN. Scrapped.
YTM-541	Ozette	11-1-73	Ex-YTB, YT. Trans./Maine Maritime Academy on 7-30-74 for further service.
YTM-703	Canarsee	1-1-75	Ex-YTB, YT. Sold.
YTM-747	Chicopee	11-1-73	Ex-YTB, YT. Sold.

Hull No.	Name	Date Stricken	Comments
YTM-753	*Naugatuck*	4-1-74	Ex-Army. Sold.
YTM-756	*Owatonna*	1-15-75	Ex-Army. Trans./MarAd, Suisun Bay for further service.
YTM-757	*Wahpeton*	3-1-74	Ex-Army. Sold.
YTM-758	Unnamed	3-1-73	Ex-Army. Sold.
YTM-762	*Pokanoket*	7-15-72	Ex-Army. Trans./South Vietnam.
YTM-763	Unnamed	7-1-72	Originally stricken on 5-1-64 as *Sabeata* (YTB-287). Reclassified YTM in 1965. There is no record of this YTM being reinstated on the NVR, but she continued in service until stricken as indicated. Sold.
YTM-769	*Hombro*	7-15-72	Ex-YTB, YT. Trans./South Vietnam.
YTM-771	*Nootka*	7-15-72	Ex-YTB, YT. Trans./South Vietnam.
YTM-772	*Makah*	10-1-71	Ex-YTB, YT. Sold.
YTM-774	*Carascan*	10-1-72	Ex-YTB, YT. Sold.
YW-85	Unnamed	7-1-74	Sold.
YW-90	Unnamed	7-15-74	Sold.
YW-95	Unnamed	5-1-74	Sold.
YW-103	Unnamed	10-15-74	Sold.
YW-104	Unnamed	6-1-74	Sold.
YW-105	Unnamed	2-1-74	Sold.
YW-106	Unnamed	6-1-74	Sold.
YW-107	Unnamed	6-1-74	Sold.
YW-111	Unnamed	10-15-74	Sold.
YW-112	Unnamed	5-1-74	Sold.
YW-114	Unnamed	12-17-73	Sold.
YW-116	Unnamed	12-17-73	Sold.
YW-117	Unnamed	5-15-74	Sold.
YW-118	Unnamed	1-1-74	Sold.
YW-130	Unnamed	10-15-74	Sold.
YW-132	Unnamed	6-1-74	Sold.
YWN-59	Unnamed	10-15-74	Sold.

C. U.S. COAST GUARD SHIPS AND CRAFT

Since the Coast Guard does not strike ships per se, the date given in the "Date Action Taken"
column is the date that the ship or craft ceased to be a Coast Guard ship or craft.

Hull No.	Name	Date Action Taken	Comments
WAGB-279	*Eastwind*	7-31-72	Sold.
WAGO-377	*Rockaway*	10-25-73	Ex-WHEC, WAVP, USN AVP-29. Scrapped.
WAGW-387	*Gresham*	10-25-73	EX-WHEC, WAVP, USN AGP-9, AVP-57. Scrapped.
WAK-186	*Kukui*	2-29-72	Ex-USS *Doddridge* (AK-176). Only AK in Coast Guard. Trans./USN for further transfer to the Philippines.
WHEC-42	*Sebago*	4-14-72	Trans./MarAd for disposal. Scrapped.
WHEC-44	*Wachusett*	9- -74	Scrapped.
WHEC-66	*Klamath*	9- -74	Scrapped.
WHEC-374	*Absecon*	5-9-72	EX-WAVP, USN AVP-23. Trans./USN for further trans. to South Vietnam.
WHEC-375	*Chincoteague*	5-9-72	Ex-WAVP, USN AVP-24. Trans./USN for further trans. to South Vietnam.

continued

Hull No.	Name	Date Action Taken	Comments
WHEC-383	Castle Rock	12–21–71	Ex-WAVP, USN AVP-35. Trans./USN for further trans. to South Vietnam.
WHEC-384	Cook Inlet	12–21–71	Ex-WAVP, USN AVP-36. Trans./USN for further trans. to South Vietnam.
WHEC-386	McCulloch	5–9–72	Ex-WAVP, USN AGP-8, AVP-56. Trans./USN for further trans. to South Vietnam.
WLB-270	Cactus	10–9–73	Sold.
WLB-289	Woodbink	6–9–72	Donated to a private organization for further service.
WLB-328	Magnolia	11–15–72	Ex-USN Barricade (ACM-3). Sold.
WLB-332	Willow	7–28–71	Ex-USN Picket (ACM-8). Sold.
WLB-398	Redbud	3–1–72	Ex-USNS Redbud (T-AKL-398), USCG Redbud (WAGL-398). Trans./USN for further trans. to the Philippines.
WLI-234	Maple	8–8–73	Trans./USN.
WLI-248	Tamarack	8–2–71	Sold.
WLI-255	Zinnia	3–1–72	Trans./USAF.
WLM-227	Lilac	6–6–72	Donated to a private organization for further service.
WLR-213	Goldenrod	9–26–73	Trans./National Service Foundation.
WLR-241	Poplar	9–26–73	Trans./National Service Foundation.
WLR-304	Fern	6–19–72	Sold.
WLV-196	Unnamed	5–20–72	Donated to a private organization for further service.
WLV-523	Unnamed	9–25–71	Trans./South Vietnam.
WLV-530	Unnamed	12–29–71	Donated to a private organization for further service.
WLV-532	Unnamed	3–30–72	Donated to a private organization for further service.
WLV-538	Unnamed	8–25–71	Trans./National Park Service.
WLV-539	Unnamed	8–9–73	Donated to a private organization for further service.
WMEC-147	Morris	11–5–71	Trans./Sea Scouts in 12/71 for further service as their training ship.
WTR-410	Courier	1–31–72	Trans./MarAd for disposal.
WTR-885	Tanager	11–3–72	Ex-USN MSF-385. Scrapped.
WTR-899	Lamar	11–8–71	Ex-USN PCE-899. Scrapped.

FOURTEEN: FORMER NAVAL VESSELS IN MARAD RESERVE FLEET

By the middle of FY 1975, there were 183 former naval vessels of merchant and navy design laid up in the three Maritime Administration (MarAd) reserve fleets throughout the country. The list of ships is arranged alphabetically by classification and within each classification by hull number. A type breakdown of the ships laid up in MarAd is as follows:
AD: 1; AE: 7; AF: 8; AG: 4; AGM: 3; AGP: 1; AGR: 1; AGS: 1; AH: 1; AK: 6; AKA/LKA: 14; AN: 8; AO: 16; AOG: 3; AP: 16; APA/LPA: 37; AR: 2; AGR: 2; ARS: 1; ARVH: 1; AS: 1; ATA: 9; ATF: 13; LCC: 4; LSD: 8; LST: 13; MCS: 2

Abbreviations used in this section are as follows:
Berthing Areas:
Suisun—Suisun Bay, San Francisco, Calif.; James—James River, Va.; Beaumont—Beaumont, Texas.
Miscellaneous:
*—Indicates the date the ship was transferred to the custody of MarAd, but has not been stricken from the Naval Vessel Register (NVR). The asterisk appears immediately after the date in "Date Stricken" column. If it appears after the date and there is no "(temp.)" immediately after the ship's name (see following abbreviation), the ship in question has been transferred to the permanent custody of MarAd.
(temp.)—Appearing immediately after a ship's name in the "Name" column, this abbreviation indicates that the ship has been transferred to the temporary custody of MarAd. The abbreviation is used *only* in conjunction with an asterisk appearing after a date in the "Date Stricken" column. In all cases, the temporary or permanent transfer of former U.S. naval ships to MarAd is for layup only. A naval ship cannot be disposed of without first being stricken from the NVR.
[1]—Indicates a ship will be disposed of in the immediate future; appears immediately after the Reserve Fleet location in the "Berthing Area" column.

MERCHANT SHIP TYPE NOMENCLATURE
Classification of Vessels

Type		Length in Feet at Load Water Line			
		1	2	3	4
C	Cargo	Under 400	400–450	450–500	500–550
P	Passenger	Under 500	500–600	600–700	700–800
N	Coastal Cargo	Under 200	200–250	250–300	300–350
R	Refrigerated Cargo	Under 400	400–450	450–500	500–550
S	Special (Navy)	Under 200	200–300	300–400	400–500
T	Tanker	Under 450	450–500	500–550	550–600

TYPE POWER—NUMBER PROPELLERS—PASSENGERS

Power	Single Screw		Twin Screw	
	1/12 Passengers	13+ Passengers	1/12 Passengers	13+ Passengers
Steam	S	S1	ST	S2
Motor (Diesel)	M	M1	MT	M2
Turbo-Electric	SE	SE1	SET	SE2

Example: R1-M-AV3. R1 = refrigerated cargo ship under 400' long; M = diesel powered; AV3 = 3rd variation ("3") of the 22nd modification ("V") of the original design ("A").
Notes: Prefix "E" stands for emergency as in EC2 (*Liberty* ships); "V" stands for VC2 *Victory* ships; "Z" indicates a special conversion of standard designs.

Hull No.	Name	Date Stricken	Type	Berthing Area	Hull No.	Name	Date Stricken	Type	Berthing Area
AD-29	Isle Royale	9-1-71*	Mod. C3	Suisun	AN-13	Buckeye	7-1-63	Navy design	Suisun
AE-3	Lassen	7-1-61	C2	Suisun	AN-15	Ebony	9-1-62	Navy design	Suisun
AE-8	Mauna Loa	9-1-71*	C2	James	AN-24	Mango	9-1-62	Navy design	Suisun
AE-10	Sangay	7-1-60	C1-A	Beaumont	AN-79	Etlah	7-1-63	Navy design	Suisun
AE-12	Wrangell (temp.)	4-29-71*	C2-S-AJ1	James	AN-86	Passaconaway	7-1-63	Navy design	Suisun
AE-13	Akutan	7-1-60	Mod. C2	Beaumont	AN-87	Passaic	7-1-63	Navy design	Suisun
AE-14	Firedrake (temp.)	7-21-71*	C2-S-AJ1	Suisun	AO-25	Sabine	9-1-71*	T3-S2-A1	James
AE-18	Paricutin	6-1-73	C2-S-AJ1	Suisun	AO-36	Kennebec	9-1-71*	T2-A Mod.	Suisun
AF-28	Hyades	9-1-71*	C2-S-E1	James	AO-37	Merrimack	2-1-59	T2-A	Beaumont
AF-34	Kerstin	6-16-50	R1-M-AV3	Suisun	AO-42	Monongahela	2-1-59	T2-A	Beaumont
AF-41	Athanasia	1-8-46	R1-M-AV3	Suisun[1]	AO-43	Tappahannock	9-1-71*	T2-A	Suisun
AF-49	Zelima	9-1-71*	R2-S-BV1	Suisun	AO-54	Chikaskia (temp.)	9-4-70*	T3-S2-A1	James
AF-52	Arcturus (temp.)	10-18-73*	C2-S-B1	James	AO-56	Aucilla (temp.)	10-7-71*	T3-S2-A1	James
AF-54	Pictor (temp.)	8-11-70*	R2-S-BV1	Suisun	AO-67	Cache	5-6-72*	T2-SE-A1	Beaumont
AF-55	Aludra (temp.)	10-1-69*	R2-S-BV1	Suisun	AO-69	Enoree	2-1-59	T3-S-A1	Beaumont
AF-61	Procyon (temp.)	2-4-71*	R2-S-BV1	Suisun	AO-72	Niobrara	2-1-59	T3-S-A1	Beaumont
AG-68	Basilan	5-22-47	EC2-S-C5	Suisun	AO-75	Saugatuck (temp.)	11-5-74*	T2-SE-A1	James
AG-71	Baham	5-22-47	EC2-S-C5	Suisun	AO-78	Chepachet	3-13-72*	T2-SE-A1	Suisun
AG-154	Observation Island (temp.)	1-26-73*	C4-S-1A	Suisun	AO-93	Soubarissen	7-1-61	T2-SE-A2	Beaumont
AG-169	Pvt. Jose E. Valdez	9-1-71*	C1-M-AV1	James	AO-97	Allagash	6-1-73	T2-S2-A1	James
AGM-4	Richfield	10-9-69	VC2-S-AP2	Suisun	AO-117	Mission Los Angeles	8-13-59	T2-SE-A2	James[1]
AGM-14	Rose Knot	10-9-69	C1-M-AV1	Suisun	AO-134	Mission Santa Ynez	3-6-75	TS-SE-A2	Suisun
AGM-17	Timber Hitch	10-9-69	C1-M-AV1	James	AOG-68	Peconic	11-12-57	T1-M-BT1	Beaumont
AGP-13	Cyrene	7-19-46	C1-A	Suisun	AOG-81	Alatna (temp.)	8-8-72*	T1-MET-24a	Suisun
AGR-11	Protector	9-1-65	ZEC2-S-C5	James	AOG-82	Chattahoochee (temp.)	2-22-72*	T1-MET-24a	Suisun
AGS-36	Coastal Crusader	4-1-70*	C1-M-AV1	Suisun	AP-110	General John Pope	5-1-70*	P2-S2-R2	Suisun
AH-7	Hope	5-21-46	C1-B	Suisun	AP-111	General A. E. Anderson	12-11-58	P2-S2-R2	Suisun
AK-91	Betsy Ross (ex-USN Cor Caroli)	12-19-45	EC2-S-C1	James	AP-112	General William A. Mann	12-1-66	P2-S2-R2	James
AK-227	Boulder Victory	9- -57*	VC2-S-AP2	Suisun	AP-114	General William Mitchell	12-1-66	P2-S2-R2	Suisun
AK-228	Provo Victory	11- -53*	VC2-S-AP2	Suisun	AP-117	General William Gordon	4-23-70*	P2-S2-R2	James
AK-235	Red Oak Victory	7-19-46	VC2-S-AP2	Suisun	AP-119	General William Weigel	4-7-70*	P2-S2-R2	Suisun
AK-236	Lakewood Victory	6-5-46	VC2-S-AP2	Suisun	AP-120	General Daniel I. Sultan	10-9-69	P2-SE2-R1	Suisun
AK-267	Marine Fiddler (temp.)	9-14-73*	C4-S-B5	James	AP-121	General Hugh J. Gaffey	10-9-69	P2-SE2-R1	Suisun
AKA-12	Libra	7-1-60	C2-F	James	AP-122	General Alexander M. Patch	5-26-70*	P2-SE2-R1	James
LKA-19	Thuban	9-1-71*	C2-S-B1	James	AP-123	General Simon B. Buckner	3-24-70*	P2-SE2-R1	James
LKA-54	Algol	9-1-71*	C2-S-B1	James	AP-124	General Edwin D. Patrick	10-9-69	P2-SE2-R1	Suisun
AKA-55	Alshain	7-1-60	C2-S-B1	Beaumont	AP-125	General Nelson M. Walker	4-16-70*	P2-SE2-R1	James
LKA-57	Capricornus	9-1-71*	C2-S-B1	James	AP-126	General Maurice Rose	6-8-70*	P2-SE2-R1	James
LKA-61	Muliphen	9-1-71*	C2-S-B1	James	AP-127	General William O. Darby	6-30-70*	P2-SE2-R1	James
LKA-93	Yancey (temp.)	3-18-71*	C2-S-B1	James	AP-176	General J. C. Breckenridge	12-1-66	P2-SE2-R1	Suisun
LKA-94	Winston (temp.)	2-17-70*	C2-S-B1	Suisun	AP-197	Geiger (temp.)	4-26-71*	P2-S1-DN3	Suisun
LKA-97	Merrick (temp.)	12-15-69*	C2-S-B1	Suisun	APA-20	President Hayes	10-1-58	C3-IN-P&C	Suisun[1]
LKA-103	Rankin (temp.)	8-12-71*	C2-S-AJ3	James	APA-138	Braxton	7-19-46	VC2-S-AP5	James[1]
LKA-104	Seminole (temp.)	5-20-71*	C2-S-AJ3	Suisun	APA-140	Brookings	10-1-58	VC2-S-AP5	James[1]
LKA-106	Union	9-1-71*	C2-S-AJ3	Suisun	APA-153	Laurens	5-1-46	VC2-S-AP5	James[1]
LKA-107	Vermilion (temp.)	7-27-71*	C2-S-AJ3	James	APA-154	Lowndes	5-1-46	VC2-S-AP5	James[1]
LKA-108	Washburn	9-1-71*	C2-S-AJ3	Suisun	APA-156	Mellette	7-1-60	VC2-S-AP5	James[1]
AN-8	Boxwood	9-1-62	Navy design	Suisun	APA-157	Napa	6-19-46	VC2-S-AP5	James[1]
AN-12	Cinchona	9-1-62	Navy design	Suisun	APA-158	Newberry	3-12-46	VC2-S-AP5	James[1]

Hull No.	Name	Date Stricken	Type	Berthing Area	Hull No.	Name	Date Stricken	Type	Berthing Area
APA-164	Edgecombe	10-1-58	VC2-S-AP5	James[1]	ATF-88	Narragansett	9-1-61	Navy design	Beaumont
APA-168	Gage	10-1-58	VC2-S-AP5	James[1]	ATF-91	Seneca (temp.)	11-18-71*	Navy design	James
APA-169	Gallatin	5-8-46	VC2-S-AP5	James[1]	ATF-102	Hidasta	7-1-63	Navy design	Suisun
APA-176	Kershaw	10-1-58	VC2-S-AP5	James[1]	ATF-104	Jicarilla	7-1-63	Navy design	Suisun
APA-177	Kingsbury	5-1-46	VC2-S-AP5	James[1]	ATF-115	Tenino	9-1-62	Navy design	Beaumont
APA-180	Lavaca	10-1-58	VC2-S-AP5	James[1]	ATF-118	Wenatchee	9-1-62	Navy design	Beaumont
APA-188	Olmstead	7-1-60	VC2-S-AP5	James[1]	ATF-148	Achomawi	9-1-62	Navy design	Beaumont
LPA-194	Sandoval	9-1-71*	VC2-S-AP5	James	ATF-151	Chawasha	7-1-63	Navy design	Suisun
APA-197	Lubbock	10-1-58	VC2-S-AP5	Suisun[1]	ATF-154	Chirariko	7-1-63	Navy design	Suisun
APA-198	McCracken	10-1-58	VC2-S-AP5	Suisun[1]	LCC-7	Mount McKinley	9-1-71*	C2-S-AJ1	Suisun
LPA-199	Magoffin	10-31-68*	VC2-S-AP5	Suisun	LCC-12	Estes	9-1-71*	C2-S-AJ1	Suisun
APA-202	Menifee	10-1-58	VC2-S-AP5	Suisun[1]	LCC-16	Pocono (temp.)	2-1-72*	C2-S-AJ1	James
APA-203	Meriwether	10-1-58	VC2-S-AP5	Suisun[1]	LCC-17	Taconic	9-1-71*	C2-S-AJ1	James
APA-204	Sarasota	7-1-60	VC2-S-AP5	James[1]	LSD-13	Casa Grande	9-1-71*	Navy design	James
APA-206	Sibley	10-1-58	VC2-S-AP5	Suisun[1]	LSD-14	Rushmore (temp.)	2-10-71*	Navy design	James
APA-207	Mifflin	10-1-58	VC2-S-AP5	Suisun[1]	LSD-15	Shadwell	9-1-71*	Navy design	James
LPA-208	Talladega	9-1-71*	VC2-S-AP5	Suisun	LSD-16	Cabildo (temp.)	7-9-70*	Navy design	Suisun
LPA-213	Mountrail	9-1-71*	VC2-S-AP5	James	LSD-18	Colonial	9-1-71*	Navy design	Suisun
LPA-215	Navarro	9-1-71*	VC2-S-AP5	Suisun	LSD-20	Donner (temp.)	4-27-71*	Navy design	James
APA-221	Oneida	10-1-58	VC2-S-AP5	Suisun[1]	LSD-26	Tortuga	9-1-71*	Navy design	Suisun
LPA-222	Pickaway	9-1-71*	VC2-S-AP5	Suisun	LSD-27	Whetstone	9-1-71*	Navy design	Suisun
APA-225	Bingham	7-3-46	VC2-S-AP5	James[1]	LST-399	USNS LST-399	11-1-73	Navy design	Suisun
APA-226	Rawlins	10-1-58	VC2-S-AP5	James[1]	LST-566	USNS LST-566	6-30-75	Navy design	Suisun
APA-227	Renville	6-30-68	VC2-S-AP5	Suisun	LST-715	USNS De Kalb County	11-1-73	Navy design	Suisun
APA-230	Rockwall	12-1-58	VC2-S-AP5	James[1]	LST-758	Duval County (temp.)	4-5-73*	Navy design	James
APA-232	San Saba	10-1-58	VC2-S-AP5	Suisun[1]	LST-1146	Summit County	3-16-70*	Navy design	Suisun
APA-235	Bottineau	7-1-61	VC2-S-AP5	James[1]	LST-1158	USNS Tioga County	11-1-73	Navy design	Suisun
LPA-237	Bexar (temp.)	8-7-70*	VC2-S-AP5	Suisun	LST-1160	USNS Traverse County	11-1-73	Navy design	Suisun
APA-239	Glynn	7-1-60	VC2-S-AP5	James[1]	LST-1162	USNS Wahkiakum County	11-1-73	Navy design	Suisun
AR-12	Briareus (temp.)	6-7-72*	C3	James	LST-1163	USNS Waldo County	11-1-73	Navy design	Suisun
AR-21	Dionysus	9-1-61	EC2-S-C1	Beaumont	LST-1164	USNS Walworth County	11-1-73	Navy design	Suisun
ARG-5	Oahu	7-1-63	EC2-S-C1	Suisun	LST-1165	USNS Washoe County	11-1-73	Navy design	Suisun
ARG-10	Palawan	7-1-63	EC2-S-C1	Suisun	LST-1177	Lorain County (temp.)	1-31-73*	Navy design	James
ARS-33	Clamp	7-1-63	Navy design	Suisun	LST-1178	Wood County (temp.)	8-15-72*	Navy design	James
ARVH-1	Corpus Christi Bay	12-31-74	Navy design	Beaumont	MCS-2	Ozark	4-1-74	Navy design	Suisun
AS-15	Bushnell (temp.)	8- -75*	Navy design	James	MCS-4	Saugus	7-1-61	Navy design	Suisun
ATA-178	Tunica	9-1-62	Navy design	Beaumont					
ATA-181	Accokeek (temp.)	9-19-72*	Navy design	James					
ATA-183	Nottaway	9-1-62	Navy design	Beaumont					
ATA-190	Samoset	9-1-71*	Navy design	James					
ATA-193	Stallion	9-1-71*	Navy design	James					
ATA-203	Navigator	9-1-62	Navy design	Beaumont					
ATA-205	Sciota	9-1-62	Navy design	Suisun					
ATA-213	Keywadin	9-1-71*	Navy design	James					
ATA-245	Tuscarora	9-1-61	Navy design	James[1]					
ATF-69	Chippewa	9-1-61	Navy design	Beaumont					
ATF-71	Hopi	7-1-63	Navy design	James					
ATF-82	Carib	7-1-63	Navy design	Suisun					
ATF-87	Moreno	9-1-61	Navy design	Beaumont					

GLOSSARY OF TERMS AND ABBREVIATIONS

A. SHIP AND CRAFT CLASSIFICATIONS

AALC	Amphibious Assault Landing Craft
AD	Destroyer Tender
ADG*	Degaussing Ship
AE	Ammunition Ship
AF	Store Ship
AFDB	Large Auxiliary Floating Dry Dock (non-self-propelled)
AFDL	Small Auxilliary Floating Dry Dock (non-self-propelled)
AFDM	Medium Auxiliary Floating Dry Dock (non-self-propelled)
AFS	Combat Store Ship
AG	Miscellaneous
AGDE*	Escort Research Ship
AGDS (Auxiliary)	Auxiliary Deep Submergence Support Ship
AGDS (Service Craft)*	Auxiliary Deep Submergence Support Vehicle
AGEH	Hydrofoil Research Ship
AGER	Environmental Research Ship
AGF	Miscellaneous Command Ship
AGFF (ex-AGDE)	Frigate Research Ship
AGM	Missile Range Instrumentation Ship
AGMR	Major Communications Relay Ship
AGOR	Oceanographic Research Ship
AGP	Patrol Craft Tender
AGS	Surveying Ship
AGSS	Auxiliary Submarine
AH	Hospital Ship
AK	Cargo Ship
AKD*	Cargo Ship Dock
AKR	Vehicle Cargo Ship
AKS*	Stores Issue Ship
AKV*	Cargo Ship and Aircraft Ferry
ANL*	Net Laying Ship
AO	Oiler
AOE	Fast Combat Support Ship
AOG	Gasoline Tanker

AOR	Replenishment Oiler
AP	Transport
APB	Self-Propelled Barracks Ship
APL	Barracks Craft (non-self-propelled)
AR	Repair Ship
ARB	Battle Damage Repair Ship
ARC	Cable Repairing Ship
ARD	Auxiliary Repair Dry Dock (non-self-propelled)
ARDM	Medium Auxiliary Repair Dry Dock (non-self-propelled)
ARG*	Internal Combustion Engine Repair Ship
ARL	Landing Craft Repair Ship
ARS	Salvage Ship
ARSD*	Salvage Lifting Ship
ARST*	Salvage Craft Tender
ARVA*	Aircraft Repair Ship (aircraft)
ARVE*	Aircraft Repair Ship (engine)
ARVH*	Aircraft Repair Ship (helicopter)
AS	Submarine Tender
ASPB	Assault Support Patrol Boat
ASR	Submarine Rescue Ship
ATA	Auxiliary Ocean Tug
ATC	Mini-Armored Troop Carrier
ATF	Fleet Ocean Tug
ATS	Salvage and Rescue Ship
AV*	Seaplane Tender
AVM	Guided Missile Ship
BB	Battleship
CA	Heavy Cruiser
CC	Command Ship
CCB	Command and Control Boat
CG	Guided Missile Cruiser

* Classification no longer in use.

CGN	Guided Missile Cruiser (nuclear propulsion)	MCS*	Mine Countermeasures Ship
CLG*	Guided Missile Light Cruiser	MHA*	Minehunter, Auxiliary
CPC	Coastal Patrol Boat	MHC*	Minehunter, Coastal
CPIC	Coastal Patrol and Interdiction Craft	MMC	Minelayer, Coastal
CV	Aircraft Carrier	MMD (ex-DM)*	Minelayer, Fast
CVA	Attack Aircraft Carrier	MMF*	Minelayer, Fleet
CVAN	Attack Aircraft Carrier (nuclear propulsion)	MON	Monitor
CVB*	Battle Aircraft Carrier	MSA*	Minesweeper, Auxiliary
CVN	Aircraft Carrier (nuclear propulsion)	MSB	Minesweeping Boat
CVS	ASW Support Aircraft Carrier	MSC	Minesweeper, Coastal (nonmagnetic)
CVT	Training Aircraft Carrier	MSCO*	Minesweeper, Coastal (old)
DD	Destroyer	MSD	Minesweeper, Drone
DDG	Guided Missile Destroyer	MSF*	Minesweeper, Fleet (steel hull)
DE*	Escort Ship	MSI	Minesweeper, Inshore
DEG	Guided Missile Escort Ship	MSL	Minesweeping Launch
DER*	Radar Picket Escort Ship	MSM	Minesweeper, River (converted LCM-6)
DL*	Frigate	MSO	Minesweeper, Ocean (nonmagnetic)
DLG*	Guided Missile Frigate	MSR	Minesweeper, Patrol
DLGN*	Guided Missile Frigate (nuclear propulsion)	MSS	Minesweeper, Special (device)
DSRV	Deep Submergence Rescue Vehicle	MSSC	Medium SEAL Support Craft
DSV	Deep Submergence Vehicle	NR	Submarine Research Vehicle (nuclear propulsion)
FF (ex-DE)	Frigate	PB	Patrol Boat
FFG (ex-DEG/PF)	Guided Missile Frigate	PBR	River Patrol Boat
FFR (ex-DER)	Radar Picket Frigate	PCF	Patrol Craft (FAST)
IX	Unclassified Miscellaneous	PCH	Patrol Craft (hydrofoil)
IXSS*	Unclassified Miscellaneous Submarines	PF*	Patrol Frigate
LCA	Landing Craft, Assault	PG	Patrol Combatant (ex-Patrol Gunboat)
LCC (ex-AGC)	Amphibious Command Ship	PGH	Patrol Gunboat (hydrofoil)
LCM	Landing Craft, Mechanized	PHM	Patrol Combatant Missile (hydrofoil) (ex-Patrol Hydrofoil Guided Missile)
LCPL	Landing Craft, Personnel, Large	PTF	Fast Patrol Craft
LCPR	Landing Craft, Personnel, Ramped	RPC*	River Patrol Craft
LCSR	Landing Craft Swimmer Reconnaissance	SDV	Swimmer Delivery Vehicle
LCU	Landing Craft, Utility	SES	Surface Effect Ship
LCVP	Landing Craft, Vehicle, Personnel	SS	Submarine
LFR (ex-IFS/LSMR)*	Inshore Fire Support Ship	SSBN	Fleet Ballistic Missile Submarine (nuclear propulsion)
LHA	Amphibious Assault Ship (general purpose)	SSG	Guided Missile Submarine
LKA (ex-AKA)	Amphibious Cargo Ship	SSN	Submarine (nuclear propulsion)
LPA (ex-APA)	Amphibious Transport	SST*	Target and Training Submarine (self-propelled)
LPD	Amphibious Transport Dock	SWAL	Shallow Water Attack Craft, Light
LPH	Amphibious Assault Ship	SWAM	Shallow Water Attack Craft, Medium
LPR (ex-APD)	Amphibious Transport (small)	SWOB	Ship Waste Off Loading Barge
LPSS (ex-APSS)	Amphibious Transport Submarine	WAGB	Icebreaker (Coast Guard)
LSD	Landing Ship Dock	WAGO	Oceanographic Cutter (Coast Guard)
LSSC	Light SEAL Support Craft	WAK*	Cargo Ship (Coast Guard)
LST	Tank Landing Ship	WAT (later WATA)*	Oceangoing Tug (Coast Guard)
LWT	Amphibious Warping Tug		
MAC	Mobile Inshore Underseas Warfare Craft		

* Classification no longer in use.

continued

GLOSSARY

WHEC	High Endurance Cutter (Coast Guard)
WIX	Training Cutter (Coast Guard)
WMEC	Medium Endurance Cutter (Coast Guard)
WTR	Training Ship (Coast Guard)
X*	Submersible Craft (self-propelled)
YAG	Miscellaneous Auxiliary (self-propelled)
YC	Open Lighter (non-self-propelled)
YCF	Car Float (non-self-propelled)
YCV	Aircraft Transportation Lighter (non-self-propelled)
YD	Floating Crane (non-self-propelled)
YDT	Diving Tender (non-self-propelled)
YF	Covered Lighter (self-propelled)
YFB	Ferryboat or Launch (self-propelled)
YFD	Yard Floating Dry Dock (non-self-propelled)
YFN	Covered Lighter (non-self-propelled)
YFNB	Large Covered Lighter (non-self-propelled)
YFND	Dry Dock Companion Craft (non-self-propelled)
YFNX	Lighter (special purpose) (non-self-propelled)
YFP	Floating Power Barge (non-self-propelled)
YFR	Refrigerated Covered Lighter (self-propelled)
YFRN	Refrigerated Covered Lighter (non-self-propelled)
YFRT	Covered Lighter (range-tender) (self-propelled)
YFU	Harbor Utility Craft (self-propelled)
YG*	Garbage Lighter (self-propelled)
YGN	Garbage Lighter (non-self-propelled)
YHLC	Salvage Lift Craft, Heavy (non-self-propelled)
YLLC*	Salvage Lift Craft, Light (self-propelled)
YM	Dredge (self-propelled)
YMLC*	Salvage Lift Craft, Medium (non-self-propelled)
YNG	Gate Craft (non-self-propelled)
YO	Fuel Oil Barge (self-propelled)
YOG	Gasoline Barge (self-propelled)
YOGN	Gasoline Barge (non-self-propelled)
YON	Fuel Oil Barge (non-self-propelled)
YOS	Oil Storage Barge (non-self-propelled)
YP	Patrol Craft (self-propelled)
YPD	Floating Pile Driver (non-self-propelled)
YR	Floating Workshop (non-self-propelled)
YRB	Repair and Berthing Barge (non-self-propelled)
YRBM	Repair, Berthing, and Messing Barge (non-self-propelled)
YRBM (L)*	Repair, Berthing, and Messing Barge (Large) (non-self-propelled)
YRDH	Floating Dry Dock Workshop (hull) (non-self-propelled)
YRDM	Floating Dry Dock Workshop (machine) (non-self-propelled)
YRR	Radiological Repair Barge (non-self-propelled)
YRST	Salvage Craft Tender (non-self-propelled)
YSD	Seaplane Wrecking Derrick (self-propelled)
YSR	Sludge Removal Barge (mnon-self-propelled)

YTB	Large Harbor Tug (self-propelled)
YTL	Small Harbor Tug (self-propelled)
YTM	Medium Harbor Tug (self-propelled)
YW	Water Barge (self-propelled)
YWN	Water Barge (non-self-propelled)

B. FLEET STATUS ABBREVIATIONS

AA	Active, Atlantic Fleet
AR*	In reserve, out of commission, Atlantic Fleet
ASA	Active, in service, Atlantic Fleet
ASR*	In reserve, out of service, Atlantic Fleet
DAA	Scheduled for disposal, active, Atlantic Fleet
DAR*	Scheduled for disposal, in reserve, out of commission, Atlantic Fleet
DPA	Scheduled for disposal, active, Pacific Fleet
DPR*	Scheduled for disposal, in reserve, out of commission, Pacific Fleet
MarAd	Transferred to permanent custody of the Maritime Administration, but not stricken from the Naval Vessel Register (NVR) (see Section 14)
MAR*	In reserve, out of commission, Atlantic Fleet in temporary custody of the Maritime Administration
MPR*	In reserve, out of commission, Pacific Fleet in temporary custody of the Maritime Administration
MSC	Assigned to the Military Sealift Command (see Section 8)
NRT	Assigned to Naval Reserve Training (see Section 7)
PA	Active, Pacific Fleet
PR*	In reserve, out of commission, Pacific Fleet
PSA	Active, in service, Pacific Fleet
PSR*	In reserve, out of service, Pacific Fleet
(Stricken)	Stricken from the Naval Vessel Register (NVR) after completion of the manuscript for this book (see Sections 13 and 14)
TAA	Active, MSC, Atlantic Fleet
TAR	In ready-reserve, MSC, Atlantic Fleet
TPA	Active, MSC, Pacific Fleet
TPR	In ready-reserve, MSC, Pacific Fleet
TWWR	Active, MSC, World-wide routes

C. SHIPBUILDERS

Alabama	Alabama Dry Dock and Shipbuilding Corporation, Mobile, Ala.
Albina	Albina Engine and Machine Works, Inc., Portland, Ore.
American	American Shipbuilding Company, Toledo, Ohio
Avondale	Avondale Shipyards, Inc., Westwego, La.
Bath Iron	Bath Iron Works Corporation, Bath, Me.
Beth., Baltimore	Bethlehem Steel Corporation, Baltimore, Md.
Beth., Fore River	Bethlehem Steel Corporation, Fore River, Mass.

* Classification no longer in use.

Beth., Hingham	Bethlehem Steel Corporation, Hingham, Mass.
Beth., Quincy	Bethlehem Steel Corporation, Quincy, Mass.
Beth., San Pedro	Bethlehem Steel Corporation, San Pedro, Cal.
Beth., S.F.	Bethlehem Steel Corporation, San Francisco, Cal.
Beth., Sparrows Pt.	Bethlehem Steel Corporation, Sparrows Point, Md.
Beth., Staten Is.	Bethlehem Steel Corporation, Staten Island, N.Y.
Boeing, Seattle	The Boeing Company, Seattle, Wash.
Boatservice, Norway	Boatservice Ltd. A/S, Mandel, Norway
Boland	Boland Marine and Manufacturing, Inc., New Orleans, La.
Boston Navy	Boston Naval Shipyard, Boston, Mass.
Brooks	Brooks Marine, Lowestoft, England
Brown, Houston	Brown Shipbuilding Company, Houston, Tex.
Charleston Navy	Charleston Naval Shipyard, Charleston, S.C.
Christy	Christy Corporation, Sturgeon Bay, Wisc.
Consol. Steel	Consolidated Steel Corporation, Orange, Tex.
Cramp	Cramp Shipbuilding Company, Philadelphia, Pa.
Defoe	Defoe Shipbuilding Company, Bay City, Mich.
Dillingham	Dillingham Shipyard, Honolulu, Hawaii
Dravo, Neville Is.	Dravo Corporation, Neville Island, Pa.
Electric Boat	Electric Boat Company, Groton, Conn.
Federal	Federal Shipbuilding and Drydock Company, Kearny, N.J.
Gen. Dyn., Groton	General Dynamics Corporation, Electric Boat Division, Groton, Conn.
Gen. Dyn., Quincy	General Dynmaics Corporation, Quincy Shipbuilding Division, Quincy, Mass.
Gibbs	Gibbs Corporation, Jacksonville, Fla.
Grumman	Grumman Aircraft, Stuart, Fla.
Gulf, Chickasaw	Gulf Shipbuilding Corporation, Chickasaw, Ala.
Ingalls	Ingalls Shipbuilding Division, Litton Systems Inc., Pascagoula, Miss.
LB Navy	Long Beach Naval Shipyard, Long Beach, Cal.
Lockheed	Lockheed Shipbuilding and Construction Company, Seattle, Wash.
Lockheed, Sunnyvale	Lockheed Missile and Space Company, Sunnyvale, Cal.
Manitowoc	Manitowoc Shipbuilding Company, Manitowoc, Wisc.
Mare Island	Mare Island Naval Shipyard, Vallejo, Cal.
Marinette	Marinette Marine Corporation, Marinette, Wisc.
Marietta	Marietta Manufacturing Company, Marietta, W. Va.
National Steel	National Steel and Shipbuilding Company, San Diego, Cal.
Newport News	Newport News Shipbuilding and Drydock Company, Newport News, Va.
Norfolk Navy	Norfolk Naval Shipyard, Norfolk, Va.
Norfolk SB & DD	Norfolk Shipbuilding and Drydock Company
NW Marine	Northwest Marine Iron Works, Portland, Ore.
NY Navy	New York Naval Shipyard, Brooklyn, N.Y.
NY Shipbuilding	New York Shipbuilding Corporation, Camden, N.J.
Peterson	Peterson Builders, Inc., Sturgeon Bay, Wisc.
Phil. Navy	Philadelphia Naval Shipyard, Philadelphia, Pa.
Portsmount Navy	Portsmount Naval Shipyard, Kittery, Me.
PS B & DD	Puget Sound Bridge and Dry Dock Company, Seattle, Wash.
PS Navy	Puget Sound Naval Shipyard, Bremerton, Wash.
Pullman	Pullman Standard Car Manufacturing Company, Chicago, Ill.
Seattle-Tacoma	Seattle-Tacoma Shipbuilding Corporation, Seattle, Wash.
Sewart Seacraft	Teledyne, Inc., Sewart Seacraft Division, Berwick, La.
SF Navy	San Francisco Naval Shipyard, San Francisco, Cal.
Tacoma	Tacoma Boat Building Company, Tacoma, Wash.
Tampa	Tampa Shipbuilding Company, Tampa, Fla.
Todd-Pacific	Todd-Pacific Shipyard, Seattle, Wash.
Todd, San Pedro/Todd Shipyards	Todd Shipyards Corporation, San Pedro, Cal.
Todd, Seattle	Todd Shipyards Corporation, Seattle, Wash.
Trumpy	John Trumpy and Sons, Inc., Annapolis, Md.
Upper Clyde, Scot.	Upper Clyde Shipbuilding, Glasgow, Scotland
Western	Western Pipe and Steel Company, Los Angeles, Cal.
Wheeler	Wheeler Shipbuilding Company, Whitestone, N.Y.
Willamette	Willamette Iron and Steel Corporation, Portland, Ore.

D. ENGINE MANUFACTURERS

A.C.	Allis-Chalmers
Alco	American Locomotive Co.
Beth.	Bethlehem Steel Co.
B.S.	Busch-Sulzer
B&W	Babcock and Wilcox Co.
C.B.	Cooper Bessemer
C.E.	Combustion Engineering
C.H.	Cutler-Hammer
CTC	Caterpiller Tractor Co.
DeLaval	DeLaval Turbine Co.
Detroit	Detroit Diesel Co.
Ell.	Elliott Co.
Enterprise	Enterprise Diesel Co.
F.M.	Fairbanks Morse Co.
F.W.	Foster Wheeler
G.E.	General Electric
G.M.	General Motors
Gen. Mach.	General Machine Co.
Grey	Grey Marine Diesel Co.
Harn.	Harnischfeger Corp.
N.D.	Napier-Deltic Co.
N.N.	Newport News Shipbuilding and Dry Dock Co.
Nordberg	Nordberg Diesel Co.
NYS	New York Shipbuilding Corp.
Packard	Packard Diesel Co.
Paxman	Davey-Paxman Diesel Co.

continued

Proteus	Bristol Siddeley Marine Proteus Co.	
R.R.	Rolls-Royce	
Skinner	Skinner-Unaflow Co.	
West.	Westinghouse	
Winton	Winton Diesel Co.	

TACAN	Tactical Air Navigation System
VDS	Variable Depth Sonar
VTOL	Vertical Takeoff and Landing

E. MISCELLANEOUS ABBREVIATIONS

AA	Antiaircraft
AAW	Antiair Warfare
ASROC	Antisubmarine Rocket
ASW	Antisubmarine Warfare
B	Boilers
BPDMS	Basic Point Defense Missile System
D	Diesels
DASH	Drone Antisubmarine Helicopter
ECM	Electronic Countermeasures
ECCM	Electronic Counter Countermeasures
EM	Electric Motors
FAST	Fast Automatic Shuttle Transfer System
FRAM I	Fleet Rehabilitation and Modernization Program (extended ship's life 8 years)
FRAM II	Fleet Rehabilitation and Modernization Program (extended ship's life 5 years)
F/S	Fleet Status
FY	Fiscal Year
GT	Geared Turbines
GST	Gas Turbine
ILP (ex-MDAP)	International Logistics Program
Mack	Combination mast and smoke stack
MarAd	Maritime Administration
MarComm	Maritime Commission
MDAP	Military Defense Assistance Pact
MK	Mark
mm	millimeter
mod.	modification
mts.	mounts
NRT	Naval Reserve Training
NTDS	Naval Tactical Data System
NVR	Naval Vessel Register
PUFFS	Passive Underwater Fire Control Feasibility System
RS	Reciprocating Steam
SCB	Ship Characteristics Board Number
SINS	Ships Inertial Navigation System
ST	Steam Turbines
SUBROC	Submarine Rocket
SUBSAFE	Submarine Safety Program

ADDENDA

Closed 29 July 1975

1. WARSHIPS

A. AIRCRAFT CARRIERS

General: On 30 June 1975, *Hancock* (CVA-19), *Oriskany* (CVA-34), *Midway* (CVA-41), *Franklin D. Roosevelt* (CVA-42), *Coral Sea* (CVA-43), *Forrestal* (CVA-59), *Ranger* (CVA-61), *Constellation* (CVA-64), and *America* (CVA-66) were all reclassified from CVA to CV. On the same date, *Enterprise* (CVAN-65) and *Nimitz* (CVAN-68) were reclassified from CVAN to CVN. *Dwight D. Eisenhower* (CVAN-69) will be reclassified CVN upon commissioning.

CVN-73 class: The current Navy construction program calls for the construction of six nuclear-powered aircraft carriers (CVN) to replace *Forrestal*, *Kitty Hawk* and *John F. Kennedy* class carriers. Hull numbers will be CVN-73/78. They will be larger than the *Nimitz* class; cost is estimated at $1.5 billion each.

Nimitz class (CVN): The *Nimitz* (CVN-68) was commissioned 3 May 1975. Two additional units of this class, CVN-71/72 are planned. They will replace the *Forrestal* (CV-59) and *Saratoga* (CV-60). Construction funds for CVN-71 are to be requested in the FY 1977 ship-building program.

Hancock class (CV): The remaining two active *Essex* class carriers, *Hancock* (CV-19) and *Oriskany* (CV-34), are scheduled to be decommissioned. *Hancock* is scheduled to begin deactivation on 30 December 1975 and decommission August 1976. Due to her age, it is most likely that *Hancock* will be scrapped rather than retained in the reserve fleet. *Oriskany* is scheduled to begin deactivation on 30 June 1976 and decommission in February 1977. However, the deactivation schedule for *Oriskany* may not hold as a few countries have expressed interest in purchasing *Oriskany* for further service in their Navy.

B. SURFACE COMBATANTS

CRUISERS

Nuclear-Powered Guided Missile Strike Cruisers (CSGN): This new class of cruiser will total 8 units. First unit will cost $1.2 billion to construct; the remaining units will cost approximately $875 million each. Primary mission of ship will be to protect the big carriers (CVN/CV). Ships will be armed with the AEGIS system, antiaircraft missiles, and possibly lightweight 8″ mounts and antiship missiles. Probable builder will be Newport News Ship-building and Drydock Company. Construction funds for the first unit will be requested under FY 1977 shipbuilding program. Probable hull numbers will be CSGN-42/49.

Virginia class (CGN): *Virginia* (CGN-38) is scheduled to commission 31 May 1976.

Des Moines class (CA): *Newport News* (CA-148), the last active all gun cruiser, was decommissioned on 27 June 1975 at Norfolk and laid up.

DESTROYERS

Coontz class (DDG): *Mahan* (DDG-42) completed her antiair warfare modernization on 22 March 1975 and was recommissioned on 1 April 1975. *King* (DDG-41) is scheduled to recommission on 26 February 1976 after completion of her antiair warfare modernization.

DD-999 class: A successor to the *Spruance* class DDs is projected. Class will number 16

Hull (DD-945): Testing the new 8″ MK71 gun which uses a laser-guided projectile. Projectile is aimed and fired the same as a conventional gun, but is stabilized in flight by tail fins. The wings are controlled by a seeker device which detects a laser beam trained on the target. Objective is to fill the gun gap left by the decommissioning of last U.S. 8″ gun cruiser, *Newport News* (CA-148). 4–17–75. **Hull** class.

units. Will be larger than the *Spruance*s and armed with AEGIS system. First unit will cost $850 million to construct; the remaining units $550 million. Probable hull numbers will be DD-999/DD-1015. Class is meant to complement the CSGN class, rather than augment it.

Spruance class (DD): The contract for the construction of DD-986/992 was awarded to Ingalls on 1–15–75. *Spruance* (DD-963) is scheduled to commission on 31 August 1975, *Paul F. Foster* (DD-964) on 26 November 1975, *Kinkaid* (DD-965) on 28 January 1976, *Hewitt* (DD-966) on 18 March 1976, and *Elliot* (DD-967) on 2 May 1976. *Elliot* will be assigned to the Pacific Fleet.

Gearing class (DD): The following units of this class are scheduled to be stricken from the Naval Vessel Register (NVR): *Epperson* (DD-719) on 1 December 1975, *Wiltsie* (DD-716), *Rowan* (DD-782), *Gurke* (DD-783) and *Richard B. Anderson* (DD-786) all on 30 January 1976. *Epperson* is scheduled to be sold to a foreign country for further service and it is more than probable that all or most all of the remaining four will be sold overseas.

Allen M. Sumner class (DD): *Laffey* (DD-724) was not replaced as NRT ship at Washington, D.C. Ship will be sunk as a target in lieu of being memorialized at Alexandria, Va.

La Vallette class (DD): The last unit of this class, popularly known by its original name of *Fletcher* class, has been stricken (see strike section of addenda).

FRIGATES

Knox class (FF): The former name of *Robert E. Peary* (FF-1073) is spelled CONOLLY not CONNOLLY.

C. PATROL COMBATANTS

Pegasus class (PHM): *Pegasus* (PHM-1) will commission on 30 September 1975 and join the Pacific Fleet.

Asheville class (PG): *Asheville* (PG-84), *Gallup* (PG-85), *Crockett* (PG-88), *Marathon* (PG-89) and *Canon* (PG-90) were transferred to the Naval Reserve Force on 7–1–75. Transfer of *Chehalis* (PG-94), originally scheduled for 7–1–75, has been delayed for an unknown duration of time.

Tacoma (PG-92) and *Welch* (PG-93) are scheduled to transfer to the Naval Reserve Force on 31 December 1975. The two non-gas turbine *Asheville* class units building for South Vietnam were actually built for South Korea (correction). Construction of both was completed 1974/75.

E. SUBMARINES

Lafayette/Benjamin Franklin class (SSBN): Poseidon (C-3) Conversions—Conversion of *Alexander Hamilton* (SSBN-617) was completed on 11 April 1975. Contract for the conversion of *Henry Clay* (SSBN-625) was assigned to Portsmouth Naval Shipyard (not General Dynamics, Groton) on 31 March 1975. Conversion begun on 29 April 1975.

Los Angeles class (SSN): *Los Angeles* (SSN-688) is scheduled to commission on 28 November 1975. *Philadelphia* (SSN-690) is scheduled to commission on 27 December 1975 (she will join the Atlantic Fleet).

Sturgeon class (SSN): The last unit of this class, *Richard B. Russell* (SSN-687), was commissioned on 16 August 1975. She was placed "in service" on 5–20–75.

A basic point defense missile launcher (BPDMS) is seen aboard the frigate *Francis Hammond* (FF-1067). No reloads are carried by the ship. 1972.

Halibut class (SSN): *Halibut* (SSN-587) will be decommissioned in June 1976 at Mare Island. She was replaced by *Seawolf* (SSN-575) as experimental submarine.

2. AMPHIBIOUS WARFARE SHIPS

Tarawa class (LHA): *Tarawa* (LHA-1) is scheduled to commission on 31 October 1975. *Saipan* (LHA-2) is scheduled to commission on 30 June 1976 (she will join the Atlantic Fleet).

Laning/Knudson class (LPR): The *Begor* (LPR-127) of the *Laning* class and the *Balduck* (LPR-132) of the *Knudson* class have been stricken from the Naval Vessel Register (NVR).

LST-1/511 class (LST): All the LSTs of these two classes, including the LSTs assigned to MSC, have been stricken from the Naval Vessel Register except for *Duval County* (LST-758) and *Summit County* (LST-1146) which are in the MarAd Reserve Fleet at James River and Suisun Bay, respectively. They are the last of the WW II-built LSTs.

3. MINE WARFARE SHIPS

Falcon/Redwing class (MSC): All surviving units of these two classes, except *Thrush* (MSC-204), that were assigned to the NRT force have been stricken from the Naval Vessel Register. *Thrush* (MSC-204) was loaned to Virginia Institute of Marine Science on 7-1-75, for 5 years, for use as a research vessel.

Aggressive class (MSO): *Illusive* (MSO-448) caught fire in her engine room in 1/75, 5 miles off Charleston, S.C. Repaired. One man found guilty of sabotage.

4. COMBATANT CRAFT

High Point class (PCH): *High Point* (PCH-1) was temporarily loaned to the Coast Guard in 3/75 as USCGC *High Point* (WMEH-1). Returned to USN on 5-5-75.

B. LANDING CRAFT

LCU: LCU-1637 was converted to an "at-sea simulator platform" (non-seagoing) in 1975 and is based at the Armed Forces Weapon Range (AFWR), Roosevelt Roads. She retains her LCU classification.

C. MINE COUNTERMEASURES CRAFT

MSS: MSS-1 has been disposed of, effective 10 February 1975.

D. RIVERINE WARFARE CRAFT

PBR: A MK III version of this type is not being built as planned.

5. AUXILIARY SHIPS

Rigel class (AF): *Rigel* (AF-58) was decommissioned on 6-23-75 and transferred to MSC on the same date for further service as USNS *Rigel* (T-AF-58).

Flyer class (AF): *Flyer* (AG-178) has been stricken from the NVR.

Eltanin class (AGOR): The Naval Electronics Command assumed operational control of *Mizar* (AGOR-11) on 1 July 1975.

Bowditch class (AGS): *Michelson* (AGS-23) has been stricken from the Naval Vessel Register.

Tang class (AGSS): *Tang* was reclassified from SS to AGSS on 30 June 1975.

Haven class (AH): *Sanctuary* (AH-17) was decommissioned on 28 March 1975, not 26 March (correction).

Mispillion class (AO): *Pawcatuck* (AO-108) and *Navasota* (AO-106) were decommissioned on 15 July 1975 and 13 August 1975, respectively, and were transferred to MSC on the indicated dates for further service as USNS *Pawcatuck* (T-AO-108) and USNS *Navasota* (T-AO-106).

Neosho class (AO: *Mississinewa* (AO-144) is scheduled to be decommissioned on 2 February

1976 and transferred to MSC for further service as USNS *Mississinewa* (T-AO-144).

Compass Island class (AG): *Compass Island* (AG-153) is currently serving as the test ship for at-sea evaluation of the TRIDENT missile navigation system. *Compass Island* played a prominent part in the development of SINS, not *Observation Island* (AG-154) (correction).

Suamico class (AO): *Tallulah* (AO-50) has been transferred to the temporary custody of MarAd and laid up at James River.

Patapsco class (AOG): *Chewaucan* (AOG-50) and *Noxubee* (AOG-56) have been stricken from the Naval Vessel Register.

Wichita class (AOR): *Roanoke* (AOR-7) is scheduled to commission on 15 April 1976. She is scheduled to join the Pacific Fleet.

Aeolus class (ARC): *Thor* (ARC-4) has been stricken from the Naval Vessel Register.

Cherokee class (ATF): *Luiseno* (ATF-156) has been stricken from the NVR.

6. SERVICE CRAFT

AFDL: Total Reserve should read 3 and total ILP should read 9. The transfer of AFDL-25 to the Khmer Republic was cancelled when the country fell to the Communist insurgents.

AFDM: Total Active should read 3 and total Reserve should read 1. AFDM-5 is currently inactivating at Bremerton.

YC: Summary should read as follows: Active 194; Reserve: 24; Loan: 3. Delete YC-1459 from the Unit list.

YD: Summary should read as follows: Active: 65; Reserve: 6; Loan: 1; ILP: 9. YD-235 and 236 were acquired from the Army on 1 May 1975 and instated on the NVR on the same date.

YFNX: YFNX-32 is fitted out as a floating PX and is based at Norfolk. She is the first of her kind.

YFRT: Delete YFRT-411 from the Unit listing. In the Summary change Active total from 5 to 4.

YFU: Delete YFU-53 from the Unit listing. In the Summary change Active total from 13 to 12.

YHLC: YHLC-1 was placed out of service on 28 March 1975 and YHLC-2 was placed out of service on 14 March 1975. Both are berthed at the MarAd Reserve Fleet at James River.

YM: In the Unit listing delete YM-22. In the Summary total change the Reserve total from 1 to 0.

YO: Summary should read as follows: Active: 15; Reserve: 11; Loan: 0; ILP: 3.

YOG: Delete YOG-89, *Lt. Thomas W. Fowler* (YOG-107) from the Unit listing. Summary totals should read as follows: Active: 4; Reserve: 6; Loan: 0; ILP: 2.

YOGN: Add YOGN-125 to the Unit listing and increase Active count to 15. YWN-154 was reclassified YOGN-125 on 1 May 1975. YWN-154 was originally YOGN-116.

YR: Add YR-84 to Unit listings. In Summary section change Reserve total to 6. YR-84 was acquired from the Army on 1 May 1975 and instated on the NVR on the same date.

YTL: Change Summary totals to read: Active: 9; Reserve: 2; Loan: 3; ILP: 11.

YTM: Delete the following from the Unit listings: *Black Fox* (YTM-177), *Olathe* (YTM-273), *Washakie* (YTM-386), *Connewango* (YTM-388), *Abinago* (YTM-493), *Barboncito* (YTM-495) and *Chohonaga* (YTM-766). Change Summary totals to read as follows: Active: 69; Reserve: 17; Loan: 1; ILP: 4.

YWN: Delete YWN-154 from the Unit listings. Summary totals should read as follows: Active: 7; Reserve: 2.

7. NAVAL RESERVE TRAINING SHIPS

Make the following changes to the Naval Reserve Training Force list:

a. *Hamner* (DD-718) was transferred to Portland, Oreg., effective 6–1–75 as replacement for *Ozbourn* (DD-846).

b. *Epperson* (DD-719) has been stricken from the Naval Vessel Register.

c. *McKean* (DD-784) was transferred to Seattle, Wash., effective 10–1–75 as replacement for *Epperson* (DD-719) not *Theodore E. Chandler* (DD-717) (correction).

d. *Higbee* (DD-806) was transferred to Portland, Oreg., effective 7–1–75 as replacement for *Theodore E. Chandler* (DD-717) vice *Ozbourn* (DD-846) (correction).

e. *Ozbourn* (DD-846) has been stricken from the Naval Vessel Register.

f. *Tulare* (LKA-112) replaced *Hamner* (DD-718) at San Francisco, Calif.

g. *Peacock* (MSC-198), *Phoebe* (MSC-199), *Shrike* (MSC-201), *Thrasher* (MSC-203), *Vireo* (MSC-205), *Warbler* (MSC-106), *Whippoorwill* (MSC-207) and *Woodpecker* (MSC-209) have been stricken from the Naval Vessel Register without replacement as NRT ships. *Thrush* (MSC-204) was removed from the NRT force and loaned commercially.

8. MILITARY SEALIFT COMMAND

Make the following changes to the Military Sealift Command Fleet List:

Name and Hull Classification	MSC F/S	Type of Change
USNS *Rigel* (T-AF-58)	TAA	Add
USNS *Pvt. Leonard C. Brostrom* (T-AK-255)	TPR	Change in Fleet Status
USNS *Victoria* (T-AK-281) (FBM)	TAR	Change in Fleet Status
USNS *Tallulah* (T-AO-50)	TWWR	Delete
USNS *Navasota* (T-AO-106)	TPA	Add
USNS *Pawcatuck* (T-AO-108)	TAA	Add
USNS *Mississinewa* (T-AO-144)	TAA	Add
USNS *Sealift China Sea* (T-AO-170)[4].	TWWR	Add
USNS *Sealift Arctic* (T-AO-175)[4].	TWWR	Add
USNS *Thor* (T-ARC-4)	TPR	Delete
USNS LST-47, 230, 287, 491, 579, 607, 613, 623, 629, 649, *Daviess County* (T-LST-692), *Harris County* (T-LST-822), *Orleans Parish* (T-LST-1069), 1072	TPR	Delete all 15 units.

10. AIRCRAFT

SKYHAWK, A-4 Series (A4D): Lockheed has rebuilt six A-4 SKYHAWKS into three TA-4S for Singapore. The three aircraft look like regular A-4s, except each has two separate canopies and sets of controls, with the forward position for the trainee and the after position for the instructor. The aircraft can also be used as a fighter, with the forward position being used by the pilot and the after position by the intercept officer. These three

are in addition to the 40 A-4Bs being modified as A-4Ss for Singapore. The Marine Corps plans to modify about 70 units of the A-4M series to a super A-4M (A-4Y). The craft will have improved HUD and a redesigned cockpit; provision is being made for the installation of a Hughes angle rate bombing system.

PHANTOM, F-4 Series (F4H-1): The Marine Corps plans to update their F-4B versions to F-4N versions and their F-4J versions to F-4S versions.

TOMCAT, F-14 Series: USN plans to modify and update 20 pre-production F-14A's for use as training aircraft. Probable classification will be TF-14A.

F-18A (unnamed): McDonnell-Douglas/Northrop has been awarded the prime contract for the construction of the F-18A. The contract could mean the construction of as many as 800 aircraft. This variation of the YF-17A will have an F404-GE-400 power plant with a thrust of approximately 16,000 pounds. Length overall will be 56'; wing span 37'6"; width of the fuselage will be 4" larger than that of the YF-17A. Further, the nose will be enlarged so it can house a 28" diameter radar dish. The Air Force transferred two YF-17As to the Navy for preliminary tests. Further details on this project are not available at this time.

TIGER II, F-5 Series (F-5E): The Navy has acquired 20 F-5E versions of the FREEDOM FIGHTER from the Air Force; they were originally part of an order of 71 F-5Es intended for shipment to South Vietnam. Named TIGER II by the Navy, they are based at the Fighter Weapons School, where they replace the T-38s that had been previously based there. The F-5Es performance and tactical air combat capabilities closely simulate those of some of the latest Soviet fighter aircraft, such as the MIG-23s. Therefore, they are used as the "enemy" in simulated war games against such Navy aircraft as the F-14.

11. MISSILES AND CONVENTIONAL ORDNANCE

BRAZO: This is first U.S. air-to-air radiation missile; it is designed to intercept enemy aircraft by homing in on their control radar. BRAZO's assigned designation is not known at this time. The project is a joint Navy/Air Force development. The missile system integrator is manufactured by Hughes Aircraft Company. BRAZO uses a SPARROW missile airframe and employs a broadband frequency receiver. Early test firings resulted in three hits out of three launches.

76mm OTO/Melara COMPACT gun: Characteristics are as follows: Mark/Mod: none assigned; Total weight of assembly: 14,219 pounds; Length of barrel from turret centerline to tip: 204.33"; Maximum range: not available; Maximum altitude: not available; Rate of fire: 85 rounds per minute; Elevation limits: −15° to +85°; Muzzle velocity: 3038 feet per second.

12. FOREIGN TRANSFERS

Make the following additions, corrections and deletions for the list of foreign transfers:

a. Add: *Chewaucan* (AOG-50) transferred to Colombia on 7–1–75 as sale: Renamed *Tumaco* (BT-65).

b. Add as second entry: *Umpqua* (ATA-209) transferred to Colombia as sale in 1975 for cannibalization and scrapping.

c. Add: Foreign name and hull number of ex-USS *Apache* (ATF-67) is *Ta Wan* (ATF-551).

d. Add: *Luiseno* (ATF-156) transferred to Argentina as sale on 7–1–75 as *Francisco De Gurruchaga* (A-).

e. Add as second entry: *Eugene A. Greene* (DD-711) transferred to Spain as sale in 1975 as *Churruca* (D-61) for further service.

f. Add as second entry for each ship: *Chevalier* (DD-805) and *Everett F. Larson* (DD-830) transferred to South Korea in 1975 as sale for further service as *Chung Buk* (DD-95) and *Jeon Buk* (DD-96), respectively.

g. Add as second entry for each ship: *Noa* (DD-841), *O'Hare* (DD-889), *Leary* (DD-879) and *Furse* (DD-882) transferred to Spain as sale in 1975 for further service as *Mendez Nunez* (D-63), *Blas De Lezo* (D-65), *Langara* (D-64), and *Gravina* (D-62), respectively.

h. *Norris* (DD-859) was originally transferred to Turkey for cannibalization and scrapping. When the Turkish Air Force accidentally sank the *Kocatepe* (D-354) (ex-USS *Harwood*, DD-861) during the invasion of Cyprus in July 1974, permission was obtained to activate the *Norris* as replacement. She was commissioned into the Turkish Navy on 24 July 1975 as *Kocatepe* (D-354).

i. Add: *Thrasher* (MSC-203) and *Whippoorwill* (MSC-207) will be transferred to Singapore as sales in November 1975 for use as minesweepers.

j. Add: *Vireo* (MSC-205), *Warbler* (MSC-206), and *Woodpecker* (MSC-209) will be transferred to the Fiji Islands as sales in November 1975 for use as patrol craft.

k. Add: *Beacon* (PG-99) and *Green Bay* (PG-101) were scheduled for transfer to Greece as sales on 30 June 1976.

l. Change: *Becuna* (SS-319) was not transferred to Peru on 7–31–74. She will be scrapped.

m. Add: *Clamagore* (SS-343) and *Tiru* (SS-416) are being retained for eventual transfer to Turkey. The current arms embargo to Turkey is preventing their transfer. Should the arms embargo continue, the two submarines will be disposed of by other means.

n. Add: YO-221 was transferred to Peru on 24 February 1975 as a sale.

o. Add: YTB-837 and 838 were transferred as Sales(b) to Saudi Arabia on 6–28–75 as EN-311 and EN-312, respectively.

p. YTL-244 was returned to the USN by Japan on 6–14–75 and sold in August 1975. She had previously been transferred to Japan as Grant Aid, having been stricken from the NVR at the time of transfer.

q. The transfer of *Goodrich* (DD-831) and *Becuna* (SS-319) to Venezuela, as sale, for cannibalization and scrapping, has finally been cancelled and the two ships will be disposed of by scrapping.

r. On 16 July 1975, the following service craft were transferred to the Philippines as loans, having previously been stricken from the Naval Vessel Register on 15 October 1974: YOG-61, YO-115, YO-116, YW-103, YW-111 and YW-130. The Philippine names and hull numbers of these craft are unknown at this time.

s. *Derrick* (YO-59), YO-179, MSB-2, and LCU-531 were sold to South Korea on 2 July 1975 for further service, having previously been on loan.

Khmer Republic (now Cambodia): On 17 April 1975, the Khmer Republic surrendered. Just prior to the surrender, three vessels of the small Marine Nationale Khmer fled to the West, bringing with them a small number of refugees. The vessels that escaped are as follows:

E-312 (ex-French *L'Inconstant*, P636, USS PC-1171)
P-111 (ex-French LSIL-9039, USS LSIL-875)
P-112 (ex-M/V *Medecin Capitaine Le Gall*, USS LSIL-   )

On 16 May 1975, after reportedly taking part in the SS *Mayaguez* incident and tossing their Communist captain and guards overboard, 10 of the crew of the Cambodian E-311 (ex-French *Flamberge*, P-631, USS PC-1086) seized control of the ship and sailed it to Sattahip, Thailand, and asked for political asylum. As of this writing, the PC is still in Thailand. Ultimate disposition is unknown.

Republic of South Vietnam: On 30 April 1975, the Republic of South Vietnam surrendered. Just prior to the surrender and immediately after it, 30 vessels of the South Vietnamese Navy escaped to the West, carrying some 30,000 refugees with them. In addition, rather than turn them over to the enemy, three South Vietnamese naval vessels were scuttled by their crews. Altogether, 30 percent of the 112 seagoing vessels in the South Vietnamese Navy were kept from falling into Communist hands. The breakdown of 33 vessels that escaped, plus those known to have been captured, are as follows:

Scuttled: The following ships were scuttled by the South Vietnamese Navy on or about 0335 ZULU on 2 May 1975:

Keo Ngua (HQ-604) (ex-U.S. PGM-68)
Lam Giang (HQ-402) (ex-USS LSM-226)
HQ-474 (ex-U.S. YOG-131)

Captured: The following South Vietnamese naval vessels are known to have been captured by the Communist forces:

Tran Knanh Du (HQ-04) (ex-USS *Forster*, FFR-334)
Ky Hoa (HQ-09) (ex-USS *Sentry*, MSF-299)
HQ-9550 (ex-U.S. *Pokanoket*, YTM-762)
HQ-9951 (ex-U.S. *Hombro*, YTM-769)
HQ-9952 (ex-U.S. *Nootka*, YTM-771)

Ex-USS *Forster* was undergoing a restricted availability in a Saigon shipyard when South Vietnam surrendered. Due to her yard period and the fact that she did not put to sea, it is assumed that work was being done on her engines and this rendered her immobile.

Escaped: The following vessels of the South Vietnamese Navy are known to have escaped from the Communists on or about 2 May 1975:

Tran Hung Dao (HQ-01) (ex-USS *Camp*, FFR-251)
Tran Quang Khai (HQ-02) (ex-USCGC *Bering Strait*, WHEC-382, USN AVP-34)
Tran Nhat Duat (HQ-03) (ex-USCGC *Yakutat*, WHEC-380, USN AVP-32)
Tran Binh Trong (HQ-05) (ex-USCGC *Castle Rock*, WHEC-383, USN AVP-35)
Tran Quoc Toan (HQ-06) (ex-USCGC *Cook Inlet*, WHEC-384, USN AVP-36)
Dong Da II (HQ-07) (ex-USS *Crestview*, PCE-895)
Chi Lang II (HQ-08) (ex-USS *Gayety*, MSF-239)
Chi Linh (HQ-11) (ex-USS *Shelter*, MSF-301)
Ngoc Hoi (HQ-12) (ex-USS *Brattleboro*, PCER-852)
Van Kiep II (HQ-14) (ex-USS *Amherst*, PCER-853)
Ly Thuong Kiet (HQ-16) (ex-USS *Chincoteague*, WHEC-375, USN AVP-24)
Ngo Kuyen (HQ-17) (ex-USCGC *McCulloch*, WHEC-386, USS *Wachapreague*, AGP-8)
Doan Ngoc Tang (HQ-228) (ex-French *Hallebarde*, L-9023, USS LSSL-9)
Lulu Phu Tho (HQ-229) (ex-Japanese *Tsutsuji*, LS-422, USS LSSL-101)
Nguyen Ngoc Long (HQ-230) (ex-Japanese *Shobu*, LS-440, USS LSSL-96)
Nguyen Duc Bong (HQ-231) (ex-Japanese *Botan*, LS-442, USS LSSL-129)
Thien Kich (HQ-329) (ex-French L-9038, USS LSIL-872)
Loi Cong (HQ-330) (ex-French L-9034, USS LSIL-699)

Tam Set (HQ-331) (ex-French L-9033, USS LSIL-871)
Hat Giang (HQ-400) (ex-French LSM-9011, USS LSM-355)
Han Giang (HQ-401) (ex-French LSM-9012, USS LSM-110)
Huong Giang (HQ-404) (ex-USS Oceanside, LSM-175)
Cam Ranh (HQ-500) (ex-USS Marion County, LST-975)
Thi Nai (HQ-502) (ex-USS Cayuga County, LST-529)
Nha Trang (HQ-505) (ex-USS Jerome County, LST-848)
Phu Du (HQ-600) (ex-U.S. PGM-64)
Minh Hoa (HQ-602) (ex-U.S. PGM-66)
Hon Troc (HQ-618) (ex-U.S. PGM-83)
1 unidentified 100-ft. PGM
Nuynh Van Cu (HQ-702) (ex-USCGC Point Clear, WPB-82315)
My Tho (HQ-800) (ex-USS Harnett County, AGP-821, LST-821)
Can Tho (HQ-801) (ex-USS Garrett County, AGP-786, LST-786)

Vinh Long (HQ-802) (ex-USS Satyr, ARL-23)
HQ-470 (ex-French L'Aulne, U.S. YOG-80)
HQ-471 (ex-U.S. YOG-33)

NOTES: (a) Tam Set (HQ-331), Loi Cong (HQ-330), Nguyen Ngoc Long (HQ-230), Minh Hoa (HQ-602) and an unidentified PGM appeared off Singapore on 8 May 1975. On 13 May, all five craft departed Singapore and put to sea with the announced intention of heading for Subic Bay or Guam. However, during the weekend of 23 May they put in to Saigon, the crews evidently having decided to return to South Vietnam.

(b) Except for the five craft noted above and Cam Ranh (HQ-500), which is moored at Guam, the other 29 vessels of the former South Vietnam Navy that escaped are moored at Subic Bay in an out-of-the-way channel, under the custody of the Commander-in-Chief, Pacific Fleet, awaiting disposition.

13. STRIKE LIST

The following ships have been stricken since the manuscript for the main text of this publication was submitted:

A. COMMISSIONED NAVY SHIPS

Hull No.	Name	Date Stricken	Comments
AG-178	USNS Flyer	7–17–75	Trans./MarAd for disposal.
AGS-23	USNS Michelson	4–15–75	Trans./MarAd for disposal.
AGSS-419	Tigrone	6–27–75	Ex-SSR, SS. Disposition pending (corrected entry).
AK-244	USNS Sgt. Morris E. Crain	4–1–75	Trans./MarAd for disposal. Scrapped.
AO-60	Nantahala	7–2–73	Fuel oil storage hulk at Philadelphia Naval Shipyard (1973–75). Trans./MarAd for disposal. Sold. (corrected entry).
AO-64	Tolovana	4–15–75	Trans./MarAd for disposal.
AOG-50	Chewaucan	7–1–71	Sold/Colombia.
AOG-55	Nespelen	7–1–75	Trans./MarAd for disposal.
AOG-56	Noxubee	7–1–75	Trans./MarAd for disposal.
ARC-4	USNS Thor	8– –75	Ex-Vanadis (AKA-49). Trans./MarAd for disposal.
ARVH-1	Corpus Christi Bay	12–31–74	Ex-Albermarle (AV-5). Trans./MarAd for disposal. Scrapped (Change in disposition).
ATA-188	Penobscot	2–28–75	Sold.
ATA-209	Umpqua	7–1–75	Ran aground on 2–16–75 while on loan to Colombia. Beyond salvage. Sold/Colombia. Hulk blown up.
ATF-92	Tawasa	4–1–75	Sold.
ATF-156	Luiseno	7–1–75	Sold/Argentina.
CA-135	unnamed (ex-Los Angeles)	1–1–74	Scrapped (Change in disposition).
CLG-8	Topeka	12–1–73	EX CL-67. Scrapped (Change in disposition).
CVS-9	Essex	6–1–73	Ex CVA, CV. Scrapped (Change in disposition).
CVS-15	Randolph	6–1–73	Ex CVA, CV. Scrapped (Change in disposition).
DD-519	Daly	12–1–74	Possible memorial (Change in disposition).
DD-566	Stoddard	6–1–75	Last USN Fletcher class on the NVR. Scrapped.
DD-587	Bell	11–1–72	Sunk as target 5–11–75.

Hull No.	Name	Date Stricken	Comments
DD-614	*MacKenzie*	7-1-71	Sunk as target 5-6-74, 150 miles East of Jacksonville, Fla.
DD-631	*Erben*	6-2-75	Sold/South Korea.
DD-642	*Hale*	6-2-75	Sold/Colombia.
DD-673	*Hickox*	6-2-75	Sold/South Korea.
DD-682	*Porterfield*	3-1-75	Scrapped.
DD-685	*Picking*	3-1-75	Scrapped.
DD-686	*Halsey Powell*	6-2-75	Sold/South Korea.
DD-711	*Eugene A. Greene*	6-2-75	FRAM I. Ex-DDR. Sold/Spain.
DD-717	*Theodore E. Chandler*	4-1-75	FRAM I. Scrapped.
DD-724	*Laffey*	3-29-75	FRAM II. Last of class on the NVR. Sunk as target (Change in disposition).
DD-805	*Chevalier*	6-2-75	FRAM II. Ex-DDR. Sold/South Korea.
DD-830	*Everett F. Larson*	6-2-75	FRAM II. Ex-DDR. Sold/South Korea.
DD-831	*Goodrich*	2-1-74	FRAM II. Ex-DDR. Scrapped.
DD-841	*Noa*	6-2-75	FRAM I. Sold/Spain.
DD-846	*Ozbourn*	6-1-75	FRAM I. Scrapped.
DD-879	*Leary*	6-2-75	FRAM I. Ex-DDR. Sold/Spain.
DD-882	*Furse*	6-2-75	FRAM I. Ex-DDR. Sold/Spain.
DD-889	*O'Hare*	6-2-75	FRAM I. Ex-DDR. Sold/Spain.
DE-168	*Amick*	6-15-75	Returned from loan to Japan on 6-14-75. Scrapped.
DE-169	*Atherton*	6-15-75	Returned from loan to Japan on 6-14-75. Scrapped.
DER-324	*Falgout*	6-1-75	Ex-DE-324. Sunk as target in PHALANX CICWS tests.
DER-386	*Savage*	6-1-75	Ex-DE-386. Sunk as target in HARPOON tests.
DER-387	*Vance*	6-1-75	Ex DE-387. Sunk as target.
DER-391	*Chambers*	3-1-75	Ex DE-391. Scrapped.
DER-400	*Hissem*	6-1-75	Ex DE-400. Sunk as target.
IXSS-246	*Croaker*	12-20-71	Ex AGSS-246, SSK-246, SS-246. Scrapped (Change in disposition).
LPR-127	*Begor*	5-15-75	Ex APD, DE-711. Scrapped.
LPR-132	*Balduck*	7-15-75	Ex APD, DE-716. Last LPR on the NVR. Scrapped.
LST-47	USNS LST-47	6-30-75	Sold.
LST-230	USNS LST-230	6-30-75	Sold.
LST-287	USNS LST-287	6-30-75	Sold.
LST-491	USNS LST-491	6-30-75	Sold.
LST-566	USNS LST-566	6-30-75	Trans./MarAd for layup. (correction).
LST-579	USNS LST-579	6-30-75	Sold.
LST-607	USNS LST-607	6-30-75	Sold.
LST-613	USNS LST-613	6-30-75	Sold.
LST-623	USNS LST-623	6-30-75	Sold.
LST-629	USNS LST-629	6-30-75	Sold.
LST-649	USNS LST-649	6-30-75	Sold.
LST-692	USNS *Daviess County*	6-30-75	Sold.
LST-762	*Floyd County*	4-1-75	Scrapped.
LST-819	*Hampshire County*	4-1-75	Scrapped.
LST-822	USNS *Harris County*	6-30-75	Sold.
LST-824	*Henry County*	4-1-75	Scrapped.
LST-854	*Kemper County*	4-1-75	Possible ILP sale.
LST-901	*Litchfield County*	4-1-75	Scrapped.
LST-980	*Meeker County*	4-1-75	Scrapped.

continued

ADDENDA

Hull No.	Name	Date Stricken	Comments
LST-1069	USNS *Orleans Parish*	6–30–75	Ex MCS-6, LST-1069. Sold.
LST-1072	USNS *LST-1072*	6–30–75	Sold.
LST-1082	*Pitkin County*	4–1–75	Scrapped.
LST-1096	*St. Clair County*	4–1–75	Scrapped.
LST-1123	*Sedgewick County*	5–15–75	Scrapped.
LST-1150	*Sutter County*	9–15–74	Scrapped.
MCS-2	*Ozark*	4–1–74	Trans./MarAd permanently for layup 9–1–71. Later scrapped (correction).
MSC-198	*Peacock*	7–1–75	Scrapped.
MSC-199	*Phoebe*	7–1–75	Scrapped.
MSC-201	*Shrike*	7–1–75	Scrapped.
MSC-203	*Thrasher*	7–1–75	Sold/Fiji.
MSC-205	*Vireo*	7–1–75	Sold/Singapore.
MSC-206	*Warbler*	7–1–75	Sold/Singapore.
MSC-207	*Whippoorwill*	7–1–75	Sold/Fiji.
MSC-209	*Woodpecker*	7–1–75	Sold/Singapore.
PG-99	*Beacon*	6– –75	Sold/Greece.
PG-101	*Green Bay*	6– –75	Sold/Greece.
SS-324	*Blenny*	8–15–73	GUPPY IA. Ex-AGSS, SS. Sunk as target (correction).
SS-343	*Clamagore*	6–27–75	GUPPY III. Sold/Turkey but transfer held up.
SS-417	*Tench*	8–15–73	GUPPY IA. Ex-AGSS, SS. Sunk as target (correction).

B. NON-COMMISSIONED SERVICE CRAFT

Hull No.	Name	Date Stricken	Comments
AFDB-6	unnamed	1–1–74	Ex-ABSD. Sold.
MSS-1	unnamed	2–10–75	Not on NVR, but declared for disposal this date. Trans./MarAd for disposal.
YC-1459	unnamed	4–21–75	Sold.
YD-20	unnamed	3–1–75	Sold.
YD-84	unnamed	3–1–75	Sold.
YF-886	unnamed	9–15–74	Trans./A.I.D. for further transfer to Panama (correction).
YFN-960	unnamed	4–1–75	Trans./Guyana for further service 8–1–75.
YFNB-16	unnamed	3–1–75	Ex-YFN. Sold.
YFND-16	unnamed	3–15–75	Ex-YFN. Sold.
YFP-13	unnamed	3–15–75	Ex-YFN. Scrapped.
YFRT-411	unnamed	5–1–75	Sold.
YFRT-519	unnamed	5–1–75	Sold.
YFU-53	unnamed	6–1–75	Ex-LCU. Target for HARPOON tests (1975–).
YM-22	unnamed	5–1–75	Sold.
YMLC-5	unnamed	2–15–75	Ex HMS LC-23. Purchased from Royal Navy in 1967. Sold.
YMLC-6	unnamed	2–15–75	Ex HMS LC-24. Purchased from Royal Navy in 1967. Sold.
YO-59	*Derrick*	4–1–75	Sold/South Korea.
YO-60	unnamed	2–1–75	Sunk as target.
YO-115	unnamed	10–15–74	Trans./Philippines (correction).
YO-116	unnamed	10–15–74	Trans./Philippines (correction).
YO-126	unnamed	10–15–74	Sunk as target (correction).
YO-179	unnamed	4–1–75	Sold/South Korea.
YO-211	unnamed	2–1–75	Sunk as target.

Hull No.	Name	Date Stricken	Comments
YO-248	unnamed	5-1-75	Trans./Army (11/73–1/75). Sold.
YOG-61	unnamed	10-15-74	Trans./Philippines (correction).
YOG-89	unnamed	5-1-75	Sold.
YOG-107	Lt. Thomas W. Fowler	5-1-75	Ex-YO. Sold.
YR-66	unnamed	4-1-75	Sold/Colombia.
YSD-21	unnamed	3-15-75	Sold.
YTM-177	Black Fox	5-1-75	Ex-YTB, YT. Sold.
YTM-190	Orono	3-15-75	Ex-YTB, YT.Trans./Guyana for further service 5-20-75.
YTM-273	Olathe	5-1-75	Ex-YTB, YT. Sold.
YTM-386	Washakie	5-1-75	Ex-YTB, YT. Sold.
YTM-388	Connewango	5-1-75	Ex-YTB, YT. Sold.
YTM-493	Abinago	5-1-75	Ex-YTB, YT. Sold.
YTM-495	Barboncito	5-1-75	Ex-YTB, YT. Sold.
YTM-533	Shahaska	3-1-75	Ex-YTB, YT. Sold.
YTM-765	Chiquito	5-1-75	Ex-YTB, YT. Sold.
YTM-766	Chohonaga	5-1-75	Ex-YTB, YT. Sold.
YW-103	unnamed	10-15-74	Trans./Philippines (correction).
YW-111	unnamed	10-15-74	Trans./Philippines (correction).
YW-115	unnamed	2-1-75	Sunk as target.
YW-129	unnamed	2-1-75	Sunk as target.
YW-130	unnamed	10-15-74	Trans./Philippines.

14. FORMER NAVAL VESSELS IN MARAD RESERVE FLEET

Delete the following ships from the list in the main text: Mission Los Angeles (AO-117), President Hayes (APA-20), Laurens (APA-153), Mellette (APA-156), Napa (APA-157), Newberry (APA-158), Gage (APA-168), Gallatin (APA-169), Kershaw (APA-176), Kingsbury (APA-177), Lavaca (APA-180), Lubbock (APA-197), McCraken (APA-198), Menifee (APA-202), Meriwether (APA-203), Sarasota (APA-204), Sibley (APA-206), Mifflin (APA-207), Oneida (APA-221), Bingham (APA-225), Rawlins (APA-226), Rockwall (APA-230), San Saba (APA-232), Bottineau (APA-235), Glynn (APA-239), Corpus Christi Bay (ARVH-1), Tuscarora (ATA-245) and Ozark (MSC-2). All have been sold for scrapping or non-transportation use.

Make the following changes to the list in the main text: Change the date in the "Date Stricken" column for LST-566 from 11-1-73 to 6-30-75.

Add the following ships to the list in the main text:

Hull No.	Name	Date Stricken	Type	Berthing Area
AO-50	Tallulah	5-29-75*	T2-SE-A1	James

INDEX

This book is set in seven point Helvetica with two points of leading. The chapter titles are twenty-four point Eurostile Bold Extended.

The book is printed offset on Bergstrom's fifty-pound Literature II Smooth. The cover material is Kivar 3-17, Chrome texture.

Composition by Monotype Composition Company, Baltimore, Maryland.

Printing and binding by George Banta Company, Incorporated, Menasha, Wisconsin.

Editorial production by Louise Gerretson.

Design by Beverly Baum.